Praise for *FDR Goes to War*

"Merits a wide readership."　　　　　　—*History Book Club*

"The Folsoms educate Americans on the facts we should have known but were never taught ... shocking and refreshing."
　　　　　—Lawrence W. Reed, President of the
　　　　　Foundation for Economic Education

"A compelling look at the FDR concealed for over half a century by liberal academics and biased journalists."
　　　　　—Paul Kengor, author of *Dupes*, professor of
　　　　　political science at Grove City College

"A page-turning tour de force. ... Be prepared to rethink much of what you think you know about FDR, the war, and the post-Depression U.S. economy."
　　　　　—Don Boudreaux, chairman, George Mason
　　　　　University department of economics

Praise for Burton W. Folsom, Jr.'s groundbreaking book
New Deal or Raw Deal?

"A must-read to help understand our current fiscal crisis."
　　　　　　　　　　　　　　—Glenn Beck

"Folsom peels away the parchment wrapping the Roosevelt myth to reveal the flawed figure beneath. ... Enjoyable and eye-opening."
　　　　　　　　　　　　　—*National Review*

"I have been proud to support research for this book."
　　　　　　　　　　　—William F. Buckley, Jr.

"Folsom convincingly indicts FDR for morally corrupting the office of the president."

　　　　　　　　　　　　　　—Steve Forbes

"A rare kind of book, one thoroughly researched by a scholar and yet written in plain language, readily understood by anyone."
　　　　　—Thomas Sowell, syndicated columnist and author of
　　　　　Basic Economics: A Common Sense Guide to the Economy

ALSO BY BURTON W. FOLSOM, JR.

New Deal or Raw Deal?:
How FDR's Economic Legacy Has Damaged America

The Myth of the Robber Barons:
A New Look at the Rise of Big Business in America

FDR

HOW EXPANDED EXECUTIVE POWER,

GOES

SPIRALING NATIONAL DEBT,

TO

AND RESTRICTED CIVIL LIBERTIES

WAR

SHAPED WARTIME AMERICA

Burton W. Folsom, Jr., and Anita Folsom

Threshold Editions

New York London Toronto Sydney New Delhi

Threshold Editions
A Division of Simon & Schuster, Inc.
1230 Avenue of the Americas
New York, NY 10020

First Threshold Editions paperback edition January 2013

THRESHOLD EDITIONS and colophon are trademarks of Simon & Schuster, Inc.

For information about special discounts for bulk purchases, please contact Simon & Schuster Special Sales at 1-866-506-1949 or business@simonandschuster.com.

The Simon & Schuster Speakers Bureau can bring authors to your live event. For more information or to book an event, contact the Simon & Schuster Speakers Bureau at 1-866-248-3049 or visit our website at www.simonspeakers.com.

Manufactured in the United States of America

10 9 8 7 6 5 4 3 2 1

Library of Congress Cataloging-in-Publication Data

Folsom, Burton W.
    FDR goes to war / Burton Folsom, Jr. and Anita Folsom.
        p. cm.
1. Roosevelt, Franklin D. (Franklin Delano), 1882–1945—Military leadership.
2. World War, 1939–1945—United States. 3. United States—Politics and government—1933–1945. 4. United States—Economic conditions—1918–1945.
I. Folsom, Anita. II. Title.
    E806.F639 2011
    973.917092—dc22

                                    2011008528

ISBN 978–1–4391–8320–5
ISBN 978–1–4391–8324–3 (pbk)
ISBN 978–1–4391–8322–9 (ebook)

To Our Parents:
Our fathers served in Europe,
and our mothers worked and waited at home.

CONTENTS

INTRODUCTION

BY M. STANTON EVANS

"War," to quote the famous phrase of Randolph Bourne, "is the health of the state."

By which Bourne meant—along with a lot of other things—that war permits the state to encroach on personal freedoms, increasing its scope and power while systematically shrinking the liberties of the people. The comment was obviously true, historically speaking, as for many ages kings, nobles, and eventually parliaments avidly sought authority, revenue, and other resources to wage their seemingly endless battles.

Bourne's axiom would be more valid yet in the modern era, as corvées numbering in the millions were mobilized in wars of global mass destruction, and newfangled methods of coercion and surveillance brought ever more aspects of daily life under the sway of state compulsion.

This study of World War II by Burton and Anita Folsom is an instructive treatment of such matters, adding in significant fashion to our understanding of President Franklin Roosevelt, his subalterns, and their performance in that titanic conflict. In numerous ways, the picture the Folsoms sketch for us is in stark contrast to the standard histories we've been given dealing with Roosevelt and his conduct of the struggle.

It has become fashionable in recent years to speak of the Americans who fought World War II as "the greatest generation."

For those who stayed to the bitter end at Corregidor, stormed the shores of Normandy, or raised the flag at Iwo Jima, such praise is not excessive. The heroism of the soldiers, sailors, Marines, and airmen who fought the battles of Europe and the Far Pacific should be remembered as long as there is an American nation.

At the level of political-diplomatic leadership, however, there is a less-edifying story to be told, fragments of which have emerged in piecemeal fashion across the decades from formerly confidential records, official archives, and the memoirs of leading actors in the drama. In this ongoing process of discovery and revision, the authors of the present study have brought together many revealing fragments and thus made a much-needed contribution to the genre.

Though FDR is treated in many histories as a far-seeing statesman waging a great crusade for freedom, the record provided by the Folsoms, backed by their extensive researches, shows us something different. In lack of preparedness during the run-up to the war (while contriving to get us in it), thereafter in many phases of its conduct, and most of all in the end game played out with Soviet dictator Stalin at Teheran and Yalta, Roosevelt made countless tragic blunders, to put the matter no more strongly. In particular, by various wartime stratagems he pursued and postwar policies he favored, he materially increased the strength of the Soviet Union and so helped consign untold numbers of suffering victims to its despotic rule.

While the Folsoms deal with issues of this sort in their discussion, it is in the realm of domestic policy and its impact on the nation that they make their most distinctive contribution. They show in detail the extent to which FDR used the war emergency (with the best of motives, per his defenders, but motives here are not the issue) to seek a further concentration of the Federal power that had been growing steadily in the New Deal era.

These wartime methods included exorbitant levels of taxation, massive increases in Federal spending, a vast proliferation of Federal bureaus, controls on prices, production, commerce, energy, and countless other facets of national life—all on the premise that the emergency called for such draconian measures. Here was the "health of the state" indeed, on a scale that far exceeded the earlier doings of Woodrow Wilson, which had led Bourne to make his sardonic comment.

Equally to the point, as the Folsoms further show, was the use Roosevelt made of the power at his disposal—going after domestic foes and critics via wiretaps by the FBI, tax audits, regulatory crackdowns, and indictments for sedition, plus the well-known internment of Japanese Americans (a measure favored by Earl Warren but opposed by J. Edgar Hoover). Roosevelt's efforts to punish and silence such opponents as Col. Robert McCormick of the *Chicago Tribune* and the Patterson newspaper family were many and relentless.

Indeed, virtually everything done and deplored some decades later in the Watergate affair was originally done—and outdone— by FDR, though one would scarcely know this from the usual hagiographic tellings of his story.

All of this makes for important reading, including in the final wrap-up some hopeful lessons also. For one thing, it's worth recalling, Pearl Harbor *was* avenged and Hitler *was* defeated—though replacing him with the equally murderous and even more powerful Stalin was no boon to the cause of democracy Roosevelt professedly was serving.

On the home front, meanwhile, there were many in Washington and media-academic circles who wanted in peacetime to continue the controls, massive spending, and taxation that were imposed in the course of the struggle. To this, however, the American people and a brand-new Congress would say no, moving instead to trim Federal power back at least to its former levels. This brought much outcry and many prophecies of doom, but resulted instead in a surge of postwar prosperity and growth that made the economy stronger. The relevance of which to happenings of the present day doesn't need much stressing.

On these topics, and many others, the Folsoms have given us a fast-moving, lucid, and informative survey that corrects the record of World War II in numerous significant aspects. The result is a major contribution to understanding events of the twentieth century that far too many histories have neglected.

M. Stanton Evans

The president nervously flicked the ashes from his cigarette and stared past the microphones. His eyes were on the guests seated in the White House radio room, but his mind was on the marching columns of Adolf Hitler's troops, who had just stormed through Belgium, Luxembourg, Holland—even France was on the verge of collapse. Many Americans had hoped that Great Britain and France could contain the Nazi menace and handle the war themselves. But the sudden and incredibly swift successes of Germany's "lightning war" had tipped the balance in Hitler's favor. France's army, once vaunted as the premier fighting machine of the world, was led by old men using outdated tactics. French troops were throwing down their weapons and surrendering en masse. Even as Franklin Delano Roosevelt sat before the microphone, the British Army in France was fighting for its life while evacuating to a beach called Dunkirk.

The Fireside Chat was Roosevelt's ingenious invention for stopping time and seizing the attention of sixty to seventy million Americans, many of whom had already tuned in their radios, coast-to-coast, eager to hear his familiar voice. Roosevelt performed these timely talks only when he absolutely had to establish a connection with the American people, either to maneuver for their votes or to persuade them of his point of view. Oddly enough, tonight, May 26, 1940, he was doing both of these things. He was preparing to run for a historic third term in the White

House, and he was also preparing the nation for war. His urgent need to rebuild America's defenses had changed his priorities and his presidency. To generations unborn he knew his presidency would forever be connected with the forthcoming world war; therefore, the United States simply had to win it. He was in reality, after tonight, a war president. The coming war, not the New Deal, would now become his top priority.

The chief radio engineer was ready; there was a hush over the guests. The president put out his cigarette nervously, and took a sip of water. He had to talk peace, think war, and use his New Deal war chest to lead him to victory in November.

Suddenly the radio man gave the signal; then came the announcements from each of the networks. Roosevelt shuffled the pages of his speech and heard the announcer's voice: "The president of the United States." He looked up and smiled forcibly. "My friends," he said, and his nervousness vanished, "at this moment of sadness throughout most of the world, I want to talk with you about a number of subjects that directly affect the future of the United States." From there he briefly described the "almost incredible eyewitness stories" of devastation from Hitler's rapid invasions: bombings of city centers, machine guns aimed at fleeing civilians, civil rights suspended. Then came the subtle nudge. He urged Americans to give to the Red Cross, thereby loosely binding the United States to the Allied cause.[1]

And he went further: "There are some among us who closed their eyes, . . . honestly and sincerely thinking that the many hundreds of miles of salt water made the American Hemisphere so remote that the people of North and Central and South America could go on living in the midst of their vast resources without reference to, or danger from, other continents of the world." Roosevelt discarded those arguments: "Today we are now more realistic."

So as Roosevelt gave his radio address on May 26, foremost in his mind was the need for war materiel, especially ships and aircraft. Already he was being blamed for the lack of preparation in the U.S. military. He knew that the country must arm itself quickly to catch up with other world powers. With two coasts to defend, the United States was woefully unprepared. Gaps in industrial production of ships, planes, and other armaments were far larger than most of the public knew. American industry could make the difference, both in defending the United States and in shoring up the democracies in Europe. In the next few minutes, Franklin Roosevelt would change the course of his presidency and call upon American industry to stand *with him* in the breach.

"Yes, we are calling upon the resources, the efficiency, and the ingenuity of American manufacturers of war material of all kinds—airplanes and tanks and guns and ships, and all the hundreds of products that go into this materiel." Roosevelt had reached the heart of his speech.

"The government of the United States itself manufactures few of the implements of war. Private industry will continue to be the source of most of this material; and private industry will have to be speeded up to produce it at the rate and efficiency called for by the needs of the times."

Some listeners must have paused in disbelief. The president was pivoting. Franklin Roosevelt—for the first time in his seven years as president—urgently needed, and publicly requested, help from the nation's largest business owners.

A bigger shock was yet to come. Not only was the president courting these "malefactors of wealth," as he used to call them, he was offering to help them, to give them financial incentives to produce.

"I know that private business cannot be expected to make all of the capital investments required for expansions of plants and factories and personnel which this program calls for at once. It would be unfair to expect industrial corporations or their investors to do this, when there is a chance that a change in international affairs may stop or curtail orders a year or two hence.

"Therefore, the government of the United States stands ready to advance the necessary money to help provide for the enlargement of factories, the establishment of new plants, the employment of thousands of necessary workers, the development of new sources of supply for the hundreds of raw materials required, the development of quick mass transportation of supplies."

As if to underscore his remarkable turnabout, he added, "We are calling on men now engaged in private industry to help us in carrying out this program, and you will hear more of this in detail in the next few days."

Careful students of the Roosevelt presidency knew that war must be near because FDR had decided to change the tone of the political debate in Washington. For almost eight years, Wall Street bankers and corporate leaders had been his favorite scapegoats for explaining why the Great Depression was persisting. The premise of his New Deal, after all, was that businessmen had failed and that government should regulate, plan, and direct much of the American economy to break the hold of the Great Depression.

Earlier, during national elections, the president could use class warfare and federal subsidies to win votes. After all, bad economies come and go in U.S. history. But when wars come, they must be won. Few remember the Panic of 1873—or even who was president then—but everyone remembered the Mexican War, the Spanish-American War, and, of course, the Civil War. U.S. presidents could fail when they worked to end depressions, as FDR had shown, and still survive politically—if they had a viable scapegoat. But they could not lose wars because those losses would be all the historians and the textbooks would ever remember. Lincoln was great because Lincoln was a successful war president. His high taxes and abuse of civil liberties were largely forgotten. If the forthcoming war were lost, FDR could, of course, attack business again for not making enough weapons. But historians would still hold Roosevelt accountable for losing any war on his watch.

Just ten days earlier, on May 16, 1940, Roosevelt had addressed Congress and asked for more than a billion dollars for defense, with a commitment for fifty thousand military aircraft. But addressing Congress was not enough. Business leaders held back their complete support, concerned that their industries would be nationalized or their profits attacked. If they committed large amounts of capital for defense plants, could these plants be converted to produce civilian goods when the hostilities ended? Would their industries lose money on costly innovations to produce war materiel?

Roosevelt had to have their cooperation. He could not win the war without them. Thus, he was finally ready for a truce with businessmen. No more would he call them "privileged princes" who were "thirsting for power." He desperately needed their help. He had already urged Congress to spend more on defense; now, beginning on May 26, he had to persuade businessmen to start making the planes, tanks, guns, and ammunition that were already needed to overpower Hitler and his allies. Of course, Roosevelt would pretend, for the sake of the 1940 elections, that America could avoid war, but he believed he was only buying time to rebuild the nation's defenses.

Franklin Roosevelt knew that this international crisis called for drastic action. To save his legacy as president, he would work with big business to arm the United States. What he signaled the nation in his Fireside Chat on May 26 was this: He would finally work with the businessmen, and if they would help the United States defeat Hitler, then FDR and the businessmen could share the pot together—the capitalists would win profits, FDR would win votes, and America would win the war.

1

HELLO TO ARMS, FAREWELL TO NEW DEAL

Professors Rexford Tugwell and Raymond Moley left their meeting with Franklin Roosevelt and looked at each other in disbelief. They could barely absorb the ideas that FDR had just unveiled. As two of his advisors, they had signed on to Roosevelt's "brains trust" with expectations of changing American society: Government programs, not free enterprise, would plan the economy in the future. Now, in January 1933, President-elect Roosevelt had thrown a wrench in their social planning by telling them that he favored "war with Japan now rather than later." Those words stunned both men.[1]

Tugwell and Moley were discovering that Franklin Roosevelt's mind touched on a hundred topics a day. As FDR waited for his inauguration in March, he remained in his home state of New York, where he had just served four years as governor. He used the interim to discuss policy with his advisors. But his was no orderly mind. As one cabinet official later admitted, "It literally is government on the jump."[2]

Days earlier, Roosevelt's nimble mind had been influenced by the current secretary of state, Henry Stimson. Stimson attended the funeral of former president Calvin Coolidge in Northampton, Massachusetts, and two days later joined Roosevelt for lunch at FDR's estate at Hyde Park, New York. Roosevelt and Stimson talked privately for over five hours. Stimson disliked Japan. When Japan invaded Manchuria in 1931, Stimson refused to recognize

Japan's claims. He wanted embargoes to cut off their oil and steel, to end the atrocities in China. America must actively intervene in world affairs—that was Stimson's position.[3]

And here was Roosevelt with his love for China. Since his grandfather Delano had made money in China in the opium trade, FDR felt that he had a connection with the country and its people. Stimson's ideas on foreign policy in Asia meshed well with Roosevelt's. The following week, FDR announced that "American foreign policy must uphold the sanctity of international treaties," which was a direct slap at Japan's invasion of Manchuria.[4]

Would Roosevelt go so far as to provoke war with Japan? Moley and Tugwell spent hours trying to dissuade FDR from this interventionist foreign policy, but the president-elect rebuffed them: "I have always had the deepest sympathy for the Chinese. How could you expect me not to go along with Stimson on Japan?"[5]

Tugwell wrote in his diary:

I sympathize with the Chinese, too. But I firmly believe it is a commitment which may lead us to war with Japan. . . . [FDR] has a strong personal sympathy with the Chinese. . . . *He admitted the possibility of war and said it might be better to have it now than later.* This horrified me and I said so.[6]

Three months later, now-president FDR focused on domestic issues, especially the economy, and not on foreign policy. With unemployment over 20 percent, he launched his New Deal, a flurry of government programs that he hoped would put people back to work. But instead, the economic downturn became the Great Depression, and unemployment remained high throughout the 1930s.[7]

Oddly, even while considering such an aggressive foreign policy, Roosevelt slashed defense spending as a percentage of the national budget.[8] Playing the role of pacifist, FDR pleased millions of American voters who wanted to avoid war. Noninterventionist leaders from the Midwest also led the Senate and the House and strongly opposed military spending. Senator Gerald P. Nye of North Dakota, a progressive Republican and New Deal supporter, stood in the Senate chamber in 1934 to denounce bankers and arms dealers for profiting from the military slaughter of the First World War.

The public responded by demanding guarantees of isolation from foreign wars. Congress then passed the Neutrality Acts, designed to prevent America from joining in another foreign war. In 1935 and 1936, the first two Neutrality Acts were meant to be temporary, but then the third act became law in May 1937 and permanently covered a wide range of activities so that the United States would not aid other nations at war.[9] Roosevelt went along with this policy.

Much of the isolationist sentiment was a backlash against World War I, which had killed almost 120,000 Americans. Many U.S. citizens vowed never again to be drawn into a European conflict. With newer weapons and modern aircraft, military experts predicted even higher casualties in future wars. "No," Americans said in vast numbers, "if we avoid any armed conflict short of an invasion of North America, that is the way for a safe future for American boys." And at any rate, Americans believed that no foreign power was strong enough, or foolish enough, to cross the ocean to attack the United States on its home land.

"War is a vain policy, except a war fought at home to establish or preserve the freedom of a nation," wrote Senator Robert Taft of Ohio in 1941, summing up the ideas of this movement in the United States called isolationism. Most isolationists were not pacifists; they wanted a strong *defense*, even as they distrusted foreign governments, which might look to the size and strength of the United States as a military reservoir to help them fight their neighbors.[10]

The United States was not alone in its revulsion at the horrors of World War I. During the 1920s, governments around the world decided they could limit armaments and even outlaw war itself. The disarmament movement worldwide was reinforced in 1928 by the Kellogg-Briand Pact, which supposedly outlawed war. The United States and dozens of other nations signed this utopian agreement.[11]

At naval disarmament conferences in the 1920s, American leaders agreed to mothball much of the U.S. Navy. Then they closed factories for making weapons and military planes. War administrator Donald Nelson, an expert on the U.S. military, noted that postwar tax laws shifted production from military to civilian goods. For example, "The biggest rifle manufacturing firm in the world, the Eddystone plant of Remington [near Philadelphia], was swept away." American corporations were also "not permitted to write off equipment that was not obsolete or worn out. The new facilities were too expensive to maintain and pay taxes on, so Bethlehem [Steel and other corporations] demolished them."[12]

Adding to the antiwar mood were revelations from traumatized veterans. The facts about trench warfare had been withheld from the public during the war, when censorship was widespread. But soldiers who survived the conflict began writing plays, novels, and short stories about their experiences.

Goodbye to All That, by Robert Graves, published in both America and England in 1929, gave readers a glimpse of trench warfare as described by a traumatized soldier. The stage drama Journey's End by R. C. Sheriff played to thousands of audiences all over the world from 1928 through the 1930s, telling the story of a British infantry company in the trenches. And the success of Erich Maria Remarque's novel All Quiet on the Western Front also showed how interested the public had become in learning the truth about the war. Within eighteen months, the book sold 2.5 million copies in twenty-five languages. Hollywood adapted the story to the silver screen, and it won 1930 Academy Awards for both Best Picture and Best Director.

Throughout Europe and the United States, the public was

stunned by the carnage of World War I, by the raw destruction, by the sheer numbers of dead or maimed. How could the British Army suffer sixty thousand casualties on the first day of the Battle of the Somme—without gaining a yard of territory? How could almost half the Frenchmen between the ages of twenty and thirty-two perish—killed on Europe's battlefields between 1914 and 1918?[13]

As isolationist sentiment in the United States increased during the 1930s, Franklin Roosevelt kept his ideas about containing Japan to himself and his closest advisors. Secrecy was not new to FDR. As a victim of polio, he could not stand without help and spent most of his time in a wheelchair. Yet the public had no idea of the extent of his disability. During his presidency, if a photographer captured a picture of FDR in his wheelchair or being carried by aides, his Secret Service detail confiscated the film. Roosevelt managed to conceal the degree of his paralysis from the public until the last days of his presidency.[14] Likewise, during his first term, few people knew that Roosevelt wanted to push back the Japanese and place the United States in the middle of foreign crises.

Even though FDR favored an interventionist foreign policy that could lead to war, he was unwilling to rebuild the military. Roosevelt had worked in Woodrow Wilson's administration as assistant secretary of the navy in World War I. As president, FDR continued to favor the Navy, but he wanted low numbers of sailors and ships. For the Army, he tended to think in traditional terms of cannons, cavalry, and small numbers of troops. Although Congress had authorized a fighting army of 280,000 men, it refused to vote the funds to make that happen, so the actual size of the U.S. Army remained about 140,000 soldiers in the mid-1930s, with National Guard units available to fill in during emergencies. FDR approved of this strategy and continued to keep national defense budgets low.[15] He would skimp on the country's defense to spend on his New Deal.

By the mid-1930s, the U.S. Army's pitiful stocks of supplies had hit rock bottom. Appropriations for the War Department had dropped from $345 million under Herbert Hoover in fiscal year 1931 to $243 million under FDR in 1934. What's more, World War I weapons and equipment were simply worn out. The entire Army owned only eighty semiautomatic rifles, with the infantry still using the 1903 bolt-action Springfield rifle. Ammunition stores were so low in 1935 that General Douglas MacArthur, Army chief of staff, proposed the "hopeful" goal of stockpiling a thirty-day supply of ammunition for all calibers of weapons.[16]

What Roosevelt did was to make the military the small step-child of the New Deal. Perhaps this allowed him to hide military expenses while bolstering the amounts he could claim the New Deal had pumped into the U.S. economy. Also, the larger New Deal projects allowed FDR and his supporters to target subsidies for key election districts.[17] In May 1934, the keel of the aircraft carrier USS *Yorktown* was laid, using Public Works Administration (PWA) funds, as well as that of the USS *Enterprise* in July. That same year the PWA also spent $10 million for the Army's motorized vehicles and $15 million for military aircraft. In 1935, PWA's figure grew to $100 million for military posts and equipment. During the 1930s, the PWA built submarines, four cruisers, four destroyers, thirty-two army posts, and fifty military airports.[18]

Roosevelt's use of New Deal programs for military projects upset many progressives. "We had a big PWA building program. Roosevelt took a big chunk of that money and gave it to the Navy to build ships. I was shocked. All the New Dealers were shocked," said White House staffer James Rowe.[19]

Works Progress Administration (WPA) funds also benefited the military: "In the years 1935 to 1939 when regular appropriations for the armed forces were so meager, it was the WPA worker who saved many Army posts and Naval stations from literal obsolescence."[20]

Roosevelt so disdained the U.S. Army that he appointed Harry Woodring, an isolationist, as secretary of war in 1936. A lackluster politician, Woodring became governor of Kansas in 1930 in a controversial three-way race with Republican Frank Haucke and write-in candidate—and goat-gland transplant specialist—Dr. John Brinkley. FDR was pleased that Woodring defeated the Republicans in Kansas and then jumped on the Roosevelt bandwagon in 1932. Woodring's isolationist views coincided with those of most Americans when he entered FDR's cabinet.

Woodring clung to his office for four years, despite an ongoing feud with the assistant secretary of war, Louis A. Johnson. Johnson backed universal military education and military aid to Great Britain, and he also coveted Woodring's position. Johnson insisted that FDR had promised *him* the secretary's position on at least seven occasions, as soon as Woodring was gone. From time to time, Johnson "leaked" to the press that Woodring planned to resign, but Woodring continued as secretary of war.[21]

The Woodring-Johnson feud was intensified by something an earlier Congress had passed in the National Defense Act of 1920. Under that law, the assistant secretary directed the nation's industrial preparedness in case of war, and in peacetime also approved military supplies. Thus, Johnson often exercised more authority than his supposed boss Woodring. "The Woodring-Johnson fight, characterized by Secretary of the Interior Harold L. Ickes as a 'holy show,' grew out of Roosevelt's unfortunate habit of sweeping embarrassing administrative problems under the rug," observed historian Forrest Pogue.[22]

An early warning signal of trouble in Germany occurred when Adolf Hitler sent troops into the Rhineland along Germany's western border in March 1936, violating the Treaty of Versailles. He cunningly denied any further territorial aims in a speech the same day. Some isolationists, hoping that war was a thing of the past, embraced Hitler's soothing words and ignored those of Winston Churchill, who called Hitler's speech "comfort for everyone on both sides of the Atlantic who wished to be humbugged."[23]

In October 1937, in response to Japan's aggression—and photos of Hitler and Mussolini cozying up in Europe—Roosevelt decided the time was right to reconsider foreign policy. FDR had publicly gone along with the isolationists until then, but as he traveled to Chicago to dedicate the Outer Drive Bridge, a multimillion-dollar PWA project, he decided the time had come for a change.[24]

With three major radio networks broadcasting the speech, the president spoke for less than a minute about the bridge. He then switched to an emotional appeal, asking the world to "quarantine" aggressors. Such a speech was straight out of Henry Stimson's playbook. The *New York Times* supported Roosevelt's stance and published positive comments from a sprinkling of other newspapers. The much larger response from isolationists was, in Secretary of State Cordell Hull's words, "quick and violent." Even Hull believed that "quarantine" was too strong a word; he rightly predicted that the American public must be led out of isolationism gradually, if at all. Six pacifist organizations issued a joint statement that FDR's speech "points the American people down the road that led to the World War." The American Federation of Labor came out against it. Members of Congress, red-faced and vitriolic, talked of impeaching FDR.[25]

In Tokyo, America's ambassador, Joseph C. Grew, received a copy of the text of the quarantine speech. Grew had tried for years to strengthen communication between the United States and Japan, without pushing the Japanese into a war over natural resources. Still, the war faction of the Japanese government had been gaining power. Aghast at FDR's tone, Grew exclaimed when he read FDR's comments: "There goes everything I have tried to accomplish in my entire mission to Japan."[26]

After the brouhaha caused by his quarantine speech, FDR abandoned the idea. Despite the newspaper accounts of atrocities overseas, the American public clung to the concept of "no involvement in foreign wars," and savvy politicians told them what they wanted to hear. Franklin Roosevelt wanted above all to stay in office. If the American people were comforted by a façade of isolationist rhetoric from the Oval Office, he would give it to them. In David Brinkley's words, "It was many months before Roosevelt again dared to mention the threat of war." [27]

Few Americans could ignore, however, the impact of the Munich Agreement in September 1938. Hitler threatened war if Germany could not annex the Sudetenland, which was a vital area of Czechoslovakia. Great Britain's prime minister, Neville Chamberlain, flew to Munich and agreed to hand over the Sudetenland to the Nazis, even though he had no authority to do so. With crumbling support from Britain and France, Czechoslovakia's president signed the ignominious Munich Agreement, transferring the Sudetenland to Germany. Losing this territory cost Czechoslovakia its best geographical defenses, as well as armament factories, and left the small country vulnerable to further Nazi demands. Many Americans began to doubt the will of France and England to challenge Germany. Polls showed that after Munich, 43 percent of Americans believed the United States could not avoid hostilities if Europe erupted in another war. [28]

On October 13, just two weeks after Munich, Franklin Roosevelt met at the White House with William C. Bullitt, ambassador to France, until late into the night. Bullitt drew a stark picture of Germany's ever-growing military, especially its air force, and told FDR that France's only chance to expand its air force rapidly was to buy military aircraft from the United States. [29] With similar reports of British interest in American planes, FDR startled the press corps the following day when he announced that he was considering "vastly increased expenditures" for both the Army and Navy. [30]

One month later, on November 14, Roosevelt convened a White House conference with his cabinet and War Department leaders. Included in the meeting was General George Marshall, deputy chief of staff of the Army. Insiders rumored that Marshall was being groomed as the next chief of staff, but General Marshall was new to FDR's White House.

At the meeting, Roosevelt announced a plan for America to build 10,000 planes, sell most of those to Great Britain and France, and use the remainder to discourage attacks on North America. He favored no new funds for training crews to man the planes, nor any funds for manufacturing the munitions needed for the bombers, and he did not see the need for a large ground army to protect air bases. FDR admitted that privately owned factories should build 8,000 aircraft, but in addition he proposed that the government's WPA build seven new aircraft plants on WPA "reservations," which would build the remaining 2,000 planes and stand by for more orders in the future. As General Marshall listened to the discussion, he noted that FDR did most of the talking. Others in the room "agreed with him entirely. . . . He finally came around to me . . . and said, 'Don't you think so, George?' I replied, 'I am sorry, Mr. President, but I don't agree with that at all.' I remember that ended the conference. The President gave me a . . . startled look and when I went out they all bade me good-by and said that my tour in Washington was over."[31]

Possibly because FDR's close advisors, such as Harry Hopkins, held General Marshall in such high regard, he escaped the anticipated demotion.

FDR's idea of using WPA workers with no experience in armaments drew attention from the press. Obviously, Roosevelt was hoping to strengthen one of his pet New Deal projects, the WPA, by making it more a part of the military establishment. However, the usually sympathetic *New York Times* editorialized that "it is not desirable to mix relief with national defense in the same program."[32] The idea of WPA aircraft plants gradually disappeared from discussions, although Roosevelt and other New Dealers touted the value of WPA workers in industry.

Often Roosevelt could hide his interest in helping European powers arm against the Nazis despite the restrictions of the Neutrality Acts. In late 1938, the French government finally awoke to the danger posed by the air strength of the German Luftwaffe and approached FDR with a request to purchase one thousand military aircraft. FDR asked his old friend Henry Morgenthau, the treasury secretary, to handle the French government's request. FDR wanted Morgenthau to work quietly on this project, which many on Capitol Hill would consider illegal. In January 1939, France sent a captain in its air force to inspect an American military plane in California, and as luck would have it, the plane crashed while on a test flight with the French captain on board. The American pilot was killed, and local newspapers were left asking why the hospitalized French officer had been on an American military test flight.[33]

A startled Congress immediately wanted to know what was going on. The ensuing uproar in Washington did not add to Roosevelt's credibility. On January 31, 1939, the president met in a closed meeting with the seventeen members of the Senate Military Affairs Committee at the White House. During the meeting, Roosevelt reportedly made the statement that "the frontier of the United States is the Rhine," meaning France's border with Germany. One of the senators leaked that comment to the press, and isolationists across the country roared their disapproval. When asked about his statement, FDR's denial became front-page headlines in the *New York Times*: "Defense Story Work of 'Boob,' He Says . . . '100% Bunk,' He Adds."[34]

Throughout 1939, most Americans remained isolationists, although they sympathized with the victims of Germany and Japan. Nazi aggression seemed more odious every day. Then, in April 1939, Italy invaded Albania. A week after the invasion, Roosevelt sent a personal message to Hitler and Mussolini, asking them to consider peaceful solutions.

Both dictators ridiculed his efforts. America had disarmed, and FDR's New Deal had fostered almost 20 percent unemployment, compared with about 11 percent for most of Europe. Why should Europeans respect U.S. opinions or strength? Even Great Britain's prime minister, Neville Chamberlain, disdained FDR's peace initiative as "Yankee meddling."[35]

Also in April 1939, President Roosevelt had to select a new Army chief of staff, and many senior officers coveted the position. George Marshall showed uncanny perception in seeking it. Knowing full well the depth of the Woodring-Johnson feud, Marshall asked both men to keep their support for him quiet and discuss his appointment only with the president: "Johnson wanted me for Chief of Staff, but I didn't want Woodring to know he was for me. . . . Woodring was for me, but I didn't want the others to know. . . . Let things take their course and perhaps I will get it."[36] With support from FDR advisor Harry Hopkins, Marshall won the appointment.

Marshall would not assume the actual office for a few months, but he was learning fast. He brought experience, wisdom, and self-control to his office. According to columnist Arthur Krock, "Marshall's unusual manner was that of a man who had forced his personal emotions below the surface and bade them stay there."[37] After graduating from the Virginia Military Institute in 1901, Marshall was assigned posts in the United States, the Philippines, and China. During World War I, he served in France and was mentored by General John J. Pershing. During these early years, Marshall learned to lead men by sound judgment and strong personal integrity. As a member of Pershing's inner circle, Marshall came into conflict with a fellow officer, Douglas MacArthur, who later opposed promotions for Marshall. With his career at a standstill for years, Marshall also developed patience.

During the interwar military slump, Marshall commanded a battalion at Fort Leavenworth, Kansas. His unit should have boasted five hundred men. Instead, Marshall said, it was "a battalion only in name, for it could muster barely two hundred men when every available man, including cooks, clerks, and kitchen police were present for what little training could be accomplished."[38]

Marshall also worked closely with training programs for young men in FDR's Civilian Conservation Corps (CCC). He spent five years at Fort Benning, Georgia, where he observed the best of the American officer corps. He compiled lists of the most capable officers in a little black book, to which he planned to refer if war ever came.[39]

In Washington, Marshall was enough of a diplomat to work well with both FDR and members of Congress. After learning not to contradict the president too openly, Marshall avoided private meetings with FDR: "I found informal conversation with the president would get you into trouble. He would talk over something informally at the dinner table and you had trouble disagreeing without creating embarrassment. So I never went. I was in Hyde Park for the first time at his funeral." Also, if Marshall had talked often with FDR, the general's frustration might have erupted: Why did the U.S. Army have only nine divisions on paper, and not one ready to fight at the strength authorized by Congress? By contrast, Germany boasted ninety divisions in the field, Japan had fifty in China alone, and Italy listed forty-five.[40]

General Marshall realized that building the Army and training air crews took time and money, both of which were in short supply. President Roosevelt, by contrast, did not understand the time involved. He believed that volunteers could quickly become soldiers or sailors if necessary. Later, in dealing with the Navy, the president told Admiral Richardson, commander of the Pacific fleet, that "men in mechanical trades in civil life could be quickly inducted and made adequate sailormen, if their services were suddenly required." The admiral countered by saying that "a seasick garage mechanic would be of little use at sea, and that it took time for most young men to get their sea legs."[41] Despite Roosevelt's cheery outlook about filling quotas for the military, Marshall and Richardson worried that the United States was not prepared for war.[42]

During the summer of 1939, Franklin Roosevelt found Congress increasingly hostile to his New Deal projects and his ideas about arming the European democracies. In the wee hours of the morning of July 1, Congress once again retained the arms embargo that FDR and Secretary of State Cordell Hull were so eager to abolish. As the fiscal year ended, sixty-one Democrats in the House voted with isolationist Republicans to keep the embargo in place. In a Senate filibuster, FDR's other proposals went down in defeat; Senator Millard E. Tydings (D-Md.) gave the final speech during the filibuster as time ran out. (FDR had tried to purge Tydings from the Senate during the previous election, and Tydings enjoyed the payback.)

Roosevelt, meanwhile, seemed unable to organize efficiently for defense. He did put the powerful Army and Navy Munitions Board (ANMB) under his own authority, but Assistant Secretary Johnson was in charge, not Woodring. Their continued feuding was a recipe for problems, and Marshall was amazed that FDR let the situation continue for so long.[43] Then, on August 9, 1939, Roosevelt appointed Edward R. Stettinius, Jr., as head of a new committee, the War Resources Board, with representatives from MIT, AT&T, the Brookings Institution, GM, and Sears, Roebuck. Johnson saw the creation of the board as a necessary step in the country's preparedness, but many New Dealers resented further military planning.[44]

As the heat of summer continued, and with Congress adjourned, headlines focused on European developments. Much of the world waited to see where gray-uniformed soldiers of the German Reich would appear next, but the deserted streets of Washington were "like the streets of Topeka on a Saturday night." The only top-ranking official in the nation's capital was Senator Key Pittman (D-Nev.), head of the Foreign Relations Committee, "who remained on the job to keep in touch with the ever-changing situation in Europe and the Far East." Both Secretary of State Cordell Hull and President Roosevelt kept to their usual routine of August vacations in order to escape the stifling heat.[45]

The president could not even get much support that month when he tampered with Thanksgiving. Americans were upset when FDR announced a change in the traditional date of Thanksgiving from the last Thursday of November (which would be November 30 in 1939) to the fourth Thursday (November 23), to increase the number of shopping days before Christmas.[46] The citizens of Plymouth, Massachusetts, protested, saying that the traditional date was sacred to their community. Several governors, particularly those in strongly Republican states, announced that their citizens would not observe FDR's change in the holiday.

On August 23, when Germany announced that its government had reached a nonaggression pact with Moscow (and therefore a Nazi attack on Poland was imminent), the shock waves that went through Europe finally reached American shores. Roosevelt and Hull rushed back to Washington to plan for a possible declaration of neutrality.[47] The War Resources Board met to review military preparedness. On August 24, the *New York Times* headlines ran across the width of the front page:

Germany and Russia Sign 10-Year Non-Aggression Pact Hitler Rebuffs London; Britain and France Mobilize

The naval attaché at the Paris embassy cabled his report: "Estimate all German forces in position enter Poland not later than Friday night. . . . [H]ostilities inevitable with drive to southeast through Hungary possible. My opinion England and France will fight. French mobilization proceeding rapidly."[48]

In response to these events, Roosevelt sent another appeal for peace to Germany, Poland, and to King Victor Emmanuel of Italy.

As tensions mounted, FDR took no responsibility for the nation's weak military; instead, he criticized Congress for failing to revise the Neutrality Acts, which "helped to encourage Chancellor Hitler to assume his present stand in the European crisis."[49] On August 30, Roosevelt held his one and only meeting with the War

Resources Board, which lasted for fifteen minutes, and asked for a detailed report on its proposals.[50]

At 3 A.M. on September 1, the telephone rang beside Roosevelt's bed. Ambassador William Bullitt was calling from Paris: "Mr. President, the German Army has crossed the border of Poland!"[51] Europe was at war.

With so much attention on Europe, few people noticed that General Marshall also became Army chief of staff on September 1. During the next two years, he worked on "a wartime basis with all the difficulty and irritating limitations of peacetime procedure."[52] In talking with congressmen about military appropriations, Marshall found that often Republicans were "willing to help him because they could tell their constituents they were following his advice, not Roosevelt's. 'He [Roosevelt] had such enemies that otherwise members of Congress didn't dare, it seemed, to line up with him. . . . And that was true of certain Democrats who were getting pretty bitter.'"[53]

On September 3, Roosevelt spoke to the nation in a Fireside Chat asking for Americans to maintain "true neutrality." Publicly, FDR continued to play the role of a peace-loving president, intent upon keeping America out of the war: "I hope the United States will keep out of this war. I believe that it will. And I give you assurance and reassurance that every effort of your government will be directed toward that end." But behind the scenes, Roosevelt wanted the United States involved in the war, so much so that even the president's speechwriter, Robert Sherwood, later admitted that Roosevelt's Fireside Chat "may be denounced as at worst deliberately misleading or at best as wishful thinking."[54]

On September 5, FDR issued another proclamation—required by the Neutrality Act of 1937—placing an immediate embargo on shipments of arms, munitions, airplanes, and airplane parts to any belligerent, including Great Britain and France. American diplomats across Europe rushed to assist stranded Americans as they nervously booked passage back to the United

States. When the passenger liner *Athenia* was sunk by a German submarine off the coast of Ireland, Ambassador to Great Britain Joseph Kennedy sent his second son, John F. Kennedy, to help the American survivors find other transport back to America. The State Department was also flooded with thousands of requests from Europe's Jewish refugees, begging for visas that would allow them to enter the United States.

In early September, when Roosevelt received the requested report from the War Resources Board, he called it "a very comprehensive blueprint prepared by the Stettinius committee, from which it appeared that this committee was prepared to take over all of the functions of the Government." The War Resources Board submitted a final report six weeks later and faded from view.[55]

Instead, Roosevelt created the Office for Emergency Management (OEM) in the Executive Office of the President. Through executive orders, FDR eventually set up a series of agencies in the OEM to manage the defense effort. By mid-1941, fifteen defense agencies reported directly to him. The *New York Times* noted that FDR's advisors, nicknamed the "brains trust," were "out the window" now that the president was setting up the OEM.[56]

While asking the American people to remain neutral, FDR secretly opened communications with the strongest war advocate in the British cabinet, Winston Churchill. Ambassador Joseph Kennedy thought Churchill lacked leadership qualities, but FDR believed that Churchill would play a huge role as war leader in Britain. Once Churchill became Great Britain's First Lord of the Admiralty, Roosevelt quickly opened a correspondence. His first letter to Churchill, dated September 11, 1939, went through traditional diplomatic channels. FDR invited Churchill to keep in touch through sealed letters in their diplomatic pouches, saying that he welcomed "anything you want me to know about."[57]

Roosevelt intensified his courtship of the new cabinet member and bypassed the cranky Neville Chamberlain the following month when a possible conspiracy appeared that endangered U.S.

shipping. Churchill was dining at his pied-à-terre in London with two guests when the phone rang, and a servant appeared to summon Churchill. Since he did not know who was calling, Churchill declined at first to take the call, but the servant insisted, which was unusual. One of the guests later recalled:

> Annoyed, Churchill went, and it was his guests' turn to be perplexed, at his answers to his caller: "Yes, sir. . . . No, sir . . ."
>
> [T]here were "few people whom he would address as 'sir' and we wondered who on earth it could be. Presently he came back, much moved and said: 'Do you know who that was? The President of the United States. It is remarkable to think of being rung up in this little flat in Victoria Street by the President himself in the midst of a great war.' He excused himself, saying, 'This is very important. I must go and see the Prime Minister at once.'" [58]

The shipping emergency proved to be a false alarm, but Roosevelt had used this excuse to strengthen ties with Churchill. Roosevelt's political instincts were proven to be correct when Churchill became Britain's great wartime leader.

Roosevelt continued to lobby Congress for changes in the Neutrality Acts during the fall of 1939, as more European countries were drawn into war. By November, with Poland overrun by the Nazis, and Great Britain and France asking for help, Congress revised the laws to provide for cash-and-carry purchases of armaments. Stalin's Russia joined in the aggression in late November by attacking Finland. Although the Finns fought magnificently, they were soon forced to cede disputed territory to Russia in a wretched peace agreement in March 1940. One month later, on April 9, Germany used more excuses to invade Denmark and Norway.

The world awakened to news on May 10, 1940, that Hitler's troops had poured across the borders of Belgium, Holland, and France, crushing the opposition. England's government was in chaos; Neville Chamberlain had finally agreed to resign only the night before. Churchill was Great Britain's prime minister at last—just as Europe was bursting into flames.

On May 13, as Hitler's troops swept through France, Roosevelt met with his cabinet and General Marshall to review the situation. Once again, several cabinet officers appealed to the president to allow Marshall to ask Congress for a huge increase in defense appropriations. National elections were less than six months away, so FDR was wary of looking too warlike either to Congress or to the American people. When FDR was obviously going to skip Marshall's comments during the cabinet meeting, the general walked over to the seated president and resolutely asked for three minutes. Roosevelt could not refuse. Marshall poured out his list of the Army's critical needs in a very intense, almost angry, torrent, ending with this declaration: "If you don't do something . . . and do it right away, I don't know what is going to happen to this country." [59] Roosevelt listened to Marshall's statements. Afterward, Marshall pointed to that committee meeting as the breaking up of the logjam on defense preparations.

That same week, Great Britain's prime minister, Winston Churchill, sent Roosevelt an urgent cable on May 15, 1940, asking for the loan of fifty destroyers, antiaircraft guns, and other military supplies. Great Britain was losing far more in the fight in France than anyone had imagined possible. Churchill understood America's industrial capacity, but he did not grasp the full extent of America's weakness due to the continuing depression and military neglect. He thought that the United States could provide tremendous amounts of supplies, and quickly. But when Secretary Morgenthau asked General Marshall about aid to Britain, Marshall replied, "The shortage of [antiaircraft guns] is terrible and we have no ammunition for anti-aircraft and will not for six months. . . . So if we gave them the guns, they could not do anything with them." [60]

When FDR spoke to a joint session of Congress on May 16, he asked for more than a billion dollars for defense and a commitment for fifty thousand military aircraft. He appealed to Congress "not to take any action which would in any way hamper or delay the delivery of American-made planes to foreign nations which have ordered them." The *New York Times* gave testimony to Roosevelt's reception on the Hill: "Rarely, if ever before, has Mr. Roosevelt received such an ovation as that which greeted his appearance . . . in what could only be interpreted as a demonstration of national unity in a time of international crisis." [61] Rebuilding the military was now a vote getter, and Roosevelt followed up his dramatic speech to Congress with the previously discussed Fireside Chat of May 26. At last, he abandoned his New Deal rhetoric and asked for industry's cooperation in arming the nation.

On Capitol Hill, military estimates for new weapons had FDR's support. By the end of June, France had fallen to the Nazis, and defense of the Western Hemisphere was on everyone's mind. In the nineteen fiscal years from 1922 to 1940, Congress had appropriated a total of $6.5 billion for the War Department. Now, the nation's defenses reached a turning point, as Congress passed the Munitions Program of June 30, 1940, giving the U.S. Army a budget for 1940 of $9 billion, with additional billions for the Navy and Marines.[62]

With the fall of France, the plight of Europe's Jews worsened dramatically. France had been the last haven for antifascist leaders who fled there as Hitler occupied country after country. The collapse of France's military meant the imminent arrest of these refugees. On June 27, 1940, two Austrian socialists, Joseph Buttinger and Paul Hagen, traveled from New York City to Washington, D.C., to meet with Eleanor Roosevelt. Both men had only recently emigrated from Europe, where they had opposed Hitler. And both men needed help. The U.S. State Department had not eased its policies when it came to issuing visas for European refugees. Buttinger and Hagen knew that the Nazis would move quickly through France, rounding up their enemies, because by 1940 "almost the entire active anti-Nazi population of occupied Europe found itself crammed into that chaotic and panic-stricken country." [63]

Buttinger and Hagen explained the terrible position of thousands of intellectuals, political leaders, writers, and artists who were caught in France by the Nazi onslaught, many of whom were Jews. Mrs. Roosevelt immediately called her husband at the White House, and for twenty minutes she tried to persuade him to grant the necessary visas. Finally, resorting to a more threatening tone, Mrs. Roosevelt went on:

> If Washington refuses to authorize these visas immediately, German and American émigré leaders with the help of their American friends will rent a ship, and in this ship will bring as many of the endangered refugees as possible across the Atlantic. If necessary the ship will cruise up and down the East Coast until the American people, out of shame and anger, force the President and the Congress to permit these victims of political persecution to land.[64]

The threat of a refugee ship may have hit a nerve with Roosevelt, because in the spring of 1939 he had refused to allow the passengers of the SS *St. Louis* to land in the United States. Its passengers, more than eight hundred European Jewish refugees, were forced to return to Europe, where many were now trapped. To prevent a repeat of that public relations disaster, FDR directed the State Department to make emergency visas available to "prominent" refugees.

Roosevelt's policy on Eastern European immigration reflected that of the State Department, which argued, "If these people were in trouble, then they must be troublemakers—probably 'Reds' or Nazi spies—and not the kind of immigrants that America wanted."[65] The anti-Jewish immigration policy within the State Department often came from Breckinridge Long, an old friend of FDR's and contributor to his presidential campaigns. In June 1940, Long wrote: "We can delay and effectively stop for a temporary period of indefinite length the number of immigrants into the United States. We could do this by simply advising our consuls to put every obstacle in the way and to require additional evidence and to resort to various administrative devices which would postpone and postpone and postpone the granting of the visas." Long believed that Nazi agents were entering the United States posing as refugees, and he was determined to stop them.[66]

During Long's tenure, 90 percent of the quota slots available to immigrants from countries under German and Italian control were never filled. He obstructed immigration both before and after America's entrance into the war. Literally tens of thousands of available visas were never used at U.S. consulates, under orders from Washington.

As Hagen and Buttinger returned to New York City, they did not realize how difficult the work of getting refugees out of France would become. Even with Eleanor Roosevelt's support, the State Department was hindering their rescue efforts. But Hagen and Buttinger were only a small part of a much larger, determined group called the Emergency Rescue Committee, which had just organized and begun raising money. Even the *New York Times* supported the Rescue Committee and urged its readers to donate to the cause.[67]

As one of the committee's leaders, Paul Hagen wanted to go to southern France personally to supervise the escapes, but he was too well known. Finally, he asked a fellow committee member, Varian Fry, to spend two months in France while contacting as many refugees as possible. Fry agreed to go, and he received a cover letter from the Red Cross, stating that he was an aid worker.

Varian Fry was an unlikely candidate for such a dangerous undertaking. Educated at private prep schools and Harvard, he studied philosophy and classical languages in college. But he had the courage of his convictions after witnessing an anti-Jewish riot in Berlin in 1935. Nazis beat Jewish victims and then left them unconscious in the streets all night. Appalled at this behavior, Fry publicized the atrocities in articles in American newspapers.[68]

A small, physically unimpressive man, Fry hoped to pass unnoticed on the streets of cities like Marseilles, which was filled with refugees trying to leave France. With his Harvard background, Fry had connections with the Roosevelts and other Washington leaders. Eleanor Roosevelt helped him receive the proper travel documents for entering the war zone. With his cover letter as an aid worker, Fry could travel to southern France from Spain. He planned to spend two months in Marseilles, using the funds he smuggled into the country to help as many refugees as possible.[69]

Once he arrived in Marseilles, Fry realized the seriousness of the problem. Many intellectuals and artists were on the Nazis' lists for arrest or already in French internment camps, where the terrible conditions were killing thousands.[70] Fry continued to work in southern France long past his two-month deadline. With the Emergency Rescue Committee raising funds in America, for over a year Fry helped more than fifteen hundred people reach freedom. He also set up escape routes followed by hundreds of British soldiers. Among his more famous escapees were the writer Heinrich Mann, the painter Marc Chagall, and novelist and playwright Franz Werfel with his wife, Alma.

Fry received almost no help from the American consulate. Breckinridge Long, for example, constantly tried to stifle immigration: "We have just tightened our immigration restrictions for very good and sufficient reasons, and I am not going to recede one inch from the line of national defense and security."[71] Eventually Varian Fry and his friends resorted to forgery to get around France's refusal to issue exit visas to Eastern Europeans, especially Jews. But in sending so many Eastern Europeans to America, Fry also became persona non grata to Breckinridge Long and other American diplomats.[72]

By opposing the policies of Breckinridge Long at the State Department, Varian Fry found that he was, in effect, opposing Franklin Roosevelt. By October 1940, the refugee problem had inflamed working relations among staff members in the Roosevelt administration. Some bureaucrats were eager to help these desperate people; other staffers wanted no new immigrants allowed into the country at all, especially if they were Jews. Eleanor Roosevelt remained a champion of aiding Germany's enemies, no matter their politics or religion. Breckinridge Long found himself at odds with Mrs. Roosevelt and FDR's Advisory Committee on Refugees; consequently, he went to the White House to discuss the matter with FDR. According to Long:

> the whole subject of immigration, visas, safety of the United States, procedures to be followed; and all that sort of thing was on the table. I found that he was 100% in accord with my ideas. . . . The President expressed himself as in entire accord with the policy which would exclude persons about whom there was any suspicion that they would be inimical to the welfare of the United States no matter who had vouchsafed for them and irrespective of their financial or other standing.[73]

Franklin Roosevelt gave lip service to the cause of freedom during the following weeks, while quietly approving restrictions against immigration by Eastern Europeans. The president did ease immigration restrictions for British citizens, to please Winston Churchill. The crisis in Europe, however, meant that Roosevelt could quietly exclude Jews and cite national security over and over again, whether or not the international crisis really warranted such a response.

Polls showed that in this crisis, a majority of Americans preferred an experienced FDR, not a novice, to guide the country. Before the war, Roosevelt's poll numbers had slumped, but now his popularity soared once more. He might have outraged Congress in the past, tried to rewrite sections of the Constitution, and mired the United States in enormous debt, but the specter of Adolf Hitler's marching troops had frightened Americans. They were ready to accept Roosevelt as a presidential candidate, and Roosevelt was determined to win that third term.

2

THE ELECTION OF 1940: A THIRD TERM

When Roosevelt gave his Fireside Chat on May 26, 1940, the United States was totally unready for war. He vowed to change that and supported "the largest appropriations ever asked by the Army or the Navy in peacetime." Most businessmen who listened to Roosevelt that night were cautious. Was the president sincere about rebuilding America's defenses? Would he drop his animus toward business and give them incentives to make planes, tanks, and ammunition? Or were businessmen being set up again to take the blame for a country woefully ill-prepared for war? One of the skeptical businessmen was the former president of the Commonwealth and Southern (C&S), a utility holding company that sold electricity and appliances in many states from Michigan to Alabama. His name was Wendell Willkie.

The Indiana-born Willkie was a bundle of energy: six feet one inch tall and forty-eight years old, with brown tousled hair, a rumpled look, and arms that gestured openly when he spoke. After college and law school, Willkie specialized in utility law and mastered the business of creating and selling electric power. He became president of the C&S in part because he innovated ways to sell electricity cheaply. For example, he gave customers greater discounts when they bought more appliances and used more electricity. That was the principle of "economies of scale": The more electricity customers bought, under Willkie's formula, the lower their cost per unit. But under Roosevelt, the more electricity he sold and the more profits he and others made, the more Roosevelt attacked them and tried to redistribute their wealth through high taxes. Many businessmen, after years of public beatings and high taxes, had urged the eloquent Willkie to run for president and restore conditions for investors to earn profits.[1]

Five days after the president's Fireside Chat, Willkie went on the offense. "Planes and guns are not built by emotional appeals over the radio," Willkie told a Denver audience, "and they are not built by attacks on business." Yes, Willkie agreed, we do indeed need to replenish our arsenal of weapons. But FDR, with his years of hostility toward business, was not the man for the job. "Let's remove from power those who have sought to divide us into classes, who have sought to turn industry against the people and make the people fearful of industry," Willkie responded. He then warned, "Unless we start the wheels of our economy functioning, that cost of defense will come only out of the standard of living of the ordinary fellow." We could not afford a New Deal and a buildup in national defense as well.[2]

Willkie had been a lifelong Democrat, but he left the party when FDR launched his crusade against the private power industry. Willkie bragged that the C&S sold electricity almost 30 percent cheaper than other utilities, and he had power lines offering cheap electricity throughout the Tennessee Valley. FDR, however, supported the building of the Tennessee Valley Authority (TVA) as an experiment in government-generated power. A clash was inevitable. Willkie protested loudly when TVA built power lines alongside those of the C&S. TVA, Willkie complained, "offered its power at a less-than-cost rate, with the loss subsidized out of the federal treasury." Then another New Deal agency, the PWA, "would approach the municipal authorities and offer to give them free 45 percent of the cost of a new distribution system and to lend them the rest at a very low interest rate."[3]

Willkie was squeezed by the TVA, and he knew it. He resented the intrusion of the federal government into the utility business, and he finally met with FDR in 1934 to discuss it. When Willkie strolled into the Oval Office, FDR remarked, "I am glad to meet you, Mr. Willkie. I am one of your customers." Willkie retorted, "We give you good service, don't we?" After their talk, Willkie wired his wife, "[His] charm greatly exaggerated."[4]

The C&S challenged TVA encroachment in the courts, but lost their plea. "A privately owned corporation," Willkie lamented, "has no standing to challenge either the direct business competition of the federal government or indirect competition made possible by federal gifts to state agencies, however unconstitutional the competition may be."[5]

Ultimately the C&S sold its Tennessee Valley facilities to the TVA, but Willkie had some parting shots. The C&S had paid $3 million in taxes that would now be lost to the nation; also, more tax dollars would be needed to expand and operate the TVA. "Since the TVA is apparently selling its power at less than cost it should say so," Willkie charged. "If the people who live in New York City, for example, are to pay part of the electric bill of people who live in Corinth, Mississippi, the people in New York should know about it."[6]

Willkie argued that the utility bill to the nation's taxpayers was likely to increase because government had a poor track record of economic efficiency. "Government has never created an invention, never founded an industry, and never successfully operated a business," Willkie noted. The Post Office, for example, "has been operated at a very considerable deficit ever since it was organized." Willkie asked, "Would we consider it to be efficient operation if the government were to run the light and power industry as it runs the Post Office?"[7]

In fact, Willkie found evidence that the TVA was operating inefficiently in selling electricity and in flood control as well. But he used that point to argue that businesses run privately could easily outperform those run by the government. If a company like

AT&T "should take over the administration of the Post Office," Willkie said, "it is my belief that we should have an even more efficient mail service, at present rates, without any deficit at all." Why? Because "more than 50 percent of all telephones in the world are in the United States, and they cost the consumer a smaller part of his income than anywhere else." The Post Office, by contrast, had racked up $1,601,569,000 in operating debts over the last century, and that didn't include building costs.[8]

Entrepreneurs, Willkie stressed, had a strong stake in their enterprise that government bureaucrats simply could not match. In speeches, Willkie stirred audiences with many examples of entrepreneurs' borrowing capital, learning their industry, and then taking risks to bring quality products to Americans at ever cheaper prices. "In fifteen years," Willkie explained, the radio industry "by large scale production, has cut the price of its product by three-fourths and sold it to nearly 25,000,000 families." Similarly, the price of gasoline had steadily declined, and "no country pays refinery workers as high a wage as they receive here."[9]

The auto industry was another example Willkie used. From 1928 to 1932, even in the midst of depression, the car companies "made a low priced car which was better than the highest priced car in 1926. The public got a better car for considerably less money; and the reduction in price did not come out of the pockets of labor because automobile labor continued to be among the highest paid of all manufacturing industries."[10]

Willkie did endorse some New Deal programs, and he even supported unionization at the C&S and elsewhere; but he abhorred the New Deal's stifling regulations and high taxes, "which take up to 83 percent of a rich man's investment." Such interference created fear and a climate of uncertainty that made business experience impossible. "In short, it is fear—fear as to what the government is going to do, fear as to what may happen to industry—that has kept the investor from providing business with capital." He complained that "business is increasingly aware that the government is gradually taking over the functions of private enterprise."[11]

Willkie gained a national reputation by effectively debating New Dealers on the stump and over the radio. For example, he debated Attorney General Robert Jackson, an FDR favorite, in a dramatic town hall meeting that aired on national radio. Willkie criticized the New Deal, defended entrepreneurs, and impressed listeners all over the nation. Afterward, Hugh Johnson, former head of the NRA, announced that Willkie had made "a perfect monkey" of Jackson. Raymond Moley, a speechwriter and former brains truster, concluded that Willkie "utterly outclassed him" in the debate. Willkie had become a celebrity. After that event, he gave rebuttals to radio speeches by William O. Douglas, then chairman of the Securities and Exchange Commission, and Thurman Arnold, the leading trust buster in the Justice Department.[12]

These public triumphs led many Republicans to push Willkie for president in 1940. At first, the idea seemed laughable. No major party in U.S. history had ever nominated a pure business-man for president—especially one with no political experience whatsoever. However, unemployment still persisted at 17 percent after almost eight years of Roosevelt. Thus, a talented corporate executive like Willkie generated more and more excitement among Republicans with each passing month.

Willkie's business savvy created his candidacy, but, oddly, the European war would win him the Republican nomination. Unlike other Republican contenders, Willkie was an internationalist, who agreed with Roosevelt's massive defense buildup and his desire to confront aggressors. France fell to the Germans on June 22, two days before the Republicans met in Philadelphia to nominate their candidate. That event hung over the convention, and Americans increasingly wanted the more aggressive stand toward Hitler that Willkie offered. With the galleries at the convention chanting, "We want Willkie," the Republicans amazingly nominated him on their sixth ballot.[13] In other words, they selected a corporate executive who had never held a political office in his life to challenge the third-term bid of one of the shrewdest politicians in the nation's history.

Roosevelt conceded that Willkie was "grassroots stuff." He added, "The people like him very much. . . . We are going to have a heck of a fight on our hands with him." True, the 1940 campaign would be tough for the president, but the fall of France—and his pivoting toward business in his famous Fireside Chat of May 26—spurred his candidacy in the polls.[14]

In August 1939, before the war began, fully 60 percent of Americans in a poll said "no" to Roosevelt's run for a third term. The Depression was still raging and his New Deal had failed to turn the economy around. "We had 12,000,000 unemployed in 1932," Willkie observed, and "we have today nearly 11,000,000 unemployed." No wonder FDR was down in the polls and Republicans looked expectantly toward recapturing the White House. The persistence of high unemployment had contributed to the Democrats' losing eighty-one seats in the midterm election in 1938. Unemployment even hit 20 percent again during mid-1939.[15]

Hitler's march through Europe and FDR's truce with business changed the political landscape. By June, 57 percent of Americans endorsed the president for a third term. The idea of breaking the two-term tradition seemed less important to voters than having an experienced commander in chief in the White House who could help the British, stop the Germans, and keep America safe from attack. The president's truce with business was also timely because it blunted Willkie's appeal. The challenger's candidacy was launched on the premise that the nation needed someone in charge who wanted to improve the climate for investment—and that's what FDR publicly said he was now doing.[16]

In the month between his Fireside Chat and the Republican convention, FDR moved carefully to undermine the appeal of a business challenger. On May 28, the president established the

National Defense Advisory Commission (NDAC), and brought seven prominent businessmen to Washington to help him strengthen the country's defenses. These businessmen included Edward Stettinius, the chairman of the board at U.S. Steel, and William Knudsen, the president of General Motors. Both men ran companies essential for rebuilding the nation's defenses. Then the president began working on tax laws that would make these industrialists eager to build the weapons of war. He sent public signals that businessmen would have incentives to produce. On a shipbuilding contract given in June, for example, FDR opposed a law limiting the profit margins businessmen could make on defense projects; then he committed to using one of his New Deal agencies, the Reconstruction Finance Corporation, to provide funding for industrialists to expand existing factories and build new ones as well. On June 23, the day before the Republican convention, even that paragon of commerce the National Association of Manufacturers (NAM) endorsed the president's defense buildup.[17]

The president always had a special political touch and he showed it the week before the Republican convention. The wily FDR invited two prominent Republicans to join his cabinet. For secretary of war, FDR appointed Henry Stimson, a former secretary of war and secretary of state under Presidents Taft and Hoover. For secretary of navy, Frank Knox, the Republican candidate for vice president in 1936, entered the cabinet. Those choices put a damper on the Republican convention, and made the president appear open and bipartisan.[18]

Willkie was perplexed by the administration's truce with business, and by the new Republicans in the cabinet. He decided to support the president's foreign policy in general, and his defense buildup in particular. Instead, he made the continuing depression and the various New Deal failures the heart of his campaign. "This administration stands for principles exactly opposite to mine," Willkie charged in his opening speech of the campaign. "It does not preach the doctrine of growth. It preaches the doctrine of division. We are not asked to make more for ourselves. We are asked to divide among ourselves that which we already have. The New Deal doctrine does not seek risk, it seeks safety." Willkie's emphasis was different: "I say that we must substitute for the philosophy of distributed scarcity the philosophy of unlimited productivity."[19]

The challenger argued that lower taxes and more freedom were the road to jobs and prosperity. Under the stifling New Deal, by contrast, "The businessman has been afraid to expand his operations, and therefore millions of men have been turned away from employment offices." The result, Willkie said, was that "for the first time in our history, American industry has remained stationary for a decade." Willkie stressed, "It is a statement of fact, and no longer a political accusation, that the New Deal has failed in its program of economic rehabilitation." Sure, the president had unleashed a flood of federal spending. "The New Deal believes, as frequently declared, that the spending of vast sums by the government is a virtue in itself. They tell us that government spending insures recovery. Where is the recovery?" Willkie dramatically concluded that "this course will lead us to economic disintegration and dictatorship."[20]

Since many of Willkie's attacks were irrefutable, the president chose to lie low for a while. No, he would not debate the challenger, which Willkie had demanded. The president was too busy, he said, attending to important affairs of state. He would not descend to political squabbling. That strategy seemed safe. The war had pushed Roosevelt into the lead in the polls, and he hoped to hold it by keeping attention on Hitler, on the defense buildup, and off the New Deal and the two-term tradition. The president avoided overt political speeches during much of the campaign; instead, he visited defense plants and rejoiced that employment there was whittling down the national unemployment rate, which he praised, at the expense of an enlarged national debt, which he ignored.[21]

With the economy a Republican issue, Roosevelt wanted to get foreign policy into the campaign, and wanted to help Britain as well. Winston Churchill was losing multiple ships each week to German submarines, and with the fall of France, was preparing for German attacks on his country. The British had left much of their military hardware on the continent when they had to evacuate quickly at Dunkirk, and Churchill's treasury was also running out of cash to buy more. Therefore, he asked Roosevelt in May for a loan of fifty destroyers, along with torpedo boats, antiaircraft guns, rifles, and ammunition. Not only Churchill but even King George VI wrote a letter to Roosevelt asking for destroyers.[22]

When the British request for destroyers became public, many isolationists protested it immediately. Senator Gerald Nye, for example, said that sending destroyers to Britain "would be a belligerent act making us a party to the war and would in addition weaken our own defense." In secret, however, FDR and his staff and cabinet worked on a deal to bypass Congress and give Britain fifty destroyers in trade for leases on military bases owned by the British and located from the Caribbean to Newfoundland. It was no loan; it was a trade. But the Neutrality Acts posed a problem. When Great Britain had earlier requested torpedo boats, Attorney General Robert Jackson had declared that transaction illegal, but this time he squirmed around the federal statute by declaring the destroyers "nonessential" to the defense of the United States, and therefore available for "trade" to Great Britain.[23]

On such a thin legal and constitutional thread, Roosevelt agreed to the destroyers-for-bases deal in September 1940, but only after he was safely nominated for a third term. He even spent $50 million refurbishing the destroyers for war. Choosing to tell the press corps while on a train in a remote area of West Virginia, FDR also had no press copies of the documents giving the details of the negotiations with the British. The press had to write their initial stories using only "facts" provided by Roosevelt. FDR trumpeted the trade to the newsmen as "the most important since the

Jefferson Administration completed the Louisiana Purchase in 1803."[24]

Even the Louisiana Purchase, however, had to be ratified by the Senate. But Roosevelt wanted to make the destroyers-for-bases trade on his own as a so-called "executive agreement." So he ignored Congress completely and sent the legislators a written announcement after he had already told the press. "Congress is going to raise hell about this," Roosevelt knew, but he didn't want the delays that a debate, and possible defeat, might bring. "I might get impeached" for what I am about to do, Roosevelt told advisor Bernard Baruch before the announcement, but it would be so "sensational," he told Harold Ickes, that he, as president, was excited to do it. And the Louisiana Purchase comparison would make the deal sound historic.[25]

Sure enough, when Roosevelt announced the destroyers-for-bases deal, many congressmen and newspapermen were shocked. "Mr. Roosevelt today committed an act of war. He also became America's first dictator," said the *St. Louis Post-Dispatch.* "The U.S. has one foot in the war, and one foot on a banana peel," concluded the *New York Daily News.* "Once again we seem to have given England a blank check, to draw on as needed." Wendell Willkie and others asked, "Why wasn't Congress consulted?" Willkie approved of the trade, but not the method Roosevelt used to achieve it. The "method by which that trade was effected," Willkie said, "was the most arbitrary and dictatorial action ever taken by any President in the history of the United States." Willkie was accustomed to the business world, where the CEO and the board of directors had to work in tandem. "It does us no good to solve the problems of democracy if we solve them with the methods of dictators or waive aside the processes of democracy," Willkie insisted. Even the *New York Times* said, "The present agreement would be even more desirable if it had the formal stamp of congressional approval on it."[26]

Roosevelt's political gamble was not as drastic as he made it seem. He believed that accusations of "dictator" and talk of impeachment would wane if he could persuade voters that England was in danger, and that Hitler was a direct menace to the United States. The president had asked George Gallup to conduct secret opinion polls on the public's response to the idea of sending destroyers to Britain. FDR also watched polls from *Fortune* and those by two Princeton University professors that showed public opinion had swung in favor of the trade. Even some isolationists heartily approved of lining America's offshore waters with bases from the Caribbean to Newfoundland because it improved America's defenses. The ends, Roosevelt firmly believed, would justify his means.[27]

Breckinridge Long, the assistant secretary of state, wrote in his diary, "The value of the destroyers is inconsequential when compared to that of ten bases—eight of them for Caribbean defense—for 100 years. The destroyers will be gone in ten. It is an enormous step in Continental defense. Of course it is a violation of international law."[28] Constitutional lawyer Edward Corwin of Princeton, who had been a consultant to the Roosevelt administration, was appalled at the constitutional violation of the destroyer deal: "Why not any and all of Congress's specifically delegated powers be set aside by the president's 'executive power' and the country put on a totalitarian basis without further ado?"[29]

But the constitutional quibblers lost out to the vote getters. With glowing headlines from the *New York Times* and the *New York Herald-Tribune*, Roosevelt's stature as war leader skyrocketed. Even most members of Congress jumped on the bandwagon, describing the trade as "a fine deal." In the words of Robert Shogan, who has written a good book on the subject, "The destroyer deal elevated FDR above the status of candidate and, more than any other event of his presidency until then, established him as a Commander-in-Chief." Gallup polls taken two weeks after the destroyer announcement showed that Roosevelt had taken the lead over Willkie.[30]

But the election was still a close contest. Roosevelt took the lead only because foreign policy had trumped the bad economy. The first test of the president's strength was the Maine elections on September 10. Maine historically held its state elections early in September, and the results always gave a clue to where the campaigns were going. Maine was a Republican state, but the large margin of victory for the Republicans there in 1940 gave the Willkie campaign "a rise in enthusiasm." Republicans won the Senate seat, the governor's race, and the three House seats by margins of about two to one. As Arthur Krock noted, "The percentage of victory was above the point which has often, historically, been followed by success for a Republican national ticket." The most conspicuous defeat for the Democrats was that of their two-term governor, Louis Brann.[31]

The Maine vote was especially ominous for FDR because Republicans had also done well in all seven previous special elections for House seats in 1940. That pattern was national. But in Maine, the Republican margin of victory had increased even more sharply than usual from the 1938 results. Joseph Martin, chairman of the Republican National Committee, was gleeful. "These results are concrete evidence of our contentions that the country has tired of waiting for recovery." On the front page of the *New York Times*, Martin said, "The Maine election definitely heralds the end of the Roosevelt administration, with all its inefficiency, bungling, extravagance and radicalism."[32]

Martin, however, was boasting too early. He must have forgotten what happened when the New Deal coalition sprang into action in 1936. In that year, FDR artfully mobilized political subsidies into the most devastating electoral weapon ever seen in American presidential politics. Congress had allocated $4.8 billion to the WPA in 1935, and Roosevelt used much of this money to target key political districts with projects to build roads and various buildings. V. G. Coplen, the Democratic county chairman of Indiana, explained this strategy: "What I think will help is to change the WPA management from top to bottom. Put men in there who are . . . in favor of using these Democratic projects to make votes for the Democratic Party." In fact, one WPA director in New Jersey answered his office phone, "Democratic headquarters." Congressman Frank Towey of New Jersey expressed the attitude of many Democrats when he said, "In this county there are 18,000 on WPA. With an average of 3 in a family you have 54,000 potential Democratic votes. Can anyone beat that if it is properly mobilized?" The president had a hired pollster assigned to detail where federal funds were going and give the Democrats bragging points about them—so that voters in each state could be reminded that keeping the Democrats in power keeps the federal faucet running. On election day, Roosevelt carried 46 states and defeated Republican Alf Landon by an electoral vote of 523 to 8. As Democratic Senator Carter Glass of Virginia said, "The 1936 elections would have been much closer had my party not had a four billion, eight hundred million dollar relief bill as campaign fodder." [33]

Many Democrats were just waiting for the flow of federal funds to come in for their 1940 campaign. The WPA would be a major force again that year. According to James Doherty, a New Hampshire Democrat, "It is my personal belief that to the victor belongs the spoils and that Democrats should be holding most of those [WPA] positions so that we might strengthen our fences for the 1940 election." C. Roger Dunn, a popular statistician of the 1930s, published the Dunn Survey on elections, and he estimated that each person on the WPA was worth four votes at the polls for FDR. [34]

FDR and his New Dealers had a special system for mobilizing the WPA to win elections. During election years, they had increased the WPA rolls (and those of other federal programs as well). Those who received government jobs were grateful and were expected to campaign vigorously for Democrats on election day. After the election, the WPA laid off workers because they were not needed until the next campaign—thereby cutting some federal spending to make the budget deficits smaller. Some members of

Roosevelt's cabinet were nervous about moving poor Americans on and off the WPA for political purposes. After the election of 1936, for example, Harry Hopkins, director of the WPA, told a private gathering that he was ready to lay off hundreds of thousands of WPA workers, including 150,000 from the cities. Henry Morgenthau, one of those present, asked this penetrating question: "If you can find 150,000 people now on relief rolls who you say now are not in need of relief, how are you going to answer the charge that you must have known before November that these people were not in need of relief?"[35]

Morgenthau's occasional moral qualms are interesting to study. Sometimes his conscience bothered him, and he would lament the targeted subsidies and the failure of New Deal spending to dent high unemployment. Other times he would join in the fun and plan subsidies, IRS audits, and congressional investigations to achieve political ends. In 1940, however, Morgenthau wanted Roosevelt to be reelected. So he had few moral compunctions about using federal subsidies to attract voters. For example, during the summer of 1939, with unemployment stuck at 20 percent, Democrats were glum, but Morgenthau became a cheery presence with a plan to target public works projects for the 1940 elections. On June 14, 1939, Morgenthau visited the president alone in the White House and advocated making a map, county by county, of public works projects that had been built under the New Deal. Then Morgenthau suggested picking out ten strategic states— those necessary for presidential victory the next year—and targeting most federal projects to them. "Of course," the president quickly responded, "that's the thing to do. . . . Have you got a list of the money ready for me?" Morgenthau had done his homework and gave the list to FDR. The president was thoroughly delighted, and Morgenthau later wrote in his diary, "I haven't enjoyed any meeting that I have had with the President as much as this one in . . . a year and a half."[36]

The planning done in 1939 came to fruition in 1940 with New

Dealers using their federal programs to win votes for the president. The Republicans could do little to stop it. Although the WPA had actually decreased its numbers during much of 1940, suddenly its numbers increased by 43,142 between September 25 and October 2. The Republicans protested, but with no effect.[37] The *New York Times*, which observed WPA activity carefully, editorialized, "The WPA program in its present form is clearly an obstacle to the defense program. When the great bulk of our present unemployed labor will now be needed either directly to produce the materials of defense or to be trained for such work, or to take the jobs vacated by others for defense work, the WPA program continues to go on the assumption that it is still necessary to invent all sorts of miscellaneous projects to keep men busy." In other words, we need to train for a defense buildup, not for busy work.[38]

Not just the WPA, but other New Deal agencies seemed to be coordinating to reelect the president. The AAA, according to Republicans, "was rushing out payments [in October] ordinarily made in November and December." R. M. Evans, an AAA administrator, denied the charges and said, "I feel all fair-minded persons will agree that any speeding up on payments under the program is an evidence of increasing efficiency . . . and in no way connected with politics."[39] Democrats wanted to pump their urban vote as well. Four days before the election, Claude Wickard, secretary of agriculture, revealed a new free milk program for children in the swing state of New York. In a front-page story, the *New York Times* reported, "All of the 149,000 children under the age of 16 on the New York City home relief rolls will receive [starting in December] a pint of milk a day without cost to their families."[40]

The president also saw great potential in signing defense contracts in targeted political areas. That way he not only achieved his truce with business, but he was also able to reward those men loyal to him in the past, and others who would become loyal to him in the future. The first naval contract, for example, that Roosevelt signed was on June 13, 1940, less than two weeks before the Republican convention. The key politician rewarded was Congress-man Lyndon Johnson of Texas. Johnson, only thirty-two years old, had become fascinated with the way federal subsidies could be used to win votes. He modeled his career after Roosevelt and helped the president whenever he could. By influencing Texas politics, for example, Johnson made the president's job easier. In 1939, Vice President John Nance Garner decided to run for presi-dent; he was criticizing FDR in cabinet meetings throughout the year. Johnson helped the president by undermining Garner's cam-paign in Texas, and also by reporting to the president the actions of fellow Texan Sam Rayburn, the new Speaker of the House. By 1940, Garner's campaign was in shambles, and Roosevelt was will-ing to give Johnson a large federal subsidy for his reward.[41]

Johnson's request was for a large naval base at Corpus Christi, Texas. Brown & Root was the construction company Johnson wanted to win the contract because they had loyally funded John-son during his political campaigns. On June 13, only eighteen days after his Fireside Chat, the president approved the contract for Johnson's naval base, and the $25 million in federal funding largely went to Brown & Root. Since the contract was a cost-plus fixed fee contract, it gave Brown & Root a guaranteed profit regardless of their efficiency. In fact, with cost overruns, the final payment for the base was closer to $100 million. As political operative Thomas Corcoran observed, "Mr. [James] Forrestal [undersecretary of the navy] twisted a hell of a lot of tails to" keep the whole project in the hands of "Lyndon's friends."[42]

With the naval contract secure, and Brown & Root flush with cash, Johnson was in position to wield power. George Brown, the financial man at Brown & Root, made that point clear. Lyndon, Brown said, you only need to say "when and where I can return at least a portion of the favors. Remember that I am *for* you, right or wrong, and it makes no difference if I think you are right or wrong. If you want it, I am for it 100%."[43] Johnson decided to use some of the abundant cash now available to him to change the outcome of the 1940 elections. While Roosevelt was focused on winning a third term, Johnson decided to increase his influence in the party he hoped to someday lead by helping several dozen Democrats in close races try to win their House seats.

In 1940, small amounts of cash—even $300—could buy radio time, or fund a late campaign rally, that could swing a close election. Johnson, with the approval of the Democratic Party, set up an office in Washington, D.C., and began contacting Democratic candidates and offering them cash. George Brown gave Johnson an initial $30,000 (campaign finance laws had some restrictions) and leveraged his influence to get more cash to the young congressman. Johnson, meanwhile, began sending checks and wiring cash all around the country to eager and desperate Democratic candidates.[44]

One needy incumbent was Martin Smith, a four-term congressman from Hoquiam, Washington. Smith needed not only cash, but help from Johnson in unraveling the WPA bureaucracy. Smith had seemingly won a WPA airport project for his district, but "this delay," he wrote Johnson on October 26, in getting federal funds flowing into his district "is not doing me any good politically." Johnson swung into action, using his influence with FDR. One week later, Johnson sent Smith this telegram: "Your WPA application has been approved by WPA and is at the White House awaiting the President's signature. Will do my best to get this signed for you and wire you by Monday."[45] With Johnson's help, Smith won his fifth term in Congress, but in 1942, without Johnson to bail him out, Smith lost his seat. In a similar manner, Congressmen Charles M. McLaughlin, John F. Hunter, William Sutphin, and Alfred Beiter received cash from Johnson, and all won their elections in 1940, but all lost in 1942.

Roosevelt's single decision to support a naval base for Johnson was thus winning votes for Democrats all across the nation. Roosevelt also used the new defense plants to win votes in the cities where they were being built. During the last two weeks of the

campaign, Roosevelt gave speeches and radio addresses in key cities boosted by defense plants. In Boston, he said, "You good people
here in Boston know of the enormous increase of productive work
in your Boston Navy Yard." In Seattle, the president, in a radio address, said, "Citizens of Seattle—you have watched the Boeing
plant out there grow." Philadelphians heard Roosevelt say, "Last
month, September, another five hundred thousand workers went
to work in our industries." And in Buffalo, Roosevelt announced, "I
have been inspecting some plants this morning—plants which are
turning out weapons of war, pursuit airplanes." Even before the
campaign began, the president had told Morgenthau that defense
plants could be translated into votes. "These foreign orders mean
prosperity in this country," Roosevelt said, "and we can't elect a
Democrat Party unless we get prosperity and these foreign orders
are of the greatest importance."[46]

Roosevelt had a delicate challenge. He wanted to exploit the
new jobs from the defense plants, but he wanted to avoid talk
about the taxes to pay for them, or talk that building defense
plants might be a step toward war. To accomplish that purpose,
Roosevelt decided to tell audiences he was not sending American
boys to war "except in case of attack."

Willkie was aghast at Roosevelt's tactics. On the issues of economic policy, voters consistently preferred Willkie to Roosevelt.
That was why the Republicans had nominated a businessman. But
the war had intruded as an issue, and voters trusted the experienced president over a novice like Willkie. And building defense
plants traded jobs for debt, which worked in Roosevelt's favor in
the short term. Therefore, Willkie challenged Roosevelt's ability to
build for war and keep the peace. "We do not want to send our
boys over there again," Willkie said in St. Louis. "If you elect the
third-term candidate, I believe they will be sent." The challenger,
he insisted, was the peace candidate. In the Chicago area, Willkie
said again and again, "And I promise that when I am President I
shall not send one American boy into the shambles of a European

war." In Portland, he said that Roosevelt "has left us virtually alone in the world and brought us to the brink of war."[47]

Roosevelt responded to Willkie by making an even stronger pledge of peace. In Boston, on October 30, Roosevelt promised, "I have said this before, but I shall say it again and again: Your boys are not going to be sent into any foreign wars."[48] He left out "in case of attack" to strengthen his hand as a peace candidate. Behind the scenes he was working with Churchill, Britain's new prime minister, to prepare for war, but in this election he wanted voters to think he was the candidate of peace.

On election night, early returns initially suggested the president might lose. Roosevelt, preparing for the worst, asked to be alone. Would the combination of businessmen, newspaper publishers, and isolationists, among others, "at last knock him down and write his epitaph in history as a power-grasping dictator rebuked by a free people?"[49] As more returns came in, Roosevelt began to win, and he had his doors opened to friends and family.

One call he made that night was to Lyndon Johnson. Walter Jenkins, Johnson's assistant, answered the phone: "Mr. Roosevelt called and asked how many seats we were going to lose, and Mr. Johnson said, 'We're not going to lose. We're going to gain.'" Roosevelt was very impressed, because pundits had predicted the Democrats would lose thirty seats. Instead, the Democrats gained eight seats in the House, but lost three in the Senate, where Democrats had to campaign without Johnson's cash. Polls showed that without the war, Willkie had a 5.5 percent edge over the president; but with Hitler on the move, voters preferred Roosevelt—the man who promised the American people, "Your boys are not going to be sent into any foreign wars."[50]

The 1940 election was a milestone in U.S. history. FDR had maneuvered to run for a third term, and voters reelected him. Of course, this election was different from others—war was on the horizon and Roosevelt had shed his animus toward business. In the campaign he celebrated the anticipated abilities of American industrialists to make fifty thousand planes, and a host of war weapons. He gave them incentives and encouragement to gird for war. As usual, Roosevelt kept the Republicans off balance. With the failure of the New Deal—unemployment was still 14.6 percent in 1940—the Republicans nominated the businessman Willkie and planned to campaign on the economy, and Roosevelt's eight-year failure to grasp the nature of markets, taxes, and incentives. Instead, Roosevelt used the European war to his political advantage.

But the 1940 election, for all its uniqueness, was a typical Roosevelt performance. First, he mobilized the WPA and other New Deal agencies to win votes. He added defense plants to his list as well. Defense plants were vote getters from Boston to the West Coast. But the president's biggest vote getter may have been the naval base in Corpus Christi that gave Brown & Root the profits to give Lyndon Johnson the campaign money that he spent to capture House seats for Democrats across the country.

Second, Roosevelt increased executive power even further with his destroyers-for-bases deal with Britain. In his first two terms, he expanded executive power on the domestic scene with a slew of federal programs that expanded executive powers beyond what the Constitution proscribed. In the destroyers-for-bases deal, the president bypassed Congress to negotiate a trade directly with Churchill. As the United States moved toward war, and into war, FDR's powers would expand further. He ushered in a new political order and used the powers of government to help him win an unprecedented third term in office. Could he ever be beaten? some critics wondered.

Finally, Roosevelt continued his success in winning over American intellectuals to his goal of expanding the federal government. During the Founding era, by contrast, most American thinkers wanted limited government and argued the case for liberty with logic and vigor. Alexander Hamilton and James Madison wrote *The Federalist Papers* to defend limited government, checks and balances, and natural rights. Those intellectuals who opposed them mainly argued that the executive and legislative branches of government still had too much authority to guarantee liberty for future generations of Americans. But the Progressive Era dimmed the case for limited government. By 1940, most intellectuals supported Roosevelt's imperial presidency, and he, in turn, brought many of them into his administration to help him run the many new programs.

In 1948, after the guns of war were silenced, historian Thomas Bailey of Stanford University emerged to defend Roosevelt's actions in 1940 and 1941. "Franklin Roosevelt repeatedly deceived the American people during the period before Pearl Harbor . . . ," Bailey wrote. "He was like the physician who must tell the patient lies for the patient's own good. . . . Because the masses are notoriously shortsighted, and generally cannot see danger until it is at their throats, our statesmen are forced to deceive them into an awareness of their own long-run interests."[51]

Bailey would teach at Stanford for almost forty years, and write *The American Pageant*, which, at more than 2 million copies sold, may have been the best-selling college textbook of the postwar period. His student and coauthor, David Kennedy, wrote a book in 1999 favorable to the presidency of Franklin Roosevelt, and that book won the Pulitzer Prize. Bailey and Kennedy are typical. In 1996, the historians in the Arthur Schlesinger presidential poll again ranked Roosevelt as a "Great President," even ahead of George Washington.[52] Roosevelt had swept through the ranks of the historians almost as thoroughly as he swept past the Republicans in 1940.

3

THE BATTLE OF THE ATLANTIC

In late August 1940, seven British scientists and military experts sailed for America with an incalculably valuable cargo contained in one black box about the size of a footlocker. Inside were top-secret blueprints and diagrams for gun sights, self-sealing fuel tanks, and rockets. Most important, the black box contained a working model of a spectacular breakthrough in radar, the cavity magnetron. James Phinney Baxter, science historian and Pulitzer Prize winner, later called the cavity magnetron the single most valuable cargo brought to American shores.[1] Winston Churchill had decided that, given the dire plight of his government, Great Britain would offer the United States virtually every armament secret with no strings attached. During the voyage, the scientists worried that the black box would float if the ship were torpedoed and possibly be discovered by German submariners, so holes were drilled in each end of the box to help it sink quickly if the ship went down.[2]

In America, the newly arrived British scientists met with Vannevar Bush and members of his National Defense Research Committee (NDRC) to unveil the wonders of the cavity magnetron. This relatively simple device made possible the development of microwave rather than long-wave radar. Suddenly, the British had advanced American research by at least two years. The cavity magnetron made precise radar possible, with much smaller and better-performing equipment than earlier, bulky models. As a comparison, Luis Alvarez, one of the NDRC's scientists, said, "If automobiles had been similarly improved, modern cars would cost about a dollar and go a thousand miles on a gallon of gas."[3]

What the British needed was a way to put microwave radar into fighter aircraft. With the Luftwaffe's nightly bombings of British cities beginning in September 1940, Britain's Chain Home radar system was not accurate enough to pinpoint night bombers, so British fighters could not repel the enemy. Thousands of Britons were dying in the bombings. The electronics industry in Great Britain was strained to the limit and could not spare the effort to produce new radar equipment. Britons would have to depend on the United States for that. Vannevar Bush and the NDRC scientists had both the funds and the know-how to find solutions, and they went to work.[4]

Radar was not new to the Americans, who had worked on primitive radar systems earlier that summer, even to the point of constructing what was probably the first radar gun. When the device proved that it could track speeders on the highway, one scientist quipped, "For the Lord's sake, don't let the cops know about this." Now they aimed for a more serious goal: As British radar expert Eddie Bowen said, "Here was the cream of American scientists, hell-bent on doing all they could for the war effort—some fourteen months before America itself actually entered the war."[5]

America's NDRC had come about in June 1940, when Franklin Roosevelt met with former MIT professor Vannevar Bush. Bush had enlisted the aid of Harry Hopkins to focus FDR's attention on the need to mobilize civilian scientists for war research. When FDR looked over Bush's four-paragraph description of his proposed "committee," the president immediately approved. "That's okay," FDR told Bush. "Put 'OK, FDR' on it."[6] Such presidential backing worked wonders in the Washington bureaucracy as Bush maneuvered to get the funding and the scientists he wanted to join his committee, despite suspicions of the New Dealers.

Vannevar Bush had an important ally in a wealthy New York

philanthropist and fellow scientist, Alfred Loomis. Loomis's cousin was none other than Henry Stimson, the same cabinet member who had met with FDR at Hyde Park in 1933 to discuss Japan. During the eventful summer of 1940, Roosevelt needed strong leadership at the War Department. He finally replaced Secretary of War Woodring with Henry Stimson, even though Stimson was a Republican. Stimson's ties with Alfred Loomis would prove very beneficial to the NDRC.[7]

Stimson's new assignment drew stern criticism from isolationists such as Senator Robert Taft, who viewed the appointment as another step toward war. At a Senate hearing, Taft asked Stimson if he favored American ships' carrying war supplies to belligerents; when Stimson said that in effect he did, Taft asked a series of questions designed to point out the potential consequences of such policies: "What if a German plane sank an American ship carrying supplies to the Allies? Would that 'almost inevitably lead us into war'?" Stimson denied that, but Taft had made the point that supplying Great Britain could pull the United States into war.[8]

One benefit of Stimson's appointment was that he worked well with General Marshall and even better with Robert P. Patterson, who replaced Louis A. Johnson. Congress voted to transfer to the new secretary of war all the statutory duties that had been formerly assigned to the assistant secretary, to avoid another feud. Congress also created the position of undersecretary of war, which Patterson filled, and he proved to be a dynamo of efficiency and honesty in mobilizing American industry to meet the needs of the military. Patterson, unlike the isolationists, believed that the United States could not avoid the war in Europe.[9]

In the fall of 1940, Stimson and Patterson worked to strengthen the country's defenses. Congress had authorized billions, but how could the defense industries be organized? Earlier that year, on May 29, President Roosevelt had appointed a seven-person National Defense Advisory Commission (NDAC), answerable to FDR. The commissioners represented seven different segments of the economy, but no one man was in charge. Thus, it was ineffective. In Henry Stimson's opinion, "It was just six men too many."[10]

Progress in the defense industries was slow, because it took time and money to get designs in place and workers trained to build aircraft, tanks, and guns. The same month that FDR had announced the creation of his defense commission (NDAC), a *New York Times* editorial observed that throwing money at defense was not the only solution: "We need also a prompt revision of those governmental policies which have destroyed production capacity in this country by discouraging private enterprise."[11] American industry was so far behind that when production started, the output was tiny compared to the urgent demand. "Germany has been preparing for seven years," said Undersecretary of War Robert Patterson, while the United States during that same time had "almost legislated [its army] out of existence."[12] Within months, it was clear that the NDAC was unequal to its task.

Roosevelt himself saw the lack of military preparedness. On August 17, 1940, he traveled to Ogdensburg, New York, to review the Army and watch an Air Force flyby. When he asked General Clifford R. Powell about the state of his unit's preparedness, Powell said that during tank maneuvers, his men were using "drain pipes to simulate mortars and broom sticks to simulate machine guns."[13] About a month later, Roosevelt asked General Marshall for the total number of bombers in the U.S. military, not counting the few located in Hawaii or the Panama Canal Zone. When Marshall reported that only forty-nine serviceable bombers were in the continental U.S. air fleet, "[FDR's] head went back as if someone had hit him in the chest," Stimson wrote in his diary.[14]

Secretary Stimson summed up the clash on defense between New Dealers and big business: "The whole thing is a great clash between two big theories and interests. If you are going to try to go to war, or to prepare for war, in a capitalist country, you have got to let business make money out of the process or business won't work, and there are a great many people in Congress who think that they can tax business out of all proportion and still have businessmen work diligently and quickly. That is not human nature."[15]

Meanwhile, with concern growing about the country's defenses, in September Congress passed the Selective Service and Training Act of 1940. The first peacetime draft in U.S. history would organize not only white recruits but also African-Americans. On September 27, African-American leaders met with President Roosevelt and War Department officials to ask that military units be integrated. According to Undersecretary of War Patterson, Roosevelt replied that he was all for "progress" but he could not endorse integrated units at the present time.[16]

After the meeting, the White House released a statement that segregation of white and black troops would continue. The wording of the statement implied that the African-American leaders at the September 27 meeting had approved the policy. Walter White, one of the participants, sent a telegram to President Roosevelt, reminding him that White and his colleagues, T. Arnold Hill and A. Philip Randolph, had "specifically repudiated" military segregation. The three black leaders were profoundly disappointed that they had made no progress at the White House. "Official approval by the Commander-in-Chief of the Army and Navy of such discrimination and segregation is a stab in the back of democracy," wrote White.[17]

With White so upset by the White House's misstatements about the September conference, FDR told his press secretary, Steve Early, to get White back in the Oval Office for another talk. Walter White was secretary of the National Association for the Advancement of Colored People (NAACP), and as its leader, he refused to meet with FDR again unless the administration would retract the statement regarding segregation of black troops.

White had already asked FDR to appoint "a civilian aide or adviser on Negro affairs at secretarial level in the War Department." Mary McLeod Bethune, founder and president of the National Council of Negro Women, wrote Eleanor Roosevelt on October 5, also suggesting that the president make such an appointment. Undersecretary Patterson at the War Department supported integrating the military and also appointing an African-American to a leadership position at the War Department. Both Secretary Stimson and FDR opposed integrating troops, but Roosevelt still maneuvered to win the black vote in the coming election.[18]

On October 25, Secretary Stimson named Judge William H. Hastie, an African-American graduate of Harvard Law School and dean of law at Howard University, as "Civilian Aide to the Secretary of War." During the same week, the U.S. Army announced that Colonel Benjamin O. Davis, Sr., was promoted to brigadier general, making him the first African-American general in the U.S. military. The White House also issued new statements about its racial policies. All of these events led Mary M. Bethune to write Mrs. Roosevelt on November 1 that "the tide of loyalty among my people is rising high," meaning that they would vote to reelect Franklin Roosevelt.[19]

All draftees began reporting for military duty in October. However, members of Congress were determined that these recruits would not be sent out of the Western Hemisphere. The Army's Quartermaster Construction Division grew seventyfold as it built housing and recreation facilities for 1,216,459 men at 245 locations. Budget overruns and delays plagued many sites; original estimates said the camps would cost $516 million, but actual costs reached almost one billion dollars. However, the size of the U.S. Army grew from 267,767 men on June 30, 1940, to 1,460,998 by the summer of 1941. The defense of the country was improving. Part of the increase occurred when National Guard units were assimilated into the regular army.[20] The Marines also expanded, building a training base at New River, North Carolina, which became Camp Lejeune.

As the military grew, Roosevelt's approach in handling details such as production quotas, Army construction, and numbers of aircraft was to leave such matters up to his staff. FDR would coin wonderful phrases, but he often overstated the defense buildup. During November and December 1940, aircraft manufacturers Douglas and Lockheed delivered twenty-nine commercial aircraft while producing only six military planes. The U.S. Army Air Force also experienced severe shortages of spare parts, including engines, propellers, and landing gear.[21]

To help solve the problems with aircraft production, Robert A. Lovett, a New York investment banker and World War I pilot, was appointed special assistant to Patterson. Lovett toured American aircraft factories to learn more about their methods and reported back to the War Department: "By European standards, the American aircraft industry was in the horse-and-buggy age . . . alarmingly small, inadequately capitalized, and technologically backward."[22] Especially in the design of war planes, the United States was far behind the other world powers.

Fortunately for the United States, Undersecretary of War Patterson and Army Chief of Staff Marshall tirelessly pushed their staffs to find available land for new bases, plan for construction of defense plants, and develop estimates of the raw materials needed in case of war. Lieutenant Colonel Brehon Somervell took command of the Quartermaster Construction Division, bringing order to what had been chaos. At the same time, the U.S. Navy expanded the number of officers and sailors and frantically ordered new ships, including 11 aircraft carriers, 9 battleships, 181 destroyers, and dozens of cruisers.[23]

Unlike FDR, Winston Churchill quoted accurate figures of production totals for fighters, bombers, all types of armaments. He enjoyed flying in military aircraft and trying out new weapons. When he had served as First Lord of the Admiralty at the beginning of World War I, Churchill's thoroughness meant that the Royal Navy was well prepared when hostilities broke out. His knowledge of the weapons of war gave his countrymen more confidence as he became a leader in the Second World War.

Franklin Roosevelt had no such technical background or interest. Thus, by December 1940, the national defense program was beginning to take shape, but Congressman Everett Dirksen of Illinois called for a congressional investigation into the "confusion, bewilderment, misdirection, chaos, discordance, inefficaciousness, and mysticism that now besets this program." He charged that thousands of defense workers had been hired, but many were still waiting for job assignments while they "twiddle their thumbs."[24]

Roosevelt responded to Dirksen and other critics that month by replacing the NDAC with the Office of Production Management (OPM).[25] FDR named William Knudsen of General Motors as director, with labor leader Sidney Hillman as associate director, and Secretary of the Navy Knox and Secretary of War Stimson as members. Knudsen's authority was muddled, because the president required unanimous agreement from the four OPM members before decisions were made.[26]

The same week that FDR created the OPM, Congress opened debate on Lend-Lease. Earlier, only days after winning his third term, Roosevelt had proposed sending Great Britain 50 percent of all defense materiel produced in the United States on a cash-and-carry basis.[27] When the British announced that their war chest was almost empty, he outlined plans in December to "lend" Great Britain war supplies, even if they couldn't pay cash. Roosevelt likened his plan to that of lending a neighbor a garden hose: If the neighbor's house is on fire, you lend him the hose at once. When the fire is quenched, the neighbor gives back the garden hose. FDR did not mention how Great Britain would return burned-out tanks, crashed bombers, or sunken destroyers. As Senator Taft said, "Lending arms is like lending chewing gum. You don't want it back."[28] Roosevelt's garden hose analogy gave the impression that the United States would lend armaments that were lying around, unused, to the Allies.

In another Fireside Chat on December 29, 1940, FDR called

upon the United States to be "the arsenal of democracy," but he had to use caution. His own party's platform said that the United States was not to declare war "except in case of attack." In his State of the Union message the next month, he emphasized America's role in sending supplies *but not men*: "Let us say to the democracies: 'We shall send you, in ever-increasing numbers, ships, planes, tanks, guns.'" Roosevelt's supporters in Congress introduced the Lend-Lease bill.

The stated purpose of Lend-Lease was (1) to build and ship armaments to Great Britain and other nations no matter when they ran out of dollars, and (2) to meet immediate needs by authorizing "the president to transfer, lease, exchange, or give any finished armament in the possession of the United States." Thus, if Congress approved Lend-Lease, the president would have enormous power to control and allocate what the United States produced and where supplies went.[29] Such unfettered power frightened Roosevelt's critics. Senator Bennett Clark of Missouri argued that Lend-Lease "is simply a bill authorizing the President to declare war."[30] Senator Taft believed that Lend-Lease "certainly authorizes him to take us into the midst of the war, and once we are there his powers will be unlimited. . . . [B]efore we get through with that war the rights of private property in the United States will be to a large extent destroyed."[31]

Ties with Great Britain continued to multiply, and much of that was the work of Winston Churchill. Years later, Churchill's son, Randolph, related a conversation he had with his father in the early days of the war, when Britain was fighting alone. Randolph asked his father how he would win the war, and Churchill answered, "I shall drag the United States in."[32] Given that Franklin Roosevelt was president of the United States, Churchill didn't have to "drag" all that hard to find an enthusiastic war partner. Roosevelt "entirely lacked an isolationist mentality," in the words of historian Waldo Heinrichs.[33]

During (and after) the debate on Lend-Lease, the British

worked openly to influence American opinion. Newsman David Brinkley explained, "By mid-1941, there were over 3,000 British businessmen, military officers, and Foreign Office officials working in Washington to promote their country's cause. At one point, [British ambassador] Halifax had a truck that had been dented by German bombs shipped over from London, placed signs on it saying 'Buy British,' and sent it off around the city [Washington, D.C.]."[34]

On March 8, Lend-Lease passed the Senate by a vote of sixty to thirty-one. (Gallup polls had shown in February that a majority of voters favored aid to Britain.) After passage in the House, the bill went to the White House for FDR's signature on March 11. Alistair Cooke attended FDR's press conference that day. When asked by a reporter if ships in America were already loading supplies for Britain, Roosevelt spoke up with an innocent look on his face: "We work fast, but we're not that fast!" Actually, Cooke's friends in England told him that American ships loaded with military supplies sailed into Liverpool harbor almost as soon as the bill was signed into law, contrary to FDR's denial.[35] The United States also transferred twenty-eight torpedo boats to the British on the day Roosevelt signed the legislation.[36]

Now that Lend-Lease was law, FDR's challenge was getting a steady stream of armaments to Great Britain, even when the United States military needed them. Roosevelt responded to critics that he had no intention of weakening the United States because of Lend-Lease, but increasingly the American military felt the shortages.[37]

The Germans responded to Lend-Lease with submarine warfare, and sinkings in March were disastrous. January had seen twenty-one Allied ships go down; in March, the total was forty-one. Precious military supplies were all too often going to the bottom of the ocean. With a genius for language, Churchill called it "the Battle of the Atlantic," a phrase that helped draw the United States into the conflict. "German surface and U-boat raiders are blazing a trail of shattered ships and floating wreckage across the tumbled wastes of the western ocean," wrote *New York Times* columnist Hanson Baldwin.[38] When the *Times*'s headlines announced that the "Battle of the Atlantic Is On," it also reported that the week ending March 2 had the third-largest losses in shipping since the war began.[39]

Antiaircraft guns were shipped to Great Britain, despite glaring needs at American bases, especially in the Pacific. Lack of ammunition and other supplies affected the training of American Army and Navy personnel. The crews of the USS *Ericsson*, USS *Nicholson*, and USS *Mayo* sailed in the summer of 1941 as part of the escort service with "no gunnery practice at all."[40]

Although problems abounded, American entrepreneurs and scientists also made significant breakthroughs in 1941. One success story was the "midget reconnaissance truck." Army leaders realized that their hodgepodge of command cars and motorcycles needed updating. In July 1940, the Quartermaster Corps released specifications for an all-purpose reconnaissance vehicle powerful enough to carry a machine gun and several passengers. After several attempts and much red tape, in the spring of 1941 both the American Bantam and Willys-Overland car companies helped to produce a prototype, which was christened "the jeep." Ford Motor Company also contributed to the final design. Controversy still rages over the origin of its unusual name, but the U.S. Army found the boxy-looking jeeps extremely useful. By March 1941, soldiers were driving jeeps in training maneuvers.[41]

Meanwhile, the scientists of Vannevar Bush's committee had made remarkable progress with new radar systems. The British adapted early radar improvements for their large search planes at sea, which could accommodate bulkier equipment. In May, the Catalina flying boat that located Germany's battleship *Bismarck* in the Atlantic did so with the help of onboard radar.[42] The British navy then sank the *Bismarck*, ending that threat in the Atlantic.

While radar was top-secret, Americans could read headlines

about a new committee in Washington to investigate mismanagement of the war effort. In February, Senator Harry Truman had asked for authority to check into construction of Army camps, after receiving letters from his constituents in Missouri about problems at Camp Leonard Wood. On his first visit to the camp, Truman saw building supplies out in the snow and rain, ruined; he talked with construction foremen who had never built anything before. Truman then visited camps from Florida to Michigan, and everywhere he went, there were problems with awarding contracts and getting the work done on time.

Truman was savvy enough about the ways of Washington to schedule an appointment with FDR before he proposed anything in the Senate. If there had to be an investigation of waste and mismanagement, FDR preferred Truman in charge rather than other options. Georgia Democrat Eugene Cox also wanted to investigate national defense, and Cox openly despised FDR. Thus, Roosevelt approved of Truman's committee but limited its budget. Truman wisely avoided direct criticism of the White House in discussing defense investigations. On March 1, 1941, the Senate voted unanimously to create the Truman Committee, but gave it a paltry $15,000 for operating expenses.[43]

As all of these war developments unfolded, FDR decided that his speech at the annual White House correspondents' dinner on March 15 was the right time to pull public opinion even further toward aiding Britain. Most Americans certainly did not know that since early January, in the words of historian Waldo Heinrichs, "British army, navy, and air planners secretly met with their American counterparts in Washington. The result was an American-British-Canadian plan (ABC-1), in case the United States entered the war, for protection of Atlantic shipping, defense of Britain, buildup of forces there, and eventual invasion of the Continent."[44] Roosevelt would keep those plans secret, but his speech would urge America to be the arsenal of democracy, while praising Churchill and the toughness of the British people.

With his address broadcast by three American radio networks and also overseas in a dozen languages, Roosevelt spoke to the world: "Let not dictators of Europe or Asia doubt our unanimity now. Before the present war broke out on September 1, 1939, I was more worried about the future than many people, indeed, than most people. *The record shows that I was not worried enough*," he said. Roosevelt went on to use his oratory to rouse the nation to action (and his critics would note that he did not mention the possible consequences, including the loss of American lives, if the United States entered the conflict). Roosevelt asked for an "all out effort" from both industry and labor; he expected industry to be content with lower profits, workers with longer hours, and there would be higher taxes. He wanted no war profiteering and no strikes. (Labor would not go along with his request.) And he now ascribed the idea of Lend-Lease as *coming from* the American people: "And so our country is going to be what our people have proclaimed it must be: the arsenal of democracy." Also unknown to the public on that same day, Roosevelt ordered the Atlantic fleet to return to home ports to apply camouflage paint and prepare for battle conditions. Admiral Stark notified Admiral King, commander of the Atlantic fleet, this was "in effect an Atlantic war mobilization."[45]

As usual, Roosevelt's oratory fanned out across the country in a way that changed attitudes. FDR's friends in the press, such as Anne O'Hare McCormick of the *New York Times*, supported his speech, declaring that he had "awakened the country to a sense of danger people in general did not feel before. The sense of emergency quickens throughout the land. With the full recognition of our involvement and our explicit commitment to a British victory the reality of war has been brought very near." Before FDR's speech, most people in Washington were talking about aid to Britain as the best way to avoid war, but afterward McCormick claimed that "it is hard to find anyone who does not admit that we are already in and that it will be a miracle, either of circumstance or of statesmanship, if we are not drawn in farther as the critical months lengthen."[46]

Three days after FDR's speech, in London, Churchill praised American involvement in the war when he welcomed U.S. Ambassador John Winant: "You, Mr. Ambassador, share our purpose. You'll share our dangers. You'll share our secrets. And the day will come when the British Empire and the United States will share together the solemn but splendid duties which are the crown of victory." In his speech, Churchill stated that German U-boats had increased their range as far as the coast of Newfoundland. Churchill painted a picture of submarines prowling along America's East Coast, interfering with shipping and threatening the country's security. He also did not miss the opportunity to praise FDR: "At such a moment and in such an ordeal, the words and acts of the President and people of the United States come to us like a draught of life and they tell us by an ocean-borne trumpet call that we are no longer alone."[47]

But on the labor side of industry, production problems slowed both America's defense program and Lend-Lease shipments. In the last half of 1940, more than twenty major strikes affected defense plants. Striking workers at Seattle's Boeing aircraft plant slowed aircraft production; in November, Vultee Aircraft's workers in California walked out. During the first quarter of 1941, fifty-seven strikes made headlines. Again, at the Boeing plant that spring, the American Federation of Labor competed with the Congress of Industrial Organizations for union membership, and another strike there stopped work on B-17 bombers. Similar infighting between unions shut down work on P-40 aircraft in Buffalo, New York, and heavy bombers in Baltimore.[48]

Suspicions grew during 1940 and early 1941 that Russia was agitating behind the scenes of labor unrest. Even FDR's attorney general, Robert Jackson, was convinced that the strike leaders at Vultee Aircraft were communists. Soviet leaders were encouraging workers to sit on the sidelines during the war, since Russia had signed a nonaggression pact with Germany. The leader of a very disruptive strike at the Allis-Chalmers powder plant in Milwaukee turned out to be a communist.[49]

When President Roosevelt refused to intervene during most strikes, columnist Arthur Krock analyzed the situation:

> The administration is anxious that no legislation be passed which will eliminate the gains and unilateral advantages given to organized labor since 1933. But these are being used by some labor leaders to acquire more through the necessities for speed and volume in the defense program. And the Communists in labor, boring from within, are helping them in the hope that a violent class struggle will be the result in which the program will be sabotaged.[50]

The following month, Krock summed up the problems with FDR's leadership during the rearmament crisis. Krock had first come to Washington, D.C., from his native Kentucky in 1909 as a correspondent for the *Louisville Times*. He had studied at Princeton University and eventually made his way to New York, where he worked at the *New York World*. Over the decades, his brilliant writing earned three Pulitzer Prizes. By 1941, Krock had directed the *New York Times* Washington bureau for nine years, and he was one of the few reporters not under FDR's spell:

> To every visitor Mr. Roosevelt talks of the unhappy condition of the world and the grim portents for humanity. In every speech and at every press conference he uses language to project this viewpoint of the future, rhetoric to impress the need for common sacrifice. But there is no present sign that he or his political advisers and allies are taking their own advice. . . . [T]hey are following the same New Deal social-economic strategy that produced five national electoral victories and a third term for Mr. Roosevelt. If the New Deal's present alliances and their subsidies were not being cher-

ished as primary policy in such an hour, it would not be so serious. But the pattern of New Deal theory and the prod of New Deal political ambition (to stay in office permanently) are jamming the defense production machine, imperiling the British cause and slowing up the rate of construction progress of our own "arsenal." [51]

New Deal programs such as the WPA and the CCC consumed precious federal funds and manpower, but FDR continued to protect them. "At a time of growing skilled labor shortage, WPA is an obstacle to defense because it puts workers on projects invented to 'give jobs' . . . but only a small minority of WPA projects are really essential to defense," ventured another editor at the *New York Times*. [52]

Another defense plant was affected when the communist-led workers at North American Aviation's plant in Inglewood, California, walked out. The strikers also kept other workers from entering the plant through threats and beatings. The prolonged strike brought even Roosevelt's patience to an end. He ordered the Army to take possession of the plant on June 9, 1941, restore order, and allow those workers willing to return to do so. The twenty-five hundred soldiers who marched on the plant with their bayonets fixed did restore order, and the plant was back in production in three days. After three weeks, the union had been reorganized, the Army departed, and overall, the American public approved. [53]

Not only strikes held up aircraft production. General Marshall had warned Americans for months that modern technology meant "there was a time lag of one to two years between the initial order and the delivery of the finished product to the soldier." [54] In the fall of 1940, the United States had sent B-17s to Great Britain not only to help in the fight against fascism, but also to see how the new aircraft would respond in combat, since tests were still incomplete. When British pilots flew the B-17s and the planes proved to have serious design problems, production teams had to work on necessary changes. Consequently, the United States produced only *one heavy bomber* in July 1941. [55]

Likewise, in the area of tank design, the German Army could send tank spearheads racing across France while the U.S. Army still drove antiquated tank models that were more like armored trucks. In 1940, American tanks had no periscope at all and were guided by the tank commander's sticking his head out of the top and nudging with his foot either the right or left shoulder of the tank driver below him to indicate turns. Only eighty obsolete medium tanks were in service in the entire army. On August 31, 1940, plans for a new tank, the M4 Sherman, were finally submitted, but they were not approved until April 1941. Meanwhile, the U.S. Army purchased twenty thousand more horses for its cavalry.[56]

In spring 1941, military strategy in Europe unfolded quickly as the weather improved. On April 6, Hitler renewed his offensive and invaded Yugoslavia and Greece, while Germany's Afrika Korps pushed British troops from Tripoli all the way back to the borders of Egypt. On April 30, Roosevelt purchased the first U.S. savings bond and urged Americans to buy bonds "to pay for our arming and for the American existence of later generations."[57] Yet the country had no clear policy of rearmament and few priorities. In similar fashion to his New Deal strategy, FDR piled layer upon layer of bureaucracy as he appointed new commissions to deal with defense.

On May 27, FDR announced that the Nazis threatened to take over the Azores or the Cape Verde Islands. With such a move, he said, they would dominate shipping routes in the South Atlantic and also be poised for an invasion of South America: "The war is approaching the brink of the Western Hemisphere itself. It is coming very close to home." In reality, no German armies were about to invade South America, but Roosevelt ended the speech by proclaiming an unlimited national emergency, which he could legally do only if war was "imminent." The proclamation gave FDR extraordinary powers over communications, public utilities, transportation, trade, and aliens. Once more, he had used war developments outside the United States to increase his executive power. FDR's speech received "vociferous" support in the press and in mail to the White House, and from April to June Roosevelt's popularity rose from 73 to 76 percent.[58]

One unknown factor continued to be the Soviet Union. Winston Churchill agonized that Russia could ally itself with Germany, making the two totalitarian countries the most powerful coalition the world had ever seen. But in the spring of 1941, intelligence reports noted concentrations of German troops in Eastern Europe. Foreign offices of Sweden, Romania, Bulgaria, and most of all Great Britain, passed on reports to the United States that Russia was the real target.

Before dawn on June 22, 1941, Germany attacked Russia, meaning that the danger of the two dictatorships working together was over. Both Churchill and Roosevelt were optimistic, if not downright relieved, that Germany's might was not focused solely upon Great Britain. From Tokyo, American ambassador Joseph Grew thought "it was the best thing that could have happened. Dog eat dog. Let the Nazis and the Communists so weaken each other that the democracies will soon gain the upper hand or at least will be released from their dire peril."[59] Secretary Stimson predicted, "Of course . . . the chances are that she will surrender."[60] Stimson grossly underestimated Joseph Stalin, leader of the Soviet Union.

Roosevelt and Churchill were determined to keep the Soviets in the war. FDR thought that the democracies need not fear Soviet expansion in Europe and approved a billion dollars of Lend-Lease shipments to Russia by the fall of 1941. Stalin did not hesitate to ask for what he wanted. American military supplies were running so low that many requests had to be ignored for the time being. Ironically, America's industry would have had more weapons for the Soviets if strikes, often led by communist sympathizers, had not disrupted production during the previous twelve months. The Russians asked for 3,000 P-40 fighter planes but were promised only 200, and 59 of those fighters were shipped lacking spare parts. They also asked for 3,000 bombers, 20,000 antiaircraft cannon, 5,000 antitank guns, and 25,000 rifles, but received only 1,000 rifles and 315,000 tons of aviation gasoline, along with lubricating oil. Stalin was demanding 500 "fighting planes" a month—a figure unreachable for the near future. Since the British also wanted 500 planes per month, that meant the United States would need to produce 1,000 military aircraft a month just to satisfy the needs of Lend-Lease. And that didn't include Lend-Lease shipments to the Chinese, which had begun in May 1941—all of these war goods paid for by American taxpayers.[61]

At the same time, Roosevelt agreed to patrol Iceland as part of America's defense of the western Atlantic. Reykjavík approved the arrangement, and an American presence there would free British troops who had been patrolling Iceland to prevent a Nazi invasion. After making the decision, Roosevelt informed Congress of the impending deployment. American ships docked in Iceland on July 7 and unloaded U.S. Marines. General Marshall agonized over the policy of sending Marines to hold an area that should have been handled by the U.S. Army, but there simply were not enough trained infantrymen.[62]

With the Germans smashing through the Ukraine, Roosevelt and Churchill planned a secret meeting off the coast of Newfoundland for mid-August. Roosevelt arrived on the heavy cruiser *Augusta*, while Churchill sailed into the bay on the battle-scarred *Prince of Wales*. Churchill had come to insist that the United States enter the war immediately. Roosevelt's chief aim was to establish the political basis for the war effort, which would also guide international policy after victory.

During the next several days, the two leaders and their military staffs discussed war policy. The schedule included a joint church service aboard HMS *Prince of Wales*, with the singing of "Onward, Christian Soldiers." As a series of affirmations, their agreement became the Atlantic Charter, and sounded very much like the platform of President Woodrow Wilson twenty-five years earlier. Their eight points renounced territorial gains by the United States and Britain, promised territorial adjustments only with approval of the participating citizens, and affirmed self-determination, freedom of trade, freedom of the seas, abandonment of force, disarmament, and eventually a system of worldwide security. Announced on August 14, the Atlantic Charter later became the basis of the United Nations Charter. The importance of the charter was its promise of self-determination and freedom for war-torn countries such as Poland.[63]

When Churchill returned to London, he gave his war cabinet a private account of his conversations with Roosevelt: "If he [Roosevelt] were to put the issue of peace and war to Congress, they would debate it for months. The President had said he would wage war but not declare it and that he would become more and more provocative. If the Germans did not like it, they could attack American forces." Churchill went on to describe an agreement with FDR in regard to convoys crossing the Atlantic: "The President's orders to these [United States Navy] escorts were to attack any [German] U-boat which showed itself, even if it were 200 or 300 miles away from the convoy. Everything was to be done to force an incident."[64]

While the specific military discussions during the Newfoundland conference remained secret, the drama of the meeting between the two leaders became a sensation when released to the press.[65] The *New York Times* splashed the headlines across the entire front page in end-of-the-world type:

Roosevelt, Churchill Draft 8 Peace Aims, Pledging Destruction of Nazi Tyranny

As the summer of 1941 passed, the original 1940 army draftees completed their one-year enlistments. While the House debated extending the enlistments, Roosevelt lobbied for the bill's passage, and finally the House approved longer enlistments by one vote. In their barracks, some soldiers painted "O-H-I-O" on the walls, meaning "Over the Hill in October" when their original one-year enlistments would be up, but few deserted.[66]

Although the United States avoided a declaration of war, FDR's policies throughout the fall of 1941 skirted the limits of American law and invited a confrontation with the Nazis. On September 11, after a German submarine fired torpedoes at the American destroyer *Greer* near Iceland, Roosevelt ordered the U.S. Navy to shoot on sight either German or Italian warships. Roosevelt did not disclose that the *Greer* had been assisting a British plane that was trying to sink the German submarine. Instead, FDR feigned indignation that "neutral" ships were attacked. The American Legion's national convention supported the president's declaration of "shoot on sight" at its fall meeting. On September 14, Secretary of the Navy Knox announced that the U.S. Navy would protect ships carrying Lend-Lease supplies from the North American coastline to Iceland.[67]

On October 17, the USS *Kearny* was hit by a torpedo off the coast of Iceland, killing eleven members of the crew. "The shooting has started" the president announced in his Navy Day speech on October 27, and "we Americans have taken our battle stations." Opponents pointed out that FDR was responding to the five words in the Democratic platform of 1940 that he had pledged to uphold, namely that the United States would avoid war "except in case of attack."[68]

On October 31, the Germans sank the first U.S. Navy vessel on patrol when the USS *Reuben James* went down west of Iceland with 115 American dead. Due to attacks on merchant shipping as well, Congress voted in November to arm the merchant marine. Looking to South America, Roosevelt also sent troops to occupy Dutch Guiana on November 24, thereby protecting its bauxite, which made up 60 percent of American aluminum production.

That fall, the Truman Committee began compiling its first annual report. Its budget had grown to $50,000 once it produced results. Before releasing the report to the press, Truman planned to give a copy to President Roosevelt. Truman warned the president that the defense effort was weak and its leadership inept.[69] FDR's Office of Production Management slowed, and sometimes altogether halted, construction of defense plants for aircraft parts, tanks, antiaircraft guns, and machine tools. The OPM was, said Truman, "a hopeless mess." In addition, FDR had layered the Supplies and Priorities Allocation Board (SPAB), directed by Donald Nelson, on top of OPM's bureaucracy. Neither agency had enough authority to direct national defense. The rush to mobilize had turned into "a scramble for natural resources," involving the Army, the Navy, and federal agencies.[70]

Truman supported appointing one man with enough authority to get results in defense. In early December, Roosevelt mulled over what to do before Truman's report became public in January.[71] An international incident could provide the excuse to ask Congress for a declaration of war, but despite so many armed American ships in the Atlantic, the Germans usually refused to oblige. Nazi submarine commanders were under strict orders not to fire on American shipping so as not to involve the United States openly in "the Battle of the Atlantic." How much longer could the United States avoid war?

4

PEARL HARBOR, DECEMBER 7, 1941

On a cold Thursday evening in Washington, D.C., Donald Nelson hosted a dinner for two dozen of the nation's leaders in the military, government, and business. Nelson, the former vice president of Sears, Roebuck, had been handpicked by Franklin Roosevelt to coordinate the country's defense industries. Nelson's job meant that he had to bring New Deal bureaucrats and independent businessmen together. The atmosphere that night was awkward. The two groups had been hostile to each other for years—each blaming the other for the continuing Great Depression.

The businessmen also disagreed among themselves on how best to arm the United States for war. Donald Nelson wanted to increase defense production, but not at the cost of major disruptions in civilian life. Others in the room wanted full rearmament, even if that included a complete government takeover of the means of production, which FDR refused to allow as being "too fascistic."[1] And the military leaders wanted their own plans, not those of civilians.

As the dinner guests assembled, the interests of two of the most prominent leaders illustrated the differences. There was Vice President Henry Wallace, an ardent New Dealer, a religious mystic, and a near socialist. Next to him was William Knudsen, the head of the Office of Production Management (OPM), a Danish immigrant with a flair for things mechanical who had risen to the top at General Motors.[2]

After the meal, the serving staff exited the room. Several guests enjoyed their cigars and after-dinner drinks. Nelson stood to make his remarks, which underscored the purpose of the evening: *We all want what is for the good of this country, and the country's defense is the number-one priority. And that means that we should all work together.* Then Nelson recognized the vice president. Henry Wallace also stood, made a short talk, and sat down. Next came Knudsen: *A big job had been given to the men in the room, but they were doing it pretty well; the war overseas would be over eventually, and things would get back to normal.* And others stood to give brief remarks.

Secretary of the Navy Frank Knox was more serious than most: "I feel that I can speak very frankly, within these four walls. I want you to know that our situation tonight is very serious—more serious, probably, than most of us realize. We are very close to war. War may begin in the Pacific at any moment. . . . But I want you to know that no matter what happens, the United States Navy is ready!" Knox repeated that before he sat down: *No matter what might happen, the Navy was prepared.*

When Knox concluded, Nelson asked him if a war in the Pacific wouldn't be "pretty much a Navy show?"

And Knox nodded yes. "We've had our plans worked out for twenty years. Once it starts, our submarines will go in to blockade them, and sooner or later our battle fleet will be able to force an action. It won't take too long. Say about a six months' war."

Often there is a fly in the ointment, a balloon-popper who appears when least expected. Tonight's voice of realism was Robert W. Horton, the director of information in the Office for Emergency Management (OEM). His long title meant that he worked for President Roosevelt, and that he had witnessed the nation's halfhearted attempts to rearm. Horton, a blunt-spoken Vermont man, rose to his feet and demolished Knox's claims of Navy preparedness with fact piled upon fact:

+ Horton had recently attended a late afternoon conference at the Navy Department, where the most important
  activity to upper-level officers was leaving to play golf.

+ On a recent trip aboard a Coast Guard patrol boat, Horton's group had cruised through the Navy yards at Norfolk. No security patrols asked for their credentials or
  authorization to be there.

+ The British aircraft carrier *Illustrious* was in the yard at
  Norfolk, awaiting repairs. Horton's boat also passed near
  that ship, without a security check as to why they were
  there.

+ On their return trip through Hampton Roads, they
  pulled into a new Navy installation. They tied up at the
  dock and went in search of a phone. Again, no security at
  all.

By this time, Secretary of the Navy Knox, red-faced, was asking
Nelson, "*Who is this son-of-a-bitch?*" Unaffected by the stir he was
causing, Horton ended his indictments with this statement: "Mis-
ter Secretary, I don't think your Navy *is* ready."[3]

What was the date of this dinner? December 4, 1941. And
shortly thereafter, statements to the effect that the United States
could defeat Japan in a few weeks permeated Secretary Knox's annual report, released on December 6, 1941.[4]

Knox, not Horton, reflected the mind-set of the Navy's upper
brass, the president's cabinet, and the mind of Franklin Roosevelt
himself. Rooted in antiquated naval strategy, these leaders tended
to be older men who loved the days when battleships ruled the
seas, and as with most nations, the Navy worked independently of
other branches of the military. Such thinking was not limited to
the American side of the Atlantic. Friends of Winston Churchill

recall that in the mid-1930s, Churchill laughed at the idea that a bomb dropped by an aircraft could sink a battleship at sea. Churchill said the only way that would happen was if the bomb went down the smokestack. Even as late as January 1939, Churchill had written for *Collier's* that "even a single well-armed vessel will hold its own against aircraft; still more a squadron or a fleet of modernized warships, whether at sea or in harbor, will be able to endure aerial attack."[5]

Roosevelt also thought in traditional patterns about the U.S. fleet, having served as assistant secretary of the navy during World War I, and he considered himself an expert on naval affairs. Roosevelt's knowledge wasn't acquired by study of naval battles or reading works of great strategic minds; he had never served in the military. FDR enjoyed the power associated with ordering ships to sea, the intrigue of foreign policy, and he believed that he knew better than most of his commanders what was best. "Roosevelt rarely took advice; he favored only the 'advice' that agreed with his own disposition," notes historian Gary Dean Best.[6] FDR was closely connected with ship movements and the dispersion of the U.S. fleet. In 1939 and 1940 he maintained a direct wire from the White House to the Ship Movements Division of the Navy Department, keeping track of vessels on neutrality patrol.[7]

Roosevelt appointed a good friend, Admiral Harold Stark, as chief of naval operations in 1939. FDR hated confrontations, even within his own cabinet, so he surrounded himself with men who reflected what he saw as important. FDR chose Stark, although several other officers were more qualified. Observers noted that "Stark was regarded in Washington as an able officer unduly responsive to Roosevelt's views."[8] FDR dealt directly not only with Stark, instead of going through the secretary of the navy, but also with several other officers in the Ship Movements Division. Thus, Roosevelt played an integral role in U.S. naval policy.[9]

Throughout the world, naval strategy was changing rapidly,

more rapidly than most American admirals (and Roosevelt) realized. As shown by Secretary Knox's statement that "we've had our plans worked out for twenty years," American strategists were not thinking of new methods using aircraft carriers, torpedo planes, and dive-bombers. Should they have known about these possibilities? Yes, they should. In 1932 the U.S. Navy simulated an aerial attack on Pearl Harbor, which proved that torpedo planes could cripple any fleet stationed there. Japanese observers secretly forwarded a report to Tokyo, where Japan's admirals studied the attack.[10]

Most of the U.S. Navy brass clung to the illusion that battleships still reigned supreme with or without air support, earning them the nickname "battleship admirals." They continued to relegate aircraft, for example, to the role of "the eyes of the fleet and to subserve battleships, scouting for them and protecting . . . [the battleships] while their 16-inch guns destroyed the enemy."[11] Likewise, in the Navy's initial strategy for its 1941 Pacific fleet, submarines would be used only as scouting vessels for the main fleet, with very cautious use in battle, even though German U-boats were showing the world what an offensive weapon the submarine could be.

One voice among the admirals sounded a warning: Throughout 1940, Admiral James O. (Joe) Richardson served as commander of the Pacific fleet then stationed in Hawaii. Even before Roosevelt ordered the fleet to stay at Pearl Harbor indefinitely, Richardson had protested to Stark that keeping the fleet there posed a danger to every ship.[12] Richardson proved his own vigilance as early as June 1940, when U.S. military intelligence lost radio contact with the Japanese fleet. He led the American fleet out of Pearl Harbor immediately to avoid being caught at anchor if attacked. The alarm proved false, but Richardson was still concerned about Japan's intentions.

Other Navy commanders warned that the inadequate number of patrol planes in Hawaii, as well as the lack of available crews to fly reconnaissance missions, left Pearl Harbor vulnerable to attack. When Captain P. N. L. Bellinger took over command of Fleet Patrol Wing Two, which was based at Pearl Harbor, he reported, "I was surprised to find that here in the Hawaiian Islands, an important naval advanced outpost, we were operating on a shoestring and the more I looked, the thinner the shoestring appeared to be." [13] Later, in February 1941, when patrol planes rolled off American production lines, Hawaii's commanders asked for additional aircraft for reconnaissance patrols. Instead, Washington ordered them sent to Great Britain under Lend-Lease. The Navy brass protested to Roosevelt, who referred them to his aide Harry Hopkins. Hopkins bluntly refused to send more planes to Hawaii. [14]

During the summer of 1940, Richardson continued to point to the potential problems of the president's plans for the Navy. With much larger congressional appropriations after the fall of France, Roosevelt had signed the Naval Expansion Act, providing for a "Two Ocean Navy" and expanding the fleet by 70 percent. FDR also continued to push for unrealistic plans to blockade Japan from reaching both Southeast Asia and the United States. Yet he planned to increase the number of men in the fleet only by 6,000. Admiral Stark reassured Richardson that he and Knox had worked to ensure an increase from 116,000 to 191,000 sailors, but the slowness of these measures also worried Richardson. Men could not be turned into sailors overnight. He argued that "it takes 24 months to make a petty officer third class out of a fairly bright recruit . . . [and] it takes at least six years to make a chief petty officer." [15]

After many letters to his superiors, Richardson "was aware that no one else had been able to deter Roosevelt from his career as a one-man general staff, working through intuition." [16] In October 1940, Richardson was ordered to report for a series of meetings with the president and Stark in Washington. When Richardson met with FDR in the Oval Office, he spelled out the dangers of keeping the fleet at Pearl Harbor, given the volatile situation with

Japan. Richardson also repeated his warning that time was required to turn civilians into experienced sailors. In Richardson's words:

> The discussion waxed hot and heavy. I could not help but detect
> that reelection political considerations, rather than long-range
> military considerations, were the controlling factor in the President's thinking. It was less than a month before the 1940 Presidential Election, and the President was reluctant to make any
> commitment to increase the number of men in the Navy, which
> due to the location of naval ships in foreign waters, would seem to
> run counter to his third-term campaign statements.[17]

Richardson also believed that the geographical port in Hawaii, or anywhere else, was not that important: The fleet would always be the primary target for enemy attacks. Richardson recommended calling the fleet back to the West Coast immediately. But when it became apparent that FDR had no intention of changing his plans, Richardson replied: "Mr. President, I feel that I must tell you that the senior officers of the Navy do not have the trust and confidence in the civilian leadership of this country that is essential for the successful prosecution of a war in the Pacific."

FDR replied, "Joe, you just don't understand that this is an election year and there are certain things that can't be done, no matter what, until the election is over and won."[18]

With the 1940 election coming up, FDR did not act on Richardson's requests. In the weeks that followed, Tokyo's leaders accused the United States of preparing to attack Japan, citing troop and armament increases in the Pacific, and the evacuation of American women and children from many locations, including the Philippines.[19] Roosevelt still kept the fleet in Hawaii, and after he was safely reelected to a third term, he fired Richardson as fleet commander.[20]

Secretary Knox also disregarded Admiral Richardson's advice.

Richardson spent two hours with Knox, warning him that FDR's understanding of the Pacific situation was a fantasy that put the fleet in grave danger. Richardson also told Knox that a Pacific war with Japan could easily take five to ten years to win at a cost of many billions of dollars.[21]

Richardson's replacement in early 1941, Admiral Husband Kimmel, submitted a traditional battle plan to Stark, who duly approved it. Kimmel's plan followed the antiquated line of thinking so dominant in Washington and took little account of any Japanese offensive aimed at the Hawaiian Islands. The logic was as follows: *Of course a Japanese offensive there was out of the question, because Japanese resources weren't deemed sufficient and Japanese pilots were inferior in skill and temperament to American pilots.* Kimmel assumed that in a Pacific war, the American fleet would steam out of Pearl Harbor to thrash the Japanese if they dared to attack Singapore or the Philippines.

A real-life scenario involving aerial attack on ships at anchor occurred in November 1940, when the British showed what could be done with a few older-model aircraft dropping torpedoes. In the harbor at Taranto, Italy, British pilots flying relatively slow Swordfish airplanes destroyed half of the Italian fleet in one night. Winston Churchill had already learned the danger of airborne attacks the hard way, by British losses in Norway and Crete. After the British victory at Taranto he sent an account of the attack to Roosevelt.[22]

Indeed, from afar the Japanese realized they could use many of the same tactics against the American fleet at Pearl Harbor, if they could only solve the problem of dropping torpedoes in the shallow waters there. The Japanese studied the Taranto attack in great detail. Secretly they also worked on air-launched torpedoes, to give them more stability and accuracy.

The American Navy had known for years that it could not depend on a strong British naval presence in the Pacific, due to the unfortunate Anglo-German Naval Agreement of June 18, 1935.

Under the direction of Prime Minister Stanley Baldwin, Great Britain had agreed to a strong German Navy in a misguided attempt at appeasement. The result simply meant that after 1935, the British Navy would have to be concentrated around the home islands and in the Mediterranean to prevent German dominance. In parliamentary debate, Winston Churchill attacked the agreement by pointing out that with a strong German Navy in the waters around Europe, Great Britain could not keep any appreciable portion of its battle fleet at the great British base at Singapore. "What a windfall this has been for Japan!" announced Churchill in the House of Commons.[23]

Seeing such international weakness, Japan invaded China in 1937 in a quest for more natural resources. Mussolini had already attacked Abyssinia in 1935, and the League of Nations did almost nothing. With a weak British presence in the Pacific and an isolationist United States, Japan's army moved quickly across the Chinese mainland. Accounts of Japanese atrocities came from missionaries and business people who saw the brutality firsthand. Secretary of State Cordell Hull repeatedly protested Japan's invasion of China, while in Tokyo, U.S. Ambassador Joseph C. Grew warned Japanese leaders "that America deeply resented bombings, indignities and manifold interference with American rights in China." The Japanese responded that they were creating "A New Order" and "Asia for Asians." Westerners should get out of the way.[24]

As Japan's Army honed its war skills against China's poorly trained troops, the Japanese Navy secretly improved its fleet. Reports coming from Japan noted that ship workers there lived in walled-off dockyards where work was highly classified. Such workers were rarely allowed to leave these sites. Japan was in fact building its navy in a closed community, in contrast to Robert Horton's reports at Donald Nelson's dinner party of wide-open U.S. Navy installations.[25]

The United States was in the hypocritical position of supplying the oil that Japan used to fuel its drive across China. Since 1911, U.S. secretaries of state had negotiated trade and navigation treaties with Japan to ensure a mutually beneficial commerce. Relations between the two countries deteriorated when the United States changed its immigration policies with Japan in the 1920s, refusing to admit more Japanese aliens. A further complication occurred when militarists took over the Japanese government and turned Japan into an aggressor nation. Many Western opponents advocated a very strong response: Cut off imports and use military force to contain Japan if necessary. The other side of this foreign policy argument pointed out that Japan was a bulwark against both the USSR and the burgeoning communist movement in Asia. Any reduction in Japan's power might create a vacuum that could be filled by Marxists, either from Russia or China.[26]

Japanese leaders were very concerned about their need for oil imports. They desperately wished to extend the trade agreement with the United States, but American voters were pressuring Congress to deny any extension. Both the American and European press covered Japanese atrocities in China, and democratic nations uniformly condemned Japan's policies. Senator Key Pittman, chairman of the Senate Foreign Relations Committee, offered a resolution in April 1939 to empower President Roosevelt to embargo shipments of war materiel to Japan, including steel, scrap iron, and oil. Roosevelt did not establish an immediate embargo but ordered Secretary of State Cordell Hull to give Tokyo the required six-month notice that the U.S.-Japanese trade agreement was ending. When Hull did so, Tokyo called the U.S. announcement "unthinkable."[27]

In the War Department, Roosevelt finally replaced Woodring with Henry Stimson in 1940, in part because many of Stimson's anti-Japanese attitudes meshed with those of FDR. Stimson had long wanted to get tough with Japan, even to the point of war. As governor-general of the Philippines in the 1920s, Stimson doubted that most Asians were capable of self-government. All of these attitudes reinforced Roosevelt's ideas about the Far East. In August 1940, Assistant Secretary of State Breckinridge Long noted Roosevelt's approach to Japan in his diary: "As a result of the interview [with Hull] I now understand that it has been discussed as a matter of high policy and the Administration has made up its mind to deal very firmly with Japan and that no steps will be spared and that those steps may even lead to war." [28]

Japan wanted oil and other natural resources, even if that meant occupying China, and the United States wanted Japan's aggression to cease. But Germany's successful military sweeps through Europe only encouraged Japanese militarism, as the leaders of one aggressor nation watched the successes of another. From Tokyo, Ambassador Grew warned, "The German victories have gone to their heads like strong wine." [29]

After Holland and France surrendered to the Nazis, Japan's leaders saw that Dutch and French colonial possessions in the Pacific were vulnerable, but the United States was in the way. Japanese diplomats traveled to Berlin in September of that year to sign the Tripartite Pact between Japan, Germany, and Italy, forming a loose alliance that came to be known as the Axis. In his diary, Breckinridge Long analyzed U.S. policy in September:

> We make a direct loan to China—twenty-five million. The next day we announce an embargo on scrap iron and steel. Each measure directed against Japan. The next day, which was yesterday, Japan signs in the axis with Germany and Italy, warning us. And so we go—more and more—farther and farther along the road to war. But we are not ready to fight any war now—to say nothing of a war on two oceans at once—and that is what the Berlin-Rome-Tokyo agreement means. [30]

As the war in Europe continued, Great Britain required more and more oil from the United States. British tankers were tempting targets for German U-boats, so sinkings were common. The drain of oil to Britain became so great that gasoline shortages plagued the eastern United States in June 1941. Roosevelt placed all petroleum products under export controls on June 20. He hesitated to enforce a total embargo on Japan, fearing that such a move would spur them to attack the oil-rich areas of Malaya, including the Dutch East Indies. Others, such as Rep. John Coffee (D-Wash.), urged further action, saying "How can we believe in quarantining aggressors in Europe while appeasing the aggressor in the Orient?"[31]

Roosevelt finally employed the devious strategy of hindering all oil exports to Japan by adding layers of red tape and freezing Japan's financial assets in the United States in what has been called "a silent embargo."[32] If Japanese buyers could get the required paperwork to buy oil or gasoline, they faced a gauntlet of restrictions in paying for it. The effect, by late 1941, was a trickle of oil actually getting to Japan from the United States. Japan's military was also aware that American military leaders had talked with the British and Dutch about defending Malaya, Singapore, and the Philippines. The United States quietly reinforced its Army units in the Philippines and sent bombers to Clark Field there, as well as troop reinforcements to Guam, Wake Island, and other locations. Tokyo steadily felt more encircled by Western powers, accusing the British and Americans of "acting like a cunning dragon seemingly asleep."[33]

Still, the attitude of FDR's administration was "So what?" Secretary Knox, of course, expected a quick American victory over Japan. Scores of articles in American newspapers predicted an easy win over Asians. *New York Times* reporter Hanson Baldwin admitted that Japan had at least thirty-six hundred combat planes, but "the plane and engine models are technically obsolescent as compared to those of Western powers." The U.S. military agreed with Baldwin; virtually all U.S. prewar plans underestimated the strength and quality of Japanese airpower.[34]

In fact, American newspapers mocked the Japanese with cartoons depicting foolish-looking Asians befuddled by modern warfare. One typical cartoon showed a powerful Uncle Sam aboard a larger, fast-moving ship, looking down at a small Japanese sailor on a clearly inferior vessel, while the caption read "Are you sure you won't run out of gas, sonny?"[35] Roosevelt and his cabinet members helped create this image. No matter how much territory Japan conquered in China, American leaders discounted the skill and planning of Japanese forces. And without natural resources, Westerners argued, Japan could not wage much of a war. British experts predicted that a total economic blockade would cripple Japanese industry in six months.[36]

Unknown to the American public, British military officers had been meeting with their American counterparts in Washington, D.C., beginning in January 1941 to plan a response to Japanese aggression in the Pacific. (The British were urging Roosevelt to send part of the U.S. fleet to Singapore.) Due to the lack of military supplies, General Marshall pleaded with FDR and Hull to propose some sort of truce with Japan. If the president could "buy" more time, the United States could strengthen its military in the Philippines and throughout the Pacific. From Tokyo, Ambassador Grew urged Roosevelt and Hull to discuss a new trade treaty with the Japanese and postpone an embargo.[37]

Roosevelt continued to side with the more aggressive views of Secretary of War Stimson. Likewise, in the State Department, Cordell Hull gave little hope of reconciling differences through negotiations. As reported by diplomat John K. Emmerson from the Tokyo embassy, three issues separated the United States and Japan in 1941: "Japan's adherence to the Axis pact, the principle of equal commercial opportunity, and Japanese troops in China."[38]

Japan was also watching the war in Russia to see if Germany would conquer that vast nation. If so, Japan could move into Siberia for easy pickings.[39] When Russia survived the German onslaught, Japan looked to the south at the weak British and American presence in the Pacific. Japan used its ties with the Nazis to great advantage by obtaining permission from Germany's puppet regime in France, the Vichy government, to set up garrisons in French Indo-China (modern-day Vietnam). Announcing the movement of fifty thousand Japanese troops to Saigon and other ports in Southeast Asia, the Japanese claimed to be protecting the interests of Vichy France and, indirectly, those of its Axis partner, Germany.

By occupying Indo-China and parts of Cambodia, the Japanese were within striking distance of Singapore, the Dutch East Indies, and the Philippines. Once again, most military observers were focusing on the Far East, not Hawaii. FDR, his cabinet, and most military leaders feared attacks on Singapore and the Philippines, and therefore Secretary Knox planned for the U.S. Navy to sail out of Pearl Harbor to the combat area after hostilities began.[40]

By early December, Franklin Roosevelt and his military advisors knew that the Japanese would launch an attack. Too many unmistakable signs pointed to that conclusion. U.S. intelligence officers could decrypt the Japanese ciphers used for communication between Japanese embassies, which showed that portraits of the emperor, sacred to the Japanese, were ordered to be shipped back to the homeland.[41] Code books were destroyed. Japanese nationals hurried home from Hong Kong, Formosa, and other ports.

America's problem was not in obtaining such intelligence but in organizing it once it was decoded. No coherent system existed for prompt dissemination of decoded messages or observations from Americans abroad, no matter the level of importance. By contrast, Great Britain had long since established a protocol for quickly using such intelligence, because of its intricate foreign relations in running the British Empire. The United States was light-years behind.

Ambassador Grew also sent warnings from Tokyo on the growing strength of the "warhawks" in the Japanese cabinet. Japan had stockpiled two years of oil supplies. Their military buildup in troops and armaments continued throughout the Pacific. Even literary agents were aware of the crisis: "Are we on the verge of a war with Japan?" asked a newspaper ad for Wilfrid Fleisher's new book on Japanese relations, *Volcanic Isle*.[42]

Roosevelt and his advisors also knew that, in 1904, the Japanese navy had launched a surprise attack on the Russian fleet at Port Arthur, and then declared war the next day. On November 25, 1941, FDR reminded the cabinet that "the Japanese are notorious for making an attack without warning."[43] U.S. bases in the Philippines, Hawaii, the Panama Canal, and even San Francisco received warnings to go on alert.

On December 6, U.S. military intelligence officers in Washington read decryptions that revealed an attack was imminent. Due to poor decisions by intelligence officers, the most vital decryptions didn't reach Marshall until Sunday morning, December 7. Marshall sent a warning to the Pacific, putting top priority on the message to MacArthur in the Philippines, which was the expected target. The message to Hawaii received a secondary rating in terms of urgency. Ever since the false alarm with the fleet in Hawaii in 1940, Washington had not included Pearl Harbor in its list of prime targets. Therefore, Marshall's warning did not receive high priority when it reached Honolulu.[44] In a series of missteps, Marshall's telegram would be in a delivery boy's bicycle pouch when the Japanese attacked.

Napoléon once said, "There is no man more pusillanimous than I when I am planning a campaign. I purposely exaggerate all the dangers and all the calamities that the circumstances make possible. I am in a thoroughly painful state of agitation. This does not keep me from looking quite serene in front of my entourage." In preparing for war in the Pacific, by contrast, FDR's commanders assumed every advantage was theirs: ability of pilots, quality of equipment, fighting spirit, strategy. Too many American planners expected the Japanese to be predictable rather than innovative, ignoring Napoléon's advice.

By sailing within a few hundred miles of Oahu under radio silence, the Japanese fleet arrived at the launch point undetected.

The fleet commander received the coded message "Climb Mount Niitaka." That message meant only one thing: "Attack!" On the morning of December 7, 1941, when the first of their 351 attack planes arrived over Hawaii, the surprise was complete.[45]

American sailors were stunned at the accuracy of the Japanese torpedo planes, at the selectivity of each pilot in knowing which ships to attack, and at the speed and rate of climb of their aircraft. American antiaircraft guns were too few. Lend-Lease policies had sent fifteen hundred to Great Britain and four hundred to other countries, but few to Pearl Harbor. At any rate, the ammunition for the antiaircraft guns they did have was stored two to three miles away because of the low-level alert.[46] Indeed, Japanese technicians had even stabilized air-launched torpedoes by adding wooden fins that broke away in Pearl Harbor's shallow waters.

Admiral Kimmel had planned to play golf that Sunday, but when he learned of the attack, he threw on his uniform and raced to the harbor. Kimmel radioed Washington, the Philippines, and all ships at sea: "AIR RAID ON PEARL HARBOR. THIS IS NO DRILL."[47]

On that tragic Sunday, President Roosevelt was in his White House study, working on his stamp collection. When Secretary Knox phoned him to announce that Pearl Harbor had been attacked, he was overwhelmed by the damage reports. A butler from the White House staff, entering the president's study during the news, recorded FDR's reaction: "I heard him remark as further details continued to come in about the destruction of the fleet. 'My God! How did it happen? I will go down in disgrace.'"[48]

When Knox entered the Oval Office later that afternoon, Roosevelt "was seated at his desk and was white as a sheet. He was visibly shaken. You know, I think he expected to get hit; but he did not expect to get hurt."[49]

Undersecretary Robert Patterson had just returned to Washington from Boston, where he had spoken the night before about the importance of labor in the nation's defense. He and his wife ate lunch with Supreme Court Justice and Mrs. William O. Douglas, and they lingered at the Douglases' home. About 3 P.M. the phone rang, and the call was for Patterson: The Japanese had bombed Pearl Harbor. "It was only a matter of time," Patterson replied. He and his wife grabbed their coats, and she drove him to the War Department.

Patterson found much of his staff already assembled, and Secretary Stimson soon joined them. Stimson reported that details were still coming in, but most of the Pacific fleet was damaged, and American airpower in Hawaii had almost been wiped out. Later that day, Patterson told his staff, "It is essential that our procurement be put in to highest gear at once. . . . You are directed to take all necessary steps to boost munitions manufacture to the highest possible level. . . . Our production must be quickly put on a 24 hour a day basis."[50]

Labor Secretary Frances Perkins and other cabinet members rushed back to Washington for a meeting that night at the White House. According to Perkins,

> The President nodded as we came in, but there was none of the usual cordial, personal greeting. This was one of the few occasions he couldn't muster a smile. . . . He began in a low voice, "You all know what's happened. The attack began at one o-clock [our time]. We don't know very much yet." Someone, I think it was Francis Biddle, spoke. "Mr. President, several of us have just arrived by plane. We don't know anything except a scare headline, 'Japs Attack Pearl Harbor.' Could you tell us?"[51]

Stimson and other staff members gave them the most current information, but either by design or because of poor communications with Hawaii, details were sketchy. Later, Secretary of State Hull asked journalist Arthur Krock for a detailed list of the losses at Pearl Harbor. For Hull, Krock's sources proved better than trying to pry information from the White House.[52]

Tragically, as reports continued to come in from Hawaii, the president learned that a bomb had hit the magazine of the USS *Arizona*, causing an explosion that killed 1,177 sailors. Of the 2,403 deaths on December 7—sailors, soldiers, and civilians—almost half were on the *Arizona*. Four battleships were sunk, and the remaining four damaged but afloat. A total of 21 ships were damaged, several needing extensive repairs. Parked wingtip to wingtip, 188 aircraft were destroyed and many more damaged.

The larger tragedy was yet to appear for the American fighting men on Guam, Wake Island, the Philippines, and throughout the Pacific. They did not know it yet, but when Japanese pilots zoomed away, the smoking wreckage of the U.S. fleet meant that the U.S. Navy could not come to their aid. British war plans for the Pacific depended on the help of the U.S. fleet as well, so their troops at Singapore, and other Allies in the Dutch West Indies, were also on their own. No troops could be resupplied or reinforced in key areas; there could be no large-scale evacuations. Instead, the U.S. fleet would have to be rebuilt by frantic repair efforts in Hawaii, and U.S. factories working twenty-four hours a day on the mainland.

According to both British ambassador Lord Halifax and Winston Churchill, FDR was looking for an international incident that would propel the United States into war with the support of its citizens (and voters), but records show that FDR thought any attack from either the Germans or the Japanese would be minor.[53] How wrong he was. The warning from Admiral Richardson in the fall of 1940 proved to be extremely accurate: The U.S. fleet was the target of the Japanese, and Roosevelt's understanding of naval tactics bordered on fantasy. Years later, Admiral Richardson wrote, "I believe the President's responsibility for our initial defeats in the Pacific was direct, real and personal."[54] Likewise, Arthur Krock wrote, "In my opinion, third-term politics accounts for the restraint of Executive policy that was reflected in the inadequate state of our military in December, 1941."[55]

Later investigations also showed a critical lack of communication between Admiral Kimmel and General Walter C. Short. The two Hawaiian commanders had not fully understood the alert status for the islands. Kimmel believed that Short had put the Army on full alert, which was not true; Short would go to his grave saying that he put his command on a low-level alert against sabotage only due to the incomplete information he received from Washington. Intelligence reports sent to the U.S. Navy at Pearl Harbor did not automatically go to General Short's office, which Short claimed kept vital information from him. General Marshall later pointed out that both the Philippines and the Panama Canal Zone went on full alert in early December, after the warnings sent to all Pacific bases, including General Short's command.[56]

The Japanese planning was not perfect. Their pilots failed to sink American aircraft carriers at Pearl Harbor because the ships were out to sea, which was a major blow to Japan's plans. Also, they did not destroy the power plant, machine shops, and oil storage tanks near the harbor. If the oil tanks had been blown up, the fuel emergency would have been acute and possibly affected the fleet for months. With the machine shops undamaged, repairs began immediately.[57]

General Douglas MacArthur also underestimated the enemy in the first days of the war. Receiving the news about Pearl Harbor in the wee hours of December 8 (Manila time), MacArthur did not coordinate well with his air commander in the Philippines. American leadership was slow and disorganized.

Nine hours after Pearl Harbor, nearly two hundred Japanese planes flew over the U.S. facilities at Clark Field, and the Japanese pilots could not believe their luck when they saw the American air force on the ground. Attacking in three waves, Japanese heavy bombers pounded the area, followed by dive-bombers and then fighters. Clark Field had no bomb shelters for its men, not even slit trenches. Virtually every building along the airstrip was flattened.[58]

After the attack, news correspondent Shelley Smith Mydans

interviewed members of the New Mexico National Guard who had manned antiaircraft guns at Clark Field. She learned that American pilots there had been ordered into the air on the morning of December 8, but they sighted no enemy planes. The American pilots returned to the base for lunch, with few scouting planes aloft. Two New Mexico sergeants told Mydans that they manned their guns, protected by sandbags, but the officers were still at lunch when the Japanese attack began.[59]

When MacArthur learned that Japanese fighters had destroyed most of his American planes in the Philippines *on the ground*, he couldn't believe the enemy planes were piloted by Japanese. The disdain for Asians was still there; MacArthur thought the Japanese had hired German pilots.[60] Again, Japanese technicians had ingeniously designed ways to extend the range of their bombers to cover the huge distances of the Pacific and reach the Philippines before the Americans thought they could get there. MacArthur's air command was not ready.

Americans were learning the bitter lessons of what Winston Churchill called "the cruel art of war." In December 1941, the U.S. military was simply not prepared for the deadly seriousness of combat, just as the British were not ready during the early months of their war in Europe. For example, in 1939, only weeks after declaring war on Germany, Great Britain assembled much of its fleet at its harbor at Scapa Flow in the Orkney Islands of Scotland. Scapa Flow was supposedly protected from enemy submarines by underwater obstacles and harbor nets. The battleship *Royal Oak* sat at anchor there on the night of October 13, with most of its 1,233 crew members asleep belowdecks. After midnight on October 14, the *Royal Oak*'s crew heard an explosion in the starboard bow of the ship; the ship's officers thought a refrigerator in the ship's stores had possibly exploded, or a British aircraft nearby had accidently released a bomb. No alarm sounded. About twenty minutes later, huge explosions rocked the *Royal Oak* as three torpedoes from German submarine *U-47* hit the ship's cordite magazine. The earlier explosion had indeed been a German torpedo. The *Royal Oak* was plunged into darkness by the massive explosion, immediately began to list, and sank thirteen minutes later. The deaths of 833 officers and crewmen served as an early lesson about Germany's grim determination to win the war.[61]

In the Pacific after December 7, the United States and Great Britain also had to adjust to Japan's skill at war. Attacking Malaya on December 8, General Yamashita's 35,000 troops landed well north of Singapore, which had a garrison of 85,000 British, Australian, and Indian troops. Yamashita had been offered a larger contingent of infantry, but he knew that larger numbers would lead to problems with supplies. Instead, he kept his forces just large enough to fight effectively. The Japanese infantry rode thousands of bicycles to circle quickly around the troops facing them, consistently outmaneuvering the British commanders.

Churchill was dismayed to learn that the British commanders in Singapore had not bothered to construct land defenses to the north of the city before the December attack. The British had also dismissed new strategies by Japan, thinking that surely the Japanese would attack Singapore from the sea—on the southern edge of the city. Another consequence of the British lack of imagination meant that they did not have enough antipersonnel ammunition for their artillery. They had stockpiled only armor-piercing shells to use on Japanese ships if they tried to steam into Singapore's waters. When Japan's infantry attacked overland through the jungles of Malaya, the British had to fall back. Japanese air forces also dominated the area because the British had kept most of their planes in Europe to fight the Germans.[62]

At Singapore, British confidence lay in its navy, represented by the battleships *Prince of Wales* and *Repulse* and four destroyers, which had arrived only a few weeks before. (The *Prince of Wales* had carried Churchill to Newfoundland for the Atlantic Charter meeting only months earlier.) On December 10, British admiral Sir Tom Phillips led his fleet out to combat the Japanese landings in the north. With almost no air cover, both the *Prince of Wales* and the *Repulse* went to the bottom, taking 840 sailors and Admiral Phillips with them, victims of Mitsubishi bombers. For the first time in the history of naval warfare, capital ships at sea had been sunk by aerial bombardment. The shock to Churchill and the British people was profound.[63]

By December 11, the United States and Great Britain were at war with both Germany and Japan. Prime Minister Winston Churchill immediately proposed that he travel in secret to Washington to confer with President Roosevelt on their future war strategy. Churchill was determined that victory in Europe should remain the first priority, and that Great Britain should continue to receive the bulk of Lend-Lease supplies. He arrived in Washington on December 22, entering the White House while very few people in the nation's capital knew of his momentous journey. When Roosevelt's press secretary, Steve Early, announced to the press that Churchill was in the White House, Early was nearly trampled by reporters running to the phones to call their papers.[64]

Churchill and Roosevelt spent the next three weeks hammering out the first steps in a war policy that would encompass much of the globe. Now that both countries were allied against a common enemy, Roosevelt welcomed Churchill to speak to the American people at the lighting of the White House Christmas tree on December 24, and to a joint session of Congress two days later.[65] Many people were questioning if the democracies could produce a war effort to overcome the central planning and efficiency of the total war economies of Germany and Japan. Churchill's soaring oratory spoke to those fears:

> The forces ranged against us are enormous. They are bitter, they are ruthless. The wicked men and their factions who have launched their peoples on the path of war and conquest know that they will be called to terrible account if they cannot beat down by force of arms the peoples they have assailed....

It is quite true that, on our side, our resources in manpower and materials are far greater than theirs. But only a portion of your resources is as yet mobilized and developed, and we both of us have much to learn in the cruel art of war. We have therefore, without doubt, a time of tribulation before us. . . . Many disappointments and unpleasant surprises await us. . . .

For the best part of twenty years the youth of Britain and America have been taught that war is evil, which is true, and that it would never come again, which has been proved false. For the best part of twenty years the youth of Germany, Japan and Italy have been taught that aggressive war is the noblest duty of the citizen, and that it should be begun as soon as the necessary weapons and organization had been made. We have performed the duties and tasks of peace. They have plotted and planned for war. This, naturally, has placed us in Britain and now places you in the United States at a disadvantage, which only time, courage and strenuous, untiring exertions can correct. . . .

Churchill did not hide his relief that the United States had entered the war:

Lastly, if you will forgive me for saying it, to me the best tidings of all is that the United States, united as never before, has drawn the sword for freedom and cast away the scabbard. All these tremendous facts have led the subjugated peoples of Europe to lift up their heads again in hope.

Franklin Roosevelt certainly joined Winston Churchill in wanting the United States to enter World War II.[66] The minutes of FDR's cabinet meetings in the fall of 1941 show that he expected the Japanese to commit an overt act that would lead to war. Secretary Stimson recorded in his diary, and stated in congressional testimony, that "the question was how we should maneuver them into the position of firing the first shot without allowing too much danger to ourselves." Before December 7, if anyone had suggested that the Japanese could mount simultaneous attacks on Hawaii, Hong Kong, Malaya/Singapore, Guam, Wake Island, and the Philippines, *and* that all of these would be successful, military commanders would have guffawed loud and long. As General Marshall said in the years after Pearl Harbor, "Of course, no one anticipated that that overt act would be the crippling of the Pacific fleet."[67]

Did FDR specifically and knowingly allow Pearl Harbor to be attacked so that he could ask for a declaration of war from Congress? The answer is no. Research shows that Roosevelt was sure that the Japanese would attack; the question was, where? And he, like most other strategists, believed that they would attack Singapore and probably the Philippines. That Roosevelt and most military leaders grossly underestimated, or even ignored, the capabilities of aerial attack is undoubtedly true. That Roosevelt and Hull could have come to some agreement with the Japanese that would have delayed war and given the United States more time to prepare is true. And that Roosevelt squandered billions of dollars on pet New Deal projects in the eight years leading up to Pearl Harbor while allowing the military to languish with archaic equipment is also true. Roosevelt's incompetence in both foreign policy and military planning certainly contributed to the disaster, but he did not plan or desire the devastation at Pearl Harbor on December 7. Now that the crisis had arrived, how would he and his country respond?

5

1942: THE WAR OVERSEAS

On December 14, 1941, a fifty-one-year-old officer in the American Army climbed down from a passenger train onto the platform in busy Union Station in Washington, D.C. He arrived alone and left the station without fanfare, because almost no one in the city knew or cared who he was. One person who did was the man who had sent for him—General George Marshall, Army chief of staff. After years of desk jobs, which included four long years serving under MacArthur in the Philippines, General Dwight Eisenhower hoped that the Army—meaning General Marshall—would offer him a command where he could lead men. Eisenhower went straight to Marshall's office at the War Department.[1]

Marshall was facing military crises on every hand. After Pearl Harbor, Germany declared war on the United States on December 11. While Marshall made plans to invade Europe, German submarine commanders began "Operation Drumbeat," sending their largest submarines across the Atlantic to attack American ships along the East Coast. Just getting an army to Europe looked like a major challenge. Fighting in the Philippines was intensifying as the Japanese landed more troops. About twenty thousand Americans served under MacArthur in the Philippines, along with a much larger force of Filipino "scouts," which meant that over five thousand miles of ocean lay between those forces and the damaged

U.S. fleet in Hawaii, and most of those miles were controlled by the Japanese.[2]

Marshall had heard good reports of both Eisenhower's military knowledge and his ability to work under pressure with others. Marshall desperately needed officers who would make informed decisions and not bring all of their plans to him for approval. Determined to use the most capable officers for high command, Marshall wanted to see what Eisenhower could do.

When Eisenhower arrived, Marshall gave him a quick briefing on the crisis in the Pacific. To the startled newcomer, he said, "What should be our general line of action?" Eisenhower asked for a few hours to formulate a plan and went to work. That same afternoon, he knew that getting reinforcements to the Philippines in time to save the American forces there from surrender was impossible. With much of the U.S. Navy sitting in the mud at Pearl Harbor, an evacuation was also out of the question. The U.S. Navy not only refused to attempt running the Japanese blockade around the Philippines, it also ignored Eisenhower's pleas for cooperation with the Army in making long-term plans. Much of the Navy brass was still concentrating on battleship tactics rather than adapting to the newer strategies using carrier task forces.[3]

For the next two months, Eisenhower was assigned to find alternatives for aiding MacArthur's forces in the Philippines. Ships, airplanes, and ammunition were in short supply, but Eisenhower spent eighteen hours a day, seven days a week, looking for solutions. Australia could serve as a staging area for the Allies. American officers were already there, trying to set up a framework for the defense of the Pacific.[4]

Searching for a way to supply American forces in the Philippines, Marshall and Eisenhower used unusual methods. They approved a bounty of $10 million to Australian privateers to break through the Japanese Navy and reach the Philippines with supplies. Only three of six privateers (Marshall called them "pirates") that tried to get through to the islands actually made it, which was not enough help to make a difference for MacArthur and his men.[5]

One significant result of Japan's "sneak" attack on Pearl Harbor was American unity. Writing in the *New York Times*, Arthur Krock noted, "The circumstances of the Japanese attack on Pearl Harbor were such that national unity was an instant consequence. You could almost hear it click into place in Washington today. . . . [N]ational unity—which has been a distant and unattained goal since and before Hitler invaded Poland in 1939—seemed visibly to arise from the wreckage at Honolulu." Krock also called the fight "World War No. 2."[6]

Most news reporters had no idea of the extent of the damage in Hawaii. H. V. Kaltenborn, a national radio broadcaster, speculated during his program on how many days and hours it would be before the U.S. Navy sailed out of Pearl Harbor to "devastate the home islands of Japan."[7] The American public expected a victory, and a quick one.

When FDR addressed the nation by radio from the Oval Office on the evening of December 9, 1941, pollsters estimated that more than 90 million Americans (or 92.4 percent of American adults) listened to that broadcast. Roosevelt accused the Japanese of committing a decade of "international immorality." He appealed to the emotions of his listeners: "We are now in this war. We are all in it—all the way. Every single man, woman and child is a partner in the most tremendous undertaking of our American history. . . . So far, the news has been all bad," Roosevelt admitted, but he continued to suppress the details of damage in Hawaii.[8]

In the weeks and months after Pearl Harbor, investigations and blame for the disaster hovered over many heads. A congressional committee, with members handpicked by FDR, began its inquiries. Admiral Stark traveled to Hawaii to examine the damage himself. Admiral Kimmel and General Short, the Navy and Army commanders in Hawaii, were scapegoats for the time being. Both were ignominiously dismissed from their posts. Roosevelt not only maneuvered to escape most criticism, but also enjoyed the highest poll ratings of his career in late January 1942, when he celebrated his sixtieth birthday.[9]

After Pearl Harbor, many White House visitors detected a change in FDR. Marshall said that after the attack, Roosevelt acted swiftly and decisively, in a direct manner the general had not seen before. Labor Secretary Frances Perkins also noticed the change. Roosevelt was indeed a wartime president now, and if his legacy was to be a great one, America had to win the war.[10] The president proclaimed that Thursday, January 1, 1942, would be a day of national prayer. Churches opened their doors to the public, regardless of denomination.[11]

The United States needed the diligence of its president and the courage and unity of its citizens, as military reports went from bad to worse. American servicemen on Guam and Wake Island had few weapons and little ammunition when they were overrun by the Japanese in mid-December; they quickly surrendered. The British fortress at Singapore had been touted as the "Gibraltar of the East" before the war, but when the British commander, General Arthur Percival, surrendered to the Japanese on February 15, 1942, more than ninety thousand British subjects, including Australian, British, and Indian troops, went into captivity. Singapore became the greatest military disaster in Great Britain's long history. The garrison at Hong Kong, manned mostly by inexperienced Canadian troops, had already surrendered on Christmas Day, 1941. In North Africa, British and Australian troops struggled to hold on to the port of Tobruk, as Germany's Afrika Korps swept across the desert.

Churchill admitted to Roosevelt that it was a difficult time for the British. A sudden increase in the number of sinkings in the Atlantic added to British gloom; the British could not use their intelligence decrypts to avoid submarine attacks, because the Germans had changed their codes. "When I reflect how I have longed and prayed for the entry of the United States into the war, I find it difficult to realize how greatly our British affairs have deteriorated since December 7," wrote Churchill. In one round of sinkings, the British lost 42 American-made tanks, 428 tons of tank parts, 236 artillery pieces, 24 armored cars, more than 5,000 tons of ammunition, and thousands of gallons of gasoline.[12]

The U.S. military found one success to cheer about: Wounded men responded amazingly well to the new sulfa drugs. Two months after Pearl Harbor, the Army Medical Corps announced that because of sulfa, not one amputation due to infection had been necessary among the wounded in Hawaii. Doctors were astounded at the difference the new drug made. During World War I, 80 percent of men with abdominal wounds had died of infection. Sulfa proved to be so beneficial in World War II that the Army supplied packets of powdered sulfa to infantrymen overseas with instructions to sprinkle it over wounds on the battlefield.[13]

The fighting in the Philippines was going badly, although the American public was not told that at first. Government briefings and newspaper headlines continued to tout American superiority, long after the Japanese obviously had the upper hand in the Pacific. Headlines such as "MacArthur Beats Off Two Divisions" or "Japanese Halted in Bataan Attack" gave the impression that Americans were winning, when in reality Japan had poured tens of thousands of troops into Luzon against General MacArthur's tired and poorly trained men.

MacArthur avoided an early surrender by pulling his forces into the Bataan peninsula, where the smaller American Army could more easily defend the hilly terrain. Sadly, years of the government's neglect of the U.S. Army bore bitter fruit. Author William Manchester, who as a young Marine served on Guadalcanal and Okinawa, later wrote that American soldiers on Bataan discovered that four out of five hand grenades failed to explode, and one platoon fired seventeen mortar shells only to find that thirteen were duds. With almost no air support and little food, MacArthur's troops were slowly retreating down the peninsula toward the island fortress of Corregidor at the mouth of Manila Bay.[14]

News dispatches about the war in the Pacific still contained such glowing descriptions as "the Pacific Fleet delivered smashing assaults" and operated "in perfect coordination" when the truth was different. Reporters such as Arthur Krock complained that the War Department and the president's Office for Emergency Management continued to portray Americans winning the war across the globe, regardless of the outcome of events.

On December 20, FDR appointed Byron Price to head the Office of Censorship. Price instituted a Code of Wartime Practices for publishers and broadcasters in the United States, heavily dependent on reporters' patriotism and common sense. Price believed in freedom of the press and asked for voluntary cooperation, calling his version of censorship "the voice of the dove." His office asked the news media to avoid mention of troop movements, ship landings, and even battle casualties. Weather bulletins were limited to emergency storm warnings. No photos of dead American soldiers from overseas battlefields were allowed in print.[15]

Overseas in combat zones, censorship was complete. Photographers were approved before traveling into combat zones, and all photos were subject to approval of government censors. What Price could not control was the White House's suppression of bad war news.[16]

In a February 10 editorial, Arthur Krock, a Pulitzer Prize–winning journalist, framed his title in a question: "Why Not Some Bad News with the Good?" Krock charged that the federal government was hiding behind the need for national security to suppress damage reports that would reflect badly on the president. "The American public has as yet no full conception of the military and naval disaster at Pearl Harbor more than two months ago." As the battle in the Philippines intensified, Krock pointed out that "the government must trust the people, as Mr. Churchill's government in Great Britain does, to be able to take promptly and without ornament all the bad news it is safe to reveal."[17]

On the evening of February 23, Roosevelt responded by addressing the nation in another Fireside Chat. His audience had already been asked to have maps available with which to follow his remarks, and many newspapers printed world maps on the day of the speech. FDR opened his address by citing the hardships of George Washington's Continental Army at Valley Forge, when Washington had provided "moral stamina" during those difficult days: "He and the brave men who served with him knew that no man's life or fortune was secure without freedom and free institutions." [18]

However, Roosevelt deviated from George Washington's advice to avoid foreign wars: "The present great struggle has taught us increasingly that freedom of person and security of property anywhere in the world depend upon the security of the rights and obligations of liberty and justice everywhere in the world." This worldwide role was never envisioned by Washington or the Founders, but Roosevelt embraced it. He went on:

> Your government has unmistakable confidence in your ability to hear the worst, without flinching or losing heart. You must, in turn, have complete confidence that your government is keeping nothing from you except information that will help the enemy in his attempt to destroy us. In a democracy there is always a solemn pact of truth between government and the people; but there must also always be a full use of discretion—and that word "discretion" applies to the critics of government as well.

Using a world map, FDR discussed the battle lines and supply lines stretching around the globe. In doing so, he finally discussed the attack on Pearl Harbor, but he understated the damage. He said that 2,340 officers and men had died, when a total of 2,403 Americans were killed, and he gave a low estimate of the number of wounded. About damage to the fleet, he claimed that only three ships were permanently out of commission, but four battleships were sunk, and seventeen other ships damaged; several couldn't be repaired. Roosevelt attacked the idea that the United States had lost more than a thousand planes in Hawaii; the reality was about 188, but he refused to give an exact number. "But I can say that to date—and including Pearl Harbor—we have destroyed considerably more Japanese planes than they have destroyed of ours." [19] Few listeners in his audience could refute this outrageous statement because losses throughout the Pacific were suppressed in the news media, including news about the aircraft destroyed on the ground in the Philippines.

Two weeks later, when Roosevelt ordered MacArthur out of the Philippines and back to Australia, the public should have known to expect more bad news. MacArthur was too valuable a commander and too much a symbol of the American military for FDR to allow his capture. Also, international politics intervened on MacArthur's behalf. With Japan threatening to invade Australia, the Aussies had demanded the return home of three divisions of Australian troops currently serving in North Africa. Winston Churchill protested that removing the Australian force could lead to a German takeover of the Suez Canal, since combined troops of the British kingdom were desperately trying to keep General Erwin Rommel and his German tanks out of Cairo. British commanders needed every Allied soldier in North Africa. Finally, Australia's prime minister, John Curtin, and his cabinet agreed to postpone their demand, but only if an American general were named as supreme commander of the Southwest Pacific war theater, with American troops soon to follow. [20]

General MacArthur agreed to leave the Philippines, but only when ordered to do so by President Roosevelt. The general still faced a twenty-four-hundred-mile journey through enemy-controlled territory. In a feat of American derring-do which would only add to the MacArthur legend, the general, his wife, and his small son boarded a PT boat at Corregidor. With only other PT boats as escorts, they traveled more than six hundred miles across open water, avoiding Japanese patrols that were watching for a potential breakout from Corregidor. Terribly seasick, MacArthur described the PT boat's day-and-a-half journey to Mindanao as "a trip in a concrete mixer."[21] Their air transport also managed to get through to the island to pick them up for the sixteen-hundred-mile flight to Australia. When MacArthur's plane finally neared Darwin, his party was diverted to another landing site because Japanese aircraft were bombing and strafing the city.

MacArthur took over Allied command of the Southwest Pacific and pledged to return to the Philippines, but to his extreme frustration, he found that he had commanded more troops on Bataan than were currently in Australia. The Australian press had issued statements about stockpiles of supplies and large numbers of soldiers in their country, but that turned out to be propaganda to fool Japan. And on May 6, the final group of American soldiers back on Corregidor surrendered to the Japanese. Almost 12,000 American and 60,000 Filipino soldiers went into POW camps in the Philippines. Very little information on the fate of the captives came out of the Philippines in the months after the surrender.

Likewise, from Burma the news was no better. General Joe Stilwell had arrived in Burma in the spring of 1942, just as the Allied front was disintegrating. During May, he led a group of 114 military men, nurses, and civilians westward on foot, with the rampaging Japanese Army not far behind. At one point, Stilwell was listed as missing in action. Surprising everyone, Stilwell and his group made it into Assam, India, without a single loss of life. The general told his superiors, "We got run out of Burma and it's as humiliating as hell."[22]

An electrifying morale boost came that spring when the American public learned that the U.S. Army Air Force had bombed Japan. Under the command of Lieutenant Colonel Jimmy Doolittle, sixteen B-25 bombers took off from the deck of the USS *Hornet*, striking several targets in the home islands of Japan in a symbolic raid that shocked the Japanese, who had been told for years they were invulnerable. The raid convinced Admiral Yamamoto that Japan should conquer Midway Island, northwest of Hawaii, to give a wider cordon of protection to the home islands. The Japanese Navy began planning another carrier-based offensive for early June. At the same time, a smaller force would attack Alaska's Aleutian Islands.

The U.S. Navy found its wartime leader in the Pacific in Admiral Chester Nimitz. Born to German-American parents in Fredericksburg, Texas, Nimitz had learned about the sea from his paternal grandfather, who had been a seaman in the German merchant marine. Nimitz graduated from the Annapolis Naval Academy in 1905, and by World War II he had served on almost every type of ship in the U.S. Navy. Appointed Commander in Chief, Pacific Fleet, only ten days after Pearl Harbor, he had the daunting task of rebuilding the battered fleet and defeating the Japanese in the central Pacific.

Nimitz quickly showed that he had the will to meet the Japanese head-on. During the same week as the American surrender at Corregidor, the Japanese military attempted to invade Port Moresby, New Guinea, and Tulagi in the Solomon Islands. Nimitz sent two American carriers and their escorts, including Australian destroyers, to intercept and destroy the Japanese fleet. In the first naval battle in history in which opposing fleets never sighted each other, aircraft from the USS *Lexington* and USS *Yorktown* attacked the Japanese task force in what came to be known as the Battle of the Coral Sea. The American aviators sank one Japanese light carrier and damaged several of its sister ships. By the end of the fight, Japanese air attacks had damaged both American carriers, whose wooden decks did not stand up well to dive-bombers. U.S. Navy planners had been slow to admit the need for steel-plated decks, already in use by the British Navy. Consequently, after direct hits that caused an internal gasoline explosion, the *Lexington* had to be scuttled, while the *Yorktown* limped back to Hawaii for repairs.[23]

Meanwhile, U.S. naval intelligence officers discovered Japan's plans for a June attack. They were sure that the target was Midway

Island, located approximately one thousand miles northwest of Hawaii. Nimitz agreed, although other staff officers argued that Yamamoto was preparing another strike against Hawaii. Still others thought the target could be the West Coast, as Japanese retaliation for the Doolittle raid. With the carriers *Hornet* and *Enterprise* ready to meet the enemy, Nimitz bet everything he had that Yamamoto would attack Midway.[24]

Nimitz needed all three of his aircraft carriers to meet what would certainly be a much larger Japanese task force. The *Yorktown* was damaged, and the repair estimates ran into weeks and months, but its flight elevators and flight deck were still working. Nimitz gave repair crews three days to patch up the *Yorktown* and get it out to sea. Repairs continued on the ship as it sailed to rendezvous with the *Hornet* and *Enterprise*. The three American carriers waited in secret to ambush the Japanese once they arrived near Midway.[25] On June 3, Ensign Jewell (Jack) Reid of Paducah, Kentucky, spotted the vanguard of the enemy fleet from his PBY patrol plane and flashed a warning.

The Japanese Navy sailed into striking distance of Midway with four aircraft carriers, hundreds of planes on board, and dozens of support vessels. On June 4, Admiral Nagumo launched his air assault, after his ships fought off land-based B-17 bombers from Midway's airstrip. In successive waves of attacks, American aviators tried to sink the Japanese fleet. Nagumo was slow to realize that carrier-based aircraft would attack his fleet because he used too few scout planes, and not all of those flew their assigned routes. Even so, when American pilots from the USS *Hornet* attacked, their slow-moving Douglas TBD Devastators were wiped out. All of the American pilots were killed save one, Ensign George H. Gay, Jr., of Houston, Texas. Ensign Gay escaped his damaged plane and, floating in the Pacific, was an eyewitness to one of the most important naval battles in the war.[26]

Japanese fighters normally flew a protective "umbrella" over their fleet, but as waves of American torpedo planes tried to sink

Japan's ships, "the Japanese fighters were simply . . . pulled in too many directions." (Northeast by a torpedo squadron from the *Hornet*; south-southwest by torpedo planes from the *Enterprise*; and southeast by fighters and torpedo planes from the *Yorktown*.) The American torpedo planes failed to sink the Japanese carriers, but they distracted the fighters long enough. When American SBD Dauntless dive-bombers from the *Enterprise* and *Yorktown* arrived minutes later, no Japanese fighters were in position to oppose them. Japanese commanders watched in shock as a "waterfall" of American dive-bombers headed for their carriers. "It was like a horrible dream in slow motion," said one of the carrier's navigators. The Americans scored hits in less than five minutes, causing major fires on board the carriers *Akagi*, *Soryu*, and *Kaga*. The Japanese fleet had been caught off balance with planes refueling, which added to the inferno. Later that day, the *Hiryu* was also hit. With four carriers lost, the devastated Japanese Navy withdrew. Never again would it mount an offensive in the Pacific war.

Ensign Gay was picked up the next day by American planes looking for survivors. Admiral Nimitz interviewed Gay to hear his firsthand account of the battle. Although the *Yorktown* had been sunk, Nimitz announced that the country had "just cause to rejoice over a momentous victory." The "miracle at Midway" gave the Americans and their allies wonderful news after six months of struggle since Pearl Harbor.[27]

The U.S. military also showed that it understood the growing importance of accurate war news, which included numbers of casualties. Newswriters praised the military's more accurate accounts of the Battle of Midway, calling them "much better than the mistakenly optimistic reports given out day by day when General MacArthur was fighting on Bataan Peninsula."[28] Japanese forces had also landed on the outer islands of the Aleutians and bombed Dutch Harbor, Alaska, in early June, but Americans rejoiced in the news of the Pacific victory.

In its June 8, 1942, issue, *Time* analyzed the first six months of the war for the United States: "On the day of Pearl Harbor, Britain had already been fighting the Axis for over 33 months, Russia had been fighting for more than five, China continuously for 59. At the end of six months a major victory for U.S. arms is still to be recorded and more defeats are all too likely." Since the magazine went to press before much was known about the success at Midway, the editors discounted the naval victories in the Pacific. More important, no Americans had wrested territory back from either the Japanese or the Germans: "At the end of six months of war the U.S. has not taken a single inch of enemy territory, not yet beaten the enemy in a single major battle on land, not yet opened an offensive campaign."[29]

Secretary of War Stimson could not reply that U.S. leadership had been working around the clock for months to plan a European ground offensive. Also, plans were already under way for Major General Carl Spaatz to travel to England on June 15, to head the American Eighth Air Force's bomber command. By August 17, Spaatz's B-17 crews were flying bombing missions over Europe. President Roosevelt was acutely aware of the public's frustration with America's seemingly slow efforts. Midterm elections were looming in the fall, and FDR wanted the U.S. Army in Europe, fighting, before the public voted on November 3.[30]

General Marshall met with British military leaders repeatedly in early 1942, knowing full well that the Brits considered American troops "green newcomers in the fight." Striking up a friendship with Lord Louis Mountbatten, chief of combined operations for the British, General Marshall asked him, "What do you need most to get ahead with planning and training?" Mountbatten's response confirmed one of the top U.S. production priorities for the duration of the war: "Double your orders for landing ships and craft in the United States and develop even a larger type of landing craft to carry infantry troops."[31]

Marshall believed that American forces would be ready to execute a limited invasion of northern France (Operation Sledgehammer) by the fall of 1942. Churchill and his generals opposed any landings in northern Europe until the Allies showed overwhelming strength. They had been thrown out of Europe once already by the Nazis, and when they returned, they wanted to stay there. Mountbatten suggested that a North African landing take the place of Sledgehammer, but Marshall thought the Mediterranean war theater would drain American troops away from the primary objective, a landing on continental Europe. Overruled by both Churchill and FDR, Marshall had to agree that U.S. forces would land in North Africa.

Once again, Marshall showed great patience in dealing with Roosevelt and his method of arriving at decisions. Closeted with Churchill, FDR had changed his mind on many points Marshall had thought were already settled. Even Secretary Stimson recorded in his diary that "Churchill and Roosevelt, despite their brilliance, were too much alike in lacking 'the balance that has got to go along with warfare.'" Marshall agreed with Stimson: "We were largely trying to get the President to stand pat on what he had previously agreed to. The President shifted, particularly when Churchill got hold of him. . . . The President was always ready to do any sideshow and Churchill was always prodding him."[32]

Marshall admitted later that he lacked FDR's sensitivity to public opinion, which was important in keeping America in the war effort. "[I] failed to see that the leader in a democracy has to keep the people entertained. (That may sound like the wrong word, but it conveys the thought.) The people demand action. We couldn't wait to be completely ready."[33] Marshall prepared for the North African landings, which would take place in the fall of 1942.

On June 21, Roosevelt once again hosted Churchill and his military advisors for a White House planning conference. Meeting in the president's office, the men had just begun their discussions when an aide entered the room and handed a note to Roosevelt.

He read it silently, then passed the note on to Churchill: "Tobruk has surrendered, with 25,000 men taken prisoner." A year earlier, Australian troops had held Tobruk against a German siege for five months, until relieved by British, Polish, and Czech soldiers under overall command of Major-General Ronald Scobie. For a total of 240 days, the Allied forces had held the Germans at bay. Tobruk symbolized British fighting spirit in the Mediterranean, marking the first time a blitzkrieg by German Panzers had been halted. Its deep-water port offered the best anchorage for supply ships in North Africa. On June 21, in a surprise attack, General Erwin Rommel's troops finally captured Tobruk. The actual count of British POWs was closer to thirty-three thousand men.[34]

For Churchill, seated in Roosevelt's office, this was one of the heaviest blows of the war. Certainly, his leadership would be questioned in Parliament. "It was then that the President made a spontaneous gesture of friendship that the Prime Minister was always to treasure. . . . [FDR] asked what the United States could do to help in the crisis. To stem the German attack that he knew would follow, Churchill asked for Sherman tanks." Marshall immediately went to work to locate tanks for the remaining British Army in Egypt, but he had to requisition them away from American units that had just received them. "It is a terrible thing to take the weapons out of a soldier's hands," Marshall told Churchill. "If the British need is so great they must have them." The United States shipped three hundred tanks and one hundred 105-mm guns by convoy as soon as possible.[35]

Meanwhile, by midsummer, Douglas MacArthur's position in Australia was desperate. Furious that his supplies were meager while so much went to the British, MacArthur had asked Roosevelt to divert America's "entire resources" to the Southwest Pacific. Roosevelt had already written MacArthur saying he understood the general's frustration, but sending an army to Europe was the first priority. The War Department was so doubtful about the chances of holding Australia that American units arriving in the Southwest Pacific were being diverted to the New Hebrides, the Fijis, and New Caledonia.[36]

On paper, MacArthur's situation looked stronger than it was, but of his sixty-two B-17 Flying Fortresses, only six could take off; the others were used for spare parts. American fighter planes had been shipped to Australia, where air crews were frantically putting them together, but the Japanese Zero was superior in handling, and its pilots highly skilled. American pilots were greatly outnumbered and definitely outgunned.[37]

The Japanese had such strength on Rabaul and other islands near Australia that invasion could come at any time. They were building airstrips at Bougainville and Guadalcanal, and when these were completed, they would have a staging area for more bombing of Australia. After being turned back at the Battle of the Coral Sea, Japanese generals still planned to take the southern coast of New Guinea and Port Moresby, which was held by only one thousand Australian troops. The Japanese knew if they could take Port Moresby, their invasion of Australia could proceed.[38]

Thinking offensively, MacArthur sent two of his best staff officers to reconnoiter the eastern end of Papua, New Guinea, near Port Moresby. Both men were horrified at what they found, reporting back to MacArthur that the dense jungles of New Guinea posed an unbelievably hostile environment for the Army. New Guinea boasts some of the highest, wettest jungles in the world, with jagged mountain peaks rising to over thirteen thousand feet. The few mountain trails over the island were slippery, tangled with roots, and often covered with green slime from the rotting vegetation and heavy rainfall. Swarms of biting insects attacked any human; malaria was rampant. Between rainstorms, the marshes that dotted the island added to the humidity, making the atmosphere a constant steam bath.[39]

MacArthur listened to their reports, and said in a low voice, "We'll defend Australia in New Guinea."[40] Knowing that he did not have enough troops to defend a continent the size of Australia,

MacArthur preferred a more compact, though more challenging, battle area. He believed that the harsh environment would be the enemy of the Japanese, just as it was for the Allies. More Australian units left for New Guinea in early July, and American troops followed weeks later.

With Japan's navy so dominant around Australia, the six-hundred-mile stretch of the Coral Sea between Port Moresby and supply depots in Australia was the Allies' logistics nightmare. Fortunately for MacArthur, an answer appeared in the person of General George Kenney, who was the new air commander and "an air-power evangelist" for getting men and supplies to New Guinea. Kenney reinvigorated the Allied air force, concentrated bombers in attack groups that sapped the enemy's strength at Rabaul, and promised MacArthur that his air force would transform Port Moresby from its current siege mentality to the main Allied base in the Southwest Pacific. Kenney used five new airfields near Port Moresby to fly in men and supplies, and even Army trucks, by cutting the trucks in half with acetylene torches, stuffing them into C-47 aircraft, and then welding them back together after the flights.[41]

In midsummer, the Japanese opened another offensive against Port Moresby by sending troops up the Kokoda Track, a winding trail through the almost impenetrable Owen Stanley Mountains that ran across New Guinea like a bony spine. Small groups of Australian soldiers attacked the climbing Japanese and then melted into the jungle to organize for the next attack. Seventy-seven Australians held off a much larger force trying to take the Kokoda airstrip, until finally the Japanese overran their position. For the next six weeks, Australian and Japanese units fought for control of Kokoda.[42]

Over on the coast on August 25, the Japanese Navy tried an amphibious assault on the Australian stronghold at Milne Bay on the eastern tip of Papua. Australian troops and American combat engineers stopped the Japanese. For the first time in the war, Allied soldiers not only threw back a Japanese landing, but forced the enemy to abandon their plan entirely. By September 17, Japanese soldiers along the Kokoda Track were eating the last of their food supplies. In New Guinea, both sides had lost far more men to jungle diseases than combat wounds. The Japanese commander ordered his emaciated men to withdraw.[43]

In the air war against the Japanese Zero, a solution for American aviators presented itself in an unusual location. When Japanese pilots bombed and strafed Dutch Harbor in the Aleutians on June 4, one Zero was caught in ground fire and crash-landed on Akutan Island. Despite heavy fog, Navy Catalina pilots finally spotted the downed plane on July 10. When a search party discovered it was a Zero, the entire aircraft was shipped to North Island Naval Air Station in San Diego, California. Test flights in the repaired Zero revealed its weaknesses in dogfights. Instructions went out to the Pacific fleet in late September 1942 on how to escape a pursuing Zero: "Go into a vertical power dive. . . . At 200 knots, roll hard right before the Zero pilot can get his sights lined up." Lieutenant Commander Eddie R. Sanders remembers that soon the answer came back, "It works!" American pilots had gained at least a small advantage in aerial combat.[44]

MacArthur's offensive in New Guinea had also temporarily taken pressure off the embattled U.S. Marines fighting six hundred miles to the east on Guadalcanal in the Solomon Islands, where American forces had landed on August 7. The Marines quickly took control of the airstrip, but the Japanese counterattacked during the next five months. Japan could not support combat operations in both New Guinea and the Solomons, so the Japanese broke off their New Guinea land offensive but continued attacking Guadalcanal until January. MacArthur moved his forward headquarters to Port Moresby on November 6. At last Allied troops were pushing back the Japanese.[45]

News dispatches gave Americans at home daily reports about the fighting on Guadalcanal. The U.S. Navy fought in five sea battles around Guadalcanal from August until November, as it supplied first the Marines and later U.S. Army soldiers. The Japanese poured men into Guadalcanal, refusing to admit defeat. The battle lingered into the fall, and President Roosevelt wanted good news before the national elections. According to historian Forrest Pogue:

> As the Japanese continued to flex their muscles, the President became seriously alarmed over the situation on Guadalcanal. On October 24, little more than a week before the fall election, he directed the Joint Chiefs of Staff to make sure "that every possible weapon gets into that area to hold Guadalcanal." When Marshall told him that shipping was the chief bottleneck, Roosevelt arranged for the War Shipping Administration to provide twenty additional vessels.[46]

Eventually, 60,000 U.S. troops, sailors, and airmen fought in the battle of Guadalcanal, with 7,100 killed (including naval personnel). For the Japanese, it was the first Pacific island battle where they had to evacuate with catastrophic losses, and many more disasters were to follow. More than 36,000 Japanese fought on Guadalcanal, and approximately 31,000 died there (including Navy losses). The United States lost 29 ships and 615 aircraft. By the time Japan removed its remaining men in early 1943, it had lost 38 ships, more than 700 aircraft, and hundreds of irreplaceable pilots.

On the other side of the world that fall, General Marshall worked to finish plans for Operation Torch, the Allied invasion of North Africa. But after the loss of Tobruk, Churchill also needed a British military victory to restore confidence. The prime minister had survived a vote of censure in the House of Commons the previous summer. Finally, on October 23, British General Bernard Montgomery opened the Battle of El Alamein with more than 1,000 tanks, including 300 Shermans from the United States, in an effort to push Rommel out of Egypt for good.

At the same time, American forces under General Patton sailed from Hampton Roads, Virginia, for North Africa. Patton had caused problems before embarkation by criticizing the Navy. Admiral King was so furious that he asked Marshall to replace Patton. "Patton and the Navy were in a scrap all the time," said Marshall, but Patton mended fences with the Navy before leaving port. Marshall was determined to keep the mercurial Patton as commander of the landing in Casablanca, because Marshall believed that Patton would be even more difficult for the Germans to handle.[47]

By November 4, as the ships carrying American forces neared North Africa, Montgomery and his troops from across the United Kingdom had given Churchill and the British people the long-awaited victory over the Germans in North Africa. After days of fighting, Montgomery's troops defeated Rommel's Panzer army, and Rommel ordered his men to retreat.

General Eisenhower and his staff waited at Gibraltar for word of the Allied landings at Casablanca, Oran, and Algiers. A nervous Eisenhower wrote Marshall: "We are standing, of course, on the brink and must take the jump—whether the bottom contains a nice feather bed or a pile of brick bats."[48]

On November 8, when American and British troops waded ashore, French troops opened fire on them. It took two days for Eisenhower and his staff to convince the French leaders, who had been working for Germany's puppet government there, to issue a cease-fire. Inexperienced American troops almost faltered, and the amphibious assault proved more complicated than expected, but finally all three landing sites were secured.

At Casablanca, Patton's troops found, instead of the predicted heavy seas, "a flat calm, the quietest sea seen by the inhabitants in many years." Writing to Marshall after the landings, Patton gave his own explanation: "In spite of my unfortunate proficiency in profanity, I have at bottom a strongly religious nature. It is my considered opinion that the success of the operation was largely dependent on what people generally call 'luck,' but what I believe to be Divine help."[49]

Finally, the American Army was in position to fight the Nazis. Even so, war historian Stephen Ambrose observes that the North African landings

> illustrated how unprepared the United States had been for the war, and how poorly it had done in the eleven months since Hitler declared war on the country. Eleven months—and the first offensive was against a demoralized, dissension-ridden, inadequately equipped French army, and even that was a chancy operation. . . . Eleven months—and the largest force the United States could throw into battle was two divisions at a time when Germany and Russia were hurling hundreds of divisions at each other on the Eastern Front.[50]

For the first time since the beginning of the war, Churchill ordered that the church bells in England be rung on November 15 to celebrate the victories at El Alamein and the successful landings in North Africa. General Marshall also felt that Americans could look back on solid achievements by U.S. troops, green as they were. The U.S. Army was fighting alongside its British allies. American bombers were flying regular missions over European targets. From their desperate summer position in Australia, General MacArthur's Allied forces were slowly pushing the Japanese out of New Guinea. The battle for Guadalcanal was in its last stages as the Army and fresh Marines mopped up the remaining pockets of enemy resistance. Australia was safe from invasion, and the convoy routes between Australia and America's West Coast were secure.

The U.S. military had grown from 1,686,000 troops (37 divisions and 67 air combat groups) on December 31, 1941, to 5,397,000 by the end of 1942 (73 active divisions and 167 air combat groups), with more than a million troops overseas. As Churchill said after El Alamein, "Now this is not the end. It is not even the beginning of the end. But it is, perhaps, the end of the beginning."[51]

6

1942: ON THE HOME FRONT

Two weeks after Pearl Harbor, surveyors showed up at Washington, D.C.'s prestigious Mount Vernon Seminary, a private girls' school at the intersection of Massachusetts and Nebraska avenues. The school's campus included classroom buildings and dormitories, nestled among the large trees and green lawns of the upscale neighborhood. When Mount Vernon's administrator asked the surveyors what they were doing, they replied, "We're staking out this property for the U.S. Navy." The Navy had decided it wanted the fifteen acres, for which it offered a meager $800,000. The school was forced to move its classrooms, finally locating space in Garfinckel's Department Store about a mile away. Students boarded with private families in the area. After negotiations, the school was paid $1.1 million. The U.S. Navy had decided it wanted that location, and with President Roosevelt's backing, the Navy had the authority to take it.[1]

Following Pearl Harbor, Roosevelt increased his executive powers enormously. On December 17, the *New York Times* reported, "Moving at wartime speed, the House and Senate today dealt with . . . legislation designed to make men and ships available on the fighting fronts abroad and to confer on President Roosevelt almost unlimited power to regulate the nation's emergency effort at home."[2] Congress erased the ban on using military draftees outside the Western Hemisphere and extended terms of service to six months after war's end. By executive order and legislative statute, FDR gained the power to disregard tariffs, close any radio station, order the military to take over any land, rent any building in the District of Columbia, close any stock exchange, and change labor regulations—and this was just the beginning.[3]

No president in American history had wielded such enormous power as Franklin Roosevelt, and government bureaucracy began regulating American life as never before. During Lend-Lease, red tape increased as military spending skyrocketed. After Pearl Harbor, the number of regulatory agencies mushroomed until no one could follow all of them: the BEW, WPB, WMC, NWLB, CAS, ODT, and OC were only a few.

Secretary of the Interior Harold Ickes, a longtime Roosevelt insider, was also the director of the Office of Petroleum Coordination (OPC). He issued orders making it a crime to manufacture, sell, or ship aviation fuel without his approval. When Ickes held a press conference to discuss the new petroleum policies, reporters asked him about the new OPC regulations. "I can't speak for the OPC," he replied. Confused reporters looked at each other with puzzled faces, "until an aide whispered in Ickes' ear that he was the *director* of the OPC. 'I'm all balled up on these initials,' Ickes explained."[4]

After Pearl Harbor, the Office of Production Management (OPM) took control of "essential" civilian manufacturing and wartime production. By executive order, President Roosevelt set up an Office of Defense Transportation (ODT) to coordinate all rail, water, and motor transportation in the United States. In one of the first waves of rationing, the use of chrome, tin, burlap, rubber, and other products was restricted.[5] OPM Director Knudsen announced that war industries would operate on a twenty-four-hour, seven-day-a-week schedule. Labor unions pledged an all-out war effort, but the *New York Times* noted that the welders' strike in San Francisco harbor continued.[6]

Finally, in January 1942, President Roosevelt established the

War Production Board (WPB), which replaced both SPAB and OPM, and named Donald Nelson as its head.[7] The purpose of the new WPB was to direct the production and allocation of materials and fuel, with enormous authority over the economy for the remainder of the war. The WPB symbol was an eagle with wings spread wide, strangely resembling the Nazi symbol of power.

And powerful it was: The War Production Board halted all construction projects that were not essential to the war effort, and it decreed what was essential. It directed the conversion of civilian industries to meet wartime needs, allocated scarce materials, and decided what services to the public would be curtailed. It rationed heating oil, gasoline, metals, rubber, paper, and plastic. The WPB's clothing section even regulated the amount of fabric that retailers could use per garment, avoiding wasteful styles such as long, full skirts for women. Clothing would be more formfitting, and skirts would be shorter. Tens of thousands of civilians worked in the WPB's twelve regional offices as well as its 120 field offices, as it became one of the most powerful agencies ever established by Franklin Roosevelt.[8]

The president also created the Office of Price Administration (OPA). As war production swelled in the months leading up to Pearl Harbor, prices rose and availability of civilian goods decreased. From September 1939 to December 1941, the price of dozens of basic commodities increased by almost 25 percent. Rents went up as defense plants hired thousands. During 1941, the cost of living increased about 1 percent per month, and wholesale prices increased even more. Roosevelt gave the OPA the authority to regulate the prices of almost all civilian goods, control rents, ration scarce commodities, and set the prices charged for military supplies.[9]

By April 1942, the OPA had frozen rents and most prices, although Roosevelt gave the agency no authority to put a ceiling on wages. The president counted on the labor vote, so he did not regulate wages and refused to intervene during most strikes as well.

During the OPA's first large rationing drive, schoolteachers registered every American for sugar rationing coupons; in New York City alone, public schoolteachers issued more than seven million sugar ration books. Cheese, butter, coffee, fish and meats, and most canned goods soon joined the ration list. Shoes were also rationed, but not clothing.[10]

Hardly were the regulations in effect when violations began. Crooks found that they made more money counterfeiting ration books than printing fake money. The books were easier to copy and distribute. Federal agents finally devised a system of emblems visible under infrared light on genuine ration coupons, but ration fraud continued to be big business.[11]

The OPA's staff also swelled as rationing increased. In 1942, 900 investigators and 300 lawyers worked in the OPA, with a total staff of more than 7,300 employees. *Time* magazine cautioned that the OPA's role as national regulator of food supplies and rationing would probably mean it needed 90,000 more employees: "OPA is likely to be the most unpopular of agencies, a sort of kitchen Gestapo."[12]

A rare instance of streamlining bureaucracy came at the top echelons of the War Department. As early as November 1941, General Marshall had begun to overhaul the Army's command structure, which had strangled efficiency since the Civil War. Under the old system, sixty officers reported directly to General Marshall. Hundreds of officers worked on overlapping details, with aged majors and colonels moving at a peacetime pace.

During the 1930s, the lax atmosphere in the neglected military meant that few men wore their uniforms to work, preferring civilian jackets and trousers. On the day following Pearl Harbor, military officers in the nation's capital were ordered to report in full uniform. Journalist David Brinkley described the results as "a rummage sale called to war."[13] Some officers were in uniforms purchased years before, and two sizes too small. Still others didn't have the insignia for their current rank or job description. Military headgear of all types and descriptions, some dating back to World War I, appeared in Washington.

Marshall's staff struggled to get their departments on a war footing. "The word went out that efficiency, tighter control, reduction in the number of General Staff officers, and a wholesale cut in the number of individuals having direct access to the Chief of Staff from some sixty to about six were essential to a successful war effort." In February, President Roosevelt followed Marshall's suggestions and restructured the War Department. Henceforth only six officers would report directly to the overworked Marshall, and deadwood in the War Department was swept away, including entire offices. Marshall forced many high-ranking officers who could not work at a wartime pace to retire. Accused of eliminating "all the brains of the Army," Marshall later observed, "I couldn't reply that I was eliminating considerable arteriosclerosis."[14]

As military plans took shape, Marshall gave Eisenhower more responsibility to see if he was up to the tasks ahead. Marshall eventually jumped Eisenhower in rank over 350 more senior men to give him command of the Allied troops in Europe. Marshall elevated many officers who would gain fame during the war, and he quickly removed anyone not up to the task. In addition to Eisenhower, Marshall promoted Omar Bradley and George Patton into major command roles.

In dealing with Patton, General Marshall showed that he expected a certain standard of behavior. In early 1942, Patton had been put in command of an armored unit that was training in the deserts of California. Marshall summoned Patton to Washington and asked him to work on battle plans for the Middle East. Early the next morning, Marshall was surprised to receive a letter from Patton changing major aspects of what Marshall had directly asked him to do. Marshall ordered a staff member to pick up Patton and "put him on a plane and send him back to California that morning."[15]

While Patton cooled his heels in California, Marshall refused to take Patton's repeated long-distance phone calls. Finally, Patton phoned Marshall's assistant and assured him that he understood now that he was not to alter Marshall's directives. Marshall then ordered Patton back to Washington for more work on overseas planning. "And that is the way to handle Patton," Marshall said later, with a smile. General Marshall chose Patton for an overseas command because he believed that Patton was one of the few American officers who understood the newer strategies of attacking with fast-moving tanks, as the Germans had done in Poland and France.

In the rush to build weapons, immediate problems surfaced because of lack of raw materials. One example was copper, which is an essential component of brass, and brass is essential for ammunition. Brass expands and contracts instantaneously during the firing of a gun. The powder within the ammunition first explodes, creating great pressure on the brass cartridge, and then the brass fitting must contract instantly. Brass was the only metal known to have these properties, but the government's scientists worked for months trying to substitute steel for brass in shell casings. Eventually, enough copper was being mined so that the military never issued steel cartridges, but copper was in such demand by 1943 that U.S. mints issued no copper pennies that year, only steel pennies—coins made of steel with a zinc coating.[16]

The shortage that led to the most problems for the most people was rubber. Japan had seized most of the world's rubber production when it invaded Malaya. David Brinkley tells the story of a man in Washington, D.C., who, with the outbreak of war, rushed to the grocery store to buy cases of canned goods and other supplies. With his station wagon overloaded, the rear of the car pressed against his tires, wearing them out by the time he reached home. To the man's shock, the government immediately began stringent rationing of car tires. The man had shopped for food thinking that it would be rationed, but rubber proved to be the most serious shortage for the rest of the war.[17]

The rubber shortage led to the federal government's authorizing local "rubber boards" to decide who would get new tires. Suddenly no citizen would be allowed to buy new tires without approval from the "rubber board." The government also rationed gasoline on the East Coast to discourage driving. Speed limits in most states were lowered to forty-five miles per hour or less to save gas and tires.

Bicycles also came under new restrictions because both the rubber for the tires and metals for the frames were in short supply. Overnight on April 2, the WPB announced that "no bicycle may leave a factory, a jobber, a wholesaler, or a retailer's place of business after 11:59 tonight."[18] The government took possession of all new bikes for workers in defense plants or for local officials, such as policemen.

Rubber rationing had been in the headlines as early as June 20, 1941, almost six months before Pearl Harbor, when the OPM announced that it was studying Americans' excessive use of rubber products and might propose rationing. Standard Oil of New Jersey also proposed a government-subsidized synthetic rubber program, but its proposals "were whittled down to virtually nothing" by the government.[19] When war broke out, FDR's administration was quick to point the finger at Standard Oil and accuse the company of working with Germany's I. G. Farben to deny access to synthetic rubber technology. Standard Oil protested, vehemently denying all charges and issuing a timeline of its proposals, most of which had been ignored by five different government agencies.

By May 1942, informed senators were telling their constituents that the tire shortage might last more than three years. As voters realized the severity of their predicament, their howls could be heard all the way to the White House. Roosevelt, when asked about the rubber shortage at a press conference, airily predicted "that everything would work out all right."

However, in the *New York Times* the following day, Roosevelt's statement and that of Missouri senator Harry Truman were side by side on the front page. Truman had already initiated a Senate committee in 1941 to investigate government waste, fraud, and mismanagement at military bases. Savvy enough to prevent FDR's friends in the Senate from loading the committee with the president's "yes men," Truman was beginning to establish a reputation for decisions based on facts. The Truman Committee released a statement on the same day as Roosevelt's press conference that "after months of studying the problem . . . the average motorist might hope to see no new rubber for his car for three years at least." [20]

Not only was rubber stringently rationed, but the government also suspended all production of civilian vehicles in early February 1942. Newspaper photos showed the last Studebaker rolling off the line at the automotive plant in South Bend, Indiana. Workers at car plants began a feverish rush to convert production lines to the manufacture of tanks, jeeps, and Army trucks. At Willow Run, Michigan, the Ford Corporation constructed a gigantic aircraft factory, which boasted the largest room in the world to house assembly lines for B-24 bombers. On the Willow Run plant alone, the government invested almost $87 million in plant construction by war's end. [21]

With hundreds of millions of dollars flowing into huge defense projects, the Truman Committee had moved on from investigations of Army camps to more complicated issues involving defense contractors. At times, questions arose about improprieties by government officials, but Truman proceeded cautiously. If his committee angered too many people, its enemies could shut it down.

Senator A. B. "Happy" Chandler, a former Kentucky governor, was running for reelection in the 1942 Democratic Senate primary. His opponent, John Y. Brown, Sr., attacked Senator Chandler for accepting expensive gifts from contractors, including a "60-foot, blue tiled swimming pool" built in Chandler's backyard in Versailles, Kentucky. Cement and other components of the swimming pool were materials rationed for the war effort. *Life* magazine featured a photo of Happy with his family in the background, swimming in his luxurious pool, and a caption that read, "It didn't cost Happy a cent." [22]

Brown alleged that the contractor, B. H. Collings, had won contracts for many miles of Kentucky highway construction. Collings also supplied concrete for a government munitions plant in southern Indiana, for which he had overcharged the government $445,170. Senator Chandler responded that Mr. Collings had built his swimming pool only because they were such very good friends. Kentucky's senior senator, Alben Barkley, was Senate majority leader, but he could not ignore the charges. The Truman Committee agreed to have its chief investigator, Harold G. Robinson, look into the allegations.

Robinson had worked as an FBI agent for many years and understood the workings of D.C.'s political elite. "Senators don't request investigations of other Senators. Democrats don't investigate other Democrats. The senior Senator from a state doesn't investigate the junior Senator from the same state," said Robinson many years later. In 1942, Robinson had told his superior on the Truman Committee staff, "If I come back from Louisville, you're going to have a report on your desk that tells you all about Happy Chandler's swimming pool. I just want to make sure you want it," said Robinson.

Hugh Fulton, the Truman Committee's top staffer, phoned Robinson the following day to say that another investigator would handle the Chandler pool investigation. Robinson continued, "[That other investigator] not only got the whitewash brush out, he got a spray gun out. He had that thing just all glossed over to a fare-thee-well. He [was] a more politically astute type of investigator than I am." [23]

The Truman Committee found no evidence that Chandler had broken the law, but Collings's cement company received a three-month suspension of "priority assistance" because the WPB had not approved the pool. No further charges were made in regard to the price of cement already invoiced to the munitions plant. Happy Chandler went on to win the Senate race and later became the second commissioner of major-league baseball.[24] But with the suspension, the Truman Committee and the WPB were warning defense contractors that their work should be reasonably priced, delivered on time, and meet the design specifications required by the military.

B. H. Collings was one of dozens of contractors who had worked on the Indiana Army Ammunition Plant (the INAAP), which would manufacture smokeless powder. The plant was funded in 1940, and planners chose the site because the nearby Ohio River provided ample water; the smokeless-powder plant would need seventy thousand gallons per minute. The location was far from the coasts and potential enemy bombers. Thousands of job seekers thronged to the area. Almost overnight, the tiny hamlet of Charlestown, Indiana, population nine hundred, became the center of one of the government's most important defense projects.[25]

During the late 1930s, the small amount of smokeless powder produced in the United States had bottlenecked the armaments industry. After Congress passed the Munitions Program of June 30, 1940, experts estimated that per day, the United States was producing only enough powder to supply one hundred thousand soldiers. Suddenly the nation needed millions of pounds of smokeless powder each month for bullets, artillery shells, and other explosives. By September 1940, INAAP construction was under way, and by December, Charlestown's population had grown to more than 13,000, with about 10,000 workers. By May 1, 1941, employees numbered 27,520.[26]

Charlestown's leaders struggled to cope with the onslaught of new faces. Historian Rob Vest found that "residents of the town rented out the rooms in their own homes, converted their garages into sleeping quarters, and turned their yards into trailer parking lots. Some people spent their nights in tents, while others slept in their cars."[27] Hotels and boardinghouses for a twenty-five-mile radius were also jammed. The sewer system in Charlestown was inadequate. Local restaurants were swamped with customers. Even the jail was full, as crime increased with the tidal wave of newcomers.

In desperation, city leaders finally appealed to Indiana governor Clifford Townsend. He approved state funds for a local engineer to serve as defense planning coordinator. The federal government sent WPA workers to build new sewers. Public health nurses arrived to give immunizations to prevent epidemics. Bus lines and shuttle trains ran along the busiest routes, especially to Louisville, Kentucky, and Jeffersonville, Indiana. More policemen helped prevent crime and improve traffic control, and improved highways shortened the commute for plant workers.

Despite the danger of working around smokeless powder, both DuPont and Goodyear Tire & Rubber, the companies operating the plant, had no trouble in finding willing workers for the six production lines. White males still made up the largest percentage of workers, but about 10 percent of the workforce was black. In the powder plant itself, about one-quarter of employees were women; in the buildings that sewed silk bags for the storage of gunpowder, women held two-thirds of the jobs.[28]

In April 1941, the plant began producing smokeless powder as well as the more volatile black powder, even as construction continued on other sections of INAAP. Secretary of War Stimson had ordered that one or two production lines should begin operating as soon as possible. When completed in May 1942, the entire site covered 10,655 acres with 1,700 buildings, 84 miles of railroad tracks, 190 miles of roads, and 30 miles of fencing. The government spent more than $146 million at the Charlestown, Indiana, plant during the war years.[29]

In speeches, in newspapers, and on radio, American leaders urged citizens to remember that even though the war caused them personal discomforts, the fighting men overseas had much worse conditions to bear. During the first six months of 1942, the men of the merchant marine were also paying a terrible price along the American coastline, from Maine to the Gulf Coast of Texas.

When the United States entered the war, Kriegsmarine submarine captain Reinhard Hardegen welcomed the challenge, after months of watching American deliveries of war supplies to Britain under Lend-Lease. Hardegen had also seen American naval vessels trying to sink German submarines in 1941, even while Hitler forbade his submariners to fire on U.S. ships; Hitler had hoped to avoid war with America. When Germany declared war on the United States after Pearl Harbor, Hardegen felt that "the charade of American neutrality was over; there was a score to settle."[30] Captain Hardegen's submarine, *U-123*, left its French home port on December 23, 1941, to join in the hunt for American shipping.

Of special interest to the Germans were the slow-moving tankers coming up the East Coast from the oil fields of Texas and Louisiana. The United States had not implemented a blackout along the coast. Ships were silhouetted against the bright lights of American cities as German submarine captains peered through their periscopes. In January, at least twelve ships were sunk or damaged along the East Coast alone, and by February, German submarines were patrolling the Gulf of Mexico. On February 16, German submarines attacked a Standard Oil refinery on Aruba, sinking three tankers and killing twenty-three workers. On February 19, the tanker *Pan Massachusetts* went down in Gulf waters with a loss of twenty crew members. *U-123* and submarines like it were devastating the tankers of the U.S. merchant marine.

In April 1942, the family of merchant marine sailor Billy Scheich received the tragic news that Billy was missing after his ship, the *Esso Baton Rouge*, was sunk by a German submarine off the Georgia coast near St. Simons Island. On the night of April 10, Billy's younger brother, Louis, sat with their grieving mother at home in Jacksonville, Florida. The lights of Jacksonville could be seen far out to sea. Hearing an explosion nearby, Louis ran down to the beach in time to see the eight-thousand-ton tanker *Gulfamerica* on fire, also torpedoed by *U-123*. The submarine was still visible on the surface as Captain Hardegen prepared to fire artillery shells to finish off the tanker. A crowd had reached the beach and, to his credit, the sub commander realized that he might harm civilians if he shot through the burning tanker toward the beach. (Later Hardegen recorded in his ship's log, "A rare show for the tourists.") Louis Scheich and the crowd of onlookers could only stand and watch as the submarine circled around to the land side to fire on the burning wreck. He could not know that this was the same submarine that had torpedoed his brother's ship just two days before.[31]

Sinkings similar to the tragedy of the *Gulfamerica* changed life all along the East Coast, as the Army put dimout restrictions and armed patrols in place. Louis Scheich recalled, "After that we were made to put in the blackout shades and they had blackout wardens walking the street. We had to paint half of the lens on our car lights on low beams. There were armed guards on the old Atlantic Boulevard. . . . Things changed."[32]

By May, the situation in the Gulf of Mexico was so serious that more than twenty ships were sunk or damaged by Nazi attacks that month alone, including the tanker *Virginia* at the mouth of the Mississippi River, with twenty-seven crew members killed. The crisis in shipping pointed to the poor record of both the British and U.S. navies against German submarines. From September 1, 1940, until March 1, 1941, the British had sunk only three U-boats in the entire Atlantic. America was also vulnerable; as early as December 22, 1941, a U.S. Navy report stated that "should enemy submarines operate off this coast, this command has no forces available to take adequate action against them, either offensively or defensively."[33]

Unknown to the public was the role of German submarines as minelayers, until newspapers warned Americans of the problem in

June 1942. For two days in June, and three in September, mines closed Chesapeake Bay to traffic. German subs also laid minefields in the waters off Cape Hatteras, North Carolina. American ports that had to be cleared of mines included Jacksonville, Florida; Charleston, South Carolina; Wilmington, Delaware; and even New York City's harbor, which was "bottled up" for three days in November 1942.[34]

American news broadcasts often stated that German subs were sunk when the reality was quite different. In 1941 and early 1942, submarines were hard to find using current technology. Depth charges and other antisub weapons were unreliable, but each time a U.S. ship dropped depth charges, the American public was told that another submarine had been sunk, whether there was proof or not.[35]

By refusing to convoy tankers along the coast, American commanders left single vessels vulnerable to being picked off one at a time. Along the entire Atlantic Coast, the Army Air Force had only nine planes for offshore patrols when the war started. By the spring of 1942, NDRC's scientists knew they needed a radar breakthrough for better submarine detection, but early attempts failed when scientists tried experimental radar in naval aircraft. After days trying to find ships at sea while flying overhead, adjusting the knobs on the sets, and looking at the radar screen, the scientists asked the pilot to find bigger targets. "That was the *Queen Mary* we just flew over," replied the disgusted officer.[36]

About a week later, after improving their equipment, the same radar team tried again with a pilot flying them along the coast near Boston. To their surprise, the radar revealed a German submarine just off the coast of Massachusetts. The frustrated pilot, with no weapons to fire or bombs to drop, opened his window and threw a wrench at the U-boat. He did not sink that submarine, but radar detection had just entered a new world of possibilities.

The NDRC recommended that the War Department begin sweeps by planes equipped with microwave radar and coordinated with patrols by the Navy, to destroy submarines. Despite improved radar systems, Admiral Ernest King, chief of naval operations, resisted the newer technology. "Admiral King had a terrible blind spot for new things—and about as rugged a case of stubbornness as has been cultivated by a human being," said Vannevar Bush.[37] Admiral King also had a fierce reputation as a loner whose knowledge of ships covered everything from the boilers to the top of the mast. Arthur Krock said that "even four-star Admirals stood in awe" of King's iron discipline, both on himself and his staff.[38] His aides quipped that he shaved with a blowtorch, but he served the U.S. Navy tirelessly during the war. Without his approval, airborne radar over American coastlines would not get far.

In early 1942, a radar-fitted destroyer could search only 75 square miles of ocean per hour, and earlier long-wave radar sets in planes only 1,000 square miles. Microwave radar covered 3,000 square miles an hour and worked in all types of weather. In order to protect American coastal waters, planes equipped with the new radar would need to travel far out to sea. Admiral King resented the intrusion into what he perceived to be the Navy's domain. King also had no confidence in submarine "killers" because of their past failures. (Even Germany's Admiral Doenitz said that "an aircraft can no more kill a U-boat than a crow can kill a mole."[39])

By June, the crisis was so severe that General Marshall wrote to Admiral King, "The losses by submarines off our Atlantic seaboard and in the Caribbean now threaten our entire war effort."[40] In the first six months of 1942, 122 ships had been sunk by the Germans along the East and Gulf coasts. When the War Shipping Administration announced that during the week of July 12 shipping losses had reached their highest level since the beginning of the war, Americans once again asked to be given the facts, not optimistic guesses, by the White House. Editorials admitted:

> The Navy cannot be everywhere at once, and the problem is at best a hard one to solve. Yet the statements coming from the Adminis-

tration, by constantly emphasizing the favorable aspects of the situation, have had the net effect of giving the public a far more optimistic view of the success of our counter-measures against the submarines than the facts themselves justify. If the full truth . . . were sufficiently impressed upon the American people they would cooperate far better than they do today in the dimout and other regulations.[41]

Fortunately, Secretary of War Henry Stimson became an advocate for the wonders of the new radar systems. Admiral King was persuaded that he must implement new methods. In May 1943, he set up the Tenth Air Fleet to coordinate all antisubmarine efforts in the Atlantic. New weapons included Allied aircraft with an airborne torpedo called Fido that could home in on submarines. The Allies sank almost one-third of the Atlantic Kriegsmarine that spring. Germany's Admiral Doenitz finally had to recall his subs, at least temporarily, or see them wiped out.[42]

Not only had FDR's administration issued optimistic reports about the submarine menace, but his nonchalant attitude had also led the public to waste rubber, critics charged. When the WPB ruled in July that a nationwide program to reduce driving was the only way to save tires, officials had actually printed the forms to introduce rationing, but at this point, "President Roosevelt intervened." FDR did not agree to nationwide rationing, which led to "the widespread cynical belief that the Administration has desired to wait 'until after the elections' before taking action which might cost votes."[43] At last, Donald Nelson named William M. Jeffers of the Union Pacific Railroad as national rubber administrator on September 15. Jeffers studied the problem and announced on September 25 a nationwide program for gas rationing.

Fewer civilian drivers were using gas and rubber as young men left home and entered military service in 1942. Their induction was often delayed in the months after Pearl Harbor, because the Army still did not have enough training bases for the men.[44] By the summer of 1942, Army camps were springing up across the country. Young men boarding buses for Army induction centers became a common sight in county seats. By that fall, dozens of new Army posts were in operation, such as Camp Van Dorn, Mississippi.

Camp Van Dorn's construction was typical of the confusion and delays in the expanding military. Two years earlier, rumors had circulated that a military base would be built in southwest Mississippi near the small town of Centreville. Local citizens welcomed the project, hoping that a training camp nearby would boost the local economy, but a year later, no construction had begun. After Pearl Harbor, suddenly both the funds and the plans for Centreville's new Army camp were in place. Texas and the Deep South were popular sites for bases, where weather conditions allowed year-round training. By late February 1942, contractors had begun work on streets and barracks. In November, the first troops appeared at Camp Van Dorn, where the military spent more than $20 million to construct facilities for forty thousand soldiers. Local communities near such bases often tried to host activities for the servicemen, to give them a taste of home during wartime.

Troop trains also became a common sight as railroads shipped men from one training base to another. The overwhelmed railroad companies pulled out all the rolling stock available, including passenger cars built during the 1800s. Travel on the crowded trains was uncomfortable and the food mediocre at best.

When citizens in the remote farming community of North Platte, Nebraska, learned that troop trains were stopping in their town every day, they decided to provide free home-cooked meals for all passengers, day or night. The North Platte Canteen began on Christmas Day, 1941, and continued until the war's end. Because the Union Pacific's main line ran through North Platte, troop trains stopped there beginning at 5 A.M. and continued at intervals through the day and into the night—as many as twenty-three trains in one day. Volunteers from 125 western Nebraska farm communities and towns donated food, served coffee, and washed dishes. Towns in eastern Colorado also sent donations. Even President Roosevelt sent a five-dollar bill when he heard what the people around North Platte were doing. For many soldiers, it was the first home cooking they had eaten in months. By war's end, the North Platte Canteen had fed more than 6 million free meals to traveling servicemen and -women.[45]

Florida was another location for large military installations, and its coastline made it useful for all branches of the service. Camp Blanding became Florida's fourth-largest city with 55,000 troops. Jacksonville's Naval Air Station included more than 700 buildings, including an 80-acre hospital and a German prisoner-of-war camp. The U.S. military operated 172 bases in Florida by 1945.

Once recruits were inducted, they experienced many supply problems. Shortages of everything from blankets to rifles to uniforms plagued the rapidly expanding Army in 1942. Recruits from the North Atlantic states on average were shorter and stockier than recruits in the South, meaning that uniform sizes had to be adjusted for various sections of the country. Teenage draftees sometimes grew into larger sizes during training.[46]

As new recruits discovered while on maneuvers in the field, only a small number of soldiers carried guns because of the shortage of weapons. The Army allotted fifteen carbines for an entire artillery battery during training. Each day the fifteen guns went to different soldiers so that they could get some experience carrying a weapon. The remaining soldiers were ordered to cut tree limbs and tie them over their shoulders with string. Each man was required to carry either a carbine or a "stick" to go through the food line. In the words of Gerhard Weinberg, military historian, few American Army divisions were "combat ready before 1943, and many soldiers fired the new M-1 rifle for the first time when they reached the front."[47]

By the fall of 1942, not even Franklin Roosevelt could hide the problems in the war and the disruptions in the American economy. The public was disgusted with the labor strikes, the shortages, the high taxes, the sinkings, and bad war news. Roosevelt knew that he had to look more effective as a war leader to do well in the mid-term elections. On October 3, he persuaded Justice James F. Byrnes to resign from the Supreme Court to become director of economic stabilization. Byrnes's duties overlapped the authority of the WPB, the OPA, and the undersecretary of war, a recipe for more confusion. At the same time, FDR also directed the OPA's Leon Henderson to place ceilings on prices of commodities making up 90 percent of the food supply in the United States.

Roosevelt also changed the way he campaigned for the 1942 elections. In previous campaigns, he had sharply attacked some groups (usually wealthy bankers and businessmen), and then redistributed their wealth to larger voter groups through the WPA, the Silver Purchase Act, the Agricultural Adjustment Act, or some other special-interest program. Roosevelt's usual campaign strategy was to mobilize the subsidized groups to get to the polls with veiled threats that otherwise they might lose their federal funds.[48]

War changed the campaign dynamics. FDR could not divide the country in the usual way because he needed a higher level of national unity to win the war. As Roosevelt declared on March 30, 1942: "The war must come first and everything else must wait." Republicans, therefore, had to be at least temporarily included in any plan to unify the nation behind production, sacrifice, and battles for victory. Republicans Stimson and Knox were in the cabinet; Wendell Willkie was on a trip to China for Roosevelt; and many positions in the wartime bureaucracy went to Republicans. Since a divided country might lose the war, Roosevelt had to wage a softer, less partisan campaign in 1942.[49]

Roosevelt appealed for unity immediately after Pearl Harbor. "In time of war," Roosevelt said on December 11, "there can be no partisan domestic politics. . . . The political truce is for the period of the emergency." Roosevelt clarified this position at a February press conference: "When a country is at war," Roosevelt said, "we want Congress, regardless of party—get that—to back up the Government of the United States."[50] The key distinction to Roosevelt was not between Republican and Democrat, but between those who supported his war policies and those who opposed them. Since Roosevelt saw himself as the "Government of the United States," and since some Republicans were backing him, he tended to avoid overtly partisan politics.

Roosevelt had problems with his pleas for unity. For example, Ed Flynn, Democratic Party chairman, suggested that Roosevelt appoint Democrat Terry Carpenter of Nebraska to the Federal Reserve Board, but Roosevelt refused to do it. Carpenter's appointment might help Democrats in Nebraska, but FDR found him unqualified for the job. In peacetime, political expediency might have tipped the balance in favor of an unqualified appointee, but wartime was different. "Americans of all parties," Roosevelt wrote publicly, "are, of course, subordinating all considerations of partisan politics to the single task of these days—defeating the enemy."

When Democratic leaders tried to spur Roosevelt to do his customary political maneuvering, he often avoided them. Of course, FDR did do some politicking in 1942, but it was tepid, especially by his usual standard. He still tried to defeat Republican Hamilton Fish for Congress in his Hyde Park district. But when New York Democrats asked Roosevelt to campaign for Attorney General John Bennett for governor, Roosevelt said, "I will not go one step further than I told Farley six weeks ago, which was that I would announce that I will vote for Bennett as against [Thomas] Dewey. Not one word more." Even that mild intervention brought forth critics. Frank Kent of the *Baltimore Sun* said what "the president is now doing is exactly the thing he has asked others not to do and which he has insisted he was not doing—to wit, concern themselves with partisan politics while the war is on." Thus, Roosevelt backed off and, except for a tour of factories in the fall, Roosevelt stayed on the job—and off the campaign trail. An election without Roosevelt's dramatic speeches and his targeted subsidies surprised many, but he believed that was his best strategy to win the war.[51]

The ultimate test of Roosevelt's willingness to suspend partisan politics was Operation Torch, the American military campaign in North Africa. During 1942, the war had gone badly for Roosevelt—Japan swept through the Pacific, and the Germans dominated Europe, bombed the British, and charged farther eastward into Russia. The United States was in retreat, and the nation was desperate for some sign of success. Operation Torch was a chance to produce that sign, and Marshall and his staff planned for the landings and combat. Roosevelt, of course, wanted a dramatic landing in late October, right before the elections. Marshall later recalled, "When I went in to see Roosevelt and told him about [planning for] Torch, he held up his hands in an attitude of prayer and said, 'Please make it before election day.' However, when I found we had to have more time and it came afterward, he never said a word. He was very courageous."[52] Military leaders prevailed, and Operation Torch began several days after Tuesday's midterm election. Unlike previous events in Roosevelt's presidency, the timing of Operation Torch was a military and not a political decision.

Many Democrats were shocked. According to Marshall, "Steve Early, Roosevelt's press secretary who was told only an hour before the attack, blew up about it because it came after the elections." In part, Early was angry because the 1942 elections were a disaster for Democrats. In a light turnout, they lost 47 House seats and 9 Senate seats—in fact, Republicans won 20 of 25 Senate races outside the South. Now, the Republicans, with help from southern Democrats, had effective control of Congress. John Harding, of the Office of Public Opinion Research, did a detailed study of the 1942 election, and concluded that most economic groups voted roughly the same way in 1942 as they had earlier. But fewer and smaller New Deal programs meant fewer Democratic votes overall. WPA workers, for example, were almost 80 percent Democratic, but with the shrinking WPA, the Democrats had a smaller base of reliable voters. Harding concluded, "It is clear that the main source of the Republican gains was the almost complete disappearance of the WPA."[53]

Many of those Democrats who lost their seats in Congress might have won in a more typical and more divisive Roosevelt campaign. Incumbent Senator Josh Lee in Oklahoma complained that he lacked patronage and federal support. Senator Prentiss Brown of Michigan helped Roosevelt establish the OPA, but when Roosevelt could not make it work efficiently for voters, and could not produce a scapegoat, Brown lost his election. One Ohio party leader complained to the president that lots of federal jobs "have gone to Republicans. . . . It seems to me that some use could be made of the people who have always been your friends." The Democrats missed their customary patronage.[54]

With Roosevelt only mildly involved in the campaign, its outcome hinged mainly on the results of his policies. Roosevelt would be judged on his economic record, and on his handling of the war. Unemployment was almost at zero, which had been a ten-year goal for FDR, but a centralized and regimented economy is inefficient. Problems with OPA, price controls, shortages, and bureaucratic snafus haunted the Democrats. They gave voters more jobs but less freedom. The Maine elections, held in September, began the political season, and they set the tone. When Republicans swept to victory, the *Portland Press Herald* editorialized that Maine was tired "of delay, of blank checks issued to the President, of stalling and wrangling; in short of making this a New Deal war."[55]

That complaint was echoed around the country in November. The *Washington Evening Star* complained of "fumbling in Washington, which threatens to bog the whole war in a mass of red tape and bureaucratic confusion."[56] The *Detroit Free Press* suggested that the OPA was "possibly the most unpopular legislation ever enacted."[57] "Under the OPA, businessmen were harassed into near-insanity," observed Senator Edwin Johnson of Colorado, who was one of the few Democratic winners that year.[58] Finally, the *Tulsa Daily World* attributed the Democratic defeat to "distrust of the leadership at Washington on account of war bungling; overloading of civilian agencies and the wild wastes of wartime; bitter .

resentment of . . . labor . . . ; censorship . . . and distortion of war news, all implying contempt for the public and resentment of its interest in its own war; the president's evasiveness in refusing to come out with candid and complete statements."[59]

Thus, Roosevelt heard from voters. Because of Roosevelt's need for a certain level of unity, he could not denounce business for the shortages and subsidize a new WPA to win votes. He had to stand on the merits of his conduct during the war, and voters responded by throwing many Democrats out of office. Roosevelt, of course, was alarmed. He shared perhaps his greatest fear about future elections with his friend Henry Morgenthau: "If the Democrats keep on fighting among themselves . . . we are going to elect a Republican president."[60] Roosevelt was trusting in business to make the weapons of war, and military leaders to use those weapons to win victories on the battlefield. If they could lead the United States to victory—or near victory—by November 1944, Roosevelt could again resume partisan politics.

7

1943: THE TIDE TURNS

Army Plans and Priorities

On January 11, 1943, the front page of the *New York Times* reported a remarkable story from Buna, New Guinea, where General MacArthur's American and Australian troops were pushing back the Japanese. At the end of the battle, a U.S. Army captain needed two soldiers to climb trees to observe mortar fire and check for Japanese snipers. However, the captain said, "I couldn't find anyone strong enough to get up a tree." His soldiers were so exhausted, fighting malaria and jungle rot as well as the enemy, they lacked enough strength to make the climb.[1]

In the words of James P. Baxter, Pulitzer Prize–winning science historian, "Their hardships and their losses focused attention on new gear for jungle fighting."[2] Once again, military and civilian authorities had to work together for solutions. For jungle fighting, the Allies developed a lighter boot for soldiers to wear, because scientists found it takes four times the energy for a soldier to carry a pound of weight on his feet as in his backpack. In both hot and cold climates, tests showed that socks were as important as boots for preventing skin diseases, so the Army issued extra socks to each man and told them to change socks every couple of days. The Army's twill uniforms were too heavy for hot climates; poplin material was lighter weight and dried faster when wet, helping men avoid heat exhaustion.[3]

As MacArthur's soldiers and Nimitz's Marines landed on other Pacific islands to fight the Japanese, new weapons gave them advantages against an enemy who would not surrender. Instead, Japanese soldiers concealed themselves in caves or camouflaged hideouts in the jungle, holding up entire companies of Allied troops and causing high casualty rates. In 1943, improvements to the portable flamethrower gave the Allied soldier an effective weapon against Japanese strongholds. OSRD scientists worked to produce other weapons that would stand up to tropical humidity. A flame-throwing tank also helped to rout the Japanese.[4]

With so many men laid low by malaria, research on the disease became a priority. In the Pacific, the Allies were losing more men to malaria than to combat wounds. To complicate matters further, when the Japanese overran Java, they had captured most of the world's supply of quinine, the best-known medical treatment for malaria. In the United States, the WPB took over control of existing supplies of quinine owned by pharmaceutical companies and regulated its use.[5]

The new Committee on Medical Research (CMR) worked with the Army's Quartermaster Corps and the surgeon general on solutions to fight malaria. When civilian scientists developed potential drugs, the military quickly arranged for field trials overseas. Eventually, the drug atabrine proved to work well for malaria patients. By 1943, the United States was producing 800 million tablets of atabrine a year, enough to treat 53 million cases.[6]

But how could the military prevent its soldiers from getting malaria in the first place? In 1941, the Germans had avoided the islands of Corsica and Sardinia in the Mediterranean because of problems there with malarial swamps. Scientists knew that the disease was spread primarily by mosquito bites. The problem proved to require multiple solutions. First, when possible, swamps had to be drained or sprayed to kill mosquito larvae. In the Pacific, combat troops needed protection in the field, where it was impossible to use mosquito nets.[7]

American scientists in Florida proved that DDT (dichlorodiphenyltrichloroethane) was effective against mosquitoes that carried malaria as well as against body lice that spread typhus and recurring fevers. The WPB selected four private chemical companies to work together on DDT and gave these companies priority assistance to expand their plants. Only 153,000 pounds of DDT had been produced in the United States in 1943, but in 1944 U.S. industry produced 10 million pounds. Eventually, soldiers overseas were sprayed once a month with DDT powder to prevent bites from both mosquitoes and lice. Troops also sprayed the inside of their sleeping tents with DDT. A year later, the rate of malaria had drastically declined. When a serious outbreak of typhus threatened troops and civilians in Naples, Italy, the use of DDT saved thousands of lives.[8]

Both in Europe and in the Pacific, by early 1943 the Allies were pushing back their enemies. If 1942 had been a year of disorganization and defeat, 1943 became the year that America and its allies began to win the war. The Russians had encircled the Germans at Stalingrad, where the Nazis finally surrendered at the end of January. A Russian winter offensive threw back the Germans along the Eastern Front, as amazed Nazi troops realized that Russian T-34 tanks worked in all types of weather, while German tanks froze up in the cold. From New Guinea, General MacArthur announced that initiative in the Southwest Pacific had swung to the Allies. And in North Africa, American troops moved eastward out of camps in Morocco and Algeria, where Patton and other American army leaders were determined to push back Rommel's forces, even as the British Army fought its way westward from Egypt.

Also in January, Franklin Roosevelt secretly traveled to Casablanca in Morocco to meet with Winston Churchill. Joseph Stalin declined the invitation to attend, saying that he was too involved in the military offensive around Stalingrad to leave the Soviet Union. During the conference, Roosevelt and Churchill, much to General Marshall's dismay, agreed that there would be no cross-Channel invasion of France in 1943. Instead, the Allies would attack Sicily. Churchill believed the Allies still were not ready for a cross-Channel invasion. Also, if the Allies invaded Sicily and eventually Italy, they would be in a better position to block Stalin from dominating Eastern Europe.

On the final day of the Casablanca meeting, Roosevelt and Churchill sat before a gathering of reporters. No press questions were allowed; FDR and Churchill would simply give comments about the conference. Roosevelt claimed that their discussions had resulted in entire agreement between British and American military staff members, which was not true. British and American generals had hammered out a compromise, but patience had worn thin on both sides. General Marshall still favored a cross-Channel landing, and he felt that the British were not committed enough to victory in the Pacific.[9]

FDR also told the reporters that he and Churchill had worked out a policy that would guarantee victory and a peaceful world after the war ended: "The elimination of German, Japanese and Italian war power means the unconditional surrender of Germany, Italy and Japan." Churchill was startled at the mention of "unconditional surrender," but he put on a grand performance in front of the reporters and pretended to agree with the president. FDR later said that the idea "just occurred" to him as he sat there, but actually he had discussed it earlier with his advisors. Also, Roosevelt thought the statement would please Stalin, who was suspicious that the United States or Great Britain would abandon the Russians and make a separate peace with the Germans.[10]

While Roosevelt was in Casablanca, on January 15, 1943, the War Department dedicated its new headquarters, "the Pentagon." Built on the site of the old Hoover Airport in Arlington, Virginia, the structure contained more office space than any other building in the world, 6.5 million square feet, which was three times the space in the Empire State Building. Choosing the site and the design of the building had delayed the start of construction in the summer of 1941, as Franklin Roosevelt dithered about putting it so close to Arlington Cemetery. Finally, in September 1941, the head of the Quartermaster Construction engineers, General Brehon Somervell, ordered the building crews to dig the foundation. By the time FDR found out about it a month later, the Pentagon was already under way.[11]

The Pentagon's construction became the responsibility of Somervell's subordinate, Colonel Leslie Groves. At a cost of $85 million, the project was completed in sixteen months, as Groves proved what he could do under pressure, especially after Pearl Harbor. At times, thirteen thousand workmen labored on the Pentagon around the clock, working under arc lights through the night. By the spring of 1942, the War Department began moving into sections of offices as they were completed, until over forty thousand staff members were located in the finished complex.[12]

Despite the dangers and discomforts of overseas combat, Colonel Groves was eager to serve in a war zone after the Pentagon was finished. He planned to escape Washington with its red tape and desk jobs. On the day after he accepted his overseas assignment, he met his superior, General Somervell, in the corridor of one of the congressional office buildings. Suddenly, the general told Groves there had been a change in plans:

"The Secretary of War has selected you for a very important assignment."

"Where?"

"Washington."

"I don't want to stay in Washington."

"If you do the job right," General Somervell said carefully, "it will win the war."

Swallowing his anger and disappointment, Groves knew vaguely that Somervell referred to research on the atomic bomb. In meetings during the next few days, Groves learned of his new duties and was promoted to brigadier general, to reflect the authority he would wield as head of the top-secret project. Groves and his aides code-named the endeavor the "Manhattan Engineer District," or MED, which was often shortened to "Manhattan Project."[13]

As the new director, Groves's ace in the hole for getting things done was the backing of both Franklin Roosevelt and Secretary of War Henry Stimson. FDR had first learned of the possibility of atomic weapons in a letter from Albert Einstein, during the tense months of the summer of 1939. Einstein wrote that scientists in France and in America had made breakthroughs in studying the atomic fission of uranium. An atomic bomb was possible. The Nazis had already set up atomic laboratories in 1937, and now they had access to large uranium deposits in Czechoslovakia. Einstein warned the president that the United States must stay ahead in this research, or face totalitarian regimes with an unspeakable advantage.[14]

Slowly at first, FDR backed minor funding for atomic research, putting all of the "Uranium Committee" matters under the authority of Vannevar Bush and the NDRC in 1940. Bush's scientists were already working on radar; now Bush's group would also help two brilliant physicists mentioned in Einstein's letter, Italian-born Enrico Fermi and Hungarian theoretical physicist Leo Szilard. The two wanted to build a graphite pile at Columbia University for their experiments with nuclear fission, but no one had the funds. The NDRC gave nuclear research clout in Washington.[15] With FDR's backing, suddenly the money was there.

Progress was slow on the atomic research project, but the work of Fermi and Szilard looked very promising; so did experiments by physicists at other American universities, who claimed that atomic fission could someday power submarines and other weapons. And other countries were rapidly exploring the possibilities. In Japan, in May 1941, Professor Tokutaro Hagiwara at the University of Kyoto had given a lecture on nuclear chain reactions using uranium-235.[16] The United States was in a race with Germany and Japan to build the bomb that could win the war.

On October 9, 1941, Bush also told the president that the British believed atomic weapons were definitely possible, and they had proposed that the two governments work together on the project. Even though the United States had not yet entered the war, FDR immediately saw the policy implications and set up his Top Policy Group: Vice President Wallace, Secretary of War Stimson, Army Chief of Staff George Marshall, Vannevar Bush, and chemist James B. Conant, president of Harvard University. Just as Roosevelt had turned businessmen loose to make weapons and chemists loose to produce DDT, so he turned his Top Policy Group of scientists loose to make an atomic bomb.[17]

Speaking to Vannevar Bush, FDR said that the funds for the top-secret project "would have to come from a special source available for such an unusual purpose and . . . he [FDR] could arrange this."[18] The president had already wrangled money from Congress when he set up his Office for Emergency Management (OEM) in 1939 and 1940. At first, the OEM budget supplied the funds. When larger sums were needed, closed-door meetings with congressional leaders gave the Manhattan Project the necessary appropriations. Bush could guide the atomic research, but without dynamic leadership for the building projects, the tangle of red tape after Pearl Harbor threatened to smother the entire enterprise. Many of the émigré scientists worried that the Germans might be making real progress on their version of the bomb. The United States had no time to waste.

The following summer, physicists at the University of California–Berkeley reported the results of their studies on U-235 and U-238 (isotopes of uranium), as well as the highly fissionable plutonium-239. Relatively small amounts of uranium and plutonium indeed had the potential to produce weapons with the same explosive power as hundreds of thousands of pounds of TNT. A committee made up of Bush's scientists issued the following report: "We have become convinced that success in this program before the enemy can succeed is necessary for victory. We also believe that success of this program will win the war if it has not previously been terminated."[19] Thus, by September 1942, when Leslie Groves became director of the Manhattan Project, Franklin Roosevelt and his Top Policy Group had learned that an atomic weapon was obtainable, that it was possibly vital to the success of the war, and they were ready to fund it.

Once Groves was head of the program, his ability to cut through red tape and steamroll anyone in his way made a difference. Immediately, he met with WPB head Donald Nelson, to explain why the Manhattan Project needed the highest possible priority rating. At first, Nelson refused, but Groves recalled that "he quickly reversed himself when I said that I would have to recommend to the President that the project should be abandoned because the War Production Board was unwilling to co-operate with his wishes."[20] Groves left Nelson's office with a letter in his pocket giving the Manhattan Project the highest priority rating, AAA, which ensured first choice in building materials, site selection, and transportation.

Within days, Groves approved the purchase of fifty-two thousand acres of land along the remote Clinch River in eastern Tennessee. The location would give the project enough water for the chemical processes and was close enough to New York, Washington, D.C., and Chicago for scientists to travel quickly between various research offices. He convinced the DuPont corporation to take over parts of the plutonium experiments already under way at the University of Chicago. Scientists had argued for months over which of two different experimental methods was better for cooling the proposed nuclear reactors; with his massive funding, General Groves simply ordered both to be built, and he gave the scientists five days in which to get the plans for the cooling systems to the head of the research committee.[21]

Lieutenant Colonel Kenneth Nichols, who worked under Groves on the Manhattan Project, called him "the biggest sonovabitch I've ever met in my life, but also one of the most capable individuals. He had an ego second to none, he had tireless energy. . . . He had absolute confidence in his decisions and he was absolutely ruthless in how he approached a problem to get it done. . . . I hated his guts and so did everybody else but we had our form of understanding."[22]

Groves brought an extraordinary work ethic to the atomic bomb project: "Our internal organization was simple and direct, and enabled me to make fast, positive decisions. I am, and always have been, strongly opposed to large staffs, for they are conducive to inaction and delay. Too often they bury the leaders' capacity to make prompt and intelligent decisions under a mass of indecisive, long-winded staff studies."[23] Amazingly, Groves and his executive assistant in Washington, Mrs. O'Leary, shared a one-room office for months, with one additional room for files; a year later, his entire office staff occupied only seven rooms.

As one of the highest-priority construction projects in the country, the site in eastern Tennessee, named Oak Ridge, would house the facilities for extracting uranium isotopes. Using powers of eminent domain, the government gave residents there two weeks' notice to leave family farms they had tended for generations. During the winter of 1942 and the spring of 1943, the Army Corps of Engineers laid fifty-five miles of railroad, built three hundred miles of paved roads and streets, widened county roads to four-lane highways, and built security fences around the entire Oak Ridge complex, which was top-secret.

Engineers also connected Oak Ridge to the Tennessee Valley Authority's electrical grid. General Groves planned to build electromagnetic isotope-separation plants and a gaseous-diffusion plant there, but the electromagnets for such a large project typically used vast amounts of electricity and tons of copper. TVA would supply the electricity. To avoid overloading a single manufacturing company, orders for power supply equipment went to General Electric, magnets came from Allis-Chalmers, and the processing bins from Westinghouse. With copper so scarce, earlier planners had already worked out an unusual solution—using silver—before Groves arrived as head of the project.[24]

During the 1930s, Franklin Roosevelt regularly won elections in western states by having the government buy silver at higher than market prices.[25] By 1941, the United States had stockpiled more than 42,000 *tons* of silver. Silver is a good conductor of electricity, and since any silver used in the electromagnets could be recovered later, the U.S. Treasury offered to make silver bullion available to take the place of copper. When Manhattan Project leaders told the Treasury Department they needed between five and ten thousand tons of silver, they received this icy reply: "We do not speak of tons of silver; our unit is the Troy ounce."[26] The Manhattan Project eventually used 395 million troy ounces of silver, equal to 13,540 tons. Groves agreed to return the same amount of silver to the Treasury Department within six months of the war's end, and he set up security precautions that were so effective that only .035 of 1 percent of the silver was lost—out of a total amount worth $300 million. The Treasury Department even continued to carry the silver on its books for security reasons, to avoid raising suspicions about such a loan to the top-secret project.[27]

Nuclear scientists also needed plutonium for their experiments, but plutonium was too dangerous for a production site within twenty miles of Knoxville. Thus, Groves and his staff searched for a second and even more remote location. On Groves's recommendation in early 1943, the government bought five hundred thousand acres near Richland, Washington, at a cost of $5.1 million. The plutonium production plant, named the Hanford site after a nearby village, would have plenty of water from the Columbia River.[28]

On Monday, March 15, 1943, another top scientist of a special research group arrived with his aides at yet a third location for work on the Manhattan Project. Years before, Robert Oppenheimer had written to a friend, "My two great loves are physics and desert country; it's a pity they can't be combined." Now his two loves came together as he reached the Los Alamos atomic research facility, forty miles northwest of Santa Fe. Teams of scientists there would use radioactive materials—uranium from Oak Ridge, Tennessee, and plutonium from Hanford, Washington—to build atomic bombs.[29]

Other scientists and their families arrived in Santa Fe during the next month. At first, the government rented all the dude ranches in the area for their lodging, because until a few months earlier, Los Alamos had been a boys' school, complete with sixty horses, saddles, and sixteen hundred books. When government officials approached the owner in November 1942, he was willing to sell the school immediately. But how would Groves's team transform such an isolated spot into an atomic research facility?

"What we were trying to do was build a new laboratory in the wilds of New Mexico with no initial equipment except the library of Horatio Alger books or whatever it was that those boys in the Ranch School read, and the pack equipment that they used going horseback riding, none of which helped us very much in getting neutron-producing accelerators," recalled John Manley, a University of Illinois physicist recruited to work with Oppenheimer.[30] Living conditions were primitive, but the scenery was beautiful and *unpopulated*, which was one of the main reasons the site had been chosen. It was the back end of nowhere.

As the scientists estimated what they needed, university laboratories around the country donated a cyclotron and other rare pieces of equipment. The Army Corps of Engineers struggled to convert Los Alamos into a top-secret research facility, complete with dormitories, housing for the families of scientists, and elaborate security precautions, including barbed wire and patrolling sentries around the entire site.[31]

The local populace in Santa Fe was naturally curious about the project. However, Groves counted on the fact that a regiment of the New Mexico National Guard had fought and surrendered in the Philippines; those soldiers were in Japanese prisoner-of-war camps, and the state of New Mexico was intensely interested in helping win the war. "The support we received was superb," said Groves. However, rumors circulated that Los Alamos had become a home for pregnant WACs (Women's Army Corps). One woman living near the highway to Los Alamos wrote frequent letters to the local paper, complaining that such expenditure must be another New Deal boondoggle.[32]

At the beginning of April, Oppenheimer convened a staff meeting of approximately thirty scientists to discuss their goals: "The object of the project is to produce a *practical military weapon* in the form of a bomb in which the energy is released by a fast neutron chain reaction in one or more of the materials known to show nuclear fission."[33] The scientists divided into teams to work on various parts of the bomb.

Also in the spring of 1943, the Japanese were studying the feasibility of atomic weapons. They understood the theory, but estimated that building an atomic bomb would require half their annual copper production and 10 percent of their electrical capacity. (At Oak Ridge, Tennessee, the uranium enrichment processes at times required more electrical power than was used in New York City.) Japanese leaders concluded that neither they nor the Germans nor the United States had enough industrial capacity to make an atomic bomb during the war. The Japanese overestimated the difficulty of producing the uranium isotopes, and they underestimated both America's industrial strength and its dedication to winning the war. Likewise, the Germans had run into difficulties with their atomic experiments, and existing German war industries required all their available resources. Neither totalitarian government made much progress on the atomic bomb as the United States raced ahead.[34]

In Washington, on January 14, WPB's Donald Nelson optimistically announced that the five most pressing areas of defense production were on target to meet their goals for 1943: synthetic rubber, high-octane gasoline, aircraft, merchant ships, and naval escort vessels. But more problems with priorities had already appeared as various industries jockeyed to be the first to receive supplies.[35]

Undersecretary Patterson testified before a joint congressional committee on February 1 that Jeffers, the rubber "czar," had tried to push through his own priorities for synthetic rubber that would delay high-octane gasoline production for four months. Patterson had already appealed to the White House for help. Jimmy Byrnes, FDR's appointed director of economic stabilization, was working on solutions.[36] Since Roosevelt kept the lines of authority unclear, who knew whether Byrnes, Patterson, or Nelson would call the shots?

Problems in production across the country had come to a head in the fall of 1942: "Even the U.S. economy, great as it was, could not undertake widely unattainable production objectives without slowing down production all along the line."[37] During 1942 and early 1943, the U.S. Army worked on a plan to allocate resources and determine priorities for defense plants as well as civilian needs. What developed was the Controlled Materials Plan (CMP), a system of channeling steel, copper, and aluminum into the most important segments of the war effort under the WPB's direction. The military devised other allocation plans similar to the CMP for tires, lumber, cotton textiles, woolens, pulp and paper, and chemicals. Slowly, during 1943, the CMP began to make sense out of the jumble of millions of manufactured items. IBM designed huge accounting machines using punch cards to tabulate all the information. The Army had used nothing like this system before.[38]

The Strain of War Production and Overregulation

In early 1943, America's industry was meeting the challenge of war production, including atomic research, but the strain was evident. Ironically, President Roosevelt spoke of the "Four Freedoms" in his

State of the Union Address in January, which included Freedom from Want. With nationwide rationing of everything from butter to tires, freedom from want was definitely not a part of the American lifestyle that year. Shortages of heating oil plagued the Northeast. Pleasure driving was banned, with gasoline strictly rationed across the country. Mayor LaGuardia of New York City discussed the meat shortage in the city's butcher shops.

In addition to materials, serious manpower shortages throughout industry and agriculture threatened production of weapons and food by 1943. In February, FDR considered asking the Army to harvest cotton in Arizona. Farmers across the country complained that the absence of young men who had been drafted into the military meant they could not find workers for their land. Absenteeism in defense plants, especially the aircraft industry, reached alarming levels (about 7 percent). One-fourth of all Boeing employees had failed to show up for work on the weekend after Christmas, 1942.[39] What was the real problem?

Columnist Arthur Krock pointed out that Jimmy Byrnes, as director of economic stabilization and a loyal FDR stalwart, was trying "to fit consistent regulations to inconsistent policies" while at the same time saying that "nothing of the sort was being attempted. . . . Because the President and his administration took the nation far into the war under peacetime regulations of production—their battle cry being, 'we must hold to the social gains of the New Deal'—expedient solutions have always been necessary." Krock also criticized FDR's labor policy: "When the unions make trouble, they have discovered the administration backs down."[40]

Investigators at aircraft plants found that wage ceilings meant that aircraft workers simply did not make as much as workers in shipyards. Americans were smart enough to flock to the shipbuilding areas, where pay was higher. Also, many former aircraft employees decided to go back into civilian work. At Willow Run, outside Detroit, only three-fifths of the required numbers of trained workers were available to build bombers; employees complained of housing and transportation problems around the plant. By the summer of 1943, U.S. aircraft production was well below projected estimates, and supply was not the problem, but manpower. For the remainder of the year, numbers of aircraft remained the only area of high-priority production that was falling behind military estimates.[41]

Senator Truman's investigating committee continued to make headlines as it looked into problems with defense contracts for airplane engines, rubber, lumber, steel—by the spring of 1943, the committee had issued twenty-one reports. On March 8, Harry Truman was on the cover of *Time*, with a spotlight behind his shoulder focused on defense industries. Later that same month, newspapers across the country carried the Truman Committee's hearing with J. Lester Perry, president of Carnegie-Illinois Steel Corporation, a subsidiary of U.S. Steel. Carnegie-Illinois had supplied steel plate for the tanker *Schenectady*, which had broken in half after launching. In testimony before the committee, Carnegie-Illinois's employees alleged that their superiors had told them to falsify reports on the tensile strength of the steel used on the *Schenectady*. In the same hearing, President Benjamin Fairless of U.S. Steel took responsibility for Carnegie-Illinois's actions:

"I intend to clean house—let the chips fall where they may," said Fairless.

Senator Truman asked Mr. Perry if anyone at Carnegie-Illinois had been fired.

"We're suspending some people," Perry replied.

"When?" Truman inquired.

"Immediately after we get through with this hearing," Perry promised.

"It's about time," Truman snapped. "I wouldn't let a cheat to work for me one minute."[42]

Truman and his committee ensured there was some accountability by defense industries. Turning entrepreneurs loose for the first time since the 1920s had dramatically boosted innovation and productivity in America. But there had to be accountability. Normally, competition and prices sorted out the winners and losers. Consumers, in effect, made producers accountable. In the war, with the government building factories and then guaranteeing contracts and fixing prices, some businesses were negligent and still made money. To millions of Americans, Harry Truman became the man who led the committee to make the defense industries accountable.

The Truman Committee could help to improve the quality of defense supplies, but it could not solve the manpower shortage throughout the country in 1943. Army officials announced that all draft-eligible, single men were in the Army. "We are scraping the bottom of the barrel on single men," said Paul V. McNutt, head of the War Manpower Commission. "Virtually the only single men out of uniform are the overage, the physically unsuitable, or the men in vital war-connected jobs."[43]

For future military quotas, draft boards would have to take married men with children. Single African-American men had already been drafted, although their induction lists were in separate articles in newspapers from draft lists of Caucasian men.[44] Throughout the American military, "colored troops" were still segregated from whites, even in hospitals and camps overseas.

By early 1943, only 6,277 conscientious objectors had registered with the government, out of millions who received draft notices. These objectors worked on projects ranging from forestation to serving as attendants in mental institutions. Some volunteered to serve as guinea pigs for studies on everything from taking vitamins to effects of high altitudes on pilots.[45]

As the need for men in the military increased, the issue of draft deferments became more important. Vannevar Bush and his research scientists had to consider if their younger scientists of draft age were more valuable to the war effort in uniform or in the laboratory. During World War I, Great Britain had issued no exemptions for its scientists; many researchers who were later needed in that war had already died in the trenches, slowing British research. During 1943, pressure increased from U.S. draft boards to recruit young scientists for the military.

On April 17, in an effort to address the manpower shortage, Paul V. McNutt announced regulations to "freeze" 27 million workers in their jobs. Except in cases that would benefit the war effort, workers were not to transfer to higher-paying jobs, and this applied to workers in government, railroads, farming, and industry. Now, in addition to price controls, wage controls, and rationing, the United States had job controls. There was little unemployment, but also little freedom and few choices.

Helping to fill the manpower gap were millions of women, many entering the workforce for the first time, as typists, file clerks, and receptionists. In Washington, D.C., paperwork reached to the ceilings in some government offices that had formerly used only male employees. Women proved that they could do the work, but traditions ran deep. Despite the manpower shortage, and stacks of fingerprint files so high that clerks had to use ladders, FBI director J. Edgar Hoover refused to have women wear trousers in his offices. Women could not work on the ladders in dresses, and Hoover would not budge, so the fingerprint stacks rose higher.[46]

Women began working in the Brooklyn Navy Yard for the first time in 1942, breaking a 141-year tradition of using only men as shipbuilders. Headlines noted that the female employees would wear coveralls or slacks on the job. By 1943, the sight of women in industrial plants wearing pants as they worked alongside men did not arouse much surprise. Women built jeeps and worked in aircraft plants, with ten thousand women employed at the Willow Run bomber plant. At first, women were paid lower wages than men for the same work, but finally the War Labor Board ordered the Brown & Sharp Manufacturing Company of Providence, Rhode Island, to award equal pay to women who performed the same work as men, setting a precedent across the country.[47] Women were serving in both the U.S. Army and Navy, having volunteered for duty.

On April 17, 1943, the president announced that women medical doctors would be inducted into the Army and Navy Medical Corps. So many nurses had already entered the Army and Navy Nursing Corps that civilian hospitals experienced nursing shortages.

The press corps in Washington also expanded from a few hundred to two thousand correspondents, many of whom were women. Major radio networks still refused to allow women to broadcast news on the air because, they argued, women were "biologically incapable of total objectivity."[48]

Women war correspondents worked around the world in uniform, giving them the same status as their male counterparts. Margaret Bourke-White, internationally known photojournalist, was one of the first American female war correspondents. In 1941, she had arrived in Moscow just as the Germans invaded the country. From the U.S. embassy, she photographed Moscow as the first German bombs fell on the capital. After the United States entered the war, she traveled to England and then to North Africa to film the fighting there. When her ship was torpedoed in the Mediterranean, she was rescued from a life raft with other survivors and, undeterred, went to work with her camera. She even talked General Jimmy Doolittle, now stationed in North Africa, into taking her on a bombing mission in a B-17 Flying Fortress, where she photographed air combat. Her story documented an American bombing raid on a German airfield near Tunis, and covered seven pages in *Life* magazine.[49]

For soldiers in North Africa and other war zones, news from back home about strikes in defense plants was demoralizing. In addition to strikes at aircraft plants and shipyards, in early 1943 the United Mine Workers (UMW) walked out of the coal mines and refused to return. By April 28, an estimated 67,300 miners were on strike, idling 130 mines in Pennsylvania, West Virginia, Kentucky, Tennessee, and Alabama.

President Roosevelt ordered the forcible seizure of the mines on May 1. On May 2, he spoke to the miners in a radio address, asking them to return to the pits for the good of the country. Steel manufacturers warned that U.S. steel plants would have to shut down if the strike continued for long. UMW president John L. Lewis sent his miners back to work, saying they would not strike again until "at least the end of October." Counting all types of industry, an incredible 3,752 strikes took place in the United States in 1943, involving more than 13 million man-days of labor.[50] From North Africa, Sergeant Billy Robertson wrote to his brother in Graves County, Kentucky:

> We are getting pretty sick of reading about strikes in rubber plants and coal mines and other war factories back in the states. We, who are making about as much per month as those fellows make in a week, are quite willing to change places with any of them. They ought to be lined up against a wall and shot or be made to lay down their tools and pick up a gun and come over here where the only "strike" they'll ever indulge in will be to strike out for a fox hole when a Stuka swoops over.[51]

About the same time, the United States finally had a breakthrough in the area of synthetic rubber production in April 1943. Rubber czar William Jeffers brought the first heavy-duty synthetic tire to Congress. Made from butadiene derived from grain alcohol, this tire was tough enough to use on jeeps and other military equipment. The rubber shortage had proven to be the most difficult supply problem of the war, and as 1943 unfolded, the controversy over synthetic production came to a head.

In the 1940s, no modern war could be fought without millions of tons of rubber. Just making a gas mask required more than one pound of rubber; more than fifty pounds of rubber went into one life raft. Armored tanks and bombers used almost one ton of rubber each; a battleship required seventy-five tons. And, of course, hundreds of tons of rubber were needed each year to make tires for military vehicles.

The crisis first hit as Japan conquered the Far East, which had supplied 90 percent of American rubber imports. The United States tried to increase imports from other areas, and many also looked at the making of synthetic rubber as a possible alternative. Experiments showed that oil could be processed and converted into a kind of synthetic rubber. But it was expensive, and whether it could be durable enough for tires and tanks was uncertain.[52]

Vice President Henry Wallace, an ardent New Dealer, weighed in on the side of importing natural rubber from new sources. "Rubber is a hobby of mine," Wallace later told a Senate committee. Specifically, Wallace wanted the United States to support new rubber plantations in Haiti and in the Amazon Valley of Brazil. He wanted millions of dollars to provide subsidized food, health care, and good working conditions for the natives, all as a part of his long-term goal of a New Deal for the world.[53]

Jesse Jones, head of the Reconstruction Finance Corporation (RFC), sharply disagreed with Wallace. Jones, a businessman, thought Wallace's schemes were risky and very wasteful at a time when all U.S. resources needed to go into the war effort. Senator Robert Taft agreed and accused Wallace of setting up "an international WPA." Sure, Jones said, the United States should try to get natural rubber whenever it could, but we would need more—therefore, we had to promote synthetic rubber to win the war.[54]

Under Jones's plan, the antitrust laws had to be suspended. Then his RFC could provide incentives to the five large American rubber companies (Firestone, Goodyear, B. F. Goodrich, General Tire, and U.S. Rubber), allowing them to share technology and profits. The RFC would build their plants, give them cost-plus contracts, and then expect them to create a durable synthetic rubber that was strong enough and cheap enough to help win the war without busting the national budget. As a counterargument, Wallace said that creating a New Deal in Haiti and Brazil was better and more certain than giving millions of dollars to rubber barons, who would either fail or become filthy rich from government grants.[55]

The United States was desperate for rubber, so Roosevelt allowed both Wallace and Jones to pursue their different paths. At first, Roosevelt trusted Vice President Wallace more than Jones. The president made Wallace head of the Board of Economic Warfare (BEW), with authority to spend millions of dollars in Brazil and Haiti. On Jones's synthetic rubber project, Roosevelt balked at helping rubber companies build the factories to do their experiments. "These wealthy rubber companies," Roosevelt told Jones, "ought to build their own plants." When Jones gingerly suggested an initial $50 million outlay for the five rubber companies, FDR cut it in half.[56]

In 1943, the results became clear. As the five American rubber companies shared ideas and technology, they began producing synthetic rubber in huge quantities—more than 300,000 tons in 1943 and 700,000 tons the next year. Germany, by contrast, which had a head start in making synthetic rubber, never produced more than 109,173 tons in any year of the war. Furthermore, American costs dropped so low that synthetic rubber became more competitive than natural rubber even after the Far Eastern plantations had been liberated from Japan after the war.[57]

Henry Wallace's experiments, however, were a disaster. The more than $5 million he invested in Haiti did produce rubber—at $546 a pound. By contrast, Firestone Tire & Rubber Company created rubber plantations in Liberia that yielded 65,000 tons of natural rubber at thirty cents a pound. For Brazil, Wallace proposed a $400 million program of free food and subsidized health care and working conditions. But, with the Haiti disaster, Jones did all he could to block Wallace and his "international WPA."[58]

On July 16, FDR sided with Jones, fired Wallace as head of the BEW, and replaced the BEW with the OEW, the Office of Economic Warfare. He did so in a way to minimize embarrassment to Wallace, but the outcome was clear to all concerned. Wallace, according to one BEW official, believed FDR "has betrayed the cause of liberalism." New Dealer Harry Hopkins, when he heard the news, lamented, "The New Deal has once again been sacrificed to the war effort."[59]

Indeed it had. When Senator Claude Pepper met with Roosevelt five days later, Pepper was amazed at how "absorbed" FDR had become in winning the war. "His immersion was so nearly total that for the first time in my memory he said not a word about politics, even though there would be a presidential election the next year," Pepper recalled. Afterward, he recorded his conversation with FDR in his diary, "Said [he] was keeping main eye on the war. No hint of politics for next year."[60]

Meanwhile, Henry Wallace took on the job of maintaining the New Deal while, in Arthur Krock's words, "the President is making a wartime detour." Wallace gave speeches and press interviews in which he extolled the accomplishments of the New Deal's agenda. Krock noted that some New Dealers excused FDR by saying that the president needed to shorten the time to victory, when an international New Deal could then be set up across the world.[61]

Franklin Roosevelt may have let down some New Dealers, but he had not entirely abandoned his old ways of doing things. Back in June 1942, he had appointed Elmer Davis as head of the Office of War Information (OWI), an agency that FDR used to influence public opinion both at home and overseas. Supposedly, OWI's duties included giving the public accurate war news, and promoting the war effort in movies, posters, and radio. OWI founded Voice of America broadcasts and worked with Hollywood screen stars on documentaries.

By February 1943, a storm arose in Congress over OWI's publication of *Victory* magazine. Opponents charged that OWI director Elmer Davis used *Victory* to tout FDR as a candidate for yet a fourth term. Articles in *Victory* labeled opponents of FDR's policies "reactionaries" while praising the New Deal. A Senate investigation also looked into the cost of producing a half million copies of the magazine in six languages, many of which were slated for South America. Evidently, South America was the target not only for rubber subsidies by Henry Wallace but for FDR's New Deal propaganda as well. When asked if shipping the magazine overseas would displace essential war supplies, Elmer Davis replied that *Victory* only took the space of eight hundred tons of shipping.[62]

With the manpower shortage in 1943 came charges that the OWI harbored draft dodgers. Davis testified before a congressional subcommittee that "insinuations that OWI is a haven for draft dodgers" were unfounded. However, his bloated agency employed more than four thousand, and one-fourth were men of draft age.[63] "Because Roosevelt hated to fire anyone, especially those loyal to him, OWI inherited much 'deadwood,'" observed George Roeder, an authority on the news media during the war.[64]

On April 15, fifteen men and women resigned as writers for the OWI, charging that they were not allowed to report the war news honestly. Instead, "high-pressure promoters who prefer slick salesmanship to honest information" for the American public wanted to control their stories. The writers called the OWI "an office of war ballyhoo."[65] By mid-June, the House voted to cut funding for OWI's domestic operations.

Adding to the difficulty of reporting war news was the need for military security. Admiral King, for instance, would have preferred not to report anything until the war was over, with a simple headline reading, "We fought the war. We won." But in a democracy, the military had to cooperate to some extent in giving the public war news.[66] However, both the Army and the Navy ignored the OWI during much of the war. Reporter David Brinkley observed that the American military, in reporting war news, "used it skillfully as the civilian agencies of government had always used it throughout history—to try to conceal their failures and blunders and to give out fulsome detail on their successes.... [I]t never was in the basic nature of government agencies, military or civilian, to tell the full truth about themselves."[67]

The controversy over OWI continued in August when OWI's overseas branch, led by Robert Sherwood (former speechwriter for

FDR), "invented" a news commentator named "John Durfee" who expressed OWI's opinions on the war with Italy. Just two months earlier, Congress had asked the OWI to stick to "authentic" news that was "on the level." After the Durfee incident, Congress voted to end OWI's funding for the next fiscal year, but finally agreed to reinstate partial funding with strict guidelines for the agency. Elmer Davis lost control of OWI's international branch as the State Department took over management of its overseas activities. For the remainder of the war, the OWI worked mainly to undermine civilian morale in enemy countries.[68]

In September 1943, the government finally allowed publication of photos of dead servicemen on the battlefield. *Life* magazine's cover featured a picture from Buna, New Guinea, of three dead American soldiers on the beach with a wrecked landing craft in the background. The government hoped that such photos would spur citizens on the home front to support the war effort even more. By late 1943, tens of thousands of American families had already received telegrams announcing the death of a relative in the service. Just about everyone knew someone who had died overseas. Surveys showed that Americans supported the realistic photos and accurate news coverage of the war.[69]

Public morale was an issue, not only because of the casualties. Price and wage controls, as well as the demands of the war industries, had led to all sorts of shortages for American consumers. During the summer, a beer shortage made newspaper headlines. The lack of beer had various causes: Grain was in short supply due to synthetic rubber production, and glass bottles were too few. OPA price ceilings on fish led to shortages of fresh fish on the East Coast, as fishermen tied up their boats rather than lose money on their catch.[70] In a similar way, cattlemen refused to take losses on their ranches because of low fixed prices. They either refused to market cattle, which created more shortages, or demanded extra payments, which scuttled the price-control system.

When the OPA tried to solve one problem with price controls, the aftereffects often created other, larger problems. For example, price controls on rents created incentives for landlords to convert their apartments into storage or for commercial use. That made the housing shortages even worse. Landlords also had incentives to demand large deposits (never to be returned), or charge tenants extra for furniture, a basement, a backyard, or permission to have a dog. From June 1942 to June 1945, the OPA received 2,612,062 official complaints from tenants, which buried civil courts and the OPA bureaucrats under a blizzard of paperwork and costs.[71]

By 1945, the OPA had issued more than 600 rent and price regulations on more than 8 million articles, with 3,100 investigators and 700 attorneys, plus support staff. Consumers needed gasoline, sugar, meat, and butter, and were willing to pay higher prices to get them on the black market. Surveys (some done by the OPA) revealed that about one-third of American business in certain products was done illegally on the black market. Thousands of OPA investigators—called "snoopers"—flooded the courts with hundreds of thousands of cases.[72]

Much fraud went unreported. Chester Bowles, the OPA director, admitted, "One of the OPA's greatest weaknesses with the public today is the fact that so many violations go unchecked." At a congressional hearing, Bowles testified, "There have been over 650 robberies of local boards involving 300,000,000 gallons of gasoline in coupons." The OPA enforcement department discovered more than one million counterfeit coupons per month during much of 1944 for gasoline alone. A WPB survey in 1943 found Americans were more annoyed at the shortages of butter, meat, sugar, soap, and canned goods than they were with the shortage of gasoline. The survey noted that most Americans were making more money than they had during the depression years of the 1930s, but there was little to buy.[73]

FDR and the Democrats took the blame for the shortages and the restrictions on buying and selling. In the by-elections of November 1943, the Republicans won impressive victories "in a showing which was already being interpreted . . . as a rebuke to the handling of the home front by the New Deal Administration." For the first time in sixteen years, Kentucky elected a Republican governor, as did New Jersey. In the race for Philadelphia's mayor, Republican Bernard Samuel defeated former ambassador William C. Bullitt, a close associate of FDR. Harrison E. Spangler, chairman of the Republican National Committee, made this statement: "The light of the New Deal has flickered out. The crystal gazers who have had fond hope of a fourth term will now gaze in darkness. The American way is on the march!"[74]

In late December, Roosevelt responded during a press conference, even as he ordered U.S. Army soldiers to take over operation of the railroads to prevent a rail strike. Comparing the New Deal to a doctor for the internal ills of the country, the president claimed that "Dr. New Deal" had saved the banks of the United States from failing, saved homes and farms from foreclosure, rescued agriculture, and worked for decent housing. On the other hand, after Pearl Harbor, the country needed "Dr. Win-the-War," who was taking care of the patient—meaning the United States— but "he isn't wholly well yet, and he won't be until he wins the war."[75]

Roosevelt went on to infer that once victory was won, the New Deal would be needed in postwar countries, although he would not give specifics. But obviously, FDR saw himself in a leadership role after the war, restoring his New Deal on an even larger scale. His will to govern and spread his New Deal philosophy had not dimmed. Republican chairman Spangler had spoken too soon. Franklin Roosevelt hadn't given up office yet. Nor was he likely to leave the office of president voluntarily, not so long as he had a living breath.

8

ENTREPRENEURS VS. THE ARSENAL OF BUREAUCRACY

When Pearl Harbor was attacked, the United States lagged way behind Germany and Japan in armed forces and war materiel. An American victory seemed uncertain and maybe even unlikely. Three years later, however, the United States significantly outproduced Germany and Japan, and victory was around the corner. How did the Americans do it?

Converting factories from making cars, pipes, and radios to making guns, planes, and bullets meant a major overhaul in equipment, training, and accounting. Would businessmen bear the costs of converting for defense? What if the war ended abruptly? Even if it lasted for many years, would FDR limit profits or sweep them away with high taxes? The business climate for defense was uncertain, and few corporations accepted war contracts, even when FDR offered them on a seemingly generous cost-plus fixed fee (CPFF) basis after his Fireside Chat of May 26, 1940.

Henry Stimson, the secretary of war, nailed the problem when he said, "If you are going to try to go to war, or to prepare for war, in a capitalist country, you have got to let business make money out of the process or business won't work."[1] In other words, people need incentives to invest. Thus, Roosevelt, who had excoriated businessmen for eight years, reluctantly made further concessions. He ended the existing legal limits on profits for war contracts; he agreed to advance payments up to 30 percent of the contract; and he gave "progress payments" on partly fulfilled contracts. Also, the RFC created the Defense Plant Corporation to build factories for defense contractors, and those contractors had the option to buy their new factories after the war. Finally, those corporations that built or converted their own factories to make war materiel could depreciate them for tax purposes over five years instead of twenty.[2]

Many New Dealers were appalled that Roosevelt was giving American businessmen the chance to earn so much money. If war was indeed inevitable, the more radical New Dealers wanted to create government-operated businesses to run the war. Most Americans, however, disagreed. They had watched the economy stagnate during the 1930s under government direction, and they had more confidence in privately run businesses.[3]

FDR agreed philosophically with his fellow New Dealers about business. But for the sake of his presidency and his future standing as a leader, he had to win any war that the United States might have to fight. In FDR's words, "The war effort must come first and everything else must wait."[4] No American president had ever lost a war, and Roosevelt intended to keep it that way.

Roosevelt did do two things to make his concessions to business more palatable. First, he urged Congress to enact a high excess profits tax (eventually reaching 90 percent) to capture most of the wealth businessmen would make. Second, he centralized power in the executive branch to run the war. He appointed businessmen he knew to run the production side of the war.

Roosevelt had created the War Production Board (WPB) in 1942 to decide what should be produced and who should do it. He appointed Donald Nelson, vice president with Sears, Roebuck, to head the WPB. Nelson either knew most major businessmen across the country or had good friends who knew them. Nelson and the WPB would ultimately set goals for how much steel, copper, and oil would be produced, and which companies would get contracts to make guns, tanks, airplanes, and ammunition.

In this arrangement, big corporations won most major contracts to make the weapons of war. In fact, the largest hundred or so corporations walked away with contracts to make more than three-fourths of the war materiel. Yes, Nelson, Stettinius, and Knudsen gave much business to their former companies, but they also gave a flood of business to their competitors—Ford, Chrysler, Bethlehem Steel, Republic Steel, and so on. For one thing, the United States had a massive need for tanks and planes, and therefore almost all large industrial companies had more business than they could handle.[5]

Smaller businesses could earn subcontracting work, but they were poorly positioned to win major contracts. Because they were small, they were untested with large orders. And sometimes the owner and key employees were drafted into the Army. What's more, smaller businessmen could grow only through profits; and the high excess profits tax, in effect, forced small companies to stay small.

Many New Dealers were outraged to see billions of dollars thrown at large corporations to build their factories, swamp them with business, guarantee their profits, and remove their risks. Roosevelt, too, hated to do this, and often said so privately. But if that was what it took to win the war and salvage his presidency, FDR would hold his nose and do it. "The job now is first and foremost to win the war," the president said again and again to protesting New Dealers.[6]

Roosevelt's New Dealers, who still had influence in his cabinet and in Congress, often tried to stifle business expansion—just as they had done in the 1930s. But during the war, Roosevelt sometimes stopped them.

FDR overruled officials in the Justice Department when they wanted to launch antitrust investigations against key war companies. Before the war, the New Deal was FDR's main concern, and he liked the idea of breaking up corporations that got too big, or that shared information with each other. For example, Thurman

Arnold of the Justice Department fingered many corporations for alleged antitrust violations starting in 1938. At that time, with no war on the horizon, the president encouraged Arnold and helped jack up his budget from $413,000 in 1938 to $2.3 million in 1942. But alas for Arnold, just as he was ready to prosecute, the war became an issue. For example, in 1942 when Arnold launched an antitrust suit against DuPont for pooling patents and sharing markets, Henry Stimson quickly protested. As secretary of war, Stimson desperately needed the munitions DuPont was making to attack the Germans. "Mr. Hitler himself could hardly have chosen a surer way to embarrass our munitions makers today," Stimson complained. The president agreed and shut down the investigation.[7]

But even here FDR was biding his time. In 1944, with the war almost won and an election at hand, the president was more willing to attack DuPont. Wendell Berge, who followed Arnold at the Justice Department, reopened the case against DuPont, and Stimson again complained to the president. But this time, as historian Ted Morgan noted, "FDR was more interested in the vote-getting potential of antitrust prosecution." By August 1944, when Roosevelt had to decide, the Germans were less than nine months from surrendering. It looked as if the war could be won without DuPont, and therefore Roosevelt wanted it investigated. "Further delay" in prosecuting DuPont, Roosevelt wrote, "should not occur in the interest of justice and the enforcement of the law."[8]

Before the president reversed himself on DuPont, the WPB had been openly encouraging the sharing of industrial knowledge among major corporations. That was, Nelson discovered, "the essence of war production." In the making of hundreds of thousands of airplanes, for example, Nelson agreed to let presidents of the nation's eight largest airplane companies share technology, patents, and manpower to meet the president's lofty goals. According to Nelson, "the eight west coast companies . . . lay down together and decided that they didn't want to murder each other half as much as they wanted to murder Japs and Germans." For example, J. H. Kindelberger, CEO of North American Aviation, told his department heads: "From now on, we are giving our competitors anything we have—processes, methods, even tools and materials—that we are not planning to use immediately."[9]

Henry Taylor, a reporter for the *Saturday Evening Post*, watched in amazement as the airlines helped one another. "From the record of exchanges I jotted down at random," Taylor said, "16 engine mount forgings [went] from Consolidated to North American; 1,000 stop nuts from Lockheed to Vultee; 150 sheets of Alcad aluminum from North American to Vultee; one-half ton of flathead Model rivets from Consolidated to Ryan. . . ." When Douglas desperately needed two thousand feet of binding braid wire to make dive-bombers, "the wire was found in the stockroom of North American in time to deliver dive bombers that played a key role in the battles of the Coral Sea and the Midway Islands."

In making a historic number of planes in record time, emergency help was only a phone call away. "Just before quitting time one evening, Mike Craemer of Vega called factory manager Paul Buckner of Northrup on the telephone." Vega was short five sets of landing gear forgings to make B-17s. Could Northrup help? "Okay," Buckner said, "send your truck over." Next week "it was turn about. Northrup was fresh out of small half pound aluminum forgings used in cowlings being built for Boeing Flying Fortresses being assembled for Douglas. Vega sent 2,500 over the back fence."

Nelson watched in amazement as hundreds of thousands of new airplanes filled the skies, bombing the Germans and giving the United States aerial supremacy. "I have been accused of cutting red tape rather brutally for the airplane firms in order to permit them to exchange materials and ideas," Nelson confessed, "and at times we may have given the anti-trust laws a rather close shave."

What the airplane and rubber companies started, the auto companies continued when they shifted from cars to tanks, jeeps, and combat vehicles. Chrysler, for example, was the nation's major tank and tool producer and that company, with Nelson's blessing, "threw open its doors, during the first year after Pearl Harbor, to newcomers so that they might study its manufacturing methods." Once the eighteen or so vehicle companies agreed to "trade skills, materials and equipment," they standardized the making of tanks and military vehicles. They "reduced battery types from twenty-nine to five; spark plugs and generators from eight to two; fan belts from eight to three. They settled on one door handle instead of eight." Then came innovations: "A method of machining turret rings cut four operations to three, saved fifteen percent in manpower and released nearly $500,000 worth of boring mills for the other jobs." In another example, "a manufacturer in need of boring mills and planers of oversize dimensions, built them to his own specifications, and then supplied them to former competitors."

Even Ford Motor Company, a stridently independent firm, shared technology and knowledge with Sperry Gyroscope Corporation to make more than one thousand M-7 antiaircraft gun directors. Just making one of these deadly weapons required 1,820 parts with 11,130 pieces and needed 721 gears, 380 nickel alloy shafts, 549 ball-bearing sets, and 39 instrument dials. But, as a Ford executive noted, "if a plane flies into its sight, and the operators of the M-7 can get the plane in their telescope, it is doomed."[10]

The rise in industrial production put a strain on railroads to deliver the goods. Freight and passenger traffic doubled from 1940 to 1943, and railroad operators responded by pooling resources, sharing competing lines, and adding cars to carry the greater traffic. Railroad owners also adopted and shared the newly developed central traffic control system (CTC), which automatically transmitted information to dispatchers, who regulated the movement of trains onto different lines.[11]

Not just in railroads, but in other industries, Americans joined in a rush to innovate. Not so in other countries. When the war began, the primary military aircraft in Japan was the Zero; little innovation occurred and Japanese pilots were still flying Zeros in

1945. The United States, in contrast, began with the B-17 and then created the leaner and wider-ranging B-24, and ended the war with the more deadly B-29 Superfortress. Also, the A-20 attack bomber was superseded by the A-26 Invader. In tank development, America began with the Sherman model and later created the "vastly superior" Pershing tank.[12]

Nelson marveled at what America's major corporations were able to make by working together. "No central authority in Washington, however stable and firm, could have integrated the various divisions of industry, large and small, simple and complex, as effectively as these free Americans did of their own volition," Nelson concluded. He added, "Voluntarily—in opposition to the policy of coercion which had made our enemies strong—voluntarily, they consolidated their skills and their energies in the interest of the commonweal, and in the end they won, hands down."[13]

Sometimes America needed inspired thinking to improve. Chrysler, for example, was stumped in creating springs strong enough to withstand the stresses of the heavier new tank designs. According to economist and journalist Eliot Janeway, "One erudite engineer found the answer in an out-of-date railroad manual." Thus, the high-stress springs used long ago for railroad cars worked fine on the new tanks. Even the best tank designs, however, sometimes needed improvising. General Eisenhower commended a Sergeant Culin for on-the-spot ingenuity. After the D-Day landing in France, American tanks couldn't maneuver through the dense hedgerows, but Sergeant Culin "[fastened] to the front of the tank two sturdy blades of steel which, acting somewhat as scythes, cut through the bank of earth and hedges."[14] American tanks could then slice through the hedgerows, moving out to support the 1944 summer offensive.

Even though industrial Germany had a head start in the war and had expert craftsmen capable of making advanced weapons, Nazi leaders dictated a top-down strategy that stifled creativity. According to historian Richard Overy, "Production schedules were set by military agencies; consultation with industrialists and engineers who had to produce the goods was rare and one-sided." Hermann Göring, for example, rigidly controlled German airplane production until the war was almost over. Albert Speer, who tried to encourage innovation and mass production, complained bitterly about "excessive bureaucratization," which he attacked "in vain." [15]

The United States avoided this trap—it tried to stay flexible and creative. For example, some ordnance experts observed that on cars, the steering gear, with its attached gearboxes, somewhat resembled a machine gun. Therefore, the ordnance officer in Detroit went to Saginaw to ask the general manager at the steering gear division of General Motors if he could create and mass-produce Browning machine guns. "If anyone else can build 'em, we can, too," the manager responded. In less than two years, the GM plant at Saginaw delivered 28,728 Browning machine guns, and even dropped the price per gun from $667 to $141. [16]

Not only with weapons but also in medicine, American business produced amazing results. Before the war, penicillin was known to have potential, but no one could produce it in mass quantities. Unlike sulfa, which was easy to produce, penicillin grew only in tiny amounts on mold in small containers. In 1939, British scientists used penicillin on mice infected with staph or strep, with a recovery rate of 93 percent. When war began, penicillin looked extremely promising against infections that produce pus within the body, which were so common among combat troops; sulfa was ineffective in the presence of pus, and deaths were all too frequent.

By 1941, with funding from the Rockefeller Foundation, British researchers still produced only enough penicillin for intravenous treatment of five seriously ill patients, three with septicemia. All five patients responded extremely well to penicillin; three survived, one died when the penicillin supply ran out, and another died from other causes. [17]

In the summer of 1941, Australian-born Sir Howard Florey came to the United States from Great Britain to meet with officials at the U.S. Department of Agriculture. Just as with radar, the British knew that penicillin was a tremendous breakthrough, but their country did not have the personnel or facilities for large-scale production. Would the Americans work on this project?

Officials asked Department of Agriculture scientists at their laboratory in Peoria, Illinois, to study penicillin research. Also, Florey met with the Committee for Medical Research (CMR), which agreed to coordinate efforts by the Department of Agriculture and four pharmaceutical companies: Merck, Pfizer, Squibb, and Lederle. How could millions of doses of penicillin be produced?

In historian James Baxter's words, "There were a great many lights burning for a great many nights in these laboratories."[18] Scientists found ways to improve the medium in which penicillin grew; also, U.S. Army Air Force personnel gathered handfuls of soil from all over the world to provide new strains of mold for experiments.

For mass production, scientists had to figure out how to grow the mold in huge vats. At first, the familiar strains of mold grew only on the surface of liquids, which did not work well for mass production. But one of the newer strains proved to be very productive and grew well in very large containers. Researchers developed processes for oxygenating, mixing, and cooling the liquid in the vats, and then, through a complicated filtration process, extracted the penicillin.

In 1942, the pilot plants produced only enough doses of penicillin to treat ten patients per month. By the spring of 1943, American pharmaceutical plants were producing enough for forty patients per month. Mass production was now possible. The WPB gave the project high priority and coordinated plant construction by choosing twenty-one chemical firms to build production facilities. Within six months, most plants were operating.

At first, all penicillin supplies went to combat troops, with shipments overseas as early as April 1943. In June 1943, available doses increased to 425 patients per month, and by December

1943 the count was up to 9,195. During the spring of 1944, Lend-Lease shipments began to include penicillin. By June 1944, a whopping 117,527 patients per month could receive the lifesaving drug. In the spring of 1944, the WPB established the Civilian Penicillin Distribution Unit in Chicago, which worked with the American Medical Association to allocate penicillin throughout the United States for civilian use as well. In the treatment of pneumonia, for example, the new drug saved tens of thousands of lives in the United States in 1945. American plants eventually produced so much penicillin that there was enough for everyone—646,818 patients per month in June 1945. And the cost of a bottle of penicillin also decreased, from about $20 to less than one dollar, and 20 percent of that was packaging.[19]

Not just the sharing of ideas, but individual entrepreneurs also helped the United States win the war. Henry Kaiser, for example, became the premier shipbuilder who delivered the goods to the Allies. Born to a German immigrant shoemaker in 1882, Kaiser grew up on a farm near Utica, New York. As he said later in life, at age thirteen, "I thought I was ready to lick the world single-handed, so I dropped out [of school]."[20] The search for work, the dead-end jobs, and even the muffed sales calls did not dampen his young spirit. He always believed he would succeed, and he loved to read about "the courage, daring, and adventurous spirit" of Teddy Roosevelt and other bold men. Like Roosevelt, Kaiser went west. Then he got married and became a builder of roads. No one could outwork Kaiser, and he eventually helped build the Hoover, Bonneville, Grand Coulee, and Shasta dams.

By 1940, with Europe at war, Kaiser switched his focus from dams to ships. "No, I had never even seen a ship launched,"[21] Kaiser told a Senate committee in 1942. But he had seen businesses launched, and he believed he could fill a niche by making ships. For one thing, Kaiser watched how slow America's existing shipbuilders were to accept the large contracts being offered in 1940.

Then, as German submarines began to decimate the British

(and, later, the American) fleets, FDR was eager to recapture the Atlantic Ocean for the United States. After the huge losses at Pearl Harbor, shipbuilding became a frantic priority. The government was willing to pay top dollar for all of the ships Kaiser could deliver. Building the standard transport ship to get goods overseas was Kaiser's goal. The older shipbuilders fashioned their ships one at a time with highly skilled craftsmen. That was too slow for Kaiser. He built massive shipyards in Portland, Oregon, and Richmond, California, and on the spot he created spacious assembly lines where unskilled laborers mass-produced "liberty ships" in record times. In his first year, Kaiser cut construction time from 355 days to 108 days per ship. Soon he was down to 40 days, then 27, while his workers always built many ships at once. Kaiser paid high wages and advertised all over the country to lure two hundred thousand workers to his assembly lines on the West Coast.[22]

He listened to suggestions and innovated constantly. Other shipbuilders, for example, relied on highly trained riveters to fit key parts of the ship together. Not Kaiser. He prefabricated the many sections of the ship on his assembly line and then welded the large sections together. Welding was much easier to learn than riveting, but was not as stabilizing. Thus, Kaiser's welded ships were not so durable, but they were built for a war, not forever. A few split in two during ocean travel, but Kaiser made adjustments by using better steel. His record became impressive.

Sometimes bureaucratic regulations almost choked Kaiser, but he "mastered evasion of bureaucratic regulations."[23] For example, he built ships so fast he often ran out of steel plate, which he could not buy at OPA prices. So he paid extra for it on the black market and was investigated by the OPA. Kaiser was popular, however, and avoided paying a fine. As columnist Ray Clapper quipped, "If you have to be a scofflaw to get steel out of the arsenal of bureaucracy, then that's okay with me."[24]

Kaiser's shipyards became virtual cities, and they swamped the sometimes smaller towns near them. Richmond, for example, had twenty-three thousand people in 1940, and Kaiser added one hundred thousand more to that in the next two years. As one wife said of her husband, "He works nights and sleeps in the car days. The children and I sleep in it nights. I just wish we were home."[25] Turnover was devastating for assembly lines, so Kaiser did all he could to entice and retain workers. High wages were a start. Then came modular houses instead of cars, trailers, and open lawns for sleeping. Next came day care services for the children of his workers; and finally he offered prepaid health care for eighty cents per family per week. Some 95 percent of his workers bought into his HMO, and Kaiser kept dozens of physicians on hand to help the sick recover, and thereby keep his assembly lines moving. When the OPA began capping wages, Kaiser and others began the tradition of offering health insurance as an incentive to retain and reward talented workers. As Kaiser became America's dominant builder of more than fifteen hundred ships, he became a "capitalist folk hero" and even a serious contender for vice president on Roosevelt's ticket in 1944.[26]

Another major war entrepreneur was boatbuilder Andrew Jackson Higgins. Born in Nebraska to a newspaper editor, Higgins—like Kaiser—hated school and left it for the world of business as soon as possible. He thrived on buying and selling and, as Higgins said, "I came south because I loved boats and forestry."[27] In New Orleans, he transformed local lumber first into speedboats, then into sailboats, and finally into his own invention—an amphibious boat with a "spoonbill bow" that could travel over sandbars and riverbanks. These shallow-draft boats caught the attention of the Navy and the Marines when Higgins "added a ramp that dropped forward onto a beach, allowing troops to charge off in rapid order."[28]

Higgins is an example of a small businessman who became a giant entrepreneur by creating a product—motorized landing craft—that was essential to military success. From 50 employees and $14,000 in plant and equipment in 1937, Higgins soared during the war to 20,000 employees working in seven plants covering 100 million square feet. They made more than 10,000 "Higgins boats," which included LCM (landing craft, mechanized), LCPL (landing craft, personnel large), and LCVP (landing craft, vehicle, personnel). He also built PT boats and antisubmarine boats. By September 1943, Higgins had designed more than 90 percent of the country's landing craft, and had built more than 60 percent of them. According to Eisenhower, Higgins was "the man who won the war for us."[29]

Why was Higgins so indispensable to an American victory? Because he was one of the very few men who could create and manufacture reliable landing craft to transport troops from ship to shore. Using landing craft in warfare was a key World War II innovation. Troop ships would bring thousands of soldiers within a mile or so of the coast. Then the soldiers would climb down the sides of the ships on cargo nets into Higgins boats, each holding thirty-six men. The landing craft would then take the soldiers in to shore—a ramp would open at the end of the boat, and the men would wade ashore. Then the boats would return to the troop ship to load more men.

Higgins's boats were so reliable, so flexible, and so fast that Americans could reach many different parts of a coastline, not just the major ports. In previous wars, invasions had to occur at major ports. Not after Higgins.

What's especially remarkable about the Higgins story is that he almost missed the chance to show the world what he could do. The biggest obstacle Higgins faced was not creating his boats or beating his competitors, but overcoming the bureaucrats in the U.S. Navy. In particular, the Bureau of Ships, which had authority to buy landing craft for the entire Navy, regularly refused to consider Higgins and his offers to supply various landing craft and PT boats. Why? First and foremost, the Bureau of Ships had its own internally designed landing craft it wanted to use. What's more, the naval leaders couldn't imagine a small-boat builder from Nebraska having the answers to the Navy's needs. Therefore, they dismissed him. When Higgins was able to challenge the Navy's landing craft in head-to-head contests, he always won; the Navy usually responded by nitpicking Higgins's design and purchasing their own vessels anyway.

To survive in business early on, Higgins sold his state-of-the-art boats to the grateful British and Finns. But when he studied the powerful Germans and Japanese, and then watched the U.S. Navy's landing craft founder, he knew his fellow Americans needed what he had. But the Navy kept saying no to him—even after Pearl Harbor. With the fate of his business and his country in the balance, he fought back. Higgins was a tall, husky man with piercing blue eyes and a blunt manner. "I don't wait for opportunity to knock," he said. "I send out a welcoming committee to drag the old harlot in." Therefore, he openly condemned the Bureau of Ships for "prejudice" against his boats. American lives were being lost, he contended, because Higgins boats were on the sidelines. To the leaders of the Bureau of Ships, he called their tank lighter—the LCM that carried tanks—"godawful." He added, "I want to say that there are no officers, whether present in this room or otherwise in the Navy, who know a goddamn thing about small boat design, construction, or operation—but, by God, I do." [30]

Of the Bureau of Ships, Higgins said, "They have erected new buildings covering acre after acre; the corridors and offices are a mystic maze. . . . If the 'red tape' and the outmoded and outlandish Civil War methods of doing business were eliminated, the work could be done in the Bureau of Ships very efficiently with about one-sixth the present personnel." [31] The bureaucrats at the Bureau of Ships loathed Higgins and rejected his superior boats, even when their own malfunctioned and killed American soldiers in transport. If the power structure in place during the early months of the war had stayed in place, Higgins would have been out of work and Americans, according to Eisenhower, would have either lost the war or had victory long delayed.

Fortunately for Higgins, the U.S. war effort was just decentralized enough to give him a chance to go outside the naval bureaucracy to prove himself. First, the Marines desperately needed amphibious boats, and after doing tests they discovered that the Navy's landing craft often didn't work, but Higgins boats did. Therefore, the Marines bought Higgins boats when possible, and they helped get a hearing for Higgins in higher tribunals. Second, Congress had authorized the Truman Committee to investigate waste, and when Higgins at last won a hearing from Senator Truman, dramatic results followed. "Produce one of your boats," Truman told the U.S. Navy. "Put it in a head-to-head operational test in competition with Higgins's product, and see what happens."[32]

That was all Higgins ever asked for. In the dramatic contest that followed at Norfolk, Virginia, on May 25, 1942, both Higgins and the Navy had to have their landing craft carry a thirty-ton tank through choppy waters. During the race, the highly touted boat built by the Bureau of Ships failed—and almost sank—while the Higgins boat dazzled the spectators. Commander E. E. Roth of the Bureau of Ships bawled, "Almost lost everybody on board, almost lost the tank." But the Higgins boat, Commander Roth admitted, "came through fine, upside in, and made the beach."[33] With the scrutiny of the Truman Committee, the Bureau of Ships had to convert to Higgins's design, and immediately he began receiving important contracts.

Truman recognized the importance of landing craft to American success, and he was shocked that the Navy had repeatedly rejected the best available. He launched a full investigation into naval purchasing and concluded that "the Bureau of Ships has, for reasons known only to itself, stubbornly persisted for over five years in clinging to an unseaworthy tank lighter design of its own. . . . Higgins Industries did actually design and build a superior lighter" but was ignored because of "a flagrant disregard for the facts, if not the safety and success of American troops."[34]

To underscore the point, Truman wrote a letter to Secretary

Knox condemning "the negligence or willful misconduct on the part of the officers of the Bureau of Ships" and its "bias and prejudiced treatment" against Higgins.[35] As a result, the leadership of the Bureau of Ships was overhauled in a manner similar to Marshall's reorganization of the Army. New men, younger and more sympathetic to Higgins, took charge of the bureau and worked with Higgins to churn out thousands more landing craft, PT boats, and other vessels to win the war. Donald Nelson, head of the WPB, joined in the praise and urged Higgins to "come into this war effort in a bigger way."[36]

Just weeks after Higgins won his boat race with the Bureau of Ships, he secured another key ally, General George Marshall. When the British told Marshall that landing craft posed one of their biggest challenges, Marshall listened carefully and put his "full strength" into finding a solution, which in large part was Higgins Industries.

With a green light from the Truman Committee, the Bureau of Ships, Donald Nelson, and George Marshall, Higgins expanded his New Orleans plant and frantically churned out landing craft. He attracted good workers from across the country for his assembly lines by paying high wages, offering free medical care, and providing great training and some community services. He hired black and white workers and, although he had to segregate them, he paid them similar wages. Getting good workers and training them was only part of his challenge. He also had to find loopholes in the new federal laws that limited wages and controlled prices and purchases. Higgins often bought steel on the black market, and once, when no bronze shafting was available for making tank lighters, he stole the needed material from an oil company in nearby Texas (he later paid for it). *Life* magazine ran a long feature on the remarkable Higgins, and Drew Pearson, perhaps the nation's most famous columnist, wrote that Higgins was "very disagreeable, likes to write insulting letters to admirals, gets on almost everyone's nerves, but is a genius when it comes to small boat design."[37]

Now that the genius was turned loose, did he have enough time to get the needed landing craft to the military to help turn the war around? In desperate battles at Guadalcanal in 1942, the Navy needed all the landing craft Higgins could produce. During March 1943, as Eisenhower prepared to invade Sicily and Italy, he had nightmares of shortages of landing craft. When I die, Eisenhower said, my "coffin should be in the shape of a landing craft, as they are practically killing [me] with worry."[38]

The next year, when the Allies launched the D-Day invasion, the Germans could not cover the entire European coast. Allied forces used thousands of landing craft to hit five Normandy beaches on D-Day, June 6, 1944. A frustrated Hitler called Higgins the "new Noah."[39]

In the Pacific, the Marines and the U.S. Army also used hundreds of Higgins boats for amphibious assaults as they island-hopped toward Japan. By Thanksgiving, 1944, Eisenhower expressed the thoughts of many when he said, "Let us thank God for Higgins Industries, management, and labor which has given us the landing boats with which to conduct our campaign."[40]

Higgins's success opened the door for other makers of landing craft. General Motors sold the Navy its previously rejected DUKW (pronounced "duck"), which was a wheeled landing craft designed to move on water and then drive on sand or roadways. More than two thousand "ducks" operated on the Normandy beaches in 1944. When Winston Churchill visited Normandy that summer, he landed on the beach in a "duck." In the Pacific, "ducks" could roll over coral reefs near island beaches, then land men and supplies safely on dry land.

With outside help, Higgins had overcome the naval bureaucracy. But one government agency that threatened all entrepreneurs was the IRS. With the excess profits tax at 90 percent, and the income tax at 94 percent on all income over $200,000, many corporations had trouble expanding to meet the huge orders for war materiel.[41] Huge corporations like General Motors, U.S. Steel, and DuPont could make tanks, planes, and ammunition from their large existing supplies of capital. Also, their size and reputation helped them win federal aid to build new plants. For smaller businessmen, the near confiscatory taxes robbed their capital and stifled their growth. Without capital to expand, how could they fulfill the ever-increasing orders for war supplies?

The case of Jack Simplot illustrates the near disaster created by high tax rates. Simplot was an Idaho potato farmer who discovered the advantages of vegetable dehydration in 1940. Using onions and potatoes, Simplot developed boilers and equipment that could dehydrate one million pounds of vegetables into 140,000 pounds of dried food. At one-seventh the original weight, the dried and shrunken potatoes and onions were easy to store and ship. True, Simplot was making small potatoes, but as the owner of the largest dehydration plant in the world, the $600,000 in profits he earned in 1940–41 was not small potatoes at all. After Pearl Harbor, Simplot was swamped with "urgent orders for huge deliveries."[42]

Simplot could have refused the large orders, or accepted some and expanded slowly. But the desperate Army officers in charge of procurement helped persuade Simplot that his country, and the men defending his country, needed his maximum production right now. So Simplot took the risks and plowed in the capital to grow his business. But with each new step of growth, he faced new hurdles. When he bought new potato farms, for example, he had to secure mineral rights on nearby land rich with phosphates to restore nutrients to his soil. Faced with millions of potato skins, he fed them to thousands of hogs he bought, and then he was in the pork business. To ship potatoes he needed boxes, so he bought acres of trees and went into the lumber business.

For each new risk, Simplot needed more men, more capital, and more lawyers. Especially lawyers—to help him salvage the capital needed to expand. "I ain't no economist," Simplot would say, but his lawyers helped him escape the 90 percent excess profits tax that threatened to swallow most of his cash. Their legal ploy was to have Simplot form "ninety-five partnerships and scores of trusts" to shelter enough capital to allow him to produce enough potatoes to feed the troops. As economist George Gilder has noted, "each one" of these partnerships and trusts was "small enough to avoid the confiscatory top tax rates."[43] Simplot had enough freedom to supply one-third of all the potatoes eaten by the U.S. Army.

His wartime production had been Herculean. Colonel Paul Logan, the U.S. procurement officer, concluded that Simplot "was asked to build a huge plant for which there was no precedent and when little construction material was available; he was asked to equip the plant with machinery that didn't exist and for which there was no blueprint, and to undertake a food processing procedure on which there was very little technical knowledge." And he did all of this, Logan observed, "working day and night for most of the war."[44]

World War II was a triumph of American business. U.S. entrepreneurs and their corporations either invented or perfected synthetic rubber, B-29 airplanes, Higgins boats, liberty ships, dehydrated food, the atomic bomb, and more. Americans produced 297,000 airplanes, 86,338 tanks, 17,400,000 rifles, carbines, and pistols, 315,000 pieces of field artillery and mortars, 64,500 landing vessels, 6,500 navy ships, and 41,400,000,000 rounds of small-arms ammunition—and gave much of this via Lend-Lease to England, Russia, and China. U.S. military strength overwhelmed the Axis powers on land, in the air, and on sea. Franklin Roosevelt deserves credit for much of this result because he chose to focus mainly on the war, not his New Deal. He was willing to give incentives to businessmen to build factories and make military hardware rather than expand the WPA, the CCC, and the NYA—all of which were canceled during the war. Furthermore, Roosevelt supported war leaders who gave ship contracts to Kaiser, boat contracts to Higgins, and food contracts to Simplot. He never endorsed a government-run steel company, as he had done during World War I with disastrous results.[45]

Clearly, however, FDR did not like most of the entrepreneurs he had to support, and he always believed that government needed to be bigger and more centralized. He still liked the New Deal, but he believed he had to turn loose unpleasant fellows like MacArthur, Higgins, and John Collyer of U.S. Rubber to give himself the best chance to beat the Axis. His concessions to business were only temporary. Even before the war was over, FDR was planning for a New Deal revival.

After the war, the New Dealers had some small revenge. FDR was, according to his son Elliott, the first president to use the IRS for political purposes. When the war ended, the IRS slapped Jack Simplot with a $2.5 million fine in back taxes. "Republics . . . ," as Andrew Higgins lamented, "are ungrateful." He added, "The people that create or build to make victory possible . . . are 'war profiteers' to be subjected to suspicion, to be investigated, to be harassed."[46] Higgins knew whereof he spoke. Not only had he been socked with an IRS audit, he also had to watch as the government sold its used Higgins landing craft at bargain rates just as the whole boat market collapsed.

Good entrepreneurs, of course, usually overcome obstacles. Simplot went into the frozen French fries business and became a huge supplier to McDonald's restaurants during the 1950s and 1960s. After the war, Henry Kaiser had much success in the steel and aluminum businesses. For a while he competed with General Motors by making the Kaiser-Fraser car. He also began building low-cost homes for veterans; later he helped develop homes in Hawaii.

The success of Simplot, Kaiser, and many other entrepreneurs after the war shows they were not dependent on government war contracts for success. The war business—with its subsidized factories, cost-plus contracts, and guaranteed markets—was the only game entrepreneurs could play in the United States in the 1940s. Thus, they played it. Even with the high tax rates, it was a better game than FDR had offered them in the 1930s—when he denounced them as "economic royalists" and created perpetual uncertainty for them through high income tax rates, new corporate taxes, a flurry of regulations, and regular subsidies for farmers, silver miners, dam builders, and many more.

Business during the war was different in other ways, too. The Allies had to beat Hitler to have an economic future. Businessmen had a focus, an enemy, and a clear goal. Entrepreneurs were willing to share secrets with competitors and work together to innovate and produce because the United States was behind early in the war, and Allied troops needed the planes, tanks, ships, weapons, and ammunition to thrash the Germans and ensure economic survival. For the four years of war, U.S. entrepreneurs endured heavy government involvement with the hope that winning the war might end the New Deal and create greater freedom in the future. FDR, however, endured giving incentives to businessmen in the hope the United States would win the war and thus allow greater growth of government in the future.

9

TAXES: "GOVERNMENT CAN TAKE EVERYTHING WE HAVE"

I said to my Uncle Sam,
"Old Man Taxes, here I am!"
And he was glad to see me.

Mr. Small Fry, yes, indeed;
Lower brackets—that's my speed,
But he was glad to see me.

I paid my income tax today.
I never felt so proud before,
To be right there with the millions more
Who paid their income tax today.

I'm squared up with the U.S.A.
You see those bombers in the sky;
Rockefeller helped to build them, so did I!
I paid my income tax today.

I paid my income tax today.
A thousand planes to bomb Berlin:
They'll all be paid for, and I chipped in.
That certainly makes me feel okay.

10,000 more and that ain't hay.
We must pay for this war somehow;
Uncle Sam was worried, but he isn't now.
I paid my income tax today.[1]

Imagine a Hollywood star belting out these lyrics in 1942. Fact or fiction? Yes, it really happened. Two weeks after Pearl Harbor, when FDR needed funds more than ever, Irving Berlin produced a propaganda masterpiece entitled "I Paid My Income Tax Today." Singer Danny Kaye recorded the song, and the Treasury Department sent it to 872 radio stations with a letter urging that it be played frequently until the March 15, 1942, tax deadline. Berlin's song appealed to pride, patriotism, and peer pressure to induce new taxpayers to part with their cash. Danny Kaye even offered to tour New York nightclubs and sing the tax song for audiences throughout the city.[2]

Radio was the medium of choice for many tax promoters. More than 90 percent of Americans listened to radio during World War II, and regular plugs on hundreds of stations emphasized the theme of "Taxes to beat the Axis." Radio stations had long been more congenial than newspapers to FDR because he could revoke their licenses. During the war, therefore, the president wanted regular radio announcements exhorting Americans to pay their taxes faithfully. Spokesmen for the OWI and the Treasury Department made regular announcements on radio, and Morgenthau even had his own weekly radio show, called *The Treasury Hour*. Morgenthau cajoled songwriter Irving Berlin to pen "Any Bonds Today," which became the theme song for the one-hour show.

More propaganda was yet to come. Later in 1942, the OWI also developed the Network Allocation Plan for radio stations. Under that plan, according to law professor Carolyn Jones, "Each network received an allocation of government messages on a regular schedule." The writers and producers of each regular network program "were asked to prepare the messages themselves but were guided by important points in a fact sheet provided by OWI. The OWI decided which messages would be placed on the network plan for a particular week." From brief radio plugs to whole shows devoted to the income tax, millions heard their favorite radio characters exhorting listeners to pay their taxes on time. Roy Rogers, George Burns and Gracie Allen, and even the radio version of Perry Mason complied with the pressure to do a tax plug. During March 1943, one Treasury official estimated "that probably 65% of the sets in the country got the tax message in the last four days . . . several of them more than once."[3]

Movies were yet another vehicle for selling taxes. As Treasury official John Sullivan told Henry Morgenthau, "What John Barrymore can't do, maybe Mickey Mouse could." Therefore, Morgenthau and his assistants persuaded Walt Disney to produce an eight-minute film, *The New Spirit*, which featured popular Disney characters. At one point in the film, Donald Duck turns on the radio and hears a typical tax plug: "[It is] your privilege, not just your duty, but your privilege to help your government by paying your tax and paying it promptly." Donald, after some anxiety, finds the tax forms easier than expected, and enjoys receiving deductions for his three nephews, Huey, Dewey, and Louie. Then Donald, with his $13 tax payment in hand, is whisked to Washington, where he sees his tax going to make guns, planes, and ships. The narrator concludes, "Taxes will keep democracy on the march."[4]

Morgenthau himself campaigned among motion picture exhibitors to show *The New Spirit* at once; Treasury officials even buttonholed the projectionists' union and told them "its exhibition is a 'must.'" According to motion picture records, *The New Spirit* was seen by more than 32 million people in twelve thousand theaters during 1942. In a Gallup poll, 37 percent said "the film had affected their willingness to pay taxes." Morgenthau himself may have been amused by such gullibility. Shortly before approaching

Disney, he had commented, "If we can get people to pay taxes with that God-awful Mickey Mouse, we will have arrived socially." After the success of *The New Spirit*, Morgenthau made sure Disney released a sequel for 1943.[5]

The Roosevelt administration trotted out Donald Duck, Irving Berlin, and Danny Kaye because in 1942 the income tax had just been transformed from a class tax on the wealthy to a mass tax—one that a majority of American families paid. Roosevelt had to do that to get the revenue he wanted because he had run out of rich people to tax. "Too many people," Roosevelt lamented, "are earning money and not contributing to the government." When a Treasury official suggested lowering personal exemptions, Roosevelt agreed: "Of course I want that. I have been trying to get it for years but nobody will help me do it." From 1939 to 1944, with Roosevelt's blessing, the personal exemption plummeted from $2,500 to $1,000 for married couples. In other words, in 1939 those couples paid no tax on the first $2,500 of their income ($37,831 in 2009 dollars); in 1944, they had to pay tax on all income over $1,000 ($15,132 in 2009 dollars). Not only did the exemption dwindle, but rates no longer started at 4 percent, but at 19 percent.[6]

Just as 1942 was the year of the first mass tax in U.S. history, 1943 would be the year of withholding taxes at the source. The case for withholding was simple: The war was expensive. FDR and Morgenthau wanted to get more revenue more efficiently and more quickly from the millions of new taxpayers. If employers could be forced to extract pay from their workers' wages each week or month, and then send that cash to Washington, the government could secure a steady flow of revenue—not only for the rest of the war, but possibly for generations to come. FDR had reached a pivotal point in American history.

Actually, the president had already experimented with withholding on a small scale. By 1936, employers had to deduct social security taxes from their employees each payday. Also, the Victory

Tax, which became law in 1942, was a 5 percent tax on all income over $624. To save the costs of collection, Congress required employers, at their own expense, to extract the Victory Tax from the wages of their employees on payday and send the revenue to Washington. Income tax payments, by contrast, were due on March 15, and those who owed money to the government had to save during the year, or pay high interest rates on overdue tax bills. Thus, FDR's next step was to require all employers to withhold a regular percentage of all income from each employee's paycheck, and send it to Washington for government use.[7]

The campaign for withholding, however, hit a snag: Tax payments in the United States were not on a current basis. The 1942 tax bill, for example, was not due until 1943. Oddly, government's hunger for revenue was what created that glitch in the first place. The Sixteenth Amendment became law in 1913, but President Wilson did not get to sign his first tax bill until October. No progressive wanted to wait until 1914 to seize a chunk of revenue from the Rockefellers, the Vanderbilts, or the Fords. Thus, Congress made the income tax passed in October 1913 retroactive for the whole year. That gave taxpayers little time to prepare to pay their taxes, so Congress extended the deadline into 1914 for money earned in 1913. Hence, March 15 became tax day for income earned the previous year. And if the taxpayer could not pay all of his 1913 taxes on March 15, 1914, he was allowed to make quarterly payments throughout 1914. This began a tradition of earning income one year and paying taxes on that income the next year on March 15, or in quarterly installments during the year.[8]

The delay of one year in collecting taxes was awkward, but it caused few problems in the 1920s and 1930s because few Americans paid income taxes. Only 4 million Americans paid any income tax in 1940, but when FDR then had the personal exemption slashed, 39 million Americans had to pay income taxes in 1942. And he wanted revenue from the tens of millions of new taxpayers right away. Instead, the new taxpayers of 1942 could delay their payments until 1943. That deprived FDR of urgently desired cash. As of 1942, those who earned more than $500 had to pay at almost a 24 percent rate, but they could delay their payments until 1943, and make them in quarterly installments starting on March 15.[9]

Granted, the president needed cash to fight the war. The United States was indeed running a large war debt, but FDR used war loan drives to raise money, and he did have a steady flow of revenue into the federal Treasury. The income tax payments for 1941 were steadily coming in during 1942. But in 1942 the income tax had become a mass tax; FDR was losing interest on income being earned in 1942, but not due in tax payments until the next year.

How could the president make the collecting of taxes current and get withholding as well? When he tried to do both, his critics, supported by millions of taxpayers, cried "double taxation." Would he ask Americans to pay both their 1942 and 1943 tax bills in the same year? If so, millions of Americans would be desperately strapped to pay household bills and two years' taxes at the same time; in fact, some Americans would owe more than they earned in 1943—which would be a wild variation on FDR's earlier effort to enact a 100 percent tax on high incomes.

The man with an answer for Roosevelt was Beardsley Ruml, a pipe-smoking professor who became a director of the New York Federal Reserve Bank and a public relations expert for Macy's, the department store chain. Ruml approached the tax problem this way: The ultimate prize for FDR was withholding. Taxpayers, of course, hated the idea of 19 percent of their wages yanked from their pay envelopes each month, but for FDR, withholding would be bliss. It gave the government immediate cash on a regular and, ideally, permanent basis. Employers had to pay the costs of collecting the cash and sending it to Washington, and because taxes were withheld, the taxpayer never saw what was taken from him. Not only did he not feel the monthly pain of losing 19 percent of his income in federal taxes, but if he overpaid, he would get a refund next year from Uncle Sam.[10]

Selling the concept of withholding to the general public was delicate, and Ruml had two marketing ideas. First, call it "pay as you go." Treat it like installment buying. According to reporter David Brinkley, "Congress and the president learned, to their pleasure, what automobile salesmen had learned long before: that installment buyers could be induced to pay more because they looked not at the total debt but only at the monthly payments. And in this case there was, for government, the added psychological advantage that people were paying their taxes with not much resistance because they were paying with money they had never even seen."[11]

Second, Ruml suggested that the 1942 tax bill should be canceled, calling it "tax forgiveness," and using it to sell withholding to taxpayers for 1943. That created an optical illusion. Taxpayers would jump for one year's "tax forgiveness" and end up in the quicksand of withholding—forever. Meanwhile, the government would get taxpayer revenue one year sooner, not later, and wealthy Americans—who stood to save much on their 1942 tax bill—still had a 70 percent estate tax waiting for them at the end of their lives. That would be payback time. And, of course, once withholding was in place, taxes could always be raised to get even more revenue. "Tax forgiveness," in other words, was a mirage.

Pollster George Gallup discovered that when "tax forgiveness" was added to "pay as you go," almost 80 percent of Americans endorsed the Ruml plan. That big jump in support triggered a national debate. Those who opposed Ruml included some conservatives, who recognized the future potential of "pay as you go" to expand the federal government, and some New Dealers, who liked "pay as you go," but also wanted double taxation because it extracted more revenue from the rich.[12]

With a large base of support for withholding, Congress held

hearings in February 1943 to change the tax system as soon as possible. Oddly, Roosevelt and Morgenthau both opposed the Ruml plan, and that was the barrier to quick passage. To Roosevelt and Morgenthau, the snag in Ruml's plan was canceling the 1942 tax bill. They wanted that revenue even if payments had to be drawn out over several years. Roosevelt increasingly began to see he could get the prize—withholding—and maybe get the 1942 tax bill thrown in as a bonus.[13]

With Roosevelt and his New Dealers wanting double taxation, the debate in Congress was guaranteed to be combative. Much was at stake. Withholding itself was a paramount issue, but double taxation meant that some higher-income Americans would pay *all* of their income (and maybe more) in taxes, and that most Americans would pay about one-fourth of what they earned to the state. Did government, even in wartime, have a right to confiscate that much property from its citizens?

The congressmen themselves recognized the seriousness of what they were doing. Robert Doughton (D-N.C.), chairman of the House Ways and Means Committee, said, "We are dealing with the most hateful, difficult problem that ever came along in the annals of mankind." Senator Robert La Follette, Jr. (R-Wisc.), observed that in his eighteen years in Congress he had never seen such a "sharp division of opinion among honest men."[14]

Of the various bills Congress considered, the basic Ruml plan drew the most support and the most fire. Frank Carlson (R-Kan.) introduced the bill in the House on March 22, 1943, and made the case that canceling the 1942 taxes was the fairest and most equitable way to make the tax system current. The government, Carlson and his supporters noted, would likely gain, not lose, revenue. "We shall all go along paying our income taxes as we have before, except they will be on a current basis." For the war, Carlson said, "our federal treasury must have more tax revenue, not less."[15] Under his plan, government would get income monthly as it was being earned and not delayed by a year. And estate taxes at 70 percent would pick up any stray profits rich people might have accumulated.

Making the tax system current by canceling one year's taxes would avoid double taxation on tens of millions of Americans. "Double taxation," Carlson argued, "is utterly unjust." In many cases it would mean that the amount of tax to be paid would be greater than the income—a "confiscation of capital." Congress had recently struck down Roosevelt's efforts to tax incomes over $25,000 at 100 percent. The notion that government should do "outright confiscation," Carlson believed, was "unconstitutional" and a horrible precedent, even in time of a world war.[16]

The Ruml-Carlson plan stirred up debate in Congress. The attack began in the House with Rep. John Dingell (D-Mich.), who called the Ruml-Carlson plan "about as legitimate as horse stealing." Fully $9 billion in income taxes would be lost, Dingell said, "as a result of the action of Congress in remitting an amount of tax money which has been legally and properly levied for the year 1942."[17] Senator Tom Connally (D-Tex.) added, "If we analyze 'abating,' 'giving away,' and any other expressions of that character under the microscope of the philologist, we find that they all mean the same thing. The government is going to lose the money. . . ." He concluded, "I am in favor of every citizen who owes the government a debt paying it in full."[18] Tax forgiveness violated that principle.

The fiscal conservatives attacked the "lost revenue" argument at every turn. "There is no loss of revenue under the Carlson bill," said Rep. Harold Knutson of Minnesota, the ranking Republican on the House Ways and Means Committee, "but on the contrary an increase in revenue because we would be tapping the higher level of 1943 incomes one year sooner than under the present law. And that is for all future years," Knutson added.[19] "From the government's point of view," asked Senator Robert Taft (R-Ohio), "how can there be any forgiveness? . . . In 1943 the government would actually receive more money under the Ruml plan. . . ." He added,

"In 1944, it would still receive more money. In the long run, the government will always receive more money when the national income is rising." Finally, because of withholding and high estate taxes, the government will get its money "more quickly" each year, and with more certainty after each death.[20]

How did New Dealers respond to the arguments of Taft and Knutson? With a touch of class warfare. In the words of Rep. John Rankin (D-Miss.), "Personally, I am not for forgiving these millionaires."[21] Others agreed. "If we allow rich people to escape a year's taxation," Rep. Dingell said, "it would make countless additional war millionaires."[22] Rep. Jere Cooper (D-Tenn.) added a twist: "The Carlson bill," he believed, "would discriminate against the small taxpayer. The forgiveness of a year's tax to those persons who in 1942 had little or no tax liability means nothing. To a man with a million dollar income in 1942 the saving is $854,000."[23]

The conservatives were appalled. "It is tragic," Rep. William Miller (R-Conn.) responded, "that we must admit that there are some people who so despise the few wealthy men and women left in the United States." On the $854,000 rebate to a millionaire, Miller said, "The Ruml plan abates the 1942 liabilities in the same manner as the progressive rates schedule of the income tax increases it. If the progressive principle of the income-tax system is fair and sound in the imposition of taxes, it is fair and sound in reverse."[24] In other words, if someone earning one million dollars pays $854,000 in income taxes, he should, if taxes are canceled, be relieved of his $854,000 debt.

Senator Connally countered with a vivid image: If we cancel taxes for 1942, that saves "$854,000 to the man of a million dollar income. His chauffeur . . . [however, will only] get $1.87." Why not, Connally implied, redistribute some of the $854,000 to the chauffeur? Either that or cancel the rebate entirely?[25] Rep. Harry Sauthoff, a Wisconsin progressive, went further and argued that rich people were not entitled to large incomes. "The Congress vetoed the President's $25,000 ceiling on wages, which I felt was a mistake," Sauthoff said. If, therefore, under double taxation, a millionaire had to pay all his income to the government, that was as it should be.[26]

To the Henry Fords, the Alfred Sloans, and the Eugene Graces, FDR was being arbitrary and unfair. These men took risks, innovated, and worked hard running industries essential to winning the war. For purposes of illustration, if Ford, Sloan, and Grace each earned one million dollars per year each year of the war, then during 1942 they were paying taxes on almost 90 percent of their 1941 income. Then, during 1943, FDR wanted them to pay $854,000 on their 1942 income and another $854,000 on their 1943 income because he wanted to make tax payments current. With this double taxation, they would each have to pay $1,708,000 on an income of $1 million. Henry Ford, who disliked FDR anyway, would have every right to ask, "Did I invent the Model T, fine-tune the assembly line, innovate on the V-8 engine, and then retool my factories to make thousands of planes for the war only to have all my income for 1943 plus much more taken by the government?"

The progressive idea that income should be limited by law raised profound questions for American society. Do rights, such as the right to property, come in a natural way from God—as stated in the Declaration of Independence—or do they come from government? If Americans have a natural right to life, liberty, and property, then high progressive taxes violate that right. If, instead, rights come from government, then the leaders of government have the legitimate authority to confiscate wealth, or redistribute it from one group to another. In time of war, Roosevelt argued, and perhaps afterward, government had the right to most, if not all, income of wealthy citizens in the national interest.

Roosevelt's view commanded some support in Congress. Emanuel Celler (D-N.Y.), for example, said, "I believe the Carlson measure will produce more revenue, because it would take the money from a taxpayer while he still has money and before he has a chance to spend it." Then Celler added: "The government can at any time make income taxes as thumping big as the necessities of war require. Thus, if any plan does not raise enough money, taxes can at any time be increased. The government always has a moral if not actual lien on all our income."[27]

In the Senate, Happy Chandler (D-Ky.) echoed Celler's point. "Mr. President," Senator Chandler said, "all of us owe the government; we owe it for everything we have—and that is the basis of obligation—and the government can take everything we have if the government needs it." Chandler wanted to be clear on this point. "The government," he added, "can assert its right to have all the taxes it needs for any purpose, either now or at any time in the future."[28]

After Chandler's speech, Senator Scott Lucas (D-Ill.) spoke next and agreed with Chandler enthusiastically. "I thank the Senator from Kentucky," Lucas said. "That is all there is to this problem. It is as simple as ABC."[29] In fairness to Lucas, he may have been praising other parts of Chandler's speech, but Lucas, the future majority leader of the Democratic Party, was still endorsing Chandler's view that "government can take everything we have."

If government had, as Celler said, "a moral lien on all our income," or, as Chandler said, a "right to have all the taxes it needs for any purpose," then all Americans, not just the rich, were servants of the state. When FDR became president, only about 3 percent of adult Americans were paying any income tax. But during the war, he expanded the tax base, and most American families began paying income taxes. As Senator Pappy O'Daniel (D-Tex.) noted, "If we keep going in the direction in which we are now headed, before we get through every citizen who earns any money will be contributing to the income tax fund."[30] And withholding was a sure way to capture income from drifters and transients who moved anonymously from job to job. As one Treasury official said, "We cannot get those fellows unless we have the collection-at-the-source method."[31] And they had to "get these fellows" because, as Senator Tom Connally said, "We cannot get much more from the very high brackets, because as to them we have already reached the point of unproductiveness."[32]

For political reasons, many New Dealers wanted to hold down inflation, and they viewed high taxes as one way to do this. According to Senator La Follette, "If we are to prevent inflation in this country, from which all persons would suffer grievously, we must stiffen the burden upon the taxpayer."[33] La Follette's comment confused a cause of inflation (government had sharply increased the money supply) with the result of inflation (higher prices for goods and services).

Rep. Wilbur Mills (D-Ark.) shared this confusion: "Only by collecting taxes—heavy taxes—can we do the job. Now that people have more money than ever before—more than can be spent on the scarce available goods—is the time to collect taxes. To forgive taxes is to present the taxpayer with increased purchasing power." Mills restated his idea this way: "The public, with money in its pockets, will inevitably try to use this money to buy what it wants, what it may need." Therefore, "to check the forces making for inflation, we must direct our tax policy toward diverting an ever larger part of the funds of persons above subsistent levels into the Public Treasury."[34]

When the time came for a vote, the House rejected the Ruml-Carlson bill. Instead, the House passed the harsher Robertson-Forand bill, which established withholding and canceled only the first 19 percent of tax liability across the board for all taxpayers. Thus, if you were in the 19 percent tax bracket, you had your tax for 1942 completely forgiven, but if you were in, say, the 50 percent bracket, you still owed 31 percent of your 1942 income to the government to be paid along with taxes on your 1943 income. As a result, as the table below indicates, people who earned $50,000 or more had a large tax bill due.

Taxes under the Robertson-Forand Bill, which Passed the House by a 313–95 Vote on May 4, 1943

Income earned in 1942 and in 1943	Taxes Owed in 1943
$10,000	$3,559
$50,000	$45,048
$100,000	$115,985
$1,000,000	$1,564,795
$5,000,000	$7,924,795

Source: Congressional Record, 78th Cong., 1st sess., May 4, 1943, vol. 89, pp. H3957-58; and May 13, 1943, p. S4344.

Naturally, the question arose, "How can we ask our wealthiest citizens, many of whom are very productive in producing war materiel, to pay more than they earn to the government?" Even if the tax debt was stretched out in smaller payments for three years, it would still exceed his income. Rep. Charles Gifford (R-Mass.) stated the problem this way: "For three long years he has to pay more than he receives. How does he pay his other taxes? How does he meet his living expenses?"[35] Rep. Jere Cooper (D-Tenn.) responded, "It may not be possible to pay more than one year's taxes out of one year's income, but, with few exceptions, persons in the higher brackets have assets that they can use to pay it."[36]

Rep. Gifford disagreed. He called such high taxes "class hatred" and said, "This administration [has] set loose the forces of prejudice and disunity."[37] John Jennings of Tennessee said of the American taxpayer, "Heretofore, we have sheared him annually—now it is proposed to skin him." Yes, Jennings conceded, "under the equality of opportunity that our system has afforded to men in every walk of life, we have some rich men." He added, "I do not hold any brief for Henry Ford, but I am glad that he started life with a pair of blue overalls and a monkey wrench and the genius that God Almighty put into his brain, and became a millionaire, because he made other men rich and paid the highest wages that up to that time had ever been paid to the American workingman and covered this whole country with a network of highways."[38]

The following discussion then ensued between Jennings and Rep. George Dondero (R-Mich.):

Rep. Dondero: I might say to the gentleman from Tennessee that the [Henry Ford] plant at River Rouge now employs 110,000.

Rep. Jennings: Of course. And at that great plant bombers are being turned out that mean victory. In my town we have a man born with inventive genius. Weston M. Fulton started from scratch. Today there is a plant in Knoxville, Tennessee, that makes instrumentalities without which we could not operate our submarines. Mr. Fulton is no longer at its head, but other men have trod in his footsteps, men who had inventive genius and vision. They are at the head of a great industry there that employs over 3,000 men, women, boys, and girls in a defense industry. Who would begrudge that man the money he made by founding that great enterprise?

Jennings then changed direction. If we want to discourage wealth and encourage modest attire, perhaps, he suggested, the House should "send for Mahatma Gandhi with his diaper and his nanny-goat and put him at the head of the Ways and Means Committee of this House." Jennings concluded, "The time will come if we continue on down the slippery, steep road we are now on to the precipice that leads to the bottomless pit, the abyss of financial bankruptcy and ruin, the time will come when we can put a taxpayer on exhibition and make money charging admission for people to see him."[39]

Rep. Everett Dirksen (R-Ill.), the future Senate minority leader, attacked high tax rates from a different angle. He noted that Europeans still owed the United States \$11 billion from debts incurred in World War I. "Yet," Dirksen observed, "there is no concern about the money that went to the people of some other country, although there is great concern over a temporary cancelation for our own people." What's more, Dirksen said, Congress had already voted \$38 billion again to Europe for the current war under the Lend-Lease arrangement. "Is there anybody who lives in a rosy, optimistic atmosphere who believes that any of it will ever come back?" he asked. With such large obligations, Dirksen noted, the United States had "the danger of wholesale default through no lack of national devotion on the part of our people but only because of incapacity to pay." Why not, Dirksen wondered, give "a temporary respite to all taxpayers, large and small. Eventually," he concluded, "there will be higher taxes to meet the debt burden and it is idle to even suggest that the large taxpayer will escape."[40]

The Robertson-Forand bill may have easily passed the House, but the Senate defeated it 52 to 27. Senator Robert Taft called the high taxes a "capital levy," and Senator Arthur Vandenberg (R-Mich.) called them "prejudicial class-baiting," and said, "I decline to be any part of it. . . . If we start discriminating, Mr. President," Vandenberg asked, "where shall we stop?" Senator James Davis (R-Pa.) agreed: "By canceling the past year's burden for some taxpayers but not for others, it results in unfairness as between different classes of taxpayers." Davis was a Welsh immigrant who worked much of his life in the steel mills, but he boldly denounced "unfairness as between different classes of taxpayers."[41]

The Senate blocked all double taxation bills, and passed a variation of the Ruml-Carlson bill that canceled income taxes completely for one year—1942 or 1943, whichever was smaller—in return for the steady flow of revenue to the Treasury through withholding. The different result in the Senate can best be explained by the presence of one man: Walter George (D-Ga.). George was chairman of the Senate Finance Committee, and he disliked the idea of confiscating the wealth of the nation's most productive citizens.[42]

But more than that, he loathed Franklin Roosevelt. In 1938, when George was running for reelection to the Senate, the president helped persuade another candidate to run against him in the Democratic primary. Roosevelt alleged that George was too conservative, but what really angered the president was George's refusal in 1937 to support the president's Court-packing plan—whereby he could add justices to the Supreme Court to protect his New Deal programs from being struck down as unconstitutional. FDR even traveled to Georgia and publicly endorsed George's opponent, but the incumbent prevailed and never forgot his snub from his party leader.[43]

Never again was Senator George reliable for the president, and the battle over withholding was one more chance for George to show his independence. Roosevelt wanted heavy taxation on the rich, and George opposed it. He called the double taxation in the Robertson-Forand bill "a complicated and, I think, a most unjust provision."[44] George did favor a small level of double taxation, but he helped prevent the House bill from passing the Senate—and in the end the bill that did pass the Senate canceled the 1942 tax burden completely.

With different bills passing the House and Senate, the two groups of lawmakers organized a conference committee of fourteen members to work out a compromise. Then President Roosevelt jumped into the dispute. He was upset that the Senate had refused to impose double taxation as the House had done. To prevent the Senate bill from being adopted, he threatened a veto if the conference committee accepted the Senate bill. "The Senate bill," the president wrote, "would result in a highly inequitable distribution of the cost of the war and in an unjust and discriminatory enrichment of thousands of taxpayers in the upper income groups." He said, "I am writing you now so that you may know my views and in the hope that a bill may be worked out in conference that I can sign." Then, he added, "I cannot acquiesce in the elimination of a whole year's tax burden on the upper income groups."[45]

Even in the best of circumstances, any conference committee would have had a tough time reconciling conflicting views on withholding and double taxation. But Roosevelt's veto threat stirred up even more emotion. By the end, Senator Vandenberg, one of the conferees, concluded, "The conference was the most difficult in which I have ever participated in all my fifteen years in the Senate."[46] Vandenberg and his fellow senators held out against double taxation, or "prejudicial class-baiting," as Vandenberg had called it. But with the veto threat and with the urgent desire to get the tax system current, the conferees finally worked out a compromise called the Current Tax Payment Act of 1943.

The main feature of the compromise was that one-fourth of everyone's income tax burden for 1942 would still have to be paid. Thus, FDR got his double taxation, but not at rates as high as the House bill. The one-fourth of the 1942 tax bill owed by many Americans could be spread out in installments and added to their tax bills in 1944 and 1945. Married people with no dependents who annually earned $500,000, for example, would have to pay a 98.7 percent tax rate in 1944 and in 1945. The rate went over 100 percent for million-dollar incomes. Those who earned $1 million each year of the war, for example, would owe $1,006,750 in both 1944 and 1945.[47] "When we get up to incomes of this size," Senator Allen Ellender (D-La.) insisted, "I submit that the taxpayer is likely to have accumulated sufficient assets with which to make the necessary income payments."[48]

The Current Tax Payment Act of 1943, signed into law on June 9, had special provisions for taxing windfall profits and included surtaxes, normal taxes, victory taxes, and special rates for soldiers. The following exchange between Senator Edwin Johnson (D-Colo.) and Senator George shows how complicated paying taxes had become:

Senator Johnson: I have just received two telegrams, and one of them, from a trust officer of one of the large Denver banks, presents this question: "Have been attempting to apply proposed Current Tax Payment Act of 1943 to specific case of the beneficiary of a large trust created by will in 1942. The beneficiary will receive an estimated one-hundred-and-sixty-odd thousand dollars of fully taxable income during 1943, and it appears that her total federal taxes payable from that income, including normal tax, surtax, unforgiven portion of 1942 tax, windfall tax, and Victory tax will aggregate slightly more than her total income from the trust during 1943. . . . [T]he beneficiary is without sufficient capital funds with which to pay deficiency and pay expenses until income from future years is received." Was provision [in the bill] made for such a condition?

Senator George: If the income was received in 1943, I assume the tax for that year was higher than the tax for 1942. In that case the second windfall tax will only apply to the year 1942, and only to that year if in excess of the income for the normal year plus $20,000. So far as the second windfall is concerned the conference agreement permits the taxpayer to take the highest income he received in 1937, 1938, 1939, or 1940, and increase that income by $20,000. Then the unabated 1942 tax which results under the second windfall is payable in four annual installments, beginning in March 1945. It is payable in four installments—that is, on March 15, 1945, March 15, 1946, March 15, 1947, and March 15, 1948. I do not, therefore, believe that this windfall provision is as harsh on the taxpayer described in the telegram as might appear at first blush.[49]

Senator George's answer didn't even address the different tax rates that applied to soldiers, the different timing of taxing for farmers, and the need for some taxpayers to send in estimated earnings for the future. Robert Doughton, chairman of the House Ways and Means Committee, was one of the conferees who forged the Current Tax Payment Act of 1943, but he was as confused as

Senator Johnson and his Denver banker. Congressman Knutson, Doughton noted, "has asked the House to instruct its conferees to accept a bill, a part of which I am sure he does not understand, and I know I do not understand. In fact, I have never found any member of this body who does understand all of it. I have discussed it with our experts, and they seem to be puzzled over parts of it."[50]

While most Americans puzzled over the new tax system, Roosevelt was ready for his next move—raising the rates. On August 1, less than two months after Roosevelt signed the Current Tax Payment Act of 1943, he warned Congress that he continued to want "a truly stiff program of additional taxes." Specifically, Roosevelt (through Morgenthau) soon urged Congress to raise $10.5 billion in new taxes in a Revenue Act of 1943. "Four-fifths of all the income of the nation is going to people earning less than $5,000 a year," Morgenthau observed. Thus, there was "a great deal of room" for higher tax rates. Congress, however, did not want to be dragged into a significant tax hike, especially near an election year. Individual taxes, Rep. Knutson complained, had gone up 2,500 percent since 1940. Should Congress further tax the wages of stenographers who made $35 a week, he asked? Instead, why not cut "unnecessary and wasteful" New Deal spending? Rep. Doughton concluded that the country had done about "all the taxing that 1944 and 1945 could endure."[51]

The Senate and the House, therefore, enacted only minor changes in the Revenue Act of 1943. Roosevelt was annoyed, and used his State of the Union speech in 1944 to prod Congress to "tax all unreasonable profits, both individual and corporate." But with the top income tax rate at almost 100 percent, and the excess profits tax on corporations reaching 90 percent, few people had any chance to make "unreasonable profits." Rep. A. Willis Robertson (D-Va.) implicitly stressed that point when he urged Congress not to reconsider FDR's old bill to tax all income over $25,000 at 100 percent—the rates were almost that severe anyway, Robertson noted.[52]

In fact, the tax code had become so complex, and it drained so much wealth, that many voting groups around the country now had strong incentives to visit Washington and lobby for special treatment. Natural gas producers, for example, wanted an exemption from the excess profits tax for their pipelines. Miners of vermiculite, potash, and feldspar (among others) wanted "depletion allowance" tax breaks for the minerals they were mining for the war effort. The Metropolitan Opera Association came to Washington to beg for an exemption from the federal tax on tickets. The governor of Florida complained about the 5 percent tax on bets at the horse races. Jewelers arrived in Washington to protest the tax on jewelry, and so on.[53] Some of these interest groups succeeded; others did not. All the while, the tax code became more complex, more arbitrary, and impossible to defend, or even understand, in its entirety.

The Revenue Act of 1943 reached the president's desk on February 22, 1944, and he was irritated that most tax rates were not raised. He vetoed the bill and called it "not a tax bill but a tax relief bill providing relief not for the needy but for the greedy." He denounced the "indefensible privileges to special groups" and lamented that little new revenue would be forthcoming. He readily admitted that tax forms were "so complex that even certified public accountants cannot interpret them," but he did not want to reduce the high tax rates that made pleas for special treatment almost inevitable. If redistributing wealth is a major goal of public policy, then the tax code is bound to become a complex instrument for social engineering.[54]

Congress was indignant at the president's veto, and in no mood to go back in session to raise tax rates. Senator George, chairman of the Senate Finance Committee, said there was such a thing as "too much taxes." He refused "to cut down the tree in order to get the fruit." On the House side, nineteen of the twenty-five members of the House Ways and Means Committee signed a statement declaring the president's proposed $10.5 billion tax hike to be "oppressive to taxpayers and dangerous to the national economy." It "would threaten the solvency of all business and undermine its ability to provide jobs when the war ends." Congress, in other words, was looking to private enterprise, not a New Deal revival, to "provide jobs when the war ends."[55]

On February 24, Congress voted to override the president's veto by 299 to 95 in the House and 72 to 14 in the Senate. Rep. Doughton said he "couldn't maintain" his "self respect" if he didn't vote to override FDR's veto. Senator Alben Barkley (D-Ky.) went further. After denouncing the president's veto, he resigned as Senate majority leader. According to Senator Claude Pepper (D-Fla.), after Barkley's speech and resignation, "The senators, with three or four exceptions, arose and applauded. Then they filed by Barkley's seat to shake his hand while the packed galleries cheered."[56] The Democrats later reelected Barkley as majority leader. This tension between a more conservative Congress and Roosevelt made the president all the more anxious to win a fourth term and elect those with him who wanted higher taxes and more government spending.

10

FDR AND CIVIL LIBERTIES

FDR amazed friends and enemies alike by his willingness to break laws and bend the Constitution. Arthur Krock of the *New York Times* described Roosevelt's "cynical approach to the trade of politics" and his desire to "punish" his critics "by questionable use of the great powers of the presidency."[1] But in defense of the president, Attorney General Robert Jackson stated FDR's beliefs this way:

> The President had a tendency to think in terms of right and wrong, instead of terms of legal and illegal. Because he thought that his motives were always good for the things that he wanted to do, he found difficulty in thinking that there could be legal limitations on them. The President was not a legalistic-minded person.[2]

Jackson has a point. On wiretapping, for example, Roosevelt broke the law and ordered wiretaps because he thought he was doing so in the national interest. In December 1939, the Supreme Court, in *Nardone v. United States*, barred federal officials from using wiretaps in law enforcement. Jackson, who became attorney general one month later, therefore ordered an end to wiretaps for gathering evidence. Roosevelt was upset with this ruling, and tried to get Congress to pass a law endorsing limited wiretaps in the national defense. When that failed, Roosevelt told Jackson that the

Supreme Court surely did not want to stop wiretaps if the nation was in danger. The *Nardone* decision might be all right for normal times, FDR conceded, but it could be ignored in wartime. "You are, therefore," Roosevelt told Jackson:

> authorized and directed in such cases as you may approve, after investigation of the need in each case, to authorize the necessary investigating agents that they are at liberty to secure information by listening devices direct to the conversation or other communications of persons suspected of subversive activities against the Government of the United States, including suspected spies. You are requested furthermore to limit these investigations so conducted to a minimum and to limit them insofar as possible to aliens.[3]

Jackson reluctantly went along with Roosevelt's illegal wiretaps with the understanding that they would be few, would be mainly restricted to aliens, and would be undertaken only in the national defense. Unfortunately, Roosevelt soon added "potential political enemies" to this list, and then added "political friends" as well. As John Roosevelt, the president's son, said later, "Hell, my father just about invented bugging. [He] had them spread all over, and thought nothing of it."[4]

For example, Roosevelt called in J. Edgar Hoover, head of the FBI, and told him that James Farley, the postmaster general, was talking to Raymond Tucker, editor of the *Hartford Courant* and sometime critic of Roosevelt. "I want you to tap Farley's wire," Roosevelt ordered. "I couldn't do that to a member of the cabinet, Mr. President," Hoover responded. "However, I will tap Ray Tucker's wire." Later, Hoover did wiretaps on Thomas Corcoran, Harry Hopkins, and Vice President Henry Wallace, all staunch friends of the president. Hoover also did wiretaps and investigations of Eleanor Roosevelt and her secretary.[5]

FDR's main targets, however, were his political opponents. For example, in 1940 Roosevelt instructed the FBI to do surveillance on former president Herbert Hoover. Roosevelt had heard a rumor that Hoover was exchanging cablegrams with French premier Pierre Laval, and the president wanted to know what was being said. J. Edgar Hoover checked any telegrams, but came up with no evidence that the two had been talking or writing to each other. In September 1941, Roosevelt tried again to catch former president Hoover in some indiscretion. He asked James Fly, chairman of the Federal Communications Commission (FCC), to see if Hoover was supplying isolationists with material to use against Roosevelt. Fly could not find such evidence, but told the president he would keep trying.[6]

Roosevelt had more success with his FBI investigation of Wendell Willkie during the 1940 presidential campaign. Hoover reported that Willkie was having a not-so-secret affair with writer Irita Van Doren. Roosevelt was willing to use such information if necessary in the campaign, but he told his staff he had to be cautious not to let anyone know the president was the one leaking the Willkie story. To Lowell Mellett, a former reporter and current FDR staffer, the president said, "Spread it as a word of mouth thing, or by some people way, way down the line. We can't have any of our principal speakers refer to it, but the people down the line can get it out." Ultimately, FDR did not expose the Willkie affair, but he always had it in reserve: "Now, now if they want to play dirty politics in the end, we've got our own people." During the campaign, Harold Ickes also asked the FBI to check on Willkie's ethnic background to see if he was Polish, but had changed his name to sound German. Ickes thought that if that was true, then leaking such information would damage Willkie with Polish-American voters. Hoover declined to do this background check, and FDR never insisted it be done. But Hoover investigated over two hundred of Roosevelt's political enemies during the 1940 campaign.[7]

Roosevelt and Hoover sometimes joked about their illegal wiretaps. For example, Hoover tried to bug the hotel room of

214 Burton W. Folsom, Jr., and Anita Folsom

Harry Bridges, a union radical in San Francisco, but was "caught in the act," he told Roosevelt. The president laughed, slapped Hoover on the back, and joyfully retorted, "By God, Edgar, that's the first time you've been caught with your pants down!"[8]

Roosevelt was especially interested in wiretapping reporters from unfriendly newspapers. Walter Trohan, for example, was a prominent reporter for the *Chicago Tribune*, perhaps the newspaper most critical of the president. Trohan deplored Roosevelt's constant wiretaps. The "taps continued on my home [and office] throughout the war," Trohan complained. "There was seldom a dull moment for me. All of my better news sources knew of the wiretaps, so we had to arrange outside meetings for transmission of news."[9]

Trohan's boss, Robert McCormick, was editor of the *Chicago Tribune* and the primary focus of FDR's wrath. McCormick embraced liberty, and he attacked FDR right from the start of his presidency. There is no question McCormick could be outrageous. He insisted that patronage dispenser James Farley was working "behind the smiling mask of Franklin Roosevelt to bring the end of self-government in the world." In 1941, McCormick called Lend-Lease the "dictator bill." After Pearl Harbor, McCormick called for Secretary Knox's resignation. Finally, during 1942, the *Tribune* announced that Roosevelt was running the war as "a bigger and gaudier WPA project." McCormick was also eccentric: He liked to swim in the nude, stockpile pineapple juice, and sing incoherently in his vegetable garden. But he had a flair for news, and his *Chicago Tribune* may have been the most widely read newspaper in the Midwest.[10]

Roosevelt always said McCormick hated him because he had stolen a girlfriend from McCormick as a young teen at Groton. McCormick brushed off this boast as "another one of Frank's shallow lies," but whatever the truth, their enmity endured during the whole of World War II. In fact, Roosevelt constantly used the power of government against McCormick. As a first step, the president confiscated at least one of McCormick's ships for government use during wartime. Early in the war, when the *Chicago Tribune* ran a story critical of the government, agents from the Treasury Department burst into *Tribune* headquarters to investigate.[11]

FDR undercut McCormick whenever possible. In 1942, when McCormick tried to publish a GI newspaper in England, FDR called Churchill to stop the project. When War Production Board officials granted an increase in supplies to the *Chicago Sun*, a newspaper favored by FDR, they denied the same request from the *Tribune*. Secretary Knox of the Navy was on salary with the *Chicago Daily News*, and he often helped his paper get exclusive coverage of naval news. When McCormick finally got a scoop on the Battle of Midway, however, he was attacked by Knox and Roosevelt for allegedly revealing wartime secrets. In fact, Attorney General Francis Biddle indicted McCormick for violating the Espionage Act of 1917, but the grand jury sided with McCormick. "We have said and proved that we cannot be intimidated," McCormick gloated. Senator Robert Taft concluded that if the *Tribune* could be indicted, "No editor in the United States is safe."[12]

Roosevelt's war with McCormick left collateral damage all over Chicago. Publishers who supported McCormick in his struggles with the president sometimes found the FBI on their cases as well. For example, the *Chicago Herald-American* decided to back McCormick in denying an Associated Press membership to the *Chicago Sun*. Soon the publisher of the *Chicago Herald-American* found FBI agents at his doorstep to cross-examine him about his decision.[13]

McCormick had two cousins, Joseph Patterson and Cissy Patterson, who published powerful newspapers in New York and Washington, D.C. Joseph Patterson's *New York Daily News* was one of the largest-circulation newspapers in the country. Cissy Patterson's *Washington Times-Herald* dominated the capital area. Both Pattersons, brother and sister, had been friendly to the New

Deal and supported Roosevelt well into 1940. But they were isolationists, and openly opposed Roosevelt's drift to war in 1941. When that happened, Roosevelt became almost as angry with them as he was with McCormick.

After the attack on Pearl Harbor, all three publishers united to win the war. Joseph Patterson, a World War I officer, spoke for many isolationists when he said in an editorial: "Well, we're in it. God knows Americans didn't want it. But let's get behind our President and fight for America first." Then, he made a special visit to FDR to offer his services. "I am here, Mr. President, to see what aid I can be in the war effort." Roosevelt, however, responded, "There is one thing you can do, Joe, and that is to go back and read your editorials for the past six months. Read every one of them and think what you've done." Patterson, the president said, had actually influenced Congress and had set back the war effort. After fifteen minutes of denunciation, Patterson said, "He told me to pass on the word to Cissy to behave herself." After that visit, both Pattersons joined McCormick in regularly denouncing Roosevelt's handling of the war.[14]

Roosevelt tried to get McCormick and the Pattersons indicted for sedition. In a conversation with Attorney General Biddle on April 22, 1942, Roosevelt attacked the "subversive mind of Cissy Patterson." He asked Biddle to make sure he "put a surveillance on her and on Col. [Joseph] Patterson," but Biddle assured the president that such surveillance was already being done. The next month, Roosevelt warned Biddle that the "tie in between the attitude of these papers [the *Chicago Tribune*, the *New York Daily News*, and the *Washington Times-Herald*] and the Rome-Berlin broadcasts" was "something far greater than mere coincidence." Earlier, when Roosevelt said, "I am convinced that Lindbergh is a Nazi," he really believed it.[15] In the same way, he also seems to have genuinely believed that McCormick and the Pattersons were either Nazis or Nazi sympathizers.

Roosevelt's minions worked overtime to get evidence on them.

The heads of the FBI, the Department of Justice, and the Office of Facts and Figures (OFF) all subjected these publishers and their newspapers to microscopic investigation for Nazi connections, but found none and had to abandon their efforts. Roosevelt could not send them to jail or shut down their papers, but he could at least humiliate them from time to time. John O'Donnell, for example, was a columnist for Patterson's *New York Daily News*, and he criticized the president's foreign policy during the first year of the war. As a result, O'Donnell was investigated by the FBI and was denied press credentials from the War Department; at a press conference in December 1942, FDR publicly awarded him the "Nazi Iron Cross" in absentia.[16]

Even the *New York Times* was suspect in Roosevelt's eyes. He was especially upset with columnist Arthur Krock, who often supported the president but sometimes opposed him. Roosevelt wrote a friend, "I am all in favor of chloroforming for certain newspaper men. Not Drew Pearson alone—but some of the more subtle murderers like Arthur Krock." As early as July 1939, FDR asked Morgenthau to do a tax audit of the *New York Times*. "I would like you to investigate a couple of companies for me especially," the president said. "Now take the *New York Times*, for example. Not that I have got anything against [its publisher] Arthur Sulzberger, but he's just plain stupid." Morgenthau asked, "What do you want me to do?" Roosevelt responded, "Well, where did they get the money from to pay their income tax?" Morgenthau said, "They got it from the Times Company. They bought back preferred stock."[17]

Morgenthau, who was loyal to the president, was clearly unnerved by FDR's investigations. For example, when Roosevelt had the Secret Service trace the source of a critical story in the *Wall Street Journal*, Morgenthau reacted, "I will not have the Secret Service used for this purpose."[18] But Morgenthau, despite his reservations, often did help Roosevelt use the IRS against political opponents.

"My father," Elliott Roosevelt observed of his famous parent, "may have been the originator of the concept of employing the IRS as a weapon of political retribution." For example, Roosevelt had the *Chicago Tribune* audited by the IRS as early as 1937, and also subjected McCormick to a personal audit. But McCormick and his newspaper had their books in order. To do so meant McCormick was paying $523,000 in taxes on $795,000 income—almost two of every three dollars he earned went to the government. Moses Annenberg, editor of the *Philadelphia Inquirer*, did not do as well. Annenberg repeatedly attacked Roosevelt and the New Deal for causing persistent unemployment, and thus the president had the Treasury Department launch an IRS investigation of Annenberg that ultimately sent him to prison.[19]

Both before and during the war, Roosevelt wanted to do the same to Congressman Hamilton Fish. Fish was a Republican congressman who represented Roosevelt's home district in Hyde Park. Roosevelt was outraged that Fish could attack him so vigorously on his home ground and yet survive so easily on election day. Fish was a regular critic of the New Deal, and later opposed Lend-Lease and other foreign interventions. Roosevelt tried to help Democrats defeat Fish, but his hard campaigning kept him winning reelection. In 1942, Fish overcame Roosevelt's active opposition and denounced the president for the "collectivism of the New Deal and its Gestapo methods that threaten free government."[20]

In 1939, Roosevelt told Cordell Hull, "I think the time has come to make a careful check-up on Mr. Fish." At the time, Roosevelt was thinking of indicting Fish for a speech he had made in Europe, but Hull suggested Fish was protected by the First Amendment. Then came the IRS. Fish had a thorough audit in the late 1930s and was assessed a fine. Fish complained that the IRS had "manufacture[d] a tax case against me" and challenged the results. Finally, after much back and forth, Fish gloated that "the Treasury Department admitted that it had erred—and gave me a refund of eighty dollars." For five years, the IRS "minutely investigated" Fish's tax returns, and those of his wife. In 1942, after another IRS audit, Fish crowed, "the Treasury Department was unable to fabricate a case against me. Quite simply, I had done nothing wrong." [21]

Roosevelt also had wiretaps put on Fish's phone. According to Fish, Senator Clyde Reed called to tell him that his "phone was being tapped, and so were those of many other Republican members of Congress." Years later, Fish said, "You might ask why I didn't complain to Speaker Rayburn when I found out that my wires were being tapped. There is a simple answer. He would have told me that there was nothing I could do about it." [22] William C. Sullivan, an FBI agent, seems to confirm Fish's view. Years after the war, Sullivan said, "Electronic devices were used freely all through World War II, with a minimum of controls. President Roosevelt made requests of various kinds." [23]

Tax audits were a key Roosevelt weapon—even when they failed, they created worry and embarrassment for the target. Charles Lindbergh, for example, was both wiretapped and audited after opposing Roosevelt and his foreign policy in 1940. When asked about the IRS, he told reporters he regularly overpaid his taxes because he was proud to be an American. Thus, the audit on him came to naught. Later, Roosevelt tried an IRS audit on John L. Lewis, head of the United Mine Workers (UMW). Roosevelt had done wiretaps on Lewis before, but no IRS audit until Lewis led his coal miners on strike in 1943. At that time, Roosevelt's staff searched for errors in Lewis's tax return. Unfortunately, as Attorney General Biddle pointed out to FDR, "When you shoot at a king you have to hit him." [24] They couldn't hit Lewis. His tax records, like those of Lindbergh, Fish, and McCormick, were in order.

With the IRS unleashed, it sometimes investigated tax dodgers who happened to be friends of the president. That created problems for Roosevelt. In the case of Lyndon Johnson, even though he was only a young Texas congressman, he was valuable to the president. During FDR's second term, Johnson spied on two Texas politicians, Vice President John Nance Garner and House Speaker Sam Rayburn. Garner opposed FDR's third term, and Rayburn was essential to helping Roosevelt get bills through Congress. Johnson's relaying of information to Roosevelt on Garner, Rayburn, and others helped him win a huge defense contract in 1940 for Corpus Christi, as discussed earlier. Johnson made sure that his friends at the construction firm of Brown & Root won the contract. Brown & Root, in turn, financed Johnson's run for the U.S. Senate in 1941. The problem was that "Brown & Root had deducted hundreds of thousands of dollars in 'bonuses' and 'fees' that IRS agents now suspected were actually disguised contributions [to Lyndon Johnson]." At Johnson's desperate urging, Roosevelt intervened with the IRS in 1944 to squelch the case. FDR called the IRS and shut down the investigation. Brown & Root made a drastically scaled-down payment to the IRS, and Johnson was never indicted, or even touched by the scandal.[25]

The IRS, the FBI, and the Department of Justice supplied much information to Roosevelt on his political opponents. But he wanted his own private espionage network. Even before the war, for example, Roosevelt asked his distant cousin Vincent Astor, who was on the board of directors of Western Union Cable Company, to spy on international callers. Breaking into international cables, like wiretapping, was a federal crime, but Astor broke into cables from Mexico, Spain, and Brazil to gather information for the president on foreign affairs. Astor assured FDR that he was eavesdropping "in accordance with your wishes." Roosevelt also hired John Franklin Carter, a pro–New Deal columnist, to assemble a staff and spy for the president. The funds Roosevelt used to finance Carter were well disguised in the federal budget, and all during World War II Carter was the president's private spy. Sometimes Carter's missions were in Europe, and sometimes in America—for example, Roosevelt wanted Carter to get something on Senator Burt Wheeler that the FBI could then use against him.

Another one of Carter's tasks was to snoop on fellow snooper Vincent Astor.[26]

Roosevelt seems to have secured the best espionage results from J. Edgar Hoover and the FBI. The president would regularly send the hostile mail he received to Hoover and ask him to "go over" the names and addresses. By wiretaps, surveillance, and even opening mail illegally, Hoover assembled files on thousands of real or imagined political enemies of the president. From A. Philip Randolph, the black leader, to Charles Coughlin, the radio priest, Hoover wiretapped and kept meticulous files. Roosevelt was able to get Coughlin taken off the radio, and then denied him use of the mail during wartime to distribute his publication, *Social Justice*. Hoover's surveillance of congressmen was so extensive that he sometimes advised the president on legislation ready to come before Congress for a vote. Some of FDR's advisors feared and deplored Hoover. Henry Stimson said, "He goes to the White House . . . and poisons the mind of the president." General Marshall called Hoover "more of a spoiled child than a responsible officer." But all agreed that Hoover was effective and powerful.[27]

Investigating political opponents was a major goal, but Roosevelt also wanted Hoover to focus on external threats. Communists Roosevelt tended to ignore because the United States was allied with Russia. In fact, Roosevelt pardoned Earl Browder, the head of the Communist Party in America, who was in prison for passport fraud. However, Roosevelt believed that the German-American Bund, the Silver Shirts, and other fascist groups warranted FBI scrutiny. Hoover concluded that by 1941, the American fascists had self-destructed; they were few in number and had little influence. Roosevelt's main target among the fascists was William Dudley Pelley, a small-time publisher who praised Hitler, attacked Roosevelt, and supported the isolationists. Six weeks after Pearl Harbor, Roosevelt wrote Hoover that Pelley had "started a new publication called 'The Galilean' and that some of the stuff appearing therein comes pretty close to being seditious."

He added, "Now that we are in the war, it looks like a good chance to clean up a number of these vile publications."[28]

Cleanup time came in March, when Pelley wrote in *The Galilean* that "Japanese bombers made Pearl Harbor look like an abandoned W. P. A. project in Keokuk." Roosevelt, Pelley proclaimed, had lied when he announced that the American fleet was largely intact. An infuriated Roosevelt had his postmaster stop Pelley's second-class mailing privileges. Then the president badgered Attorney General Biddle at cabinet meetings: "When are you going to indict the seditionists?" Biddle couldn't nail McCormick or the Pattersons, but he did indict Pelley, and the jury found him guilty of seditious libel and sentenced him to fifteen years in prison. Law professor Geoffrey Stone, at the University of Chicago, has studied that trial and contends Pelley lost the case because he had a terrible lawyer. Pelley, in Stone's view, was foolish and deceived, but he was more accurate than FDR on Pearl Harbor and was no threat to national security. Of the several dozen fascists indicted by Biddle, Pelley's was a rare conviction.[29]

Although Roosevelt used wiretaps, the IRS, and grand jury investigations as sticks against political opponents, he also liked to use carrots as incentives to encourage cooperation. The RFC, which had tens of billions of dollars to loan, was a useful carrot dispenser for the president. Jesse Jones, a wealthy Texan, was Roosevelt's man to head the RFC, and he and Roosevelt worked well together. Jones helped those the president sent his way—either through RFC loans or by using influence with others to loan the money. J. David Stern, for example, edited the *Philadelphia Record*, which was Roosevelt's newspaper in Philadelphia. Stern backed Roosevelt and other Democrats enthusiastically during election campaigns. Stern, however, almost went bankrupt before the war, so Roosevelt asked Jones to help. Jones used his influence in the banking community to secure $1 million worth of loans to keep Stern publishing.[30]

Some reporters were sensitive to the RFC money and influence offered by Jones. Walter Trohan, for example, the Washington bureau chief for the *Chicago Tribune*, often interviewed Jones, and according to Trohan, Jones would often offer RFC loans to him. "Jones frequently offered me a tool company or some other business the RFC controlled, offering to lend me the money to operate it. I turned these offers down, because I didn't know anything about such businesses and because I didn't think I would be honest in accepting." [31] If Trohan had taken an RFC loan, Roosevelt could have gained a foothold in penetrating the hated *Chicago Tribune*.

Others did not have Trohan's scruples. Hall Roosevelt, the president's brother-in-law, used White House telephones to request loans from the RFC. According to Jones, "Two or three loans were made in which it appeared Hall Roosevelt had some kind of interest." At one point, the president urged Jones to give Hall the loan he requested because, in Jones's words, "The president wanted to get Hall as far from the White House as possible." [32]

Roosevelt's son Elliott also needed Jones's help at RFC. In the late 1930s, Elliott invested in the Texas State Network, a radio chain based in Fort Worth, Texas. Despite a $200,000 loan to Elliott from John Hartford, president of the A&P chain stores, Elliott's radio network went bankrupt. On December 14, 1941, the week after Pearl Harbor, Roosevelt called Jones for help. According to Jones, FDR said that "he would appreciate it very much if I would confer with Elliott's creditors and see what, if anything, they would be willing to do about his debts." Jones had Elliott visit Hartford and had him call the White House. He did, and suddenly Hartford, who had never met the president, heard Roosevelt's voice. "Hello, John," the president said jovially. "While any business you have with my son must stand on its own merits, I will appreciate anything you do for him." Roosevelt added, "When you are in Washington come in to see me." Hartford was elated to receive that invitation because A&P, according to Jones, "was being sued by the Federal Trade Commission under the antimonopoly laws." Hartford happily canceled Elliott's debt by selling his worthless stock in Elliott's company to Jesse Jones himself. As Jones noted, "Many rich people [like Hartford] would give or spend that much for a friendship with the President of the United States and his family—especially with the Roosevelts."[33]

Roosevelt indeed used the RFC for political purposes, but to be fair so did Republicans when Hoover was in the White House and the RFC was first started in 1932. True, Hoover never used the head of the RFC to help family members, but cabinet members, such as Roy Chapin; Republican senators, such as Phillips Goldsborough of Maryland; and Republican Party officials, such as Joseph Nutt, treasurer of the Republican National Committee, all received RFC loans for banks in which they were heavily invested. In fact, Republican Charles Dawes, former U.S. vice president, resigned as head of the RFC, and less than three weeks later accepted a $90 million loan for his Central Republic Bank and Trust Company in Chicago. Thus, Roosevelt could always say to critics that with the RFC, he was merely emulating his predecessors.[34]

Roosevelt wanted to have the media be as compliant as his federal agencies. With newspapers that was almost impossible, and he would often fume at the many editorials he read each day. Roosevelt, however, was able to work his charm on some of the reporters. He usually held two press conferences per week during the war, and he often shaped news coverage through his personal touch. "If I were writing this story, here is how I would write it," Roosevelt would tell them, and then slip in his point of view. He also invited reporters to special social events, shook their hands, and bantered with them about life in Washington.[35]

Radio was much easier for Roosevelt to manipulate because radio could operate only on government-regulated airwaves. The FCC was a controlling force in the radio industry, and the president appointed the head of the FCC. Also, after a change in policy under Roosevelt, radio stations were forced to renew their licenses every six months instead of every three years. Thus, radio broadcasters needed some favor with the president to guarantee their continued operation. The war increased Roosevelt's authority over radio even more. The Communications Act of 1934 gave the president the power to control broadcasting in a national emergency. Five days after Germany invaded Poland, Roosevelt declared a "limited national emergency." Radio's independence, as Press Secretary Steve Early explained, was conditional. If radio during the war was "well mannered, it would be left to move along on its own." But if it should prove "to be a bad child, there would, I think, be a disposition to . . . correct it and make it behave itself." When many radio broadcasters moved quickly to support the president, FDR announced he would use radio more and newspapers less to convey news. By 1940, journalist Quincy Howe concluded that on foreign policy "all regular radio news broadcasts gently, firmly, and consistently support Roosevelt to the exclusion of any other point of view."[36]

Some broadcasters became cheerleaders for FDR. Raymond Gram Swing, a popular broadcaster, sought to explain "the correctness of every move toward greater overseas involvement made by Roosevelt." By 1939, New Dealer and diplomat Adolf Berle reported that Walter Winchell, the columnist and broadcaster, offered to "put his radio time at our disposition . . . to develop any angle of foreign affairs the administration might deem worthwhile."[37]

The movie industry, like radio, complied with Roosevelt's wishes for intervention sentiment before Pearl Harbor and patriotic sentiment afterward. Just as the FCC exerted control over radio, so the Justice Department supervised the movie studios. Lowell Mellett, Roosevelt's advisor on media relations, told Roosevelt in 1941 that the movie industry was "pretty well living up to its offers of cooperation." He added, "The fact [is] that the picture industry is conscious of the Justice Department just as the radio industry was of the FCC." Federal regulation had, in practice, led Roosevelt to federal control of both radio and movies even before Pearl Harbor.[38]

The most blatant violation of civil liberties under FDR was the internment of Japanese-Americans. Japan's heinous attack on Pearl Harbor naturally exposed those Americans of Japanese descent to special scrutiny. But investigators found little evidence that civilians of Japanese ancestry gave help to Japan through espionage and sabotage. Nonetheless, almost 120,000 Japanese-Americans, most of them citizens, were rounded up and herded into ten "relocation centers," mainly located in the western states. Such a violation of the Constitution was unprecedented in U.S. history, and Roosevelt had a variety of pressures that led him to make such a decision. Alleged "military necessity" was one, but political expediency was another. In both cases, Roosevelt gained more than he lost politically by the internments.

Japanese-Americans lived mostly in the western states, especially California, where many worked as vegetable farmers. The Native Sons and Daughters of the Golden West and other racist groups had long opposed Japanese immigration. Also, some entrenched farmers resented competition from foreigners. The disaster at Pearl Harbor, and rumors of espionage and sabotage by Japanese-Americans, gave these racist groups extra influence. "We're charged with wanting to get rid of the Japs for selfish reasons," said a leader of California's Grower-Shipper Vegetable Association. "We may as well be honest. We do. It's a question of whether the white man lives on the Pacific Coast or the brown man." Congressman Leland Ford in Los Angeles reflected these views when he recommended that "all Japanese, whether citizens or not, be placed in inland concentration camps." California attorney general Earl Warren, who would win election as governor in 1942, was especially sensitive to these racist pleas: "We believe that when we are dealing with the Caucasian race we have methods that will test the loyalty of them. . . . But," Warren insisted, "when we deal with the Japanese we are in an entirely different field and we cannot form any opinion that we believe to be sound." [39]

General John DeWitt was head of the Western Defense Command, and his judgment would shape the military opinion on the loyalty of the Japanese-Americans and on the safety of the Pacific Coast from espionage and sabotage. With strong cooperation from Japanese-Americans after Pearl Harbor, DeWitt at first insisted their liberty be protected. "An American citizen, after all, is an American citizen." After two months of pressure and wild, unproven rumors, however, DeWitt concluded, "A Jap's a Jap. . . . It makes no difference whether he is an American citizen or not." He recommended forcibly removing all Japanese-Americans from the Pacific Coast, and Henry Stimson accepted that view even though, as Stimson earlier noted, it would "make a tremendous hole in our constitutional system." On February 11, Stimson met with Roosevelt to promote relocation, and "fortunately found that he was very vigorous about it and [he] told me to go ahead on the line that I had myself thought the best."[40]

Roosevelt took a big step to sign an executive order that denied civil liberties to a whole ethnic group, mostly citizens, on the basis of rumor, fear, self-interest, and "military necessity." The ACLU called it "the worst single wholesale violation of civil rights of American citizens in our history." The Japanese-Americans were given no habeas corpus, no protection against search and seizure, and no protection of their property—which most of them therefore sold quickly for whatever they could get. Then they were taken to remote compounds, fenced in with barbed wire, and watched by armed sentries with searchlights, and sometimes machine guns. In those one-square-mile compounds they were lodged in flimsy pine barracks with thin walls, community bathrooms, and porous floors, which let in swirling dust and sand both day and night. They were charged with no crime, but their imprisonment was indefinite.[41]

FDR knew from his own investigations that most Japanese-Americans were loyal citizens. J. Edgar Hoover, for example, who had the best espionage network in the country, always insisted that the Japanese-Americans were overwhelmingly loyal, and should not be forcibly removed from their homes. He should know. His agents broke into Japanese consular offices and grabbed a summary they found of Japan's spy system in the United States. What spying existed, Hoover and others controlled and stopped. Thus, in Hoover's "Personal and Confidential" memo, written on February 7, 1942, he disputed charge after charge of espionage and sabotage. At one point earlier he wrote FDR, "I thought the Army was getting a bit hysterical," and he privately held to that position throughout the war. "The necessity for mass evacuation is based primarily upon public and political pressure rather than on factual data," Hoover observed. In 1943, Hoover sent Roosevelt a 480-page report on the subject, and advocated "individual" treatment, not "mass" confinement.[42]

Hoover's conclusions did not surprise FDR, because even before Pearl Harbor he had authorized John Franklin Carter, his personal spy, to investigate the Japanese-Americans. Carter hired businessman Curtis Munson to do firsthand detective work with the Japanese-Americans, and with others who knew them. In October and early November 1941, Carter and Munson sent the president glowing reports of Japanese-American loyalty. "They are pathetically eager to show this loyalty," Munson discovered. Carter concluded that while a few "Japanese in the United States" were dangerous, "for the most part the local Japanese are loyal to the United States or, at worst, hope that by remaining quiet they can avoid concentration camps or irresponsible mobs."[43]

If there was any danger, it would have been in Hawaii, where Secretary Knox fanned false rumors that Japanese-Americans had aided the attack on Pearl Harbor. But in Hawaii the Japanese-Americans were never interned. Hawaiian officials pointed out that they were needed to harvest crops and that, in any case, there were too many of them to confine anywhere. But if those rules applied to Hawaii, it was hard to apply different rules on the mainland. General DeWitt partly gave the show away when, in response to the absence of attacks by Japanese-Americans, he said,

"The very fact that no sabotage has taken place to date is a disturbing and confirming indication that such action will be taken."[44]

The political motive for FDR's move becomes clearer when we see that he never seriously considered interning large numbers of immigrants or citizens from Germany or Italy, even though we were at war with those countries. In fact, the United States had six hundred thousand Italian immigrants who were not citizens, and were therefore designated "enemy aliens." FDR chose to announce on Columbus Day, 1942, just three weeks before the midterm elections, that immigrants from Italy who were not citizens would no longer be labeled "enemy aliens."[45]

In Roosevelt's political calculations, he wanted votes from German-Americans and Italian-Americans. He also wanted to carry California and the western states. By relocating only the Japanese-Americans, he could please native Californians and not offend the many ethnic Germans and Italians he would need to win reelection in 1944. Also, by not overturning the military recommendation to remove the local Japanese, FDR was showing the military leaders he was willing to follow their lead in the war. Thus, Roosevelt issued the executive order needed to intern the Japanese-Americans. Biddle privately denounced the decision as "ill-advised, unnecessary, and unnecessarily cruel," but Roosevelt argued, "This must be a military decision." FDR knew he had to win the war to preserve his reputation; good military cooperation and leadership were essential to victory. However, from a civil rights perspective, as Biddle observed, "I do not think he was much concerned with the gravity or implications of this step."[46]

Biddle has a point. What were "the gravity or implications" of Roosevelt's abuse of civil liberties? Even if we assume that all, or most, of his breaches of individual rights helped his country win the war, is it possible for liberty and the rule of law to long endure under such a system?

11

COURTING STALIN

After Pearl Harbor, Roosevelt began a remarkable diplomatic courtship of Joseph Stalin. It started with sending the Russian dictator, usually free of charge, all the supplies he asked for. "I would go out and take the stuff off the shelves of the stores, and pay them any price necessary, and put it in a truck and rush it to the boat [to send to Stalin]," Roosevelt said on March 11, 1942. Two years later, on February 14, 1944, he was equally intense: "We must therefore continue to support the USSR by providing the maximum amount of supplies which can be delivered to her ports. This is a matter of paramount importance." Granted, Stalin was a useful ally, but he was also one of the most treacherous mass murderers in world history. Why was Roosevelt so attracted to the Russian dictator, and what resulted from this strange courtship?[1]

Ever since the communist revolution in Russia in 1917, Americans had been wisely skeptical of its totalitarian leaders, Lenin and then Stalin. Four American presidents refused to recognize the ruthless new Soviet regime. Roosevelt, however, broke tradition and extended diplomatic recognition to the Soviets in 1933. He thought they might help balance the power of Japan in the Far East. Also, with diplomatic recognition, Russia promised to repay at least part of its $636,177,226 debt to the United States from businesses the Soviets had confiscated and money they had borrowed. Sadly for FDR, the Russians reneged, but Stalin tried to offset his deception through calculated flattery. Roosevelt was, Stalin told the U.S. ambassador to Russia, "one of the most popular men in the Soviet Union." In turn, FDR told the Soviet ambassador to the United States, "A deep love of peace is the common heritage of the people of both our countries, and I fully agree with you that the cooperation of our great nations will inevitably be of the highest importance in the preservation of world peace." FDR was already listening to Stalin's words more than watching his actions.[2]

Cordell Hull, the secretary of state, and William Bullitt, the ambassador to Russia from 1933 to 1936, were both wary of Stalin and voiced their alarm to FDR. In 1939, when Stalin joined Hitler in an alliance to divide Poland and mutually carve up many countries nearby, Roosevelt was jolted back to reality; he even condemned Russia's "new resort to military force."[3]

But the president couldn't stay angry with the Russians for long, because he was enchanted by what he thought was their worldview. Sure, they were sometimes insecure and barbaric, but at heart FDR thought they were inherently peaceful, seeking the common good. When Frances Perkins, the secretary of labor, was talking with FDR about the Russians, she said she had heard they had a "desire to do the Holy Will." Roosevelt responded, "You know, there may be something in that. It would explain their almost mystical devotion to this idea which they have developed of the Communist society. They all seem really to want to do what is good for their society instead of wanting to do for themselves. We take care of ourselves and think about the welfare of society afterward."[4]

When Hitler broke his pact with Stalin and invaded Russia in mid-1941, Roosevelt was delighted to have the Russians as a partner. They were a crucial ally. As savvy as Roosevelt usually was, however, he really believed they were a selfless people, and should receive large helpings of Lend-Lease aid from the United States. When Ambassador Bullitt questioned that move, FDR responded,

"I think if I give him everything I possibly can, and ask nothing from him in return, *noblesse oblige*, he won't try to annex anything and will work with me for a world of peace and democracy." The president said almost the same thing in a letter to Prime Minister Churchill: "I think there is nothing more important than that Stalin feel that we mean to support him without qualification and at great sacrifice."[5]

Many American experts on Russia tried to warn the president. Ambassador Bullitt told Roosevelt that Stalin was a "Caucasian bandit whose only thought when he got something for nothing was that the other fellow was an ass." Senator Robert Taft offered this important distinction between fascism and communism:

> The victory of communism would be far more dangerous to the United States than the victory of fascism. There has never been the slightest danger that the people in this country would ever embrace . . . nazism. . . . But communism masquerades, often successfully, under the guise of democracy, though it is just as alien to our principles as nazism itself. It is a greater danger to the United States because it is a false philosophy which appeals to many. Fascism is a false philosophy which appeals to very few indeed.[6]

Churchill also reminded FDR of Soviet treachery, but FDR became almost blind to it. At one point in 1943, Churchill said, "The real problem is Russia. I *can't* get the Americans to see it." In part FDR couldn't see it because he perceived Churchill, not Stalin, as the imperialist. The British retained colonies from India to Kenya to British Honduras. They were a threat to self-determination and the right of people to be free. Stalin, in Roosevelt's eyes, wanted to do good for the broader society. Therefore, he thought they could work together side by side after the war to achieve world peace through the United Nations. "Of one thing I am certain," FDR said as late as 1945, "Stalin is not an imperialist."[7]

To believe that "Stalin is not an imperialist," Roosevelt had to explain away the Soviet conquest of Poland, Estonia, Lithuania, and Latvia in 1939 and 1940. "I'm not sure," he concluded, "that a fair plebiscite, if ever there was such a thing, wouldn't show that these eastern provinces would prefer to go back to Russia. Yes, I really think those 1940 frontiers are as just as any."[8]

For Roosevelt to maintain his theory of the Soviets, he also had to reinvent Stalin's atheist regime as tolerant of religion. At a press conference in November 1941, FDR spoke of "freedom of conscience" and "freedom of religion" as being somewhat similar in the United States and Russia. He cited the Russian constitution and thought he could read into it "freedom of religion. Freedom equally to use propaganda against religion, which is essentially what is the rule in this country; only we don't put it quite the same way." As late as 1945, Roosevelt told a cabinet meeting that Stalin, perhaps because he trained for the priesthood, had "something else in his being besides this revolutionist, Bolshevik thing." He added, "I think that something entered into his nature of the way in which a Christian gentleman should behave."[9]

Nothing would deter Roosevelt from his courtship of Stalin. In March 1942, FDR wrote to Churchill, "I know you will not mind my being brutally frank when I tell you that I think I can personally handle Stalin better than either your Foreign Office or my State Department. Stalin hates the guts of all your top people. He thinks he likes me better, and I hope he will continue to."[10]

Roosevelt made sure Stalin liked him by giving Russia abundant food, guns, and ammunition to fight Hitler on the Eastern Front. In July 1941, just weeks after Hitler broke his alliance with Russia, FDR sent Harry Hopkins to Moscow to find out what was needed. The United States pledged over a billion dollars of Lend-Lease aid during 1942, and raised that to more than $10 billion during the war. From October 1941 through May 1945, the United States sent the Soviets 427,284 army trucks, 13,303 tanks, 35,170 motorcycles, and thousands of other vehicles. Oil was important, and the United States sent more than 2.5 million tons of high-octane aviation fuel, which made the 15,033 planes sent from America fly more efficiently. American P-39 planes, for example, saved Moscow from German attacks as late as 1943. The United States also rebuilt Soviet railroads and sent railroad cars and machine tools. Next came clothing, and then 4.5 million tons of tinned meat, sugar, flour, and fats from American farms to feed Soviet troops throughout the war.[11]

Vice President Henry Wallace, who visited Russia in 1944, saw American goods everywhere. "I found American flour in the Soviet Far East," he said, "American aluminum in Soviet airplane factories, American steel in truck and railway repair shops, American machine tools in shipbuilding yards, American compressors and electrical equipment on Soviet naval vessels, American electric shovels in open-cut coal mines, American core drills in the copper mines of Central Asia and American trucks and planes performing strategic transportation functions in supplying remote bases." One thing Wallace was not allowed to see were the thousands of American citizens in Soviet prisons; some were POWs from the war, others were naïve visitors who had believed in Stalin and came to help him in the 1930s. Most of them were executed or died in prison, and their tragic story is told well by Tim Tzouliadis in *The Forsaken*.[12] One of the aircrews from the Doolittle raid over Japan in 1942 was interned by Stalin after they crash-landed near Vladivostock, but they had escaped to Iran by the time of Wallace's visit.

The amount of U.S. help to Russia can never be fully known, because Stalin's spy network maneuvered effectively to bring the Soviets secret documents from the U.S. government and new technology from U.S. corporations. We don't know for certain how much information was stolen, but we know how some of the theft was done. For example, the United States built a large airfield in Great Falls, Montana, to airlift military hardware to Russia. Planes would fly Lend-Lease material from Great Falls to Fairbanks, Alaska. Then Soviet pilots would fly it across the Bering Strait into Russia. Security was lax, so Russian pilots sometimes flew to Great Falls, loaded tons of cargo unsupervised onto their planes, and flew it to Russia.

Randolph Hardy, a civilian official, and Major George Jordan, a liaison officer, often tried to examine the large containers being shipped to Russia, but the Soviets called it "personal baggage" and pleaded "diplomatic immunity." Major Jordan remarked, "Here were tons of materials proceeding to the Soviet Union, and I had no idea what they were." Once, when the Soviet pilots were distracted with vodka, Jordan sneaked away to the airstrip to examine one of these trunks. "There were groups of documents which, on the evidence of stationery, had been contributed by the Departments of Agriculture, Commerce and State." He also found diplomatic reports, and even information on uranium, which was potentially useful in making an atom bomb.[13] Soviet spies also entered the United States through Great Falls, and then hooked up with the central Soviet spy networks in Washington, D.C., and New York City.

Major Jordan tried to alert the Roosevelt administration to the massive Russian thievery in Great Falls, but had no success. At one point he told influential pilot Eddie Rickenbacker about the Russian thefts and Rickenbacker told Henry Stimson, the secretary of war. According to Rickenbacker, "Stimson said that he had heard about it too but had been unable to do anything about it." How Stimson, a man in steady communication with the president, was "unable to do anything about it" was something Rickenbacker could not understand.[14]

American planes, tanks, and food supplied the Russian Army, but Stalin wanted more. He asked Roosevelt for a "second front," a U.S. and British landing in France. That would force the Germans to shift troops from attacking Russia to guarding the Western Front. The idea of a cross-Channel attack on Germany—codenamed Sledgehammer—pleased Roosevelt even if it meant the Americans and British would have to face huge casualties. A cross-Channel attack "might be the turning point which would save Russia this year," Roosevelt believed. "Sledgehammer is of such grave importance that every reason calls for accomplishment of it. . . . The principal objective of Sledgehammer is the positive diversion of German Air Forces from the Russian front."[15]

But he had to persuade the British. On April 3, 1942, Roosevelt wrote Churchill, "Your people and mine demand the establishment of a front to draw off pressure on the Russians." Harry Hopkins, after talking with Churchill, wrote the president: "I particularly stressed . . . that the disposition of the United States was to take great risks to relieve the Russian front." Emphasizing that point, Roosevelt wrote Churchill in May, "I believe German air forces cannot be defeated or indeed brought to battle to an extent which will bring them off the Russian front until we have made a landing."[16]

Churchill used all the diplomacy he could muster to dissuade Roosevelt from such a suicidal attack. The Channel, Churchill stressed, would turn into "a river of blood" and the attack "would lead to disaster."[17] Germany had veteran troops with air support hovering over the key ports in France. U.S. troops were eager but unseasoned, and they lacked the landing craft, the planes, and the weapons to challenge the Germans on the Continent. "It takes two years to make a soldier," Churchill quipped after watching the Americans train. Finally, Roosevelt, after much British negativity, conceded the Americans were not ready yet, and he regretfully had to disappoint Stalin. Thus, North Africa, an easier target, would be the place Americans would land in November 1942.

Actually, Stalin wanted a second front in Europe, but he wanted it to begin in France, as far west of Berlin as possible. Why? Because Stalin wanted Soviet troops to have a clear, uninterrupted route to Berlin. As Stalin said privately, "Whoever occupies a territory imposes on it his own social system. Everyone imposes his own system as far as his army can reach."[18] And he wanted his troops to reach as far into Western Europe as they could.

The United States could have prevented the Soviet Army from marching so far west. When the Americans and British finally defeated Germany in North Africa, they next went into Sicily, and then Italy. At that point, Churchill favored another push up the Italian or Balkan peninsula into Central Europe. Such a march would be quicker in reaching Berlin, but Stalin rejected Churchill's plan because it would cut the Russians off from reaching Berlin first.

Churchill anticipated Stalin's goal and urged the Anglo-American and the Russian armies "to shake hands as far east as possible." Churchill wrote his chiefs of staff, "Once again I draw attention to the extreme importance on grounds of high policy of our having a stake in central and southern Europe and not allowing everything to pass into Soviet hands with the incalculable consequences that may result therefrom." The success of the Italian campaign, and the urging of Churchill for a second front, initially persuaded Roosevelt to go along. FDR thought Stalin might "suggest that we stage an operation at the top of the Adriatic with a view to assisting Tito." Churchill was pleased but Stalin wasn't, and Stalin got his way in the first meeting at Teheran in November 1943. That meeting of the great powers would plan the strategy for the rest of the war.[19]

Part of the reason for conferring at Teheran was Roosevelt's eagerness to meet Stalin face-to-face. FDR believed he could charm Stalin and win him over with almost unconditional friendship. Roosevelt's letters to Stalin are filled with the president's desire to talk with Stalin—for a "meeting of the minds," to "have . . . an exchange of views," and because "I need your advice." In April 1942, William Standley, U.S. ambassador to Russia, brought a note to Stalin that said, "The president told me that he was sure that if the two of you could sit down together and talk matters over, there would never be any lack of understanding between our countries."[20]

Stalin always found excuses not to meet with Roosevelt and Churchill together. Perhaps he thought they might pressure him to restrain his postwar ambitions. Also, Stalin did not like or trust either man. He shrewdly flattered Roosevelt in public, but not in private. According to Josip Tito of Yugoslavia, Stalin said Churchill wanted to put his hand in your pocket to steal a kopeck, but Roosevelt "only goes after the big kopecks." [21]

Thus, Stalin artfully planned to use the Teheran meeting to divide Roosevelt and Churchill and solidify gains for the Soviets. First, the choice of Teheran gave Stalin almost a home field advantage. Roosevelt had an exhausting six thousand miles of plane travel overseas. Second, Stalin persuaded Roosevelt not to reside in the American embassy in Teheran, but in the Russian compound, where Stalin could charm him one-on-one. Churchill was surprised at Stalin's maneuver, and Hastings Ismay, the British general, said, "I wonder if microphones had already been installed in anticipation." They had been. Roosevelt's room was bugged, and historian Robert Nisbet found that "more than a few Soviet 'servants' were observed wearing NKVD [Soviet secret police] uniforms under outer garments of the kind waiters and room maids and others would normally wear." [22]

In three private meetings Roosevelt and Stalin had before the conference began, Stalin converted Roosevelt on the major points. Thus, in the general sessions, with Churchill present, Roosevelt suddenly opposed strengthening the Italian campaign and wanted troops there to go to France for the larger cross-Channel attack planned for 1944. "Nothing," FDR now argued, "should be done to delay the carrying out of Overlord which might be necessary if there were any operations in the Eastern Mediterranean . . . undertaken." Churchill fought hard for the Italian campaign, but made no headway against the converted FDR. Thus, the Americans would have to face the Germans in a cross-Channel landing; and the Eastern Europeans would have to face the Russians and the loss of freedom that would follow. General Mark Clark, the American commander in Italy, later lamented FDR's decision: "The weakening of the campaign in Italy in order to invade Southern

France, instead of pushing on into the Balkans, was one of the outstanding mistakes of the war. . . . Stalin knew exactly what he wanted . . . and the thing he wanted most was to keep us out of the Balkans."[23]

Stalin, with his path to Berlin now clear, next used the Teheran meeting to legitimize his control over Eastern Europe. That desire conflicted with the goals of the Atlantic Charter, which Roosevelt and Churchill had established in 1941 to promise self-determination for the nations of Europe after the war. Of special interest at Teheran was the future of Poland.

Stalin recognized that establishing hegemony over Poland was the necessary prelude to controlling the rest of Eastern Europe. In 1940, shortly after the war began, Stalin began sending hundreds of thousands of Poles to hard-labor camps in Siberia. He also had more than ten thousand Polish officers—the cream of the nation's talent and youth—executed, mostly in the Katyn Forest in Poland. The Soviet leaders shot them in the head, trampled their bodies, and buried them in mass graves. In 1943, not long before the Teheran conference, the mass graves were discovered; the Soviets professed to be startled, and blamed the Nazis. Churchill and others investigated the crime, and their evidence clearly pointed to a Soviet massacre.

Roosevelt asked John F. Carter, the president's personal spy, to investigate the Katyn massacre. Roosevelt told Carter the Soviets were probably guilty, but that he "didn't want to believe it," and if he had to believe it, he would "pretend not to." Carter's verdict was that the Poles were right to look past Soviet denials and demand independent verification.[24]

At Teheran, Stalin had to overcome the existing sympathy for Poland among the Allies. Polish men were fighting Hitler in large numbers. And the Polish government in exile in London was embracing the idea of a free Poland after the war, and in the meantime was demanding that the Red Cross investigate the Katyn massacre.

Stalin, in his last private meeting with Roosevelt, made clear his desire for hegemony in Poland. Roosevelt cared little for Poland but cared much for Stalin's goodwill. Also, FDR worried about the effect of giving Poland to Russia less than a year before the 1944 elections. He couldn't stand, as he told Stalin, "six to seven million Americans of Polish extraction" angry with him, and "as a practical man" he didn't want "to lose their votes."[25] Roosevelt also made sure Stalin understood that the United States would not object to his occupation of the Baltic states. On the principle of self-determination, Roosevelt explained, he "was confident that the people would vote to join the Soviet Union."[26]

Roosevelt had to strike a balance in 1944 between pretending to care about Poland and not deterring Stalin from taking it. Roosevelt confided to Averell Harriman, ambassador to the Soviet Union, that he "didn't care whether the countries bordering Russia became communist or not." But, as George Kennan, diplomat and expert on Russia, noted, "His anxiety was rather that he had a large body of voting constituents in this country of Polish or Baltic origin."[27] The president's task was keeping both them and Stalin happy at the same time.

The Warsaw uprising in the fall of 1944 tested Roosevelt's ability to hold the Polish vote and his desire to please Stalin. The episode began with the western surge of the Russian Army to the suburbs of Warsaw. The Germans were in full retreat, but they did hold Warsaw. The Poles in Warsaw had a Home Army of about five thousand troops, and the Russians decided to urge the Poles to revolt against the powerful German Army in Warsaw. In Moscow, Stalin warmly received the Polish premier in exile. Then the Russians issued a radio message for the Poles: "The time of liberation is at hand! Poles, to arms!"[28] With the Russian Army just outside Warsaw, the Home Army sprang into revolt and seized most of Warsaw from the startled Germans. The Poles and the Russians, allied on the Eastern Front, would, so it seemed, take Warsaw together and move the Nazi Army back into Germany.

Then came the shocker. With the Poles clashing with the Germans in the streets of Warsaw, the Russian Army stood still. They refused to aid the Home Army, which was fighting valiantly against the superior German forces. Day by day the Germans, with reinforcements, butchered the Poles and recaptured the city block by block.

Churchill was frantic to send planes and airlift supplies to help the Poles, but Roosevelt was nervous. Churchill proposed to Roosevelt that they send a letter to Stalin that read: "The massacre in Warsaw will undoubtedly be a great annoyance to us when we all meet at the end of the war. Unless you directly forbid it, therefore, we propose to send the planes."[29]

But Roosevelt said no. "In consideration of Stalin's present attitude in regard to relief of the Polish Underground in Warsaw as expressed in his messages to you and me," FDR wrote Churchill, "and his definite refusal to permit the use by us of Soviet air fields for that purpose, and in view of current American conversations in regard to subsequent use of other Soviet bases, I do not consider it advantageous in the long range general war prospect for me to join with you in the proposed message to U[ncle] J[oe]."[30]

As the slaughter of the Poles continued, Churchill refused to give up. On September 4, he wrote Stalin directly, "Our people cannot understand why no material help has been sent from outside to the Poles in Warsaw. . . . Your government's action in preventing this help being sent seems to us at variance with the spirit of Allied cooperation."[31] Stalin's army remained in place, and FDR gave some rhetoric but no action to support Churchill and the Poles. Stalin refused to allow British or American planes, which might airdrop supplies to the Poles, to land and refuel in Russian territory. By October 1, the Polish freedom fighters, along with over two hundred thousand civilians, had been wiped out.

With the Home Army removed, the Russian Army suddenly came to life and marched into Warsaw to challenge the somewhat weakened German Army. Stalin took Warsaw and, with the collapse of the Polish resistance, increased his ability to install a pro-communist government after the war. And because Roosevelt's refusal to help the Poles was not made public, he would still make a claim for the votes of Polish-Americans in the presidential elections one month away.

Stalin's daring moves in Poland startled his democratic allies. By urging the Poles to revolt, then refusing to come to their aid, and then obstructing the British and Americans from helping, didn't he risk a break with his American allies? How could Stalin have been so sure FDR would comply with Russia's wishes?

On the Polish question, and on other issues, Stalin had help from his vast network of spies in the United States—not just Soviet spies, but American spies, most of whom had secretly joined the Communist Party of the United States (CPUSA). More than three hundred communist members or supporters had infiltrated the American government and worked in Lend-Lease, the Treasury Department, the State Department, the office of the president, the office of the vice president, and even American intelligence operations—the Office of Strategic Services (OSS). These spies not only relayed information to the KGB, they constantly tried to shift U.S. policy in a pro-Soviet direction. The opening of the Soviet archives in 1995 revealed the extensive espionage network that effectively operated inside the U.S. government.[32]

The CPUSA had existed since 1919, but its members began to seriously infiltrate the U.S. government in the 1930s. Naturally, they supported Roosevelt's recognition of the Soviet Union, and they also gained experience working for the AAA, the NRA, and the Treasury Department. The writings of former spies Whittaker Chambers and Elizabeth Bentley help explain how state documents were copied or microfilmed, and ultimately delivered to Russian leaders. By World War II, several of these spies were well positioned to influence policy, or at least explain policy, so that Stalin could plan his tactics carefully.

One of these spies, economist Lauchlin Currie, had direct access to Roosevelt. Currie was educated at the London School of Economics and at Harvard. He joined the Treasury Department in 1934, but became senior administrative assistant to the president in 1939. Currie went to China for Roosevelt and also worked on Lend-Lease and the Foreign Economic Administration. KGB cables show some of his messages during the war. In June 1944, he cabled the New York KGB that Roosevelt was willing to concede half of Poland to Stalin, and would pressure the Polish government-in-exile to cooperate with the Russians.[33]

Another well-positioned Soviet spy was Harry Dexter White, who became the number-two man in the Treasury Department. White was born to Jewish immigrant parents in Massachusetts, and was educated at Columbia and Stanford before taking his Ph.D. in economics at Harvard. White joined the Treasury Department in 1934, and quickly earned favor with his boss, Henry Morgenthau. During the 1930s, White began passing information to the Soviets and also influenced the hiring of at least eleven communists into the Treasury Department, including Lauchlin Currie. During World War II, White became assistant secretary of the treasury and began to influence tax policy and foreign policy. Historians have uncovered fifteen KGB messages that White sent to Russian intelligence officers late in the war. In these deciphered messages, White told the Soviets that Roosevelt would give only limited backing to the Polish government-in-exile, and that he would not resist the Soviets' annexing of Latvia, Estonia, and Lithuania. After Roosevelt died, White met with key Soviet intelligence men and told them the Soviets could press for veto power in the newly created UN because "Truman and Stettinius want to achieve the success of the [UN] conference at any price."[34]

The most famous American spy for the Soviets was Alger Hiss, who worked his way from a government official in the AAA to head of the Office of Special Political Affairs in the State Department. Educated at Johns Hopkins and Harvard Law School, Hiss clerked for Oliver Wendell Holmes and entered government with seemingly impeccable credentials. During the 1930s, he passed documents to the Soviets, and during the war he became part of the Roosevelt team that went to Yalta to negotiate with Stalin over Poland.[35]

Vice President Henry Wallace was very sympathetic to Russia, and several American communists helped influence and reinforce that kind of thinking. Lawrence Duggan, a graduate of Harvard, headed the South American division in the State Department under FDR. At some point, Duggan became a Soviet spy, and told the Russians about the British and American plan to invade Italy—information Stalin could use because he wanted a second front in France, not Italy. One cable, part of the recently declassified Venona papers, said Duggan could help the Soviets by "using his friendship" with Henry Wallace for "extracting . . . interesting information." Duggan almost did better than that. Wallace said that if he became president he would give Duggan a high position in the State Department, and make Harry Dexter White secretary of the treasury.[36]

The hundreds of Soviet spies in the U.S. government, all working to influence American policy, had a potential setback in 1939 when fellow agent Whittaker Chambers quit spying for the Soviets, changed his allegiance, and told Adolf Berle in detail about some of the communist sympathizers in government. He specifically fingered Hiss, Currie, White, and Duggan. An astonished Berle took notes and gave them to Marvin McIntyre, the White House secretary. Berle also told Dean Acheson. But they apparently dismissed Chambers as a crank, and nothing was done with his revelations during the war.[37]

The final meeting of Roosevelt, Stalin, and Churchill—at Yalta in February 1945—provided the Russians with many advantages. First was location. Yalta was Stalin's summer hideaway on the Black Sea, and very hard to reach. Roosevelt again had to travel around the world to get there. Once in Yalta, Roosevelt again stayed in rooms that were bugged. The Soviets listened to all his conversations. At one point, Stalin asked one of his spies, "What do you think? Do they know that we are listening to them? . . . It's bizarre. They say everything in the fullest detail."[38] Stalin was well prepared because of the bugging, the information gathered from Soviet spies in the United States, and the presence of Alger Hiss in the American delegation at Yalta.

As in Teheran, Stalin again began manipulating Roosevelt. Roosevelt had two goals at Yalta. First, he wanted Soviet help with Japan after the Germans surrendered. If the atomic bomb didn't work, that help would save American lives. On this point, Stalin extracted land concessions and continued Lend-Lease for his agreement to help—which, of course, he could always withdraw if necessary. Second, Roosevelt wanted Stalin to be a major partner in achieving world peace through the future United Nations. On this point, Stalin saw no harm for Russia from the future UN as long as Russia had veto power in the Security Council. Meanwhile, Roosevelt's fervent desire for the future United Nations would give Stalin a chance to make firm his own conquests in Europe. Any time Roosevelt expressed doubt about Stalin's territorial ambitions, Stalin could balk at participating in the UN. Thus, Stalin was comfortable agreeing to join the UN and help Roosevelt defeat Japan.[39]

Stalin's major goals at Yalta were to confirm and secure his dominance over Eastern Europe—including Berlin and a chunk of Germany—and to keep such rivals as France and England as weak as possible. This game, for Stalin, started with Poland. He must have Russian hegemony over Poland confirmed at Yalta. Much of Stalin's intricate maneuvering during the war was an effort to dominate Poland. It started with the alliance with Germany in 1939 and the carving up of Poland after that. The next step was the Katyn massacre to remove as much of the Polish officer corps and intelligentsia as he could. Then came the removal of tens of thousands of Poles into the Soviet Gulag during the war. The failed Warsaw uprising in 1944 was Stalin's further effort to weaken Poland and prepare it for Soviet domination.

When the Germans discovered and exposed the Russian massacre of Poles at Katyn, Stalin used that accusation to condemn the Polish government in exile in London, which demanded an investigation of the massacre, and establish his own pro-communist government for Poland in Lublin. FDR, even though his independent investigation confirmed the Soviet massacre at Katyn, refused to stand in Stalin's way.

At Yalta, Stalin knew ahead of time that Roosevelt would press for free elections in Poland. Even though the 1944 elections in the United States were over, Roosevelt still needed some support from Polish-American voters. Thus, he would ask Stalin for some pro-democratic Poles to be put into the provisional government that would rule Poland after the war. Vasili Mitrokhin, the former Soviet spy, described Stalin's public reaction at Yalta to Roosevelt's request for free elections: "On this point, after initial resistance, Stalin graciously conceded, knowing that the 'democrats' could subsequently be excluded."[40] "Free elections" for Eastern European countries meant one thing to Stalin and another to Roosevelt and Churchill. Thus, Stalin, at Yalta, was able to secure hegemony over Poland, Hungary, Romania, Bulgaria, almost half of Germany, and other territories from the Baltic Sea to the Adriatic. The "Iron Curtain," as Churchill later called it, began to fall across Eastern Europe.

Many historians have argued that once the Soviet Army had a stronghold in Eastern Europe, it would have been almost impossible to dislodge it. After all, as Stalin himself had said, "Whoever occupies a territory imposes on it his own social system." Once the Soviet Army dominated an area, Soviet hegemony could not be dislodged unless FDR wanted to take on Russia after fighting Germany. Thus, Stalin's victory, in this view, was a fait accompli, not something Roosevelt gave away.

That point, as a description of the world as it existed in February 1945, has validity. But it ignores the steps Roosevelt could have taken earlier. He could have stopped Stalin, or at least maneuvered him into a weaker position during the war. Why give Stalin such abundant Lend-Lease aid, even during 1945, with almost no strings attached? Why not weaken Soviet intelligence by listening to Whittaker Chambers and others on the subject of Soviet espionage? Why not launch the second front in Europe from Italy, as Churchill urged, and block the Soviet expansion westward? Failing that, why not give Eisenhower the green light to march into Berlin before the Soviet Army could get there and loot the city and countryside of much of its industrial equipment?

Roosevelt's failure to take any of these steps has suggested to some historians that the president was not mentally competent, that he was weakened mentally and physically by heart problems that would take his life less than two months after Yalta. True, FDR was indeed debilitated by heart problems, by the exhausting trip to Yalta, and by Stalin's tough negotiating. But Roosevelt was always mentally sound. As Charles Bohlen, Roosevelt's interpreter, noted, "While his physical state was certainly not up to normal, his mental and psychological state was certainly not affected." Sir Frank Roberts of Britain agreed. "The hand of death was on him," Roberts said, "but it didn't impede his role at Yalta. He was in charge and achieved everything he had come to do."[41] Roberts is right. After Yalta, on March 1, Roosevelt bragged to Congress that he and Stalin, working through the UN, would create a "permanent peace" that would change international relations forever.

With world peace the prize, whatever happened to Poland would be secondary. Roosevelt made that point clear at Yalta. "I am determined," he told Stalin, "that there shall be no breach between ourselves and the Soviet Union." FDR added, "The United States will never lend its support in any way to any provisional government in Poland that would be inimical to your interests."[42]

After Yalta, when Stalin began to violate his pledge to support free elections in Europe, Roosevelt finally became annoyed. He spoke as though the veil had been lifted from his eyes. "Averell [Harriman] is right," the president said. "We can't do business with

Stalin. He has broken every one of the promises he made at Yalta." But these feelings apparently passed. The day before his death, Roosevelt wrote Churchill: "I would minimize the general Soviet problem as much as possible because these problems in one form or other seem to arise every day and most of them straighten out." That sounds like the old Roosevelt. Thus, he may have seen the error of his ways, but probably not.[43]

The story of George Earle and his investigation of the Katyn massacre helps confirm Roosevelt's mind-set on Russia.[44] Earle had been governor of Pennsylvania in the 1930s; after his loss in a run for the Senate, Roosevelt appointed him minister to Bulgaria. When war broke out, Earle became part of FDR's spy team. In 1942, when the Germans discovered the mass graves in the Katyn forest, they exposed the Russians; Stalin, as we have seen, denied his crime and blamed the Nazis. The controversy that followed was critical. Could Stalin, Roosevelt's trusted ally, have secretly murdered more than ten thousand elite Polish officers? If Stalin was innocent, why did he refuse an investigation?

Roosevelt was nervous. Could Stalin really be trusted in this war, and in the peace afterward? As we have seen, John F. Carter, one of the president's spies in Europe, reported privately to Roosevelt that the Russians were the probable murderers at Katyn. To Roosevelt, that was the wrong conclusion, so he called on George Earle for a second opinion. Earle carefully gathered evidence, including more than one hundred interviews, and concluded that Stalin was guilty. According to Earle, Roosevelt reacted with these words: "George, this is entirely German propaganda and a German plot. I am absolutely convinced the Russians did not do this."[45] Earle was startled at that response, but he continued to accumulate evidence and kept telling the president that proof of Soviet guilt was conclusive. In response, Roosevelt dismissed Earle and took him off the case.

In March 1945, after Yalta, Earle reappeared in Roosevelt's life, angry that his warnings on Katyn and on Russian treachery had been ignored. Earle was now on the sidelines watching Stalin con-solidate power in Eastern Europe by murdering or imprisoning political opponents. Since Roosevelt had been ignoring all of Earle's letters and warnings, he wrote to the president's daughter, Anna, whom he also knew. I am being "forced out of the picture," Earle said, "because I told your father the truth about conditions in Rus-sia and countries occupied by Russia."

"Russia today," Earle wrote, "is a far greater menace than Ger-many ever was." Even though "your father resents the fact that I told him the truth," Earle promised to be quiet and not "hurt or embarrass" Roosevelt if the president insisted on that. But if not, Earle would begin talking with the press about Stalin and Katyn in one week.

That letter got Roosevelt's attention. On March 24, with less than three weeks to live, Roosevelt ordered Earle to keep quiet: "I have noted with concern your plan to publish your unfavorable opinion of one of our allies at the very time when such a publica-tion from a former emissary of mine might do irreparable harm to our war effort. . . . I specifically forbid you to publish any informa-tion or opinion about an ally that you may have acquired." Then Roosevelt ordered the Navy to transfer Earle to Samoa for the rest of the war.[46]

There in Samoa, in virtual exile, Earle could ponder the cen-tralization of power and Roosevelt's use of it. Earle had seen it from both sides. When Roosevelt was manipulating men and using power to help Earle, as happened in the 1930s, life could be wonderful. Earle and Roosevelt had much in common: Both were wealthy, both graduated from Harvard, and both came from old colonial families. Earle, in fact, had backed Roosevelt for president with $35,000 even before he was nominated in 1932. Two years later, Roosevelt supported Earle in his successful run to become the first Democratic governor of Pennsylvania in four decades. After he and FDR both won reelection in 1936, the *American Mercury* called Earle "the nation's number one carbon copy of

Franklin Delano Roosevelt."[47] Since Pennsylvania was a battle-ground state, which Hoover had carried in 1932, Roosevelt showered it with federal funds and let Earle distribute some of the WPA money.

Then came trouble. Earle and the Democrats had pressured many of those who received WPA jobs to campaign for Democrats at election time. That was a common tactic, and Democrats in many states used WPA funds to reward friends and win elections. But Earle and Senator Joseph Guffey left a paper trail that led to trouble. All government employees and all WPA workers in Pennsylvania received a letter signed by Senator Guffey and authorized by the Democratic State Committee that asked for funds to help Democrats win in 1938. Also, Earle was accused of receiving campaign kickbacks from a well-placed contractor. The resulting investigation was promoted by Republican Moses Annenberg, editor of the *Philadelphia Inquirer*, who blasted Earle for corruption and FDR for prolonging the Great Depression with his policies. Under Annenberg's impressive leadership, Republicans recaptured Pennsylvania in the 1938 elections. They defeated Earle, who was running for Senate, and threatened to move the state back into the Republican column in the presidential election of 1940.[48]

Roosevelt swung into action. He appointed Earle as minister to Bulgaria and had the IRS launch a tax investigation against Annenberg, who lost and went to prison. Then, with the path clear, Roosevelt carried Pennsylvania and won a third term in 1940. Safe in Bulgaria, Earle saw what Roosevelt could do for you. But then he saw what the president could do against you. Earle, like Admiral Richardson before him on Pearl Harbor, bluntly told Roosevelt momentous news he didn't want to hear. Earle persisted, as did Richardson, because the future of their country was at stake. Both men were fired. Living in exile in Samoa, Earle, like Richardson, knew a spectacular truth but could not influence world politics with it.

Roosevelt always liked to play hunches. He had lucky numbers, lucky clothes, and lucky days. And sometimes he conducted public policy on the basis of hunches. In World War II, he had a hunch he and Stalin could achieve world peace together. At the outset of the war, William Bullitt, first ambassador to Russia and then ambassador to France, argued vigorously with Roosevelt that Stalin's record showed he could not be trusted. By that time, however, Roosevelt had his hunch that Stalin could be trusted. Finally, the president said, "Bill, I don't dispute your facts, they are accurate. I don't dispute the logic of your reasoning. I just have a hunch that Stalin is not that kind of man." When Bullitt challenged that conclusion, Roosevelt retorted, "It's my responsibility and not yours, and I'm going to play my hunch."[49] His hunch was wrong. And millions were killed or imprisoned, the Cold War began, and the world became a more dangerous place.

12

THE 1944 ELECTION: A FOURTH TERM

Since 1944 was an election year, Turner Catledge, veteran reporter at the *New York Times*, was eager to cover Roosevelt's fourth run for president. Catledge had met with the president often and knew him well. Sure FDR wanted another term—despite his feeble protests to the contrary. He loved the action, loved the attention, and relished the power he could wield. The war was finally going well, and Catledge knew the champ would be hard to beat.

By mid-March 1944, Roosevelt had been to Teheran to confer with Stalin and Churchill, but since he had returned he was often on vacation. Catledge had not seen him in many months, and that was unusual. Finally, the White House secretary called Catledge and told him President Roosevelt wanted to see him again. As Catledge sauntered off to the White House for his appointment that brisk March morning, he prepared himself for a lively exchange with the master politician.

Instead, when Catledge entered the president's office, he got a jolt. "I was shocked and horrified," Catledge said, "so much so that my impulse was to turn around and leave. I felt I was seeing something I shouldn't see." There was the president, so gaunt, so thin, so white that Catledge almost thought he was face-to-face with a dead man. "He had lost a great deal of weight. His shirt collar hung so loose on his neck that you could have put your hand inside it. He was sitting there with a vague, glassy-eyed expression on his face and his mouth hanging open." Conversation was almost impossible. FDR "would start talking about something, then in midsentence he would stop and his mouth would drop open and he'd sit staring at me in silence. I knew I was looking at a terribly sick man."

To break the silence, Catledge mentioned Teheran, but the president drifted in and out of the conversation. He talked randomly about the water system in Teheran, about how Stalin joked about executing fifty thousand Germans after the war, how Churchill was indignant at that idea, and how Roosevelt airily suggested killing only forty-nine thousand Germans as a compromise. He enjoyed telling that story, and it seemed to revive him a bit; but the conversation again became disconnected. "Repeatedly, he would lose his train of thought, stop, and stare blankly at me." Finally, with a luncheon guest waiting for the president, Catledge "was able to make my escape." [1]

Roosevelt's health had greatly deteriorated since the grueling trip to Teheran, and Catledge was not the only one in shock about it. Family and cabinet members were also alarmed. Dr. Ross McIntire, the White House physician, thought the problem was mere bronchitis, but daughter Anna called in a specialist. On March 28, shortly after Catledge's visit, Dr. Howard Bruenn, a premier heart surgeon with the Navy, gave the president a thorough exam. What he found was alarming: an enlarged heart, hypertensive heart disease, cardiac failure in the left ventricle, and dangerously high blood pressure. The president was near death. Bruenn confronted the incompetent McIntire at once. The president needed regular doses of digitalis immediately for his heart, and then he needed rest and a strict diet. The president had only one year to live, but much of that year of life was made possible by Bruenn's medication and treatment. [2]

In March 1944, Bruenn could not guarantee Roosevelt would survive his current term, much less run for another one. But Roosevelt was determined, regardless of health, to seek reelection. Actually, Bruenn never told Roosevelt how sick he was, and Roosevelt never asked. When the president fell asleep in midconversation, or fell out of his wheelchair, White House servants would assist him and say nothing. To curious reporters, Roosevelt dismissed his haggard look by saying he had a touch of flu and a cough. Ever the fighter, Roosevelt conserved his energy, cut down on cigarettes, and plotted his campaign for a fourth term. Privately he would tell his staff he felt "rotten," but his mental capacity was still strong.[3] Even at death's door, FDR was still in charge.

Bad health was just one of Roosevelt's many obstacles. The polls, for example, were none too encouraging. A recent Gallup poll showed Dewey, the anticipated Republican candidate, beating FDR by a 51 to 30 percent margin if the war were over by election time. Americans resented wartime restrictions, and Roosevelt remembered well how Democrats had been ousted from power after World War I.

The discouraging polls put added pressure on Roosevelt to dump Henry Wallace as vice president. Wallace was a loyal New Dealer, but was unpopular with many Democratic leaders, especially in the South. Roosevelt's strategists told him Wallace would cost the ticket more votes than he would add. In early July, before the Democratic convention began, Roosevelt sorted through possible candidates for vice president with his advisors. They settled on Harry Truman, a border state New Dealer who satisfied Democratic leaders on most issues. His Truman Committee, which was investigating military camps and defense contractors, was effective and popular.

Roosevelt had personally made Wallace vice president in 1940 and owed him no political favors. The president could easily have asked Wallace to step down, which Wallace offered to do at one point. Instead, Roosevelt told Wallace face-to-face that he hoped to have him back on the ticket again. "I hope it will be the same old team," he assured Wallace. Roosevelt even told the delegates to the Democratic convention, "I personally would vote for his [Wallace's] renomination if I were a delegate." But behind the scenes, Roosevelt worked to sabotage Wallace's candidacy. The president's emissaries called every state delegation to tell them FDR wanted Truman. Wallace made a gallant run for vice president, but the delegates chose Truman on the second ballot.[4]

Even though Roosevelt was weak from heart problems, he had not lost his ability to persuade. Wallace later said of Roosevelt's profession of loyalty that his words were "absolutely and utterly convincing." Wallace added, "If Roosevelt had kept hands off I could have been named [by the convention]."[5] Wallace was a bit naïve. Back in 1940, Roosevelt had encouraged James Farley, Cordell Hull, and others to run for president. Then, after they announced their candidacies and did some campaigning, Roosevelt snatched the nomination from them at a carefully crafted Democratic convention.

Even with Wallace off the ticket, the president would have much more persuading to do, and limited energy to do it. Under doctor's orders, the White House staff limited Roosevelt to working at most only twenty hours a week. Historian Robert Ferrell, who has studied Roosevelt's appointment books carefully, estimates that Roosevelt was only working four hours a day, maybe less. And he was away from the White House, usually on vacation, 175 days during 1944. Thus, he had little time for the war or politics. During those few hours Roosevelt was able to work, he had to conserve his energy and use the powers of government very wisely.[6] The political problem, as Roosevelt's pollsters told him, was remobilizing Democratic voters and luring back those who had voted Republican in 1942.

The Republican-dominated Congress, elected in 1942, had wrecked much of the president's New Deal machinery for organizing voters. The WPA had been abolished in the last Congress, along with the NYA and the CCC—all of which Roosevelt had used to win votes in 1936 and 1940. Republicans also slashed the OWI, Roosevelt's major propaganda agency during the war. If

Roosevelt were to win, he would have to rebuild his election machinery and reinvigorate the Democratic Party. He started by hiring pollster Hadley Cantril to give him good political advice. "Ways must be found," Cantril recommended, "to make it possibl[e] and easy ... for men in the armed forces to vote both at home and abroad, and ... for defense workers to vote in any location to which they have moved."[7]

Since soldiers were a likely bloc of Democratic voters, Roosevelt tried to win their votes to replace those lost when the WPA was dismantled. First, Roosevelt supported the G.I. Bill to give education, housing grants, and subsidies to returning veterans. For the next step, Roosevelt supported the federal ballot, which was a shortened mass-produced ballot that would go out to soldiers. It would include federal elections only—the contests for president, Senate, and House. It would exclude other state and local races, because including them would require a huge bureaucracy to print and distribute thousands of different ballots, and find the exact soldiers for whom each of these ballots would be relevant.[8]

The Republicans, who saw through the president's tactics, argued that the Constitution put states in charge of elections; each soldier ought to have a ballot that included all state and local elections relevant to his hometown and state. Yes, that would be a bureaucratic nightmare and reduce turnout, but that was what the Constitution demanded. The political angle in FDR's federal ballot bothered the Republicans even more. "Nearly every means of communication to the men serving abroad is controlled by Government," Robert Taft noted. "If the federal ballot was approved, there was a danger that those who control ... the means of communication" would "conduct a campaign on one side against those who do not have equal facility to reach the men in the armed forces." Taft could also have argued that the federal ballot, if given to soldiers, should also be given to all Japanese-Americans eligible to vote, but currently confined in relocation centers. After a series of compromises in the House and Senate, the Republicans largely prevailed.

Under the banner of states' rights, few soldiers would use the federal ballot in 1944.[9]

Roosevelt's next step was to mobilize unions to win the urban vote. The last Republican Congress would make that hard for him to do. In the spring of 1943, John L. Lewis led his mine workers on a major coal strike. FDR took over those mines to keep war production going, and the Senate passed a bill permitting the president to seize factories closed by strikes. The House added a clause to prohibit labor organizations from making political contributions. The resulting Smith-Connally bill passed both houses in 1943, but Roosevelt was aghast at the thought of losing union donations. He therefore vetoed Smith-Connally, but the Senate and House, with strong Democratic support in the South, overrode Roosevelt's veto. Unions, therefore, could not legally raise money for FDR in 1944.[10]

Roosevelt circumvented Smith-Connally with help from Philip Murray and Sidney Hillman, the president and vice president of the Congress of Industrial Organizations (CIO). They formed a Political Action Committee (PAC), the first of its kind in U.S. history. This labor PAC was created to "educate" union members by giving speeches, printing literature and passing it out. Republicans howled that such "education" was really funding in disguise. But Francis Biddle, Roosevelt's attorney general, made a ruling that unions could "educate" their members and then organize them, help them register to vote, and even take them to the polls on election day—and not violate the letter of the Smith-Connally bill.[11]

Once the PAC was declared legal, Sidney Hillman, a longtime friend of the president, was put in charge. An immigrant from Lithuania, Hillman helped found the Amalgamated Clothing Workers of America. He had also become vice president of the CIO, and he had worked with Roosevelt on the NRA and, early in the war, on the OPM. As one of the most energetic labor leaders, he was well suited to organize voters for the president.[12]

Hillman raised money to fund a headquarters for the PAC in

New York City, and fourteen regional offices throughout the country. Hillman plowed over $1.5 million into the PAC to do newspaper ads, radio spots, voter registration, and massive canvassing of war plants and shipyards for election day. It would possibly be the most comprehensive lobby effort in U.S. history to elect a president. They covered America's major cities block by block and handed out more than 85 million pieces of campaign literature. On election day, the PAC's car pools and voter banks were used by twenty thousand volunteers and staffers in New York City alone, and more than that scattered in all major cities in the country.[13]

Republicans watched with alarm as Democrats mobilized an army of blue-collar voters for FDR. Even many southern Democrats were annoyed. Martin Dies (D-Tex.), chairman of the House Un-American Activities Committee, pointed out that many communists were involved in the PAC's activities. The communist presence in the Democratic campaign was further seen when Earl Browder, head of the Communist Party of America, also endorsed FDR. The president had pardoned Browder, who was serving time in a federal prison for passport fraud, and Browder decided to form the Communist Political Association and publicly back FDR in 1944. Roosevelt technically repudiated the endorsement of the CPA, but privately did nothing to block their influence on the PAC.[14]

With the PAC busily organizing Democratic voters, Roosevelt decided to be presidential and stay aloof from public appearances. Of course, he was too sick to campaign hard, and the fewer people who saw him—and heard him—the better. Therefore, he avoided the Democratic convention that nominated him and broadcast his acceptance speech via radio from a train in San Diego—where he was touring military facilities in presidential fashion. "I shall not campaign," Roosevelt told the convention, "in the usual sense, for the office." He artfully added, "In these days of global warfare I shall not be able to find the time."[15] During his speech, Roosevelt allowed photographers on the train to take pictures of him. Those photos revealed a gaunt and tired man, with mouth elongated, head drooping, and legs withered. Steve Early, FDR's press secretary, was "terrifically disappointed" with Roosevelt's appearance in the pictures. "Something decidedly was wrong," Early admitted.[16]

After touring various military facilities in the Northwest, Roosevelt headed to Hawaii to meet with Admiral Nimitz and General MacArthur about Japan. MacArthur later said, "I had been shocked at his personal appearance. . . . He was just a shell of the man I had known. It was clearly evident that his days were numbered." Later FDR was off to Quebec to meet with Churchill, who was so distressed by Roosevelt's appearance that he, Churchill, asked to see Dr. McIntire privately to discuss it. William MacKenzie King, the Canadian prime minister, was also "shocked at his [Roosevelt's] appearance." "It seems to me . . . ," King wrote in his diary "that he had failed very much since I last saw him."[17]

On rare occasions, when Roosevelt decided to risk a public speech, or even a public appearance, there could be problems. After returning from Hawaii, for example, he gave a speech from a ship at Bremerton, Washington, on August 12. But he was too weak to do the speech well, and he had an angina attack in the middle of it. Thus, the speech, according to his personal secretary, Grace Tully, was "one of the poorest speeches he ever made, both in form and in delivery." The president's handlers were nervous. Special Counsel Sam Rosenman, when he heard the speech on the radio, realized "something must have happened to the president."[18]

Those close to the campaign wondered if Roosevelt would survive. Speechwriter Robert Sherwood cited Roosevelt's "almost ravaged appearance," and reporter Allen Drury, after an embarrassing press conference, was "wondering if it has been the last" for the president. Newspapers raised doubts as well. The *New York Daily News* asked the president to have a physical exam, and let the public know the results. The *New York World-Telegram*, in an editorial, described "the genuine weariness of an aging man." Was the president near death? The *Chicago Tribune* and other Republican newspapers featured pictures of a haggard Roosevelt for readers to ponder.[19]

Six days after the Bremerton fiasco, Roosevelt was back at the White House, avoiding public appearances and working only a few hours each day. When Harry Truman came to the White House for lunch, he was among the many who were shocked at how ill the president looked. To reporters afterward, Truman said, "Don't let anybody kid you about it. He's keen as a briar." But privately, back at the office, Truman told his administrative assistant, "You know, I am concerned about the president's health. I had no idea he was in such feeble condition. . . . His hands are shaking and he talks with considerable difficulty."[20]

On the Republican side, Governor Thomas Dewey of New York won the nomination as expected. Short, dark, and sporting a mustache, Dewey had won recognition for cleaning up city government in New York. At age forty-two, Dewey's youth contrasted with Roosevelt's haggard appearance. In Dewey's acceptance speech at the Republican convention, he played up this contrast. The New Deal, he charged, "has grown old in office." Three terms in office, and running for a fourth, were too much for any man as the Founders of our country told us. Therefore, Dewey concluded, we should oust these "stubborn men, grown old and tired and quarrelsome in office." The New Deal, Dewey continued, started with seven years of massive spending and growth in government, but still left the nation with 10 million unemployed as late as 1940. Then we traded unemployment for war. Dewey slammed his fist and asked, "Do we have to have a war in order to get jobs?" Next Dewey looked ahead: "What are we offered now?" he asked. "Only the dreary prospect of a continued war economy after the war, with interference piled on interference, and petty tyrannies rivaling the very regimentation against which we are now at war." Then Dewey hit the president between the eyes. "This present administration has never solved this fundamental problem of jobs and opportunity." He added, "It can never solve this problem. It has never even understood what makes a job. . . . It has specialized in curtailment and restriction."[21]

Dewey's speech kept the health issue in the forefront of the campaign. FDR, so haggard and so unconvincing in his assurances, needed help from surrogates. First was Governor Robert Kerr of Oklahoma, who brought the war into focus at the Democratic convention on Roosevelt's terms. Kerr asked, "Shall we discard as a 'tired old man' 59-year-old Admiral Nimitz . . . 62-year-old Admiral Halsey . . . 64-year-old General MacArthur . . . 66-year-old Admiral King . . . 64-year-old General Marshall? No . . . we are winning the war with these 'tired old men,' including the 62-year-old Roosevelt as their Commander-in-Chief." Robert Hannegan, the chairman of the Democratic National Committee, hit on another angle: "The risks of a total war are too great to entrust . . . waging it from here on to a novice." Roosevelt liked that line of attack. In his acceptance speech, he asked the voters "whether they wish to turn over this 1944 job, this world-wide job, to inexperienced or immature hands" or keep it with the president.[22]

In one of the president's infrequent public speeches, he addressed the Teamsters union in Washington, D.C., on September 23. "You know, I am actually four years older, which is a fact that seems to annoy some people," Roosevelt quipped. Then he burdened Dewey with Hoover and the Great Depression. "Now there is an old and somewhat lugubrious adage which says: 'Never speak of rope in the house of a man who has been hanged.' In the same way, if I were a Republican leader speaking to a mixed audience, the last word in the whole dictionary that I think I would use is that word, 'depression.'"

Then Roosevelt turned the charges of wasteful spending back on the Republicans with his sharp wit:

> These Republican leaders have not been content with attacks on me, or my wife, or on my sons. No, not content with that, they now include my little dog, Fala. Well, of course, I don't resent at-

tacks, and my family doesn't resent attacks, but Fala does resent them. You know, Fala is Scotch, and being a Scottie, as soon as he learned that the Republican fiction writers in Congress and out had concocted a story that I had left him behind on the Aleutian Islands and had sent a destroyer back to find him—at a cost to the taxpayers of two or three, or eight or twenty million dollars—his Scotch soul was furious. He has not been the same dog since. I am accustomed to hearing malicious falsehoods about myself—such as that old, worm-eaten chestnut that I have represented myself as indispensable. But I think I have a right to resent, to object to libelous statements about my dog.[23]

By implication, anyone who could be so witty could not be so sick. That flustered the Republicans. "The people here who are handling Dewey," one reporter wrote, "had figured the President on basis of his San Diego picture and his Bremerton speech."[24]

But Dewey had more issues at hand than the president's health. Early in the campaign, Dewey decided to make the communist and far-left support for Roosevelt an issue in the campaign.[25] "Why are the Communists so strongly for Roosevelt?" he asked. The whole system of communist infiltration into the U.S. government puzzled Dewey and others. In agency after agency, communists—and other security risks—could be hired, and then have influence on public policy. Of course, the Russians were American allies in the war, but should that mean that U.S. government agencies should hire communists? Under Roosevelt, the answer was, "Sometimes, yes." Here is why.

Before the war, overt communists were excluded from any important U.S. government job. The Navy, for example, barred communists and Nazis from radio jobs on American ships. After all, radio work involved transmitting secret military information. In May 1942, however, Frank Knox lifted this ban. That decision is described in Navy records as follows:

The Secretary [Knox] . . . said that he had no brief for the activities of the Communist Party, but that the President had stated that, considering the fact that the United States and Russia were allies at this time, and that the Communist Party and the United States effort were now bent toward our winning the war, the United States was bound not to oppose the activities of the Communist Party, and specifically, to not disapprove the employment of any radio operator for the sole reason that he was a member of the Communist Party or that he was active in Communist affairs.[26]

By 1944, the Army was using similar procedures. Also, the U.S. Civil Service Commission canceled its ban on hiring communists. New orders told civil service investigators not to ask job applicants about their membership in the Communist Party, or in any communist front groups. Under these circumstances, communists could more easily enter the U.S. government and promote their views. The OWI and the Board of Economic Warfare, for example, had many communists and radicals in them. The recent Congress, however, had reorganized both agencies.[27]

Dewey was alarmed at the influence communists were having on American life. They and their radical sympathizers seemed to be dominating Roosevelt's campaign. Earl Browder, the head of the U.S. Communist Party, was giving speeches for FDR. Sidney Hillman was not a communist, but, as a labor leader, he often made alliances with them and even hired one as his lawyer.[28]

Hillman had flirted with communism from the time of his youth in Lithuania to his life in New York as a union president. He came to America at age eighteen, but went to Russia after the Bolshevik revolution and met with Lenin and Trotsky. Hillman called them "realistic, practical, and courageous." In 1921, the thirty-four-year-old Hillman called Lenin "one of the few great men that the human race has produced, one of the greatest statesmen of our age and perhaps of all ages." Twenty-one years later, he told FDR that he supported an excess profits tax of 100 percent on corporations. The FBI began a long file on Hillman and was especially interested in his support for the American Fund for Public Service, which donated money to the *Daily Worker*, a communist newspaper, and other causes, both communist and non-communist. Hillman also served on their board of directors.[29]

Dewey made Browder and Hillman issues in the campaign. The Democratic Party, Dewey insisted, had been kidnapped by New Dealers, the PAC, and the communists "to change our system of government." "In America," Dewey said, "a communist is a man who supports a fourth term." When Arthur Krock reported that Roosevelt had asked party leaders to "clear everything with Sidney" before choosing Truman as vice president, Dewey attacked Hillman's towering influence on the president. Dewey also attacked Hillman's method of coaxing voters. He "stalks the country squeezing dollars for a fourth term campaign out of the working men and women of America, under threat that if they do not give the dollar, they will lose their jobs." Hillman countered by calling Dewey a "red-baiter," and the attacks on communists probably persuaded few voters. Even Dewey himself had no idea how many communists were employed by the U.S. government, how much damage they were doing with their espionage, how many documents they were smuggling out of the country, and how much equipment they were stealing from the Lend-Lease airport in Montana.[30]

Since Roosevelt was campaigning on his record as commander in chief during wartime, Dewey decided to attack that record. After he had done so, FDR responded by saying, "Perhaps the most ridiculous of these campaign falsifications is the one that this Administration failed to prepare for the war that was coming. I doubt whether even Goebbels would have tried that one." The president added, "For even he would never have dared hope that the voters of America had already forgotten that many of the Republican leaders in the Congress and outside the Congress tried to thwart and block nearly every attempt that this Administration made to warn our people and arm our nation."[31]

Dewey accepted Roosevelt's challenge to debate his war preparedness. "Now I had not intended in this campaign," Dewey said, "to rake over my opponent's sad record of failing to prepare the defenses of this country for war. It's all in the past—a very tragic past. It has cost countless American lives; it has caused untold misery." Then he quoted General Marshall and General Hap Arnold on the weak state of the U.S. military in 1941. "Now Mr. Roosevelt, did those statements [by General Marshall] come from Goebbels? Was that fraud or falsification? Those are the words of General George C. Marshall, Chief of Staff of the United States Army, under oath." Then Dewey added, "After Pearl Harbor, we found ourselves woefully unprepared for war." Roosevelt was "desperately bad" in preparing for war and in defending Pearl Harbor.[32]

Other Republicans seized the Pearl Harbor issue. John Bricker, Dewey's vice presidential candidate, accused the White House of a cover-up in the "disgraceful Pearl Harbor episode." Rep. Hugh Scott (R-Pa.) wondered why the American fleet was sent to Hawaii in the first place. Dewey, with help from friends, discovered that Japanese codes had been broken before Pearl Harbor. That suggested that Roosevelt knew the war was coming but was caught napping anyway. Senator Styles Bridges of New Hampshire went on the Senate floor to say Dewey was "gathering facts" on Pearl Harbor that might suggest a presidential whitewash.[33]

When General Marshall heard about Dewey's speech and its aftermath, he sprang into action. Marshall was nervous that a Pearl Harbor debate in the midst of the war would undermine national unity and jeopardize military success by revealing publicly that the United States had broken the Japanese codes—codes still being used by Japan. Marshall sent Colonel Carter Clarke to Tulsa with a top-secret letter for Dewey, but Dewey thought it was a trap. "Marshall does not do things like that," Dewey told Clarke. "I am confident that Franklin Roosevelt is behind this whole thing." He refused to read beyond the first paragraph of the letter. Dewey told Clarke he knew all about the code breaking "and Franklin Roosevelt knows about it too. He knew what was happening before Pearl Harbor, and instead of being re-elected he ought to be impeached."[34]

Marshall was alarmed when he heard about Dewey's reaction. Shortly, Marshall and Dewey talked on the phone, and Dewey agreed to see Clarke again. In their next meeting, Dewey read Marshall's letter urging Dewey not to discuss Pearl Harbor "because the military hazards involved are so serious that I feel some action is necessary to protect the interests of our armed forces." Yes, the United States had broken the Japanese codes, Marshall admitted, but we didn't know Hawaii was the target, and bureaucratic delays kept the warnings from reaching Pearl Harbor in time. But later those broken codes had helped the United States succeed in the Coral Sea and at Midway. They were still helping us because we could gain information on "Hitler's intentions in Europe . . . from Baron Oshima's messages from Berlin reporting his interviews with Hitler and other officials to the Japanese Government. These are still in the code involved in the Pearl Harbor events." Marshall concluded, "You will understand from the foregoing the utter tragic consequences if the present political debates regarding Pearl Harbor disclose to the enemy, German or Jap, any suspicion of the vital sources of information we now possess."[35]

Dewey was angry, and let Clarke know it. Roosevelt was "a traitor" for his incompetence at Pearl Harbor, Dewey exclaimed. But he realized, for the sake of the American military, in the national interest, that he had to keep Pearl Harbor out of the campaign. Thus, he instructed his assistant to collect all of the Pearl Harbor research, "put it away securely and forget it." And so, Dewey was not able to exploit the failure at Pearl Harbor or the presence of communists in government. What's more, FDR was able to negotiate around the delicate issues of civil liberties for blacks, for Japanese-Americans, and for Poland, with Polish-Americans watching.

First was the black vote. Dewey was challenging Roosevelt by direct appeals to blacks, who had been historically Republican. For example, Governor Dewey appointed a black to the New York Supreme Court. Also, Dewey's Republican platform opposed the poll tax and favored an antilynching law—both of which Roosevelt had refused to act on. Furthermore, the Republican platform called for a "congressional inquiry" to investigate "segregation and discrimination against Negroes who are in our armed forces." Dewey's actions and positions on those issues appealed to black voters, but Hillman's PAC went into black areas of the nation's cities, passing out pamphlets and exhorting black voters to support the president. PAC workers not only helped swing the black vote to FDR, but in New York they also elected the first black congressman in Harlem's history, Adam Clayton Powell, Jr.[36]

Roosevelt, feeble as he was, had to solve some of his political problems himself. The Japanese-Americans, for example, were pressing their case for freedom to the U.S. Supreme Court, in *Korematsu v. United States*, which challenged the constitutionality of the executive order that had sent Japanese-Americans into internment camps. By March 1944, it was painfully obvious that the overwhelming majority of Japanese-Americans confined in relocation centers posed no danger to American society. Some had even been released to join the military; they were serving bravely and effectively in the armed forces. But Roosevelt wanted to keep the Japanese confined because their return to California would upset voters there and create a possible backlash against him in the 1944 elections.

From the standpoint of sabotage and espionage, General Marshall confirmed that the Japanese-Americans were not a threat to America. Major General Charles Bonesteel, who became the new head of the Western Defense Command in June 1944, agreed with Marshall. Some individual Japanese-Americans might be a threat, as were some German-Americans and Italian-Americans, but "there is no longer a military necessity for the mass exclusion of the Japanese from the West Coast as a whole."[37]

At a May 26 cabinet meeting, even Henry Stimson, who helped launch the internment policy, argued that "the ban . . . should . . . be lifted." Harold Ickes agreed: "I made the statement that unless it were determined as a matter of deliberate policy to postpone the lifting of the ban on the Pacific Coast until after election, it should be lifted right away—the sooner the better." After the cabinet meeting, Ickes confided in his diary, "My expectation now is that this issue will continue to be evaded until after the election." The problem, Ickes noted, was that Roosevelt might lose the *Korematsu* v. *United States* case before the Supreme Court in the fall. "That would leave us on the eve of election in the position of having committed an illegal act." [38]

Roosevelt urged Ickes to investigate "with great discretion how many Japanese families would be acceptable to public opinion" on the West Coast. Perhaps, Roosevelt suggested, the Japanese could again be forcibly reassigned, this time across the nation, "one or two families to each county as a start." But, as General Bonesteel noted when he heard the president's plan, the Japanese wanted to go back to their own houses, not be scattered and "isolated from their own people." Furthermore, "if they are not returned, a very large number of them will bring legal action to accomplish it." Thus, Roosevelt decided to take his chances—he would keep the Japanese-Americans in the camps, hope he won the Supreme Court case, and then hope to carry the western states in the election. [39]

During the campaign, Roosevelt won the *Korematsu* case 6–3. Many of the justices he had appointed, led by Hugo Black, backed up FDR's executive order, which had forced the whole Japanese-American community into relocation camps as a military necessity. When complaints followed, Stimson turned them over to his assistant secretary of state, John McCloy. General Bonesteel, for example, did not seem to grasp the political maneuvering going on; he kept insisting to McCloy that "mass exclusion is no longer justified." Let them go. When McCloy ignored his letters, Bonesteel said he would visit McCloy directly and make his case. McCloy then put Bonesteel off with these words: "There is a disposition not to crowd action too closely upon the heels of the election" on November 7. The administration probably would, he assured Bonesteel, "have a greater opportunity for constructive plans at a date somewhat later than November 6."[40]

Sure enough, on election day Roosevelt won reelection, he carried California, and the Democrats won four new House seats in that state. Three days after the election, at the first cabinet meeting, Roosevelt announced the end of the Japanese-American crisis; he asked Stimson to write up a plan to release the interned Japanese-Americans. FDR had escaped a political disaster.

Another delicate issue for Roosevelt was the concern of six million Polish-Americans for the independence of Poland after the war. Roosevelt had already conceded Poland to Stalin but had told him that he couldn't "publicly take part in any such arrangement at the present time" because of the Polish vote. By March 1944, however, as Stalin's Army approached Poland, the Poles in America began to worry about what Roosevelt might have given away at Teheran, and how he felt about Poland's independence. Roosevelt gave them public assurances that Poland would be fine. He committed himself in the Democratic platform to give "support to the Atlantic charter," which promised freedom and self-determination for all the countries of Europe after the war.[41]

Some Polish-Americans were uneasy about Stalin's motives and Roosevelt's backbone. They formed the Polish-American Congress to promote Poland's independence, and they had their first meeting in May in the heavily Polish city of Buffalo, New York. Roosevelt sent David Niles to the meeting as an observer, and he reported ominous irritation with the president. Niles saw "terrific resentment against the Administration which will eventually crystallize in some unfriendly form." What's worse, advisor Isador Lubin told the president that "an underground movement among the Catholics is playing up our friendship with Russia." Roosevelt was already on record denying Russian responsibility for the Katyn massacre; and by August the Russians were letting Poles die by the tens of thousands in the Warsaw uprising. Why wasn't Roosevelt taking more action to urge Stalin to help the Poles fight against Hitler?[42]

Roosevelt sought advice from Hadley Cantril, his pollster. Cantril was showing large defections of Catholic voters from the Democratic Party—18 percent among upper-income Catholics, 11 percent among middle-income Catholics, and 4 percent among low-income Catholics, a national total, Cantril estimated, of 730,000 votes, or a 10 percent reduction from Roosevelt's Catholic vote in 1940.[43]

Roosevelt knew he had to act to stanch the bleeding. On October 11 (Pulaski Day), he invited the leaders of the Polish-American Congress to the White House and met with them personally. He told them he believed "Poland must be reconstituted as a great nation." He had a big map of prewar Poland in the room, and had his photo taken pointing to the map, surrounded by a dozen or so Polish-American leaders.[44]

The president of the Polish-American Congress, Charles Rozmarek, was apparently still not persuaded that Roosevelt was being honest, so the president, two weeks later, met with him privately and promised him that Poland would be treated fairly at the forthcoming peace conference. After the meeting, Rozmarek told reporters, "The president assured me that he will carry out the pledges of the Democratic Party platform . . . that Poland is treated justly at the peace conference." Therefore, he endorsed Roosevelt for president: "I shall vote for him on November 7."[45]

Frank Januszewski, a vice president of the Polish-American Congress, still had doubts, and wrote Republican senator Arthur Vandenberg for his opinion. "We cannot prove that they have been 'sold down the river' (if they have)," Vandenberg lamented, "and we cannot conscientiously promise them that they can rely upon us for a better deal when we collide with Stalin at the Peace Table."[46]

On election day, Roosevelt, with Rozmarek's help, won almost 90 percent of Polish-American votes—and he didn't have to meet again with Stalin for four more months, at which time the Polish-Americans would finally begin to learn the bad news about Stalin's real intentions and Roosevelt's grand concessions to him. There would be no self-determination for Poland. After Yalta, Rozmarek denounced the new "illegal, Communist-dominated Warsaw government" and the "dictatorial manner in which the Polish question was settled." If only the election had been held after Yalta, Rozmarek lamented, the result might have been different. Rozmarek became an instant Republican. He endorsed Thomas Dewey for president in 1948.[47]

Roosevelt's sly outmaneuvering of Rozmarek and the Poles was part of a late-campaign development. The president had temporarily regained energy. Whether his heart briefly improved, or whether the campaign got his blood circulating better, or whether his indomitable will rose up, no one will ever know. One person who noticed the change was reporter Turner Catledge. On October 17, Roosevelt called Catledge to the White House to pump him for information on the campaign. "When I walked into his office," Catledge said, "a new man was sitting there beaming at me. He was still thin and emaciated, but he had life and spirit in his face, and I remember thinking, 'It's the campaign that's revived him—politics is this man's life blood.'" Roosevelt talked energetically about the election and asked Catledge for his opinions on strategy.[48]

Dr. Bruenn, although alarmed at Roosevelt's sudden "disregard of the rest regimen," was pleased with the president's improvement. "B[lood] P[ressure] levels have been, if anything, lower than before," Bruenn wrote. "Patient is eating fairly well and . . . appears to be well stabilized on his digitalis."[49]

Roosevelt needed all the energy he could muster. Polls showed that almost one in three voters did not think Roosevelt, if elected, would survive another term. In the last weeks of the campaign,

Roosevelt agreed to give major speeches, which he could do sitting down, in New York, Philadelphia, Chicago, and Boston. Even more dramatically, Roosevelt rode in an open car in a motorcade, covering the boroughs of New York, fifty-one miles on a cold, windy, rainy Saturday, October 21. More than one million New Yorkers could see for themselves the bundled president smiling and waving to the crowds, forcing himself for four hours to pretend he was well.[50]

Once on the campaign trail, Roosevelt attacked the Republicans with gusto. On October 28, for example, just hours after his coup with Rozmarek, an energized Roosevelt spoke to more than one hundred thousand people at Soldiers' Field in Chicago. First, he broached the health issue indirectly. "Republican orators," the president noted, attack the New Deal but then want to preserve the programs in it. "And they go on to say, 'Those same quarrelsome, tired old men—they have built the greatest military machine the world has ever known, which is fighting its way to victory; and' they say, 'if you elect us, we promise not to change any of that, either.'" Roosevelt continued, "They also say in effect, 'Those inefficient and worn-out crackpots have really begun to lay the foundations of a lasting world peace. If you elect us, we will not change any of that, either.'"[51]

Much of the speech was his plan for an "economic bill of rights" for postwar America: FDR wanted to revitalize and expand the New Deal through massive federal programs. Roosevelt had avoided the New Deal during much of the war; now that peace was near, he gingerly set forth his goals for the economy. He usually avoided that subject because it was controversial. Roosevelt's best chance to win the election, as polls confirmed, was to be the nation's commander in chief, an expert strategist, planning the end game for the war.[52]

Dewey may have been surprised by Roosevelt's late-campaign blitz. In the week before the election, Dewey said, Roosevelt "offers us nothing except a repetition of the New Deal policies which failed for eight straight years."[53] True, Dewey seemed to accept many New Deal programs, and Roosevelt was accurate to point that out. But Dewey clearly opposed the New Deal revival. On redistribution, for example, Dewey deplored setting "class against class."[54] His solution was to "reduce personal income tax rates." That way, people "can be encouraged to expand and help create the millions of jobs we need."[55] We must, Dewey insisted, "release the energies of this country and at the same time reduce these taxes on men who will make $11 a week."[56]

Dewey's campaign fell short. On November 7, Roosevelt won a comfortable 53 percent of the popular vote, and a 432 to 99 advantage in the electoral college. Still, Dewey had done better than the others who had challenged Roosevelt. In the twelve largest cities, where the PAC was the strongest, Roosevelt won 2.2 million votes more than Dewey—an edge that clearly swung New York, Michigan, and other states into the Democratic column.[57]

When Roosevelt heard the election news, he was pleased to win but upset with Dewey. "I still think he is a son of a bitch," the president told an aide before going to bed on election night.[58] Roosevelt's hostility is odd. Granted, no one likes to be criticized on the campaign trail. But Dewey was restrained. He said FDR was a "tired old man," but never said he was half dead, as many others did. Dewey accused FDR of having communists in government, but never speculated, as others did, about the breaches of security that let the Russians pilfer documents and equipment in the United States. Dewey, after prodding from Marshall, clammed up about the broken Japanese codes at Pearl Harbor. When FDR learned about Dewey's forbearance on that issue, he said Dewey was desperate even to consider bringing it up.

Maybe as Roosevelt's health weakened, so did his willingness to hear someone tarnish his legacy. Roosevelt was the longest-serving president, and he hoped to be known as the greatest. And here was Dewey publicly challenging that view. As Roosevelt said of Dewey, "He talks to the people as if they were the jury and I were the villain on trial for his life."[59] Roosevelt was always the hero of his own life.

THE WAR ENDS ON THE USS *MISSOURI*

At the White House correspondents' dinner in March 1945, Arthur Krock was there as head of the *New York Times*' Washington bureau. Krock's editorials gave the public incisive analysis of the Roosevelt administration's policies, often pointing to problems caused by FDR's management style, or lack thereof. Krock tried to avoid personal contact with Roosevelt, because it was too easy to be swayed by the charming president; FDR was just too persuasive in person. Roosevelt often retaliated to Krock's criticism by giving news stories to other journalists at the *New York Times*, including Anne O'Hare McCormick and Turner Catledge.[1]

The president had just returned a few weeks before from the Yalta conference, and Krock had seen the photographs of FDR, Stalin, and Churchill together. FDR's physical deterioration could not be hidden from the cameras. Even so, Krock said, "The White House doctors were still giving optimistic public diagnoses of his condition. So I was shocked at the President's appearance in the flesh [at the dinner]. If ever impending death was written on a human countenance, it seemed to me I saw it that night."[2]

Krock was seated near the exit ramp, which the president used at the conclusion of the dinner. Krock's expression as FDR went by in his wheelchair showed that he was concerned about Roosevelt's health. But FDR hadn't lost his quick wit and said, "Cheer up, Arthur. Things have seldom been as bad as you said they were."

Despite his ghastly appearance, Roosevelt's doctors continued to assure the press that he was in reasonably good health, "thus everyone in the world was totally unprepared for his death," observed Krock.[3] On April 12, Roosevelt was at his home in Warm Springs, Georgia, having his portrait painted by artist Elizabeth Shoumatoff, when he said, "I have a terrific pain in the back of my head." He slumped forward and was carried, unconscious, to his bedroom. He died within minutes from a massive stroke.

Even in death, FDR was still up to his old ways of getting what he wanted, but hiding so much. In the room with him that day at Warm Springs was Lucy Mercer Rutherford, his former mistress from his younger days. The portrait painter quickly escorted her away from Warm Springs after FDR died. Back in 1918, when Eleanor discovered their affair, Roosevelt promised his wife that he would never see Lucy again. FDR had ended the relationship, but renewed his ties with Lucy during later years. Eleanor had to deal with the knowledge that FDR's former mistress was the person with him on his last day.

Perhaps the most shocked person in the country when President Roosevelt died was Vice President Harry Truman. Now, as President Truman, he assumed vast power and decision-making authority during a world war. Roosevelt hadn't discussed war plans with his vice president; they had been in the same room only a few times. Truman was not yet aware of the atomic bomb project.

Immediately, Truman's administration was faced with negotiations for the surrender of Germany. The policy of "unconditional surrender" as announced by FDR at Casablanca in 1943 had hindered relations with the Nazis, who used the term as propaganda to spur on the German people to stay in the war. Also, Great Britain, the Soviet Union, and the United States could not agree on postwar plans for Germany, so no comprehensive Allied statement to reassure German citizens was possible.[4]

Adding to the confusion was Secretary Henry Morgenthau's proposal to "pastoralize" Germany after the war: strip all industrial equipment, ship it to Russia and other Allied countries as restitution, then divide Germany into northern and southern districts, which would be strictly agricultural. The Morgenthau Plan was never adopted, but when it was revealed in the press, German leaders used it as proof of what unconditional surrender would mean. The unintended consequences of Morgenthau's strategy may have been the delay of Germany's surrender, which the Allies finally celebrated on May 8.

In the Pacific, the battle for Iwo Jima during February and March had shown the world how difficult fighting the Japanese could be. Almost 19,000 Japanese soldiers on the island fought to the death, with only 216 taken prisoner. U.S. Marines battled for weeks to clean out the caves and tunnels on the rocky fortress. Almost 7,000 Americans died there, with about 19,000 wounded. The U.S. Army and Marines were fighting on Okinawa when FDR died in April. By June, the battle was won, but 7,613 Americans were dead and more than 31,000 wounded, with 110,000 Japanese casualties. Almost 5,000 American sailors had also died in the waters around Okinawa. But to invade the home islands of Japan, what would be the cost?[5]

The fate of hundreds of thousands of Allied prisoners of war also hung in the balance. In January 1944, the American public was electrified by the accounts of three escaped American officers from a POW camp in the Philippines. The officers described the Japanese brutality of the sixty-mile march from Bataan to Camp O'Donnell after the U.S. surrender in the spring of 1942. Thousands of American soldiers died during the "death march" and at Camp O'Donnell, and tens of thousands of Filipino "scouts" perished, too, as the Japanese took revenge for the Filipinos' resistance to Japanese rule. Truman and Stimson knew that POWs worked as slave laborers in Japan and Manchuria. Captives from the battles for Malaysia and the Dutch East Indies were still in labor camps throughout Asia. Many of these captives could not survive a prolonged war; they were at the end of their physical resources.[6]

Truman concluded that he must approve the use of atomic weapons on Japan. He must end the war quickly, without a bloody invasion of the Japanese islands costing hundreds of thousands of lives. On August 6, the American Air Force dropped an atomic bomb on Hiroshima, containing uranium-235. More than 100,000 Japanese died within the first days, destroyed by a blast that leveled everything within a radius of two kilometers. Still the Japanese refused to surrender. On August 9, a bomb containing plutonium-239 destroyed Nagasaki, causing at least 45,000 immediate deaths.[7]

In negotiations, Japan wanted to keep the emperor as a condition of laying down arms, although the Allies initially demanded unconditional surrender. Australia especially wanted all vestiges of prewar authority erased in Japan, including the emperor. Finally, the Allies agreed to Japan's immediate surrender, with the condition that the emperor would remain in power. On August 14, Emperor Hirohito ordered the Japanese cabinet to accept the terms of surrender.[8]

On August 30, MacArthur landed in Atsugi, Japan, on his way to his new quarters in Yokohama. Although MacArthur's staff had landed earlier to set up a perimeter around Atsugi of five hundred veteran paratroopers, no one really knew what Japan's reaction would be. Tens of thousands of Japanese soldiers were in the area. Until two weeks earlier, they had been the general's sworn enemies. Yet MacArthur was certain of his knowledge of the Japanese mind: Their emperor had commanded the Japanese to surrender, and they would do so.

Winston Churchill later said, "Of all the amazing deeds in the war, I regard General MacArthur's personal landing at Atsugi as the bravest of the lot."[9] MacArthur's small landing party encountered no problems. The general and his aides motored safely to Yokohama's New Grand Hotel with the highway lined by Japanese soldiers standing at parade rest, their backs to MacArthur as a sign of respect.

As supreme commander for the Allied powers, MacArthur would rule Japan with as much power as a medieval shogun.[10] MacArthur lived in Yokohama for several weeks, where he began the long process of rebuilding Japan. MacArthur told his aides that one of his first goals after receiving the official surrender would be to give Japanese women the right to vote; he felt that their natural abhorrence of war would mitigate Japan's former militarism and help to prevent another war.[11]

On September 2, 1945, in tribute to President Truman's home state, the forty-five-thousand-ton battleship *Missouri* was the site for the surrender ceremonies. In Tokyo Bay, row upon row of gleaming Allied ships represented the vast armada that had battled the Japanese across the Pacific. An awed Japanese witness wrote afterward, "This was the mighty pageant of the Allied navies that so lately belched forth their crashing battle, now holding in their swift thunder and floating like calm sea birds on the subjugated waters."[12] Above the decks of the *Missouri*, General MacArthur's five-star flag fluttered in the breeze, with Admiral Nimitz's beside it. Above both military flags, the Stars and Stripes flew on this day of victory. The *New York Times* reported that it was the same American flag that had flown over the Capitol Building in Washington, D.C., on December 7, 1941, the day of the Pearl Harbor attack.[13]

MacArthur directed the surrender proceedings, flanked by General Wainwright, who had surrendered at Corregidor, and General Percival, taken prisoner at Singapore. Both men had just been freed from Japanese POW camps in Manchuria. On either side of the two emaciated generals were the Allied leaders who would sign the official documents. Hundreds of naval officers and sailors watched the ceremony from every conceivable nook and cranny on the decks, while newsreel cameramen recorded the proceedings.

The eleven members of the Japanese delegation arrived for the surrender proceedings. One of Japan's delegates, Toshikazu Kase, was in charge of writing the official report for the Imperial Palace.

He later recorded his impressions: "I felt subjected to the torture of the pillory. A million eyes seemed to beat on us with the million shafts of a rattling storm of arrows barbed with fire. We waited. . . . I tried to preserve the dignity of defeat but it was difficult and every minute contained ages."[14]

After an invocation and the playing of "The Star-Spangled Banner," MacArthur stepped to the microphone: "We are gathered here, representatives of the major warring powers, to conclude a solemn agreement whereby peace may be restored." He went on to say it would be inappropriate to discuss ideologies or to meet "in a spirit of distrust, malice or hatred." He hoped that all present would rise to a higher dignity, to work toward a world of faith and understanding, dedicated to the dignity of man and the fulfillment of freedom, tolerance, and justice. As Kase listened to these words, he was deeply moved: "He can impose a humiliating penalty if he so desires. And yet he pleads for freedom, tolerance, and justice. For me, who expected the worst humiliation, this was a complete surprise. . . . [T]his narrow quarterdeck was now transformed into an altar of peace."[15]

First, two Japanese senior officials signed the surrender documents, Foreign Minister Mamoru Shigemitsu for the Japanese government and General Yoshijiro Umezu for its military. MacArthur then sat at the green-baize-covered table to sign as supreme Allied commander, using multiple fountain pens for his various signatures; the first went to Wainwright, another to Percival, the third and fourth would go to West Point and Annapolis, and the fifth he later presented to his wife, Jean. Admiral Nimitz signed as representative of the United States; then signatories from China, Great Britain, Russia, Australia, Canada, France, the Netherlands, and New Zealand added their names.[16]

As formations of B-29s and Navy fighters approached in a flyover to commemorate the victory, MacArthur announced, "Let us pray that peace be now restored to the world and God will preserve it always. These proceedings are closed."

14

DID THE WAR END THE GREAT DEPRESSION?

"World War II got us out of the Great Depression." On the surface, this popular mantra seems to be true. Before the war, the United States had a decade of double-digit unemployment. After the United States entered the war, people had jobs, factories had orders, and the economy was booming. But that observation is superficial. The quality of American life during the war was very precarious. Overseas, our soldiers risked their lives every day—405,399 were killed, 670,846 were wounded.[1] Those who survived spent their time destroying billions of dollars' worth of property with expensive weapons. At home, food was rationed, luxuries removed, taxes high, and work dangerous. Is that really the stuff of a recovery?

FDR himself recognized the war was only a short-term fix, and a very costly one at that. The national debt had skyrocketed fivefold during the war from $49 billion to almost $260 billion. And what would happen after the war—when twelve million troops came home and when strong demand for guns, bullets, tanks, and ships ended? After World War I, unemployment had skyrocketed. Would the Great Depression, with veterans in breadlines, return after World War II?

Roosevelt envisioned a New Deal revival when the war ended. In fact, he had created the National Resources Planning Board (NRPB) in 1939, and urged it during the war to plan federal programs for peacetime. The NRPB leaders believed that strong government planning was necessary to promote economic development.[2] They consciously (and sometimes unconsciously) followed ideas popularized in 1936 by John Maynard Keynes in his best-selling book *The General Theory of Employment, Interest and Money*.[3]

Capitalism was inherently unstable, Keynes argued, and would rarely provide full employment. Therefore, government intervention was needed, especially in recessions, to spend massive amounts of money on public works, which would create new jobs, expand demand, and rebuild consumer confidence. Yes, government would need to raise taxes and run large deficits, but economic stability was society's reward. If government planners could manage aggregate demand through public works, then the business cycle of boom and bust could be flattened and economic development could be managed in the national interest. No more Great Depressions. Man could indeed be master of his economic future.

Before and during the war, Keynes's ideas swept through the United States. First they transformed the universities, then the political culture of the day. With statistics in hand, and a near reverence for government, the Keynesians were the new generation of planners who would remake society. Not entrepreneurs, but economists were needed to use the powers of government to gather data, plan programs, and regulate economic life. Paul Samuelson, for example, a twenty-one-year-old economics student, was cautious at first, but then euphoric after Keynes's book was published. "Bliss was it in that dawn to be alive, but to be young was very heaven," Samuelson wrote.[4] Other economists soon accepted Keynes, and by the 1940s his ideas dominated the economics profession. In 1948, Samuelson would defend Keynes by writing the best-selling economics textbook of all time.[5]

The planners on the NRPB were among the excited disciples of Keynes. The war itself seemed to be evidence that government jobs had pulled the U.S. economy out of the Depression. Now the economists and planners would oust the entrepreneurs and take the nation's helm to plan for peace. Roosevelt encouraged them.

According to Charles Merriam, vice president of the NRPB, "It should be the declared policy of the United States government, supplementing the work of private agencies as a final guarantor if all else failed, to underwrite full employment for employables." That idea launched what Merriam and the NRPB called "A New Bill of Rights." Included were the rights to jobs "with fair pay and working conditions, . . . equal access to education for all, equal access to health and nutrition for all, and wholesome housing conditions for all."[6]

Roosevelt incorporated the NRPB's ideas into an "economic bill of rights," which he announced during 1944. "Our economic bill of rights," he said, "like the sacred Bill of Rights of our Constitution itself—must be applied to all our citizens."[7] He discussed his economic bill of rights only briefly in the presidential campaign because he wanted to win the war before announcing his New Deal revival. But Roosevelt gave an outline of what he hoped to accomplish in his State of the Union message in 1944. "A new basis of security and prosperity can be established for all—regardless of station, race, or creed," Roosevelt insisted. These new rights included:

> The right to a useful and remunerative job in the industries or
> shops or farms or mines of the nation;
>
> The right to earn enough to provide adequate food and clothing
> and recreation;
>
> The right of every farmer to raise and sell his products at a
> return which will give him and his family a decent living;
>
> The right of every businessman, large and small, to trade in an
> atmosphere of freedom from unfair competition and
> domination by monopolies at home or abroad;

The right of every family to a decent home;

The right to adequate medical care and the opportunity to achieve and enjoy good health;

The right to adequate protection from the economic fears of old age, sickness, accident, and unemployment;

The right to a good education.

Roosevelt concluded: "All of these rights spell security. And after this war is won we must be prepared to move forward, in the implementation of these rights, to new goals of human happiness and well-being."[8]

Where do Roosevelt's new rights come from? They are not natural rights, or God-given rights, because nature, or God, does not endow man with "a good education," "adequate medical care," or a "decent home." Only if government is the source of rights do Roosevelt's rights have meaning. If an American has a right to "a useful and remunerative job," then government has the obligation to tax those who have jobs and redistribute that wealth to those who don't. If an American has a right to a "decent home," whatever size and furnishings that might include, then other Americans have the responsibility to pay for that decent home. Thus, Roosevelt's new economic bill of rights was revolutionary. To provide these new rights, government would have to tax and redistribute wealth on a massive scale.

The original Bill of Rights was very different. It listed freedoms *from* government interference, not the freedom to invoke government to fulfill wants. The Founders said that free speech was a natural or human right that exists freely for all people to enjoy. If Roosevelt had a right to freedom of speech or freedom of religion, he imposed no obligation on other Americans. They could turn off the radio during a Fireside Chat or ignore the preaching at his St. James Episcopal Church. Freedom of speech and freedom of religion could be enjoyed by all Americans without hampering one another's liberty.

During Roosevelt's twelve years in office, he had increased government immensely, which had prepared the nation for the larger government he wanted after the war. His economic bill of rights presaged programs for national health care, federal aid to education, and a federal housing authority. The taxing machinery was also in place. During the war, most Americans had begun paying some income tax. That new tax was highly progressive, and withholding guaranteed a steady source of revenue to the government. An economic bill of rights was impossible in America in 1933, when Roosevelt became president, but it was very possible by 1945, when he was inaugurated for his fourth term.

Many congressmen resisted Roosevelt. They saw the new bill of rights as an invitation to class warfare, or at least an invitation to redistribute wealth. That transfer of wealth changed incentives. If rich Americans paid the top marginal tax rate of 94 percent in 1945, they had little capital and no incentive to build factories and create jobs. Likewise, those Americans who had houses, jobs, and medical care provided as rights had little incentive to work harder to fulfill their potential and create the inventions and businesses needed for America's future.

Congress abolished the NRPB in August 1943 and refused to translate any part of the economic bill of rights into policy. Roosevelt did not dwell on it. After all, winning the war always trumped the New Deal in his mind. But in a campaign speech in Chicago right before the election, Roosevelt did briefly discuss his New Deal revival, "Every full-time job in America must provide enough for a decent living." He added, "For those very low income groups that cannot possibly afford decent homes, the federal government should continue to assist local housing authorities in meeting that need." Toward the end of the speech, Roosevelt talked about "our ability to provide sixty million peacetime jobs."[9]

Since only about 47 million Americans had jobs in 1940, before the war began, the 60 million figure was high and reflected the president's belief that government needed to create jobs for peacetime. Like Keynes, FDR focused on aggregate demand. "At the end of the war," the president said, "there will be more goods available, and it is only common sense to see to it that the working man is paid enough, and that the farmers earn enough, to buy these goods and keep our factories running." [10] Roosevelt intended to have government ready to make sure "there will be more goods available."

Roosevelt died in April 1945, before he could promote any new laws. Many of his followers, however, vigorously promoted his ideas for the reconversion period after the war. Henry Wallace, for example, "had found widespread anxiety over the future of employment." He wrote a book entitled *Sixty Million Jobs*, in which he strongly endorsed FDR's economic bill of rights. "The man who made that pledge [to ensure 60 million jobs] is dead," Wallace lamented. "But we must justify his faith." [11]

For Wallace, redistributing wealth was a way to create jobs. "We must do something about bringing the bottom half of our population within the boundaries of our economic frontiers at home," Wallace urged. He wanted "all of our people to enjoy decent housing, better health, and a good education." Therefore, he urged lawmakers to secure a "People's Peace—through increasing the purchasing power of the masses of the people." [12] Job creation would follow.

Other politicians picked up the theme of using government programs to reach the goal of 60 million jobs. Senator James Murray (D-Mont.) introduced a full-employment bill into the Senate for discussion. The bill committed the government in a general way to provide jobs if unemployment became too high. Many leading Democrats and economists supported Murray's bill. "In this session of Congress," the *New Republic* reported, "one of the first bills to be introduced will no doubt be the full-employment bill of 1945, designed to carry out item number one in the Economic Bill of Rights." [13] The *Nation* joined the *New Republic* in endorsing the full employment bill. "Mr. Roosevelt's program," the *Nation* concluded, "is squarely based on the best economic authority available. It is entirely consistent with the economic doctrines of the distinguished British economist Lord Keynes." [14]

Among the mainstream economists, Dr. Leo Barnes, chief economist for Prentice-Hall, vigorously supported the full-employment bill. He noted that "to raise employment to 60 million jobs and keep it there will demand even more thoroughgoing government direction of our economic life." Americans needed to be ready for controls and regimentation: "The economic equivalent of war will require some, at least, of the economic organization of war." Harvard economists Seymour Harris and Alvin Hansen agreed with Barnes: "Many in Washington will concur that the prospects for a high level of employment are not too bright unless the government is prepared to step in." Critics argued that such intervention would curtail liberty and be costly. But Harris and Hansen defended an ever larger federal deficit. "The exaggerated fear of public debt is especially troublesome," they said. "In a growing economy, the rising debt need not concern us." They pointed approvingly to "blueprints . . . available for public projects estimated to cost around $1 billion." [15]

What did Truman think? In some ways, Truman and Roosevelt were opposites. Roosevelt was well born, educated at Harvard, and full of self-confidence. In temperament he was, as Arthur Krock observed, "clever and slick," and "was often devious when it was not necessary." [16] Truman was the son of a Missouri farmer, and never went to college. In temperament he was blunt and honest, but often insecure. Unlike Roosevelt, who wanted to be his own cabinet, Truman wanted good people around him to offer advice. But even with differing backgrounds and personalities, the two presidents shared a progressive view of politics. Truman liked the economic bill of rights and endorsed it publicly.

Fred Vinson, Truman's new secretary of the Treasury, signaled the economic views of the new president. "History shows us," Vinson argued, "that business, labor, and agriculture cannot in themselves assure the maintenance of high levels of production and employment. The government . . . must assume this responsibility and take measures broad enough to meet the issues."[17]

Once in office, however, President Truman focused mainly on Germany's surrender and the bombing of Japan. He had to learn his job and make appointments to fill his cabinet and other executive positions. Planning had to be delayed. But that was all right because most military experts predicted that Japan would persist in the war well into 1946. Even those few who knew about the atomic bomb did not know if it would work. When it did work on August 6 over Hiroshima and on August 9 over Nagasaki, Japan soon surrendered and the United States was suddenly faced with the reconversion from war to peace.

The sudden end of the war startled the planners. Few government programs were in place to give jobs to returning veterans. "We are completely unprepared for a Japanese collapse," reporter I. F. Stone lamented, "and unless we act quickly and wisely [we] may face an economic collapse ourselves."[18] The planners had no faith that existing industries could or would reemploy the 12 million soldiers and sailors coming home, or the 12 or so million civilians who were making war materiel. "The action of Congress in abolishing the National Resources Planning Board . . . ," the *New Republic* complained, "will probably be remembered as one of the silliest and most spiteful gestures of all time."[19]

Without a WPA, or even unemployment benefits, many Keynesians were frantic. I. F. Stone sounded the alarm: "New agencies, new men, new ideas, new directions are necessary—and quickly—if we are not to suffer a relapse into chronic mass unemployment now that war's blood transfusions will no longer be available to an ailing capitalism."[20]

When war ended, congressmen were in the midst of their summer recess. President Truman immediately called Congress back into session to plan for reconversion. Economists, politicians, and journalists clamored loudly for new federal programs to absorb the millions of Americans now out of work. The hastily convened Congress looked at bills for an increased minimum wage, unemployment benefits, and new public works. Senator Barkley, still the majority leader, listed a fifteen-point program to consider; point number one was the economic bill of rights.[21]

The jubilation of peace was offset by a concern that jobs would be there when the soldiers came home. Would the Great Depression return? Many experts said it would. War employment, after all, was only temporary; capitalism was unstable and without help from government the breadlines would return. Would Congress, many wondered, give the nation a new WPA for newly unemployed veterans, shipbuilders, and gunmakers?

During August and September, the experts fanned a wave of pessimism throughout the nation. Which economist, politician, or journalist could predict the greatest disaster? *Time, Newsweek,* and *U.S. News & World Report* warned that 5 to 7 million Americans, especially in industrial centers, would soon be jobless. The War Manpower Commission estimated that 5 million Americans would be unemployed in the next ninety days. The Treasury Department weighed in with an estimate of 8 million soon to be unemployed, and Sidney Hillman of the CIO predicted 10 million would be jobless in six to eight weeks. Senator Harley Kilgore (D-W.Va.), who sponsored an unemployment bill in the Senate, insisted that 18 million Americans would soon be jobless; their numbers and their distress would exceed the despair of the 1930s.[22]

President Truman was under tremendous pressure to act decisively. He assembled the best wisdom he could find and announced a call to action. On September 6, Truman delivered one of the longest messages in presidential history—sixteen thousand words—all of it devoted to reconversion. "The end of the war came more swiftly than most of us anticipated," Truman confessed. "Obviously, displaced war workers cannot find jobs until industry has been re-geared and made ready to produce peacetime goods." During this lag "the government should provide help." In the area of government help, Truman advocated both a short-term fix and a long-term program of recovery—both of which he based on the economic bill of rights.[23]

In the short term, Truman urged Congress to pass a full-employment bill, an increase in the minimum wage, and unemployment benefits of $25 per week for twenty-six weeks. For public works, he suggested that the TVA model be applied to other river valleys in the United States. He also urged labor unions to be patient and the OPA to be diligent in retaining enough controls to combat inflation. He suggested possible tax relief as well, but only "limited tax deductions" because he needed much revenue to support his long-term goal of a New Deal revival.[24]

Truman would later call his program "the Fair Deal," and in his September 6 speech, he sketched some of his ideas. He repeated FDR's economic bill of rights and declared "the attainment of those rights [to be] the essence of post-war American economic life." He thereby reiterated the right to a "remunerative" job, a "decent" home, "adequate" medical care, and a "good" education. He had covered the right to a "remunerative" job with his support for full employment and for an increased minimum wage. Then on housing, he promoted the idea of urban renewal. "A decent standard of housing for all," Truman said, "is one of the irreducible obligations of modern civilization." He did not specify any plans for education or medical care, but did so later in his Fair Deal.[25]

The reaction to Truman's speech followed partisan lines. The planners were "jubilant," but not Joseph Martin, the Republican leader in the House. "Not even President Roosevelt ever asked so much at one sitting," Martin fumed. "It is just a case of out–New Dealing the New Deal."[26]

The Republicans and the conservative Democrats rejected or stalled on all of Truman's recommendations except for his "limited tax reduction." Walter George (D-Ga.), the head of the Senate Finance Committee, warmly endorsed Truman's idea for tax cuts, but he was silent on the rest of the president's message. Rep. Harold Knutson (R-Minn.), the ranking Republican on the House Ways and Means Committee, attacked the whole message as "a continuation of the pre-war Roosevelt program." He said that a tax increase would be needed to implement it. Knutson countered that "rigid economies and sane spending" were the only way to balance the budget and support a tax cut. The unemployment benefits bill, Knutson argued, "would saddle at least another $1.5 billion onto the budget, and some estimate it may go as high as $6 billion." On full employment, Knutson said, "Nobody knows what the President's full employment bill will cost American taxpayers, but the aggregate will be enormous."[27]

Those who, like Knutson, rejected Truman's program also dismissed the ubiquitous cries of gloom if the government failed to act. Robert Wason, head of the National Association of Manufacturers (NAM), said, "The problem of our domestic economy is the recovery of our freedom." NAM and the Chamber of Commerce campaigned for fewer controls and more incentives. Lawrence M. Giannini, president of the Bank of America, argued, "The substitution of paternalistic cradle-to-the-grave philosophy for the self-reliance which built this nation is probably America's greatest weakness."[28]

Truman and his administration did make some moves toward freer markets. First, he freed gas and some food from OPA controls. Second, he encouraged the Treasury and the Federal Reserve to maintain low interest rates for borrowing money. Third, the WPB took controls off dozens of commodities—including lumber and the building of new houses. Julius Krug, who now headed the WPB, was one of the few leaders who believed that markets pointed the way to recovery.[29]

Much to the distress of the Keynesians, most congressmen balked at new federal programs. They wanted to cut spending and balance the budget. They followed Congressman Knutson and

Senator George and put tax relief at the top of their agenda. "As I see the picture," Knutson said, "the time has come to cut out all governmental activities that are not necessary to the conduct of orderly government and to future national security." With Truman's program rejected, and government spending lowered "to a sane level," Knutson recommended a 20 percent across-the-board cut in tax rates to stimulate the economy. Incentives, to Knutson, were the way to get Americans to start or expand businesses to create jobs for the returning veterans.[30]

During October, Congress passed the first bill since the 1920s that cut tax rates. Their first target was the excess-profits tax, a special tax on corporate profits that was designed for wartime only. During the war, the tax rate on corporate profits more than doubled (from 19 to 40 percent) and the marginal excess-profits tax reached as high as 90 percent. Senator George, and even Treasury Secretary Fred Vinson, wanted to repeal the tax now that the war was over. Senator Tom Connally (D-Tex.) defended the excess-profits tax as "a permanently sound tax." It needed to be continued, Connally argued, to raise $5.5 billion in revenue to balance the federal budget and reduce the ballooning national debt. Senator Joseph O'Mahoney (D-Wyo.) agreed. To abolish the tax would be to sacrifice revenue "almost as great as the amount of interest the government would have to pay the next year on the national debt." "Never," he said, "was there a more inappropriate time to cut taxes." We were "blindfolding ourselves" to the "gravity of the whole situation." The Committee for a Progressive Tax Program attacked the equity of the repeal. It would "relieve [the] 99,000 wealthiest corporations and individuals." Poorer Americans would then have to bear more of the tax burden.[31]

Conservatives defended tax rate cuts on three grounds: incentives, equity, and future revenue. On incentives, as Senator George said, the excess-profits tax "definitely is a brake on expansion and on the development of new business." Senator Wayne Morse (R-Ore.) agreed, and condemned "propaganda ... being issued urging

Senators to keep this excess profits tax." Morse added, "I believe that if we are to have full employment, and if we are to operate the private enterprise system in the interest of increased production and higher standards of living, it is very important that we do away with the excess profits tax." Senator George reinforced Morse by quoting a "typical" letter he had received from a businessman who said, "If we are to be subject to the present excess profits tax," we are being "impractical" to risk starting a business.[32]

On the issue of equity, conservatives argued that punishing the rich through high taxes was hardly equitable. Not only the tax on excess profits but also the high income tax rates were unfair. Under wartime law, an entrepreneur who earned $1 million paid $900,000 in federal income taxes alone. Of the $100,000 the government allowed him to keep, he was still liable for state income taxes, sales taxes, and excise taxes on items from gasoline to telephone calls. Under the Revenue Act of 1945, the government was taxing him "only" $838,850 of his $1 million income and allowing him to keep $161,150. That 16 percent of his income that he was allowed to keep was still so small that many congressmen were not sure risk-takers had enough incentive to start a business or expand an existing one.[33]

But beyond that, Congress made sure that the new revenue act increased freedom for all groups. For example, it repealed the capital stock tax, which taxed each share of stock issued by all corporations. Thus, the stock of all corporations benefited equally from repeal. Also, the new revenue act had across-the-board cuts on both the corporation tax and the income tax. The tax rate on corporate profits was cut by 2 to 4 percent; tax rates on incomes were cut almost 10 percent for all taxpayers. Furthermore, exemptions increased, which would remove 12 million, or one-fourth of all taxpayers, from paying any tax. From top to bottom, then, the Revenue Act of 1945 allowed all taxpayers to keep more of their property.[34]

With 12 million Americans removed entirely from the tax

rolls, and with rates slashed for all other groups, would the budget be balanced? Critics of the new revenue tax called the cuts foolhardy and irresponsible and predicted they would break the budget after a long war. But Senator Albert Hawkes (R-N.J.) disagreed. Hawkes was both a lawyer and a businessman. Before winning his Senate seat in 1942, he had been president of a chemical company, and also president of the U.S. Chamber of Commerce during the early 1940s. Hawkes knew firsthand how incentives worked, and he predicted that "the repeal of the excess-profits tax, in my opinion, may raise more revenue for the United States than would be raised if it were retained." Tax rates at 90 percent were stifling and, Hawkes noted, you "cannot get a golden egg out of a dead goose." [35]

Senator George supported Hawkes's predictions. If the revenue act "has the effect which it is hoped it will have," George said, "it will so stimulate the expansion of business as to bring in a greater total revenue." He provided a historical example from the 1920s. "The act of November 23, 1921, made more substantial reductions in [tax] rates. The recovery of the country from a state of depression in 1920 and 1921 was rapid. The Revenue Acts of 1924 and 1926 made still further tax reductions, but the income from tax revenues of the government increased through all of that period." [36]

Senator George, a veteran politician, remembered well the tax cuts of the 1920s, and how they spurred investment and raised revenue at the same time. When George entered the Senate in 1922, Warren Harding was the new president and Andrew Mellon was the secretary of the treasury. Unemployment had reached 11.7 percent in 1921, and Mellon argued against federal spending, but instead for cutting tax rates to spark new growth. By 1923, unemployment dropped below 3 percent, and it remained at about that level for the rest of the Harding-Coolidge presidency. [37]

High income tax rates, Mellon argued, "inevitably put pressure upon the taxpayer to withdraw his capital from productive business and invest it in tax-exempt securities. . . . The result is that the sources of taxation are drying up; wealth is failing to carry its share of the tax burden; and capital is being diverted into channels which yield neither revenue to the government nor profit to the people." Mellon wrote *Taxation: The People's Business*, which developed his ideas of "supply-side economics." "It seems difficult for some to understand," he wrote, "that high rates of taxation do not necessarily mean large revenue to the government, and that more revenue may often be obtained by lower rates."[38]

Mellon, of course, recognized that there was a limit to how far you could cut tax rates and still increase revenue. "The problem of government," he said, "is to fix rates which will bring in a maximum amount of revenue to the Treasury and at the same time bear not too heavily on the taxpayer or on business enterprises." Senator Hawkes clearly understood Mellon's point. "A tax bill which would take 99 percent of everything everyone makes, . . ." Hawkes observed, "would not produce any revenue. . . . We must find a tax that will produce revenue, and which is fair enough so that it will stimulate business to go back to full effort and work."[39]

Mellon's example showed Hawkes the way. During the 1920s, marginal income tax rates on large incomes were slashed from 73 to 24 percent, and on smaller incomes from 4 to one-half of 1 percent. These tax cuts helped produce an outpouring of economic development—from air-conditioning to refrigerators to zippers; Scotch tape to radios and talking movies. Investors took more risks when they were allowed to keep more of their gains.

Furthermore, Mellon was also vindicated in his astonishing predictions that cutting tax rates across the board would generate more revenue. Overall, federal receipts declined during the 1920s, but revenue from the income tax actually increased. In the early 1920s, when the highest tax rate was 73 percent, the total income tax revenue to the U.S. government was a little over $700 million. In 1929, when the top tax rate was 24 percent, the total revenue topped the $1 billion mark. What's more, in every year of the 1920s, the United States had a budget surplus. During that decade, more than one-fourth of the entire national debt was eliminated, and the American standard of living grew steadily.[40]

Senators George and Hawkes were bold and daring in making the argument that the Revenue Act of 1945 might raise revenue as well as spur job creation. They were open to massive criticism if entrepreneurs sat on their hands and budget deficits climbed through the roof. Robert Doughton, chairman of the House Ways and Means Committee, concluded: "We have given business a green light. They claimed that what they need is encouragement. Now if they don't go forward, the responsibility is on them."[41]

The Revenue Act of 1945 passed the House and Senate in October 1945. J. J. Nance, vice president of Zenith Radio, was excited: "We must create and sustain a desire for goods to steadily increase consumption." As business expanded, the stock market surged almost 20 percent in six months. At the end of 1945, unemployment stood at 2 million people—not the 6, 8, or 18 million projected by the Keynesians.[42]

Truman was pleased with American production, but he still promoted the economic bill of rights. Congress, however, was more determined than ever to let markets work; it rejected a New Deal revival. On January 3, 1946, Truman made an impassioned speech for new federal programs, but Congress either ignored him or undermined him. For example, when Truman pleaded for his plan to give six months of benefits to the newly unemployed, Congressman Doughton said that with all the new industrial expansion under way, he was concerned about a scarcity of labor; he didn't want to give any incentive for anyone to stay unemployed. Congress not only refused to act on Truman's proposal but relegated to the states Truman's United States Employment Service, which he had ready as a federal agency to help the unemployed. Then when Truman asked Congress to increase the minimum wage from 40 to 65 cents an hour, Congress said no. Truman suggested 60 cents an hour, but again, nothing happened.[43]

Truman's vaunted plans for public works also went nowhere. He wanted to extend the TVA idea to the St. Lawrence Valley and the Missouri Valley, but Congress wouldn't act on it. When Truman brought up the economic bill of rights and asked Congress to consider a health care program, Congress refused to do anything. On Truman's federal housing bill, Congress took out the major subsidy and then harmlessly passed into law what little was left. Truman trumpeted his Full Employment Bill as the centerpiece of the economic bill of rights, but Congress emasculated its provisions. By the time it passed, it was merely the Employment Bill of 1946, and it gave no power to the federal government to hand out jobs. The bill did set up a Council of Economic Advisers for the president, but Truman was slow to appoint the three advisors, and even slower to take their advice.[44]

What to do about the OPA was Truman's biggest headache. During the war, the Federal Reserve had inflated the currency, which leads to inflation. But the inflation did not officially occur because the OPA artificially fixed prices and legally prevented them from rising. Even though the money supply had more than doubled during the war, only minor rises in wages and prices were allowed. Thus, when the war ended, Americans wanted their wages to rise to their new market value, but did not want prices to rise as well. Truman reflected the confusion on this issue when he urged employers to raise wages but not prices of the products being sold. In the months after the war, the OPA lifted some prices, but not others.[45]

Chaos resulted. When some corporations refused to raise wages if prices had to be held steady, many workers protested, and some went on strike. The UAW had the auto workers strike for higher wages, and many other unions joined them during late 1945 and 1946.[46]

Consumers were frustrated as well. Because prices were fixed below their market value, producers had no incentive to make goods and send them to market. Thus, the shelves of many stores were empty, and Americans often bought items on the black market. Cabell Phillips, a reporter for the *New York Times*, described the typical family's dilemma: "Seventy nine cents and five red stamps would buy a pound of medium-grade sirloin, provided you could find a store that had sirloin. Or you could pay $2 and no stamps to a shady black marketer, and run the risk that both of you would go to jail."[47]

The solution, of course, was to abolish the OPA and let prices rise to their new market levels. But Truman didn't want consumer anger at "inflation" directed at him, so he proceeded slowly. When Congress passed a law undermining the OPA, Truman vetoed it. Then Congress passed another such law, and he reluctantly signed it in July 1946. As a result, most controls were eliminated, and all would be banished by the end of 1946. As Rep. George Fallon (D-Md.) noted, the congressmen "were extremely anxious to turn the control situation over to 'free enterprise.'"[48]

Truman would occasionally get caught between the OPA and striking workers. When two major railroad unions went on strike in May 1946, Truman threatened to seize the railroads and draft the striking workers into the Army. When the attorney general suggested that act would not be constitutional, Truman responded, "We will draft them and think about the law later." The striking workers soon agreed to return to their jobs, but Truman's heavy-handed use of government to fix prices and draft strikers made reconversion more difficult.[49]

Meanwhile, despite the strikes and the rising prices, the economy boomed in 1946. The absence of the war spending of the previous years was offset by the large expansion of American businesses. Private GDP was up 30 percent in 1946—a figure never reached before or since. Domestic investment surged from $13.4 billion in 1945 to $39 billion in 1946 (in 2009 dollars). Consumers were indeed spending more, but that was because rationing was ending and businesses were risking capital by expanding. In other words, consumer spending was not the cause of the recovery, but the result of it. Also, American consumers were saving more—they had more money to spend and were paying less in taxes. In the year after the war, the Dow Jones average soared from 165 to 212 before losing ground.[50]

Amazingly, the U.S. economy reached FDR's goal of 60 million jobs in 1946—and did so with limited federal intervention. Civilian jobs expanded rapidly from 39 million to 55 million—a one-year growth never seen before in U.S. history. With all those people in the workforce, many of them were earning more than ever, and so were the corporations who were hiring them. The sudden, unexpected job creation meant more tax revenue in the federal Treasury. Corporate and individual tax revenue in 1946 dropped only a fraction of the projected $5.5 billion—even with the excess-profits tax gone and 12 million people removed from the tax rolls. The United States was on its way to a balanced federal budget.

The next year, 1947, with the Revenue Act of 1945 still in place, the Treasury Department again greatly underestimated the projected revenue. Treasury experts predicted only $31.5 billion, but $43.3 billion came in. That meant that the U.S. Treasury generated more revenue from both corporate and individual income taxes in 1947 than during any previous year in U.S. history. Senator Hawkes and Senator George had been prophetic: Hawkes had predicted that the repeal of the excess profits tax "may raise more revenue than would be raised if it were retained," and George said he hoped that the new revenue act "will so stimulate the expansion of business as to bring in a greater total revenue."[51]

Few businessmen were surprised at what they could do. Unlike the Keynesian economists, businessmen after the war, according to forecaster Michael Sapir, "could not believe that a serious 'slump' was around the corner just because the government had stepped out of the market so fast." The CEO of General Motors, Alfred Sloan, said, "I haven't any feeling at all that we are going to have a serious recession in this country. I don't see how that can be possible." Neither did Charles E. Wilson, the president of General Electric, who criticized "some Washington economists for wrongfully predicting a depression." The unemployment rate for 1946 was 3.9 percent, a far cry from the 10 to 15—and even 20—percent predicted by many economists in 1945.[52]

The Keynesians, however, were mostly unrepentant. They had predicted a new Great Depression; then they predicted large budget deficits; now they argued for more government programs to maintain full employment. But Congress trusted incentives and expanding businesses instead. Were businessmen just lucky to support 60 million jobs after the war? Economist Leo Barnes thought so. As we have seen, Barnes argued the case for government intervention to provide jobs for returning soldiers. The "optimism of businessmen about postwar production and employment prospects" Barnes insisted, "was a lucky psychological illusion, based largely on economic and statistical errors."[53] Economist Michael Sapir was more honest. "Looking backward it seems incredible that we could have missed the signs so badly."[54] Lucky or not, America's return to prosperity allowed it great influence and prestige in world affairs.

For example, because the United States had returned to prosperity, it could save Europe from one of the worst famines in world history. With most of Europe in chaos after the war, and with bad weather and with property rights unclear, many European farmers had poor harvests in 1945, 1946, and 1947. Hundreds of American congressmen went to France and Germany and came back with sad reports of starving people, dead babies, and famine stalking the land. In a bipartisan move, Americans sent tens of millions of tons of food to Europe—to those people who had fought against us as well as those who had fought with the United States. Even the newly communist countries of Eastern Europe received some of the U.S. bounty.[55]

That food may have saved much of Europe from a social breakdown after the war. According to the *New York Times*, "Europe faces one of the bleakest, saddest winters since the chaos of the Thirty Years War. . . . The resistance of Europe is down. Tuberculosis is rife. The very young and the very old are beginning to die in droves as the Autumn leaves fall." Even before those negative reports came in, Truman insisted that "ways and means must be found to meet the irreducible minimum needs [of Europe] and to prevent starvation." He appointed a Famine Emergency Committee, which tried to balance Europe's needs with America's limited food supply. To feed Europeans with a minimal diet, Americans had to eat less—they briefly considered a national rationing plan again. Instead, the Famine Emergency Committee turned to voluntary controls. Americans, they said, needed to eat 50 percent less wheat and 20 percent less fat in 1946 so that six to eight million tons of wheat could be sent to Europe.[56] Food was power. With prosperity returning, America could conduct its foreign policy from a position of strength and abundance after the war. Before the war, when the United States had a deeper depression than most of Europe, Japan and Germany were freer to ignore or challenge FDR's suggestions and threats.

The midterm elections of 1946 were a referendum on the new economic order. Truman applauded American productivity and praised the 60 million jobs industry had provided. He called such rapid job creation "the swiftest and most gigantic change-over that any nation has ever made from war to peace." But—at the risk of more deficits—Truman continued his campaign for a New Deal revival. Government, Truman argued, needed a larger role in postwar America to guarantee American rights to houses, health care, jobs, and decent wages. In the months before the election, he retained the price control on meat, and then, under pressure from angry consumers, he lifted the controls, and lamented as meat prices rose sharply.[57]

The Republicans responded with a campaign slogan in the form of a question: "Had Enough?" Those two words meant no to the New Deal revival, to deficit spending, and to price controls, and only limited aid for federal housing and no national health care program. Republicans wanted more houses, better health care, and lower prices, but they wanted it done privately. To promote that result, they campaigned for even more tax cuts and even less federal spending. Let a free people voluntarily meet the needs of their countrymen and the hungry Europeans as well. On election day, Republicans took control of Congress for the first time since 1928. They gained fifty-five seats in the House and twelve in the Senate. To celebrate, their leaders brought brooms to Congress to symbolically sweep out the New Dealers. At last the Republicans had their referendum on the New Deal and the war's planned economy.

CONCLUSION

One month before the attack on Pearl Harbor, Earl Thacker, the vice president of Hawaiian Hotels, Ltd., attended a meeting of the American Hotels Association in New York City. When asked about the safety of tourists visiting Hawaii, Thacker replied, "People should have no mental hazard, for with our Navy in the Pacific that ocean is a safe place."[1]

Franklin Roosevelt could not have said it better if he had been asked the same question. FDR trusted the U.S. Navy so thoroughly, and disdained the Japanese Navy so intensely, that he refused to believe that any real danger could threaten Hawaii. In many ways, Roosevelt was a war hawk. He talked about confronting Japan in the Pacific even before he took office. By 1937, he was ready to "quarantine" Japan, Germany, and other aggressors. He repeatedly manipulated public opinion as he searched for a "flash point," an international incident that would goad the American public into demanding war. In the words of historian Robert Dallek, "The President's deviousness also injured the national well-being over the long run. His action[s] . . . created a precedent for manipulation of public opinion which would be repeated by later Presidents in less justifiable circumstances."[2]

Until almost too late, Roosevelt spent lavishly on New Deal programs but refused to strengthen and modernize the military (except as a stepchild of the WPA and PWA). He did little for the Army, either with its size or weapons. During the 1930s, his defense budgets were cut to the bone. In 1940 his spending for defense was a smaller percentage of the budget than it had been in his first year as president.[3] If war came to the United States, he believed his country would quickly be ready. Japan, he believed, was a second-rate power and in awe of the fleet at Pearl Harbor.

After the European war began, FDR argued that men could be quickly converted from "mechanical trades" to being sailors "if their services were suddenly required."[4] Roosevelt saw little urgency in training large numbers of men or in making weapons. Thus, the United States had decrepit planes, antiquated tanks, obsolete rifles, few antiaircraft guns, and almost no ammunition. In May 1940, with disasters in France, General Marshall interrupted the complacent Roosevelt in his cabinet meeting: "If you don't do something . . . and do it right away, I don't know what is going to happen to this country."[5]

To Roosevelt's credit, he listened to Marshall and began to rebuild American defenses. His May 26, 1940, Fireside Chat announced his changed strategy. He replaced "old Dr. New Deal" with "Dr. Win the War," who prescribed strong incentives for ailing American businessmen. Thus, Roosevelt belatedly gave America's leading industrialists contracts for making weapons and incentives to build defense plants and train workers.

When war did come, Roosevelt's lack of preparedness became apparent. He had underestimated the Japanese, and their surprise attack at Pearl Harbor devastated the American Navy and exposed the president's incompetence. To win the war, he suspended antitrust laws and allowed corporate leaders to share ideas and personnel. When entrepreneurs such as Henry Kaiser and Andrew Higgins cut red tape and broke rules, FDR often looked the other way. He mobilized scientists to develop the atomic bomb, and he often let military leaders make decisions as they thought best. Had FDR abandoned his New Deal philosophy? No, he was making "a wartime detour" but planned to spur on the New Deal after victory over fascism.[6]

During the war, Roosevelt shifted power to the executive branch and took charge of U.S. foreign policy, often with disastrous results. He joined forces with Churchill and Stalin, but Roosevelt especially liked and trusted Stalin, whom he called "Uncle Joe." Thus, when Churchill and various military leaders supported an Allied invasion of Central Europe—to stop the Russian advance—FDR listened to Stalin instead, and insisted on a second front far to the west of Germany. "Stalin is not an imperialist," Roosevelt insisted. At major conferences at Teheran and Yalta, Roosevelt trusted Stalin to grant free elections in Poland and Eastern Europe.

Roosevelt flooded Stalin with Lend-Lease aid—food, planes, tools, and supplies in large quantities. Stalin, in turn, planted spies in the United States who worked their way into key positions in the American government. They influenced U.S. policy to favor Russia; they sent copies of government documents to Russia; and they described U.S. plans in messages to Russia. In one of the great ironies of history, Stalin knew much about the development of the atomic bomb long before President Truman did.

In Europe, FDR insisted on the unconditional surrender of Germany, and in doing so prolonged the war. FDR initially supported the ludicrous Morgenthau Plan to deindustrialize Germany, and that threat kept the Germans fighting even longer.

Roosevelt also shifted power to the executive branch during the war to run the domestic economy. Donald Nelson, Roosevelt's "czar" at the WPB, dictated what products would be manufactured (few consumer goods but lots of tanks) and which corporations would get the contracts. The WPB even dictated how much fabric would be used in making clothes. The OPA set prices for 8 million products, rationed others, and controlled rents across the nation. The RFC bailed out some corporations and made huge loans to others.

Despite a slow start in 1942, American manufacturers produced a tidal wave of armaments that not only revitalized the U.S. military but provided supplies to Allies all over the world. The War Department's text on economic mobilization states, "The procurement of Army materiel for World War II represented the greatest purchasing operation ever conducted by a single agency in the history of the American economy."[7] And this did not take into account supplies for the Navy and Marines. From only eighty medium tanks in 1940, along with a hodgepodge of trucks, motorcycles, and staff cars, the U.S. Army by 1945 could move its entire force of 8 million men *at the same time* by motorized transport, if necessary.[8]

To fund the war and his planned economy, Roosevelt secured a large and regular supply of revenue by raising tax rates and requiring the withholding of pay. Before the war, fewer than 5 percent of Americans were required to pay income tax. By the end of the war, that number jumped to about 65 percent of adult Americans who had to pay income tax, and the top rate was 94 percent on all income over $200,000.

What did America's centrally planned economy look like? On the plus side, jobs were readily available, usually at decent pay. But the money spent to fund these jobs, to train millions of soldiers, and to arm and equip them to risk their lives spiraled until the national debt was out of control. Millions of Americans migrated across the country to make ships, planes, and weapons. They crowded into dilapidated trailers, unfurnished apartments, and crowded houses to work long hours (45.2 hours per week by 1944) with a 30 percent greater risk of injury than before the war. They often traveled long distances to and from work with gas and tires rationed. They stood in long lines in stores to buy scarce, rationed products, often inferior to what existed before the war. As economist Robert Higgs concluded, "In thousands of ways, consumers lost their freedom of choice."[9]

When Congress ended New Deal programs such as the WPA,

the NYA, and the CCC, Roosevelt lost much of his federal patronage, which had been so essential to greasing his election campaigns. In 1942, when Americans had a chance to vote on the war and their planned economy, the Democrats lost forty-seven seats in the House and twenty of twenty-five Senate races outside the South.

What about Franklin Roosevelt as a war leader? Although he was accountable for what the *Tulsa Daily World* labeled the "distrust of the leadership in Washington," he did not approve of the "war bungling" and the "wild wastes of wartime." Some of it was the inevitable result of waging a war. In Fireside Chats, FDR tried to speak comfort to the nation and unite it behind the task of winning the war. Many Americans liked his optimism—and it prevailed when American (and British) entrepreneurs rescued the Allies by inventing and producing radar, penicillin, DDT, landing craft, and liberty ships.

However, Roosevelt's leadership during the war was often evasive and self-serving. Toward the end of the 1940 election, he promised, "Your boys are not going to be sent into any foreign wars," but FDR wanted the United States at the center of international affairs. Once the war began, civil liberties lost ground as Roosevelt conducted illegal wiretaps on hundreds, and maybe thousands, of political opponents. Property rights were often disregarded. He also signed the executive order to intern 110,000 Japanese-Americans in tightly guarded camps and kept them there until he was safely reelected in 1944. Also, FDR harassed newspapers that opposed his policies and tried to shut them down.

Americans were willing to go along with some of FDR's abuses of civil liberties to win the war. Mothers and wives of servicemen overseas knew that government censors were reading their mail from loved ones before they received it, and scissoring out any passages with information on troop movements or other military details. Americans on the home front went along with the need for this intrusion. Likewise, most citizens cooperated with restrictions such as the dimout along the East Coast, the slower speed limits to save gas and tires, and the complete lack of new radios, typewriters, or bicycles for private citizens.

The tipping point with FDR's abuse of freedom came in the case of Sewell Avery. In the spring of 1944, Avery, as chairman of Montgomery Ward & Co., refused to comply with government labor regulations. With national elections looming in the fall, Roosevelt wanted the labor vote. FDR issued an executive order directing the U.S. secretary of commerce to take over operation of Montgomery Ward "for the successful prosecution of the war." (Roosevelt had discussed his plans with Secretary of War Henry Stimson, who refused to become involved. Stimson believed that any government seizure of Montgomery Ward had "a doubtful basis in law."[10]) Army soldiers with fixed bayonets marched into the Chicago headquarters of Montgomery Ward, and when Sewell Avery refused to leave his office, two soldiers carried him from the building. For the sixteenth time, the president had ordered the U.S. Army to seize private property during a wartime labor dispute, but this time circumstances were different. Montgomery Ward was not manufacturing aircraft or bullets or landing craft, essential to victory.

Sewell Avery maintained that his company was denied due process because the government did not want to risk having its labor policies struck down in court. FDR, in other words, was making laws and ignoring judicial process. The public, however, overwhelmingly supported Avery's position. *Time* magazine analyzed the national attention focused on the Montgomery Ward case: "That night on the radio, in the early editions of morning newspapers, in news offices and corner drugstores, the questions were asked: Is Ward's a war plant? Do the President's wartime powers cover seizure of a mail-order house?"[11] One letter to the *New York Times* concluded, "The moral absurdity of soliciting co-operation with a platoon of soldiers exposes government in its most contemptible light. It's time to do some real fighting here at home for the same cause for which we send our soldiers to fight abroad."[12] On May 9, the government ended its occupation of Montgomery Ward's offices, although it maintained the right to direct the company's operations until the war ended. World War II had provided the opportunity for Franklin Roosevelt to implement his planned economy and for the nation to see what it looked like.

What is America's legacy from World War II? For good or ill, the United States went from avoiding entangling alliances before the war to building them afterward. FDR immersed the United States in foreign affairs by his conduct of the war. America had indeed become the arsenal of democracy, and the "military-industrial complex" became a part of America's economy. Government subsidies to defense industries, which often work well in wartime, usually fail in peacetime. After World War II, a large part of the U.S. budget would be spent each year on defense, as the United States built military bases around the world. Noticeably absent from U.S. defense maps were any American installations in East Germany, Eastern and Central Europe, and areas running eastward across Asia all the way to the Pacific, the domain of Soviet Russia.

The Soviet Union had battled Germany for almost four years. In the words of historian Robert Messenger, "The Red Army did not just defeat Hitler and National Socialism, but also put an end to Prussian militarism. It was a Soviet victory over something that had menaced Europe for two centuries."[13] The United States helped Russia through Lend-Lease shipments—weapons, gasoline, food, and medicines poured in for the Soviets. The Allies' invasions of North Africa, Sicily, and Western Europe drained German men and resources from the Eastern Front, helping to stop the Nazi colossus. Even so, according to Messenger, the Soviet Union sacrificed 11.5 million soldiers and lost an estimated 15 million civilians in occupied territories as it battled the German Army all the way from the edge of Moscow to the center of Berlin.

In the wake of the Red Army's success, its legacy after the war was a vast region under Stalin's boot. FDR unwittingly encouraged that result, and the best efforts of Winston Churchill, and later Harry Truman, could do little to prevent communist domination of Eastern and Central Europe.

By contrast, the United States was the major player in the fight against Japan, with help from Australia, Great Britain, and other Allies. The United States developed the landing craft necessary to wage island campaigns. It perfected the strategy of the aircraft carrier task force to take the war all the way to the Japanese home islands. Most important, the men of the U.S. military and its Allies had the will to sustain the battle month after month, on island after island. Yes, U.S. manufacturers produced a tidal wave of armaments, but men had to use those weapons in bitter combat to defeat the highly skilled Japanese and, in Europe, the Germans. Weapons alone could not win the war. Determined soldiers, Marines, sailors, and airmen proved that they had the will to win when given the right tools.

America's legacy in foreign policy after the war differs greatly from that of the Soviet Union. U.S. policies in occupied Japan helped to rebuild the shattered country and turned Japan into a democratic ally. Then, on July 4, 1946, the United States and the Philippines signed a Treaty of General Relations; the United States relinquished sovereignty and recognized the Republic of the Philippines as an independent power. Also in 1946 and 1947, U.S. wheat and corn fed millions of starving Europeans until agriculture and commerce could once again get under way. Then, in 1948, came the Marshall Plan to rebuild Europe with U.S. aid. The Soviet Union, meanwhile, stripped eastern Germany of factories and refused to feed its hungry citizens. Thirty years later, bomb craters from World War II still pockmarked East Berlin in the Russian zone, and German citizens there still used public showers because of the lack of plumbing in apartment buildings.

With Roosevelt dead, the decision to use the atomic bomb fell on Harry Truman. Critics complain about the bomb's devastation, but Truman and his advisors used it to end the war and save more lives in the long run, both American and Japanese. A soldier in training for the invasion of Japan said it best:

> I was a 21-year-old second lieutenant leading a rifle platoon. Although still officially in one piece, in the German war I had already been wounded in the leg and back severely enough to be adjudged, after the war, 40 percent disabled. But even if my legs buckled whenever I jumped out of the back of a truck, my condition was held to be satisfactory for whatever lay ahead.
>
> When the [atomic] bombs dropped and news began to circulate that "Operation Olympic" would not, after all, take place, that we would not be obliged to run up the beaches near Tokyo assault-firing while being mortared and shelled, for all the fake manliness of our façades we cried with relief and joy. We were going to live. We were going to grow up to adulthood after all.[14]

Ironically, one unintended consequence of the atomic bomb was that it ended the war so quickly that Keynesian planners had no chance to foist a New Deal revival on America's postwar economy. As a top-secret project, the bomb was made known to New Dealers only after its first use on August 6.[15] By August 14, the war was suddenly over.

The United States had been at war for three years and eight months, with 405,399 Americans killed and 670,846 wounded. Now most of the 12 million servicemen who survived would be leaving the military. What would happen to society when so many returned home to seek jobs? On the issue of reconversion from war to peace, Congress repudiated FDR and Truman. Franklin Roosevelt had believed in a centrally planned economy since the earliest days of his presidency, and yet his high taxes, rationing, and infringements on civil liberties proved to be a poor substitute for a free society. Most voters wanted freer markets, even with risks, not the job security of a planned economy. After a spirited debate, Congress lifted most economic controls, cut tax rates, slashed federal spending, and trusted entrepreneurs to create the jobs needed for the returning soldiers. The large dose of freedom revived the economy, which grew much faster in 1946 and 1947 than government experts had forecast. Unemployment stabilized at 3.9 percent. The Great Depression was finally over.

Senator Walter George, one of the heroes of the recovery, must have felt history was on his side as he watched industries expand and returning soldiers get jobs. Cutting tax rates and federal spending in the 1920s, he argued, made the economy boom during that earlier decade. "Tax revenues of the government," he observed, "increased through all that period." Cutting tax rates and spending again in 1945, he predicted, "will . . . stimulate the expansion of business," and keep revenue flowing into the government. That is exactly what happened.

President Truman, however, dismissed this verdict of history and argued for sharply increased government spending. His strategy would have forced the U.S. to abandon limited government and instead copy FDR's massive spending of the 1930s. Thus, in 1946, Truman was slow to lift war controls and even slower to back Senator George's deep tax cuts.

When the Democrats were thrashed in the 1946 midterm elections, Truman kept his faith strong in New Deal policies but changed his tactics. He embraced the economic recovery, even calling it "the swiftest and most gigantic change-over that any nation has ever made from war to peace." But he artfully campaigned for reelection in 1948 on the theme of class warfare. He vetoed further tax rate cuts because he believed "high taxes contribute to the welfare and security of the country." From coast to coast, Truman sounded the alarm that if Republicans further cut government spending they would wipe out FDR's New Deal programs and return the nation to the days of Herbert Hoover and the Great Depression. By attacking the rich, spreading fear that Republicans would cut government benefits, and mobilizing labor to get voters to the polls, Truman was fully imitating FDR. And it worked as well in 1948 as it had earlier. Truman won reelection and captured Congress for the Democrats.

Next, Truman tried to win more special-interest groups to the Democratic Party by adopting much of FDR's economic bill of rights, and later presidents (even some Republicans) often followed this pattern. On the right to education, for example, FDR and Truman started with the G.I. bill; then federal aid to education expanded under Eisenhower (the National Defense Education Act) and Johnson (the Higher Education Act of 1965). Truman launched the campaign for the right to health care; Johnson achieved part of it with Medicare, and Barack Obama may have completed the process in 2010. Truman (and FDR) began the crusade for federal housing, but the failure of urban renewal in the next generation prompted President Carter and others to support the Community Reinvestment Act, which forced banks to make low-interest loans to high-risk applicants. Much of the campaign for the economic bill of rights—especially after the collapse of the housing market under the Community Reinvestment Act and the adoption of the Health Care and Education Reconciliation Act of 2010—has, in fact, culminated under President Obama.

The political issues that FDR and Truman launched during the war and postwar recovery have dominated the political arena for two generations, and may persist well into the twenty-first century. But few people have studied the origins and results of these issues. Therefore, we need a deeper understanding of the presidencies of Roosevelt and Truman, and the effects of their programs, if we are to know the best course to follow.

ALPHABET AGENCIES

The following is a list of agencies and boards discussed in the text, along with abbreviations to aid the reader.

Agriculture Adjustment Administration	AAA
Army and Navy Munitions Board	ANMB
Board of Economic Warfare	BEW
Central Administrative Services	CAS
Civilian Conservation Corps	CCC
Committee for Medical Research	CMR
Controlled Materials Plan	CMP
Division of Defense Aid Reports	DDAR
National Defense Advisory Commission	NDAC
National Defense Mediation Board	NDMB
National Defense Research Committee	NDRC
National Recovery Administration	NRA
National Resources Planning Board	NRPB
National War Labor Board	NWLB
National Youth Administration	NYA
Office of Agricultural Defense Relations	OADR
Office of Censorship	OC
Office of Civilian Defense	OCD
Office of Defense Housing Coordination	ODHC
Office of Defense Transportation	ODT
Office of Economic Warfare	OEW
Office for Emergency Management*	OEM
Office of Facts and Figures	OFF

Office of Government Reports	OGR
Office of Lend-Lease Administration	OLLA
Office of Petroleum Coordination	OPC
Office of Price Administration	OPA
Office of Price Administration and Civilian Supply	OPACS
Office of Production Management	OPM
Office of Scientific Research and Development	OSRD
Office of Strategic Services	OSS
Office of War Information	OWI
Public Works Administration	PWA
Reconstruction Finance Corporation	RFC
Supplies and Priorities Allocation Board	SPAB
Tennessee Valley Authority	TVA
War Labor Board	WLB
War Manpower Commission	WMC
War Production Board	WPB
War Shipping Administration	WSA
Works Progress Administration	WPA

*The Office for Emergency Management is sometimes referred to as the Office of Emergency Management.

NOTES

Prologue: May 26, 1940

1. Russell D. Buhite and David W. Levy, eds., *FDR's Fireside Chats* (Norman, Okla.: University of Oklahoma Press, 1992), xv–xx, 152–62.

Chapter 1: Hello to Arms, Farewell to New Deal

1. Rexford Tugwell Diary, January 17, 1933, in Franklin Roosevelt Presidential Library (RPL). See also Bernard Sternsher, "The Stimson Doctrine: F.D.R. versus Moley and Tugwell," *Pacific Historical Review* 31 (August 1962), 284.
2. Waldo Heinrichs, *Threshold of War* (New York: Oxford University Press, 1988), 18.
3. Heinrichs, *Threshold of War*, 18; Henry L. Stimson and McGeorge Bundy, *On Active Service in Peace and War* (New York: Harper & Bros., 1948), 292.
4. Sternsher, "The Stimson Doctrine," 283. See also Robert Dallek, *Franklin D. Roosevelt and American Foreign Policy, 1932–1940* (New York: Oxford University Press, 1979).
5. Raymond Moley, *After Seven Years* (New York: Harper and Bros., 1939), 95.
6. Rexford Tugwell Diary, January 17, 1933, RPL. See also Gary Dean Best, "Franklin Delano Roosevelt, the New Deal, and Japan," in Hilary Conroy and Harry Wray, *Pearl Harbor Reexamined* (Honolulu: University of Hawaii Press, 1990), 29.
7. Burton W. Folsom, Jr., *New Deal or Raw Deal?* (New York: Simon & Schuster, 2008), 43, 60, 81.
8. *New York Times*, July 21, 1940, p. E8.
9. Provisions of the 1937 Neutrality Act: An arms embargo would go into force if a foreign nation became belligerent, whether victim or aggressor; no loans or bank credits to belligerents; U.S. merchant ships were not to be armed; U.S. citizens were banned from traveling as passengers on ships belonging to belligerents, and there were other restrictions. Even if belligerent countries wished to purchase noncontraband goods, they must pay cash and transport them in foreign vessels. For a discussion of the Neutrality Acts, see William Langer and Everett Gleason, *The Challenge to Isolation, 1937–1940* (New York: Harper Torchbooks, 1964).

10. James T. Patterson, *Mr. Republican: A Biography of Robert A. Taft* (Boston: Houghton Mifflin, 1972), 243.
11. Robert Ferrell, *Peace in Their Time: The Origins of the Kellogg-Briand Pact* (New York: W. W. Norton, 1969).
12. Donald Nelson, *Arsenal of Democracy* (New York: Harcourt, Brace and Co., 1946), 32.
13. William Manchester, *The Last Lion, 1932–1940* (New York: Dell, 1988), 45.
14. David Brinkley, *Washington Goes to War* (New York: Ballantine, 1988), 104.
15. R. Elberton Smith, *The Army and Economic Mobilization* (Washington, D.C.: Government Printing Office, 1959), 122.
16. Smith, *The Army and Economic Mobilization*, 123–25.
17. Folsom, *New Deal or Raw Deal?*, 169.
18. *New York Times*, May 5, 1934, p. 7, and June 16, 1934, p. 7; Smith, *The Army and Economic Mobilization*, 125.
19. Studs Terkel, *"The Good War"* (New York: MJF Books, 1984), 321.
20. Smith, *The Army and Economic Mobilization*, 125.
21. Forrest C. Pogue, *George C. Marshall: Ordeal and Hope* (New York: Viking Press, 1966), 20.
22. Pogue, *Ordeal and Hope*, 20.
23. Manchester, *The Last Lion*, 182.
24. Brinkley, *Washington Goes to War*, 13. To "welcome" FDR to the city, *Chicago Tribune* publisher Robert McCormick, an isolationist, had his workmen paint "UNDOMINATED" in letters ten feet high on the side of a warehouse near the site of Roosevelt's platform for the speech.
25. *New York Times*, October 6, 1937, pp. 17, 24; Brinkley, *Washington Goes to War*, 13; *Chicago Tribune*, October 7, 1937, p. 1.
26. John K. Emmerson, "Principles Versus Realities: U.S. Prewar Foreign Policy toward Japan," in Conroy and Wray, *Pearl Harbor Reexamined*, 37. John K. Emmerson served in the Tokyo embassy before World War II and serves as an eyewitness to these events. He agrees that Hull disliked FDR's speech.
27. Brinkley, *Washington Goes to War*, 13.
28. Forrest C. Pogue, *George C. Marshall: Education of a General* (New York: Viking Press, 1963), 320.
29. Pogue, *Education of a General*, 322; Smith, *The Army and Economic Mobilization*, 127.
30. *New York Times*, October 15, 1938, p. 1.
31. Pogue, *Education of a General*, 323.
32. *New York Times*, November 16, 1938, p. 22.
33. Robert Shogan, *Hard Bargain* (Boulder, Colo.: Westview Press, 1999), 48–49; *New York Times*, January 27, 1939, p. 5.

34. *New York Times*, February 4, 1939, p. 1.

35. Folsom, *New Deal or Raw Deal?*, 243; Manchester, *The Last Lion*, 248, 421. Members of Chamberlain's inner circle privately acknowledged that the British prime minister had "an almost instinctive contempt for the Americans."

36. Pogue, *Education of a General*, 326.

37. Arthur Krock, *Memoirs* (New York: Funk & Wagnalls, 1968), 215.

38. Brinkley, *Washington Goes to War*, 58.

39. Pogue, *Education of a General*, 274–77; Pogue, *Ordeal and Hope*, 95, 237.

40. Pogue, *Education of a General*, 324, 336.

41. James O. Richardson, *On the Treadmill to Pearl Harbor* (Washington, D.C.: Department of the Navy, 1973), 434.

42. Pogue, *Education of a General*, 334.

43. Smith, *The Army and Economic Mobilization*, 42; Pogue, *Ordeal and Hope*, 23. The duties of the ANMB included joint planning by the U.S. Army and Navy for mobilization of America's economy in case of war:
    (1) What are the total supply requirements of all military branches?
    (2) How do we get those military supplies from civilian industries?
    (3) How should we divide those resources between the Army and Navy once they are produced?

44. Smith, *The Army and Economic Mobilization*, 99–100.

45. *New York Times*, August 20, 1939, p. E7.

46. *New York Times*, August 15, 1939, p. 1. "All New England Says 'No'!" was the descriptive title of one article.

47. *New York Times*, August 24, 1939, p. 3.

48. Richardson, *On the Treadmill to Pearl Harbor*, 153.

49. *New York Times*, August 30, 1939, p. 3.

50. Smith, *The Army and Economic Mobilization*, 101.

51. Brinkley, *Washington Goes to War*, 23.

52. Pogue, *Ordeal and Hope*, 11.

53. Shogan, *Hard Bargain*, 266.

54. Shogan, *Hard Bargain*, 53.

55. Smith, *The Army and Economic Mobilization*, 101.

56. *New York Times*, September 10, 1939, pp. 1, 50; Keith E. Eiler, *Mobilizing America* (Ithaca, N.Y.: Cornell University Press, 1997), 91. Some of the offices under the OEM included OPACS, DDAR, OLLA, OGR, NRPB, OPM, NDMB, ODHC, OCD, and OADR.

57. Winston Churchill, *The Gathering Storm* (Boston: Houghton Mifflin, 1948), 440–41.

58. Manchester, *The Last Lion*, 545.

59. Pogue, *Ordeal and Hope*, 31–32.

60. Shogan, *Hard Bargain*, 81.

61. *New York Times*, May 17, 1940, pp. 1, 16.

62. Smith, *The Army and Economic Mobilization*, 132–33.

63. Andy Marino, *A Quiet American: The Secret War of Varian Fry* (New York: St. Martin's Press, 1999), 38.

64. Marino, *A Quiet American*, 47.

65. Marino, *A Quiet American*, 115.

66. Breckinridge Long Diary, Box 5, June 26, 1940; memo from Assistant Secretary of State Breckinridge Long to State Department officials, June 26, 1940, Library of Congress (LC).

67. *New York Times*, August 16, 1940, p. 14.

68. *New York Times*, July 16, 1935, p. 1; July 17, 1935, p. 1; July 26, 1935, p. 8; and July 28, 1935, p. 2.

69. Marino, *A Quiet American*, 52.

70. Marino, *A Quiet American*, 73, 81–83, 165. The French government maintained internment camps at Agde, Bram, Brens-Gallac, Falaise, Gurs, Le Cyprien, Riveslates, Septfonds, St. Nicholas, and Vernet. Tens of thousands and possibly hundreds of thousands of prisoners died in these camps.

71. Breckinridge Long Diary, Box 5, July 12, 1940, LC.

72. Marino, *A Quiet American*, 142, 271.

73. Breckinridge Long Diary, Box 5, October 3, 1940, LC.

Chapter 2: The Election of 1940: A Third Term

1. Ellsworth Barnard, *Wendell Willkie* (Marquette, Mich.: Northern Michigan University Press, 1966); Joseph F. Barnes, *Willkie* (New York: Simon and Schuster, 1952); Herbert S. Parmet and Marie B. Hecht, *Never Again: A President Runs for a Third Term* (New York: Macmillan, 1968).

2. *New York Times*, June 1, 1940, p. 7.

3. Wendell Willkie, *This Is Wendell Willkie: A Collection of Speeches and Writings on Present-Day Issues* (New York: Dodd, Mead and Co., 1940), 194.

4. Steve Neal, *Dark Horse: A Biography of Wendell Willkie* (Garden City, N.Y.: Doubleday, 1984), 30.

5. Willkie, *Willkie Speeches*, 94.

6. Willkie, *Willkie Speeches*, 136.

7. Willkie, *Willkie Speeches*, 144–45, 231.

8. Willkie, *Willkie Speeches*, 65.

9. Willkie, *Willkie Speeches*, 61–62, 65.

10. Willkie, *Willkie Speeches*, 65.

11. Willkie, *Willkie Speeches*, 70, 87–88.

12. Willkie, *Willkie Speeches*, 31.

13. Neal, *Dark Horse*, 108–16.

14. Neal, *Dark Horse*, 122.

15. Willkie, *Willkie Speeches*, 96.

16. *New York Times*, June 5, 1940, p. 18. See also Hadley Cantril, *Public Opinion, 1935–1946* (Princeton, N.J.: Princeton University Press, 1951), 607, 611.

17. Robert Higgs, *Depression, War, and Cold War* (New York: Oxford University Press, 2006), 30–60; Sidney Ratner, *Taxation and Democracy in America* (New York: John Wiley and Sons, 1942), 493–99; and Roland Stromberg, "American Business and the Approach of War, 1935–1941," *Journal of Economic History* 13 (Winter 1953), 72.

18. Henry L. Stimson and McGeorge Bundy, *On Active Service in Peace and War* (New York: Harper and Bros., 1948), 320, 323–24; Neal, *Dark Horse*, 82–83.

19. Willkie, *Willkie Speeches*, 270, 273.

20. Willkie, *Willkie Speeches*, 275–77.

21. Parmet and Hecht, *Never Again*, 201, 214–15, 222.

22. The debate over the destroyers is well discussed in Robert Shogan, *Hard Bargain* (Boulder, Colo.: Westview Press, 1999).

23. Shogan, *Hard Bargain*, 231.

24. *New York Times*, September 4, 1940, pp. 1, 15–16; Shogan, *Hard Bargain*, 217, 237–38.

25. Shogan, *Hard Bargain*, 233–43.

26. James MacGregor Burns, *Roosevelt: The Lion and the Fox* (New York: Harcourt Brace, 1956), 441; Shogan, *Hard Bargain*, 244–45; Neal, *Dark Horse*, 140.

27. Shogan, *Hard Bargain*, 241–42.

28. Breckinridge Long Diary, August 31, 1940, LC.

29. Shogan, *Hard Bargain*, 260–61; Edward Corwin, *Total War and the Constitution* (New York: Alfred A. Knopf, 1947), 26–27.

30. Shogan, *Hard Bargain*, 242–43.

31. *New York Times*, September 11, 1940, p. 23.

32. *New York Times*, September 10, 1940, p. 1; Robert A. Caro, *The Path to Power: The Years of Lyndon Johnson* (New York: Random House, 1982), 622.

33. *Newark Evening News*, September 8, 1938, as quoted in a telegram to Harry Hopkins, in "WPA—Political Coercion, New Jersey," File 610, National Archives. See also James T. Patterson, *The New Deal and the States* (Princeton, N.J.: Princeton University Press, 1969), 82–83; Burton Folsom, Jr., *New Deal or Raw Deal?* (New York: Simon & Schuster, 2008), 86–88; Jim Powell, "Welfare Corruption and the New Deal," *Freedom Daily* (September 2009), 26.

34. Folsom, *New Deal or Raw Deal?*, 86; Parmet and Hecht, *Never Again*, 244.

35. John M. Blum, *From the Morgenthau Diaries*, 3 vols. (Boston: Houghton Mifflin, 1959–67), I, 277.

36. Blum, *From the Morgenthau Diaries*, III, 39.

37. *New York Times*, October 10, 1940, p. 19.

38. *New York Times*, June 7, 1940, p. 20.

39. *New York Times*, October 22, 1940, p. 17.

40. *New York Times*, November 2, 1940, p. 1.

41. Caro, *Lyndon Johnson*, 581–606. Most of our discussion of Johnson and the 1940 election comes from Caro. Caro concludes that the Corpus Christi naval base was probably FDR's first base signing after his May speeches.

42. Caro, *Lyndon Johnson*, 586.

43. Caro, *Lyndon Johnson*, 606. For a history of Brown & Root, see Joseph A. Pratt and Christopher J. Castanada, *Builders: Herman and George R. Brown* (College Station, Tex.: Texas A&M Press, 1998).

44. Caro, *Lyndon Johnson*, 606–64; Louise Overacker, "Campaign Finance in the Presidential Election of 1940," *American Political Science Review* 35 (August 1941), 701–27.

45. Caro, *Lyndon Johnson*, 640–41.

46. Samuel I. Rosenman, ed., *Public Papers and Addresses of Franklin D. Roosevelt* (New York: Random House, 1941), IX, 490, 515, 542; David Kennedy, *Freedom from Fear* (New York: Oxford University Press, 1999), 464.

47. Parmet and Hecht, *Never Again*, 235; Kennedy, *Freedom from Fear*, 462.

48. Rosenman, ed., *Public Papers*, IX, 517.

49. The quotation is from Burns, *The Lion and the Fox*, 452.

50. Caro, *Lyndon Johnson*, 654; Neal, *Dark Horse*, 176–77.

51. Thomas A. Bailey, *The Man in the Street* (New York: Macmillan, 1948), 11–13; Shogan, *Hard Bargain*, 278.

52. Kennedy, *Freedom from Fear*; Arthur M. Schlesinger, Jr., "Rating the Presidents: Washington to Clinton," *Political Science Quarterly*, 112 (Summer 1997), 182.

Chapter 3: *The Battle of the Atlantic*

1. James Phinney Baxter III, *Scientists Against Time* (Cambridge, Mass.: M.I.T. Press, 1946), 142.

2. Robert Buderi, *The Invention that Changed the World* (New York: Simon & Schuster, 1996), 31–32.

3. Buderi, *The Invention that Changed the World*, 49.

4. Buderi, *The Invention that Changed the World*, 70, 89, 100.

5. Buderi, *The Invention that Changed the World*, 39, 98.

6. Baxter, *Scientists Against Time*, 14–19; Buderi, *The Invention that Changed the World*, 34.

7. Buderi, *The Invention that Changed the World*, 38.

8. James T. Patterson, *Mr. Republican: A Biography of Robert A. Taft* (Boston: Houghton Mifflin, 1972), 238–39.

9. R. Elberton Smith, *The Army and Economic Mobilization* (Washington, D.C.: Government Printing Office, 1959), 108.

10. Henry L. Stimson and McGeorge Bundy, *On Active Service in Peace and War* (New York: Harper and Bros., 1948), 354; Smith, *The Army and Economic Mobilization*, 103. National Defense Advisory Council members: William Knudsen (industrial production), E. R. Stettinius, Jr. (industrial materials), Sidney Hillman (employment), Leon Henderson (price stabilization), Chester C. Davis (farm products), Ralph Budd (transportation), and Harriet Elliott (consumer protection).

11. *New York Times*, May 17, 1940, p. 16.

12. Keith E. Eiler, *Mobilizing America* (Ithaca, N.Y.: Cornell University Press, 1997), 43; Smith, *The Army and Economic Mobilization*, 103.

13. *New York Times*, August 18, 1940, p. 3.

14. Robert Shogan, *Hard Bargain* (Boulder, Colo.: Westview Press, 1999), 248.

15. Eiler, *Mobilizing America*, 65; Stimson and Bundy, *On Active Service in Peace and War*, 353.

16. Eiler, *Mobilizing America*, 134; *St. Louis Post-Dispatch*, September 14, 1940, p. 1.

17. Eiler, *Mobilizing America*, 135.

18. Eiler, *Mobilizing America*, 135–37.

19. Eiler, *Mobilizing America*, 137.

20. Waldo Heinrichs, *Threshold of War* (New York: Oxford University Press, 1988), 10; Eiler, *Mobilizing America*, 68, 74; Smith, *The Army and Economic Mobilization*, 122. From July 1, 1940, to March 1, 1941, the military authorized $1.738 billion in cost-plus fixed fee contracts.

21. Eiler, *Mobilizing America*, 60.

22. Eiler, *Mobilizing America*, 50.

23. Eiler, *Mobilizing America*, 72; Heinrichs, *Threshold of War*, 10.

24. *New York Times*, December 21, 1940, p. 8.

25. Stimson and Bundy, *On Active Service in Peace and War*, 354.

26. In FDR's executive order of January 7, 1941, the OPM was assigned to "increase, accelerate, and regulate the production and supply of materials, articles, and equipment" for the nation's defense and to coordinate the activities of other government agencies or departments concerned with these issues.

27. *St. Louis Post-Dispatch*, November 8, 1940, p. 1.

28. David Brinkley, *Washington Goes to War* (New York: Ballantine Books, 1988), 48.

29. *New York Times*, February 5, 1941, p. 18.

30. *St. Louis Post-Dispatch*, January 10, 1941, p. 1.

31. Patterson, *Mr. Republican*, 243. FDR's critics also believed that his administration planned to use Lend-Lease as an excuse to socialize American industry; see Arthur Krock, "In the Nation: An Undercurrent of the Lease-Lend Debate," in *New York Times*, February 7, 1941, p. 18.

32. John V. Denson, "Franklin Delano Roosevelt and the First Shot: A Study of Deceit and Deception," in John V. Denson, ed., *Reassessing the Presidency* (Auburn, Ala.: Mises Institute, 2001), 494.

33. Heinrichs, *Threshold of War*, 7.

34. Brinkley, *Washington Goes to War*, 47.

35. *The American Experience*, online at www.pbs.org/wgbh/amex/presidents/ video/fdr_21_qt.html#v122, statement by Alistair Cooke in *The Presidents*, Chapter: "FDR, The Juggler."

36. Shogan, *Hard Bargain*, 247.

37. *St. Louis Post-Dispatch*, March 15, 1941, p. 1; Eiler, *Mobilizing America*, 88.

38. *New York Times*, March 24, 1941, p. 5.

39. Winston Churchill, *The Grand Alliance* (Boston: Houghton Mifflin, 1950), 122; *New York Times*, March 12, 1941, p. 1, and March 19, 1941, p. 1.

40. Heinrichs, *Threshold of War*, 165.

41. *New York Times*, March 23, 1941, p. XX3; Smith, *The Army and Economic Mobilization*, 9, 255–56. By the end of the war, U. S. industry produced 634,569 jeeps, and soldiers drove them all over the world.

42. Buderi, *The Invention that Changed the World*, 121.

43. David McCullough, *Truman* (New York: Simon & Schuster, 1992), 255–58.

44. Heinrichs, *Threshold of War*, 39.

45. Heinrichs, *Threshold of War*, 31, *New York Times*, March 16, 1941, p. 42.

46. *New York Times*, March 22, 1941, p. 14.

47. *New York Times*, March 19, 1941, p. 1.

48. Eiler, *Mobilizing America*, 164–66.

49. Heinrichs, *Threshold of War*, 16; Eiler, *Mobilizing America*, 167–71.

50. Arthur Krock, "The Pressure for Labor Action Nears Its Peak," in *New York Times*, April 4, 1941, p. 20.

51. *New York Times*, May 16, 1941, p. 22.

52. *New York Times*, May 22, 1941, p. 20.

53. Eiler, *Mobilizing America*, 169–70; *New York Times*, June 7, 1941, p. 8, and June 10, 1941, p. 16.

54. Forrest C. Pogue, *George C. Marshall: Ordeal and Hope* (New York: Viking Press, 1966), 17.

55. Heinrichs, *Threshold of War*, 173; Pogue, *Ordeal and Hope*, 66.
56. Brinkley, *Washington Goes to War*, 56–57; Eiler, *Mobilizing America*, 122–23. Tank production posed special problems because no comparable civilian vehicle existed; new tank engines had to be developed.
57. *New York Times*, May 1, 1941, p. 1.
58. Heinrichs, *Threshold of War*, 85.
59. Heinrichs, *Threshold of War*, 101–2.
60. Heinrichs, *Threshold of War*, 94–95.
61. Heinrichs, *Threshold of War*, 140; *New York Times*, September 17, 1941, p. 10.
62. Shogan, *Hard Bargain*, 265.
63. I. C. B. Dear, ed., *The Oxford Companion to World War II* (New York: Oxford University Press, 1995), 69.
64. *New York Times*, January 2, 1972, p. 7. Churchill's statements are taken from minutes of British cabinet meetings in declassified files released to the public by the British government in 1972.
65. *New York Times*, August 15, 1941, p. 1.
66. Ohio History Central, *An Online Encyclopedia of Ohio History*, at www.ohiohistorycentral.org/entry.php?rec=534.
67. *St. Louis Post-Dispatch*, September 15, 1941, p. 1.
68. George Morgenstern, *Pearl Harbor* (New York: Devin-Adair, 1947), 87; *New York Times*, October 29, 1941, p. 4.
69. *New York Times*, April 22, 1941, p. 20.
70. McCullough, *Truman*, 267–69; Eiler, *Mobilizing America*, 94.
71. Brinkley, *Washington Goes to War*, 64; Eiler, *Mobilizing America*, 87.

Chapter 4: Pearl Harbor, December 7, 1941

1. David Brinkley, *Washington Goes to War* (New York: Ballantine, 1988), 60.
2. Brinkley, *Washington Goes to War*, 61.
3. Bruce Catton, *The War Lords of Washington* (New York: Harcourt, Brace and Co., 1948), 3–12; Donald M. Nelson, *Arsenal of Democracy* (New York: Harcourt, Brace and Co., 1946), 183.
4. George Morgenstern, *Pearl Harbor* (New York: Devin-Adair, 1947), 61.
5. Winston Churchill, "Let the Tyrants Bomb!" *Colliers*, January 14, 1939, p. 13; William Manchester, *The Last Lion: 1932–1940* (New York: Dell, 1988), 122.
6. Gary Dean Best, "Franklin Delano Roosevelt, the New Deal, and Japan," in Hilary Conroy and Harry Wray, *Pearl Harbor Reexamined* (Honolulu: University of Hawaii Press, 1990), 28.
7. Waldo Heinrichs, *Threshold of War* (New York: Oxford University Press, 1988), 17–18.

8. Forrest C. Pogue, *George C. Marshall: Ordeal and Hope* (New York: Viking Press, 1966), 125.

9. Heinrichs, *Threshold of War*, 18.

10. Thomas Fleming, *The New Dealers' War* (New York: Basic Books, 2001), 43–44.

11. Morgenstern, *Pearl Harbor*, 17, 80–81.

12. Morgenstern, *Pearl Harbor*, 57.

13. James O. Richardson, *On the Treadmill to Pearl Harbor* (Washington, D.C.: Department of the Navy, 1973), 355–56.

14. Morgenstern, *Pearl Harbor*, 93.

15. Richardson, *On the Treadmill to Pearl Harbor*, 391, 394, 433.

16. Morgenstern, *Pearl Harbor*, 57.

17. Richardson, *On the Treadmill to Pearl Harbor*, 434.

18. Richardson, *On the Treadmill to Pearl Harbor*, 435.

19. *New York Times*, November 1, 1940, p. 9.

20. Fleming, *The New Dealers' War*, 1–18, 42–43. FDR and Navy leaders also changed Pacific strategy from "War Plan Orange" to "Rainbow Five," which caused confusion.

21. Fleming, *The New Dealers' War*, 42–43; Morgenstern, *Pearl Harbor*, 56–62; Richardson, *On the Treadmill to Pearl Harbor*, 399–400.

22. Martin Gilbert, *Churchill: A Life* (New York: Henry Holt, 1991), 683.

23. Manchester, *The Last Lion*, 144.

24. *New York Times*, January 28, 1940, p. E1.

25. *New York Times*, April 14, 1940, p. 1.

26. Best, "Roosevelt, the New Deal and Japan," 31; John K. Emmerson, "Principles Versus Realities: U.S. Prewar Foreign Policy toward Japan," in Conroy and Wray, *Pearl Harbor Reexamined*, 38.

27. *New York Times*, July 27, 1939, p. 1.

28. Breckinridge Long Diary, Box 5, September 14, 1940, LC.

29. Robert Shogan, *Hard Bargain* (Boulder, Colo.: Westview Press, 1999), 256.

30. Breckinridge Long Diary, Box 5, September 28, 1940, LC.

31. *New York Times*, June 21, 1941, p. 1.

32. Fleming, *The New Dealers' War*, 18.

33. Heinrichs, *Threshold of War*, 127.

34. *New York Times*, July 31, 1941, p. 4.

35. *New York Times*, January 21, 1940, p. 65.

36. *New York Times*, July 26, 1941, p. 4.

37. Emmerson, "Principles Versus Realities," 38; Fleming, *The New Dealers' War*, 21–22.

38. Emmerson, "Principles Versus Realities," 41–42. Emmerson also lists four principles, about which Cordell Hull maintained an "all or nothing" attitude:

     (1) Respect for the territorial integrity and sovereignty of all nations;

     (2) Noninterference in the internal affairs of other countries;

     (3) Equality, including equality of commercial opportunity;

     (4) Nondisturbance of the status quo in the Pacific except as the status quo might be altered by peaceful means.

39. Heinrichs, *Threshold of War*, 120; *New York Times*, July 26, 1941, p. 4.

40. Pogue, *Ordeal and Hope*, 199.

41. Heinrichs, *Threshold of War*, 124.

42. *New York Times*, September 5, 1941, p. 17

43. Morgenstern, *Pearl Harbor*, 12, 292.

44. Pogue, *Ordeal and Hope*, 213; Henry C. Clausen and Bruce Lee, *Pearl Harbor: Final Judgement* (New York: Crown Publishers, 1992), 172–77.

45. Morgenstern, *Pearl Harbor*, 72. Radar stations in Hawaii picked up signals from the incoming Japanese squadrons, but officers thought it was merely six American bombers arriving from the West Coast. The radar stations closed down at 7 A.M. on December 7. Gen. Short concentrated on measures to prevent sabotage rather than radar training.

46. Morgenstern, *Pearl Harbor*, 16, 80–81.

47. William Manchester, *American Caesar* (New York: Dell, 1978), 229.

48. Alonzo Fields, *My 21 Years in the White House* (New York: Coward-McCann, 1961), 80.

49. Fleming, *The New Dealers' War*, 41.

50. Keith E. Eiler, *Mobilizing America* (Ithaca, N.Y.: Cornell University Press, 1997), 229–30.

51. Frances Perkins, *The Roosevelt I Knew* (New York: Macmillan, 1946), 279.

52. Arthur Krock, *Memoirs* (New York: Funk & Wagnalls, 1968), 202; Clausen and Lee, *Pearl Harbor*, 9.

53. Heinrichs, *Threshold of War*, 78.

54. Richardson, *On the Treadmill to Pearl Harbor*, 461.

55. Krock, *Memoirs*, 191.

56. Pogue, *Ordeal and Hope*, 205; Clausen and Lee, *Pearl Harbor*, 131–32.

57. Heinrichs, *Threshold of War*, 219; Morgenstern, *Pearl Harbor*, 23–25. The Japanese launched five midget submarines during the attack, but all five were sunk before they could inflict damage. Accounts of the number of Japanese planes shot down on December 7 vary; some historians estimate that American forces brought down about two dozen.

58. Manchester, *American Caesar*, 233–38.

59. Nancy Caldwell Sorel, *The Women Who Wrote the War* (New York: Arcade Publishing, 1999), 151–52.

60. Fleming, *The New Dealers' War*, 45; Manchester, *American Caesar*, 208, 212.

61. Andrew Williams, *The Battle of the Atlantic* (New York: Basic Books, 2003), 31–37.

62. Gilbert, *Churchill*, 694.

63. Gilbert, *Churchill*, 712; Heinrichs, *Threshold of War*, 218–19.

64. Brinkley, *Washington Goes to War*, 102; Gilbert, *Churchill*, 711.

65. *New York Times*, December 27, 1941, p. 4.

66. Heinrichs, *Threshold of War*, 78.

67. Morgenstern, *Pearl Harbor*, 292–93.

Chapter 5: 1942: The War Overseas

1. Stephen E. Ambrose, *Eisenhower: Soldier, General of the Army, President-Elect, 1890–1952* (New York: Simon and Schuster, 1983), 133.

2. Thomas Fleming, *The New Dealers' War* (New York: Basic Books, 2001), 46.

3. Ambrose, *Eisenhower*, 133, 141.

4. Forrest C. Pogue, *George C. Marshall: Ordeal and Hope* (New York: Viking Press, 1966), 237–39.

5. Ambrose, *Eisenhower*, 137; Pogue, *Ordeal and Hope*, 244–46.

6. *New York Times*, December 8, 1941, p. 6.

7. Brinkley, *Washington Goes to War*, 88.

8. *New York Times*, December 10, 1941, p. 1.

9. George Morgenstern, *Pearl Harbor* (New York: Devin-Adair, 1947), 42; *New York Times*, January 28, 1942, p. 17.

10. Frances Perkins, *The Roosevelt I Knew* (New York: Macmillan, 1946), 379–80; Pogue, *Ordeal and Hope*, 23.

11. *Mayfield Messenger*, January 1, 1942, p. 1.

12. Joseph Persico, *Roosevelt's Secret War* (New York: Random House, 2002), 160.

13. *Mayfield Messenger*, February 12, 1942, p. 4.

14. William Manchester, *American Caesar* (New York: Dell, 1978), 267; *New York Times*, February 2, 1942, p. 1, and February 10, 1942, p. 1.

15. Richard Polenberg, *War and Society* (Philadelphia: J. B. Lippincott Co., 1972), 51; George H. Roeder, Jr., *The Censored War* (New Haven, Conn.: Yale University Press, 1993), 8; Frederick S. Voss, *Reporting the War: The Journalistic Coverage of World War II* (Washington, D.C.: Smithsonian Institution Press, 1994), 24.

16. Roeder, *The Censored War*, 9.

17. *New York Times*, February 10, 1942, p. 18.

18. *New York Times*, February 24, 1942, p. 1.

19. *New York Times*, February 24, 1942, p. 4.

20. Manchester, *American Caesar*, 286–87.

21. Doulgas MacArthur, *Reminiscences* (New York: McGraw-Hill, 1964), 144.

22. Manchester, *American Caesar*, 336. See also Barbara Tuchman's excellent volume, *Stillwell and the American Experience, 1911–1945* (New York: Mac-Millan, 1971).

23. Ronald H. Spector, *Eagle Against the Sun: The American War with Japan* (New York: Macmillan, 1985), 158.

24. Gordon W. Prange, *Miracle at Midway* (New York: McGraw-Hill, 1982), xiii.

25. Spector, *Eagle Against the Sun*, 168; *Life*, February 18, 1946, p. 93.

26. *New York Times*, June 9, 1942, p. 1; Jonathan Parshall and Anthony Tully, *Shattered Sword: The Untold Story of the Battle of Midway* (Dulles, Va.: Potomac Books, 2005), 110, 175. Japanese air commander Minoru Genda later wrote that "it has to be admitted that the planning of the air searching was slipshod." For data on Japanese fighters and American torpedo planes, see pages 227, 236, 243.

27. *New York Times*, June 7, 1942, p. 1.

28. *New York Times*, June 14, 1942, p. E3.

29. "U.S. at War: The First Six Months," *Time*, June 8, 1942.

30. Fleming, *The New Dealers' War*, 135, 155.

31. Pogue, *Ordeal and Hope*, 310–12.

32. Pogue, *Ordeal and Hope*, 329.

33. Pogue, *Ordeal and Hope*, 330.

34. Martin Gilbert, *Churchill: A Life* (New York: Henry Holt, 1991), 723.

35. Pogue, *Ordeal and Hope*, 332–33.

36. Manchester, *American Caesar*, 329, 337.

37. Manchester, *American Caesar*, 335, 337.

38. Manchester, *American Caesar*, 339, 341.

39. Spector, *Eagle Against the Sun*, 189.

40. Manchester, *American Caesar*, 343–44.

41. Manchester, *American Caesar*, 349–50.

42. Spector, *Eagle Against the Sun*, 189, 214.

43. Manchester, *American Caesar*, 351; Spector, *Eagle Against the Sun*, 190.

44. *American Heritage*, vol. 13, issue 2, Fall 1997, online at http://www.american heritage.com/articles/magazine/it/1997/2/1997_2_56.shtml; Spector, *Eagle Against the Sun*, 178.

45. Manchester, *American Caesar*, 346, 354.

46. Pogue, *Ordeal and Hope*, 393–94.

47. Pogue, *Ordeal and Hope*, 405.

48. Pogue, *Ordeal and Hope*, 416.

49. Pogue, *Ordeal and Hope*, 417.

50. Ambrose, *Eisenhower*, 200.

51. Gilbert, *Churchill*, 734; Pogue, *Ordeal and Hope*, 397, 425.

Chapter 6: 1942: On the Home Front

1. David Brinkley, *Washington Goes to War* (New York: Ballantine Books, 1988), 116.

2. *New York Times*, December 17, 1941, p. 1.

3. *New York Times*, December 9, 1941, p. 7.

4. Brinkley, *Washington Goes to War*, 108; *New York Times*, December 14, 1941, p. 32.

5. *New York Times*, December 24, 1941, p. 10.

6. *New York Times*, December 11, 1941, p. 1, and December 23, 1941, p. 20.

7. David McCullough, *Truman* (New York: Simon & Schuster, 1992), 268–69. President Roosevelt created the WPB to replace the OPM and SPAB before the Truman Committee published its annual report, criticizing the OPM and the chaos in the defense industries.

8. Marshall Clinard, *The Black Market* (Montclair, N.J.: Patterson Smith, 1952), 266; *New York Times*, April 9, 1942, p. 1.

9. Clinard, *The Black Market*, 9, 11.

10. *New York Times*, May 3, 1942, p. 1.

11. Clinard, *The Black Market*, 13, 23.

12. "U.S. at War: The First Six Months," *Time*, June 8, 1942; Clinard, *The Black Market*, 10, 64.

13. Brinkley, *Washington Goes to War*, 90.

14. Forrest C. Pogue, *George C. Marshall: Ordeal and Hope* (New York: Viking Press, 1966), 97, 295–96.

15. Pogue, *Ordeal and Hope*, 404–05.

16. R. Elberton Smith, *The Army and Economic Mobilization* (Washington, D.C.: Government Printing Office, 1959), 28.

17. Brinkley, *Washington Goes to War*, 91.

18. *New York Times*, April 3, 1942, p. 1.

19. *New York Times*, April 2, 1942, p. 20.

20. *New York Times*, May 27, 1942, p. 1.

21. *New York Times*, February 2, 1942, p. 8; Smith, *The Army and Economic Mobilization*, 496.

22. "Summer Politics," *Life*, August 10, 1942, p. 31; *Mayfield Messenger*, July 11, 1942, p. 1.

23. Harold G. Robinson, oral history interview, March 6, 1971, conducted by J. R. Fuchs for the Harry S. Truman Library, online at www.trumanlibrary.org/oralhist/robinsoh.htm.

24. *Mayfield Messenger*, November 12, 1942, p. 1.

25. *New York Times*, January 2, 1941, p. 1.

26. *Louisville Courier-Journal*, July 25, 1940, p.1, and September 13, 1940, p.1; *New York Times*, January 2, 1941, pp. 1, 14; Smith, *The Army and Economic Mobilization*, 8, 28.

27. Rob Vest, "Charlestown, IN and the Indiana Army Ammunition Plant: The Making of a War-Industry Boom-Town," online at http://homepages.ius .edu/RVEST/INAAP.htm, p. 6.

28. Vest, "Charlestown, IN and the Indiana Army Ammunition Plant," p. 5; *Louisville Courier-Journal*, September 14, 1940, p. 2.

29. *New York Times*, January 2, 1941, pp. 1, 14; Vest, "Charlestown, IN and the Indiana Army Ammunition Plant," p. 2; Smith, *The Army and Economic Mobilization*, 501. The Indiana Ordnance Works cost $113,919,357, and the Hoosier Ordnance Plant cost $32,245,612. Both were part of the INAAP.

30. Andrew Williams, *The Battle of the Atlantic* (New York: Perseus Books, 2003), 162.

31. Williams, *The Battle of the Atlantic*, 180–81.

32. *New York Times*, April 27, 1942, p. 1; Williams, *The Battle of the Atlantic*, 183.

33. Williams, *The Battle of the Atlantic*, 114, 165.

34. James Phinney Baxter III, *Scientists Against Time* (Cambridge, Mass.: M.I.T. Press, 1946), 39; *New York Times*, June 22, 1942, p. 14.

35. Williams, *The Battle for the Atlantic*, 169.

36. Robert Buderi, *The Invention that Changed the World* (New York: Simon & Schuster, 1996), 139–40.

37. Buderi, *The Invention that Changed the World*, 142.

38. Arthur Krock, *Memoirs* (New York: Funk & Wagnalls, 1968), 211.

39. Baxter, *Scientists Against Time*, 42.

40. Williams, *The Battle of the Atlantic*, 185.

41. *New York Times*, July 24, 1942, p. 18.

42. Baxter, *Scientists Against Time*, 40; Williams, *The Battle of the Atlantic*, 266–69.

43. *New York Times*, August 6, 1942, p. 18.

44. Smith, *The Army and Economic Mobilization*, 441–42, 445–47.

45. Bob Greene, *Once Upon a Town* (New York: Harper, 2003), 5–8.

46. Smith, *The Army and Economic Mobilization*, 200.

47. Dan C. Garrott, *My World War II Story*, self-published; Gerhard Weinberg, "Franklin D. Roosevelt and the Approach of War, 1937–1941," in *One of Freedom's Finest Hours* (Hillsdale, Mich.: Hillsdale College Press, 2002), 20.

48. See, for example, Burton Folsom, Jr., *New Deal or Raw Deal?* (New York: Simon & Schuster, 2008), 168–91, for Roosevelt's campaigns in 1934 and 1936.

49. Richard Polenberg, *War and Society* (Philadelphia: J. B. Lippincott, 1972), 78.

50. Samuel I. Rosenman, ed., *The Public Papers and Addresses of Franklin D. Roosevelt* (New York: Random House, 1950), XI, 80. See also Robert E. Ficken, "The Democratic Party and Domestic Politics during World War II" (Ph.D. dissertation, University of Washington, 1973), 15.

51. Ficken, "The Democratic Party," 49. For the Kent quotation, see *Washington Evening Star*, July 29, 1942, p. A11.

52. Pogue, *Ordeal and Hope*, 402.

53. Pogue, *Ordeal and Hope*, 402; John Harding, "The 1942 Congressional Elections," *The American Political Science Review* 38 (February 1944), 56.

54. *Tulsa Daily World*, November 5, 1942, pp. 1, 10, and November 6, 1942, p. 12; *Detroit Free Press*, November 5, 1942, p. 2; *Cleveland Plain Dealer*, November 5, p. 8. See also Ficken, "The Democratic Party," 38.

55. *Portland Press Herald*, September 16, 1942, p. 8.

56. Quoted in *Detroit Free Press*, November 12, 1942.

57. *Detroit Free Press*, November 5, 1942, p. 2.

58. Quoted in Ficken, "The Democratic Party," 85.

59. *Tulsa Daily World*, November 6, 1942, p. 12.

60. John M. Blum, *From the Morgenthau Diaries*, 3 vols. (Boston: Houghton Mifflin, 1959–67), III, 54.

Chapter 7: 1943: The Tide Turns

1. *New York Times*, January 11, 1943, p. 1; William Manchester, *American Caesar* (New York: Dell, 1978), 344. Soldiers in New Guinea could not leave the battlefield until their fever went higher than 102 degrees.

2. James Phinney Baxter III, *Scientists Against Time* (Cambridge, Mass.: M.I.T. Press, 1952), 108.

3. Baxter, *Scientists Against Time*, 106–7.

4. Ronald H. Spector, *Eagle Against the Sun: The American War with Japan* (New York: Macmillan, 1985), 214–15; Baxter, *Scientists Against Time*, 108.

5. Baxter, *Scientists Against Time*, 310–11.

6. Baxter, *Scientists Against Time*, 309; *New York Times*, December 18, 1942, p. 4.

7. Baxter, *Scientists Against Time*, 106.

8. Baxter, *Scientists Against Time*, 108, 368–72.

9. Forrest C. Pogue, *George C. Marshall: Organizer of Victory, 1943–1945* (New York: Viking Press, 1973), 30–34.

10. Pogue, *Organizer of Victory*, 32–34; Thomas Fleming, *The New Dealers' War* (New York: Basic Books, 2001), 173.

11. David Brinkley, *Washington Goes to War* (New York: Ballantine Books, 1988), 71–73.

12. Brinkley, *Washington Goes to War*, 73.

13. Leslie R. Groves, *Now It Can Be Told* (New York: Da Capo Press, 1962), 2–5, 17.

14. Groves, *Now It Can Be Told*, 6–7.

15. Richard Rhodes, *The Making of the Atomic Bomb* (New York: Simon and Schuster, 1988), 338, 394–95.

16. Rhodes, *The Making of the Atomic Bomb*, 375.

17. Groves, *Now It Can Be Told*, 125–27; Rhodes, *The Making of the Atomic Bomb*, 378.

18. Rhodes, *The Making of the Atomic Bomb*, 379.

19. Groves, *Now It Can Be Told*, 8; Rhodes, *The Making of the Atomic Bomb*, 421.

20. Groves, *Now It Can Be Told*, 22.

21. Groves, *Now It Can Be Told*, 13–14; Rhodes, *The Making of the Atomic Bomb*, 421–31.

22. Rhodes, *The Making of the Atomic Bomb*, 426.

23. Groves, *Now It Can Be Told*, 28.

24. Groves, *Now It Can Be Told*, 97; Rhodes, *The Making of the Atomic Bomb*, 486–87.

25. Burton W. Folsom, Jr., *New Deal or Raw Deal?* (New York: Simon & Schuster, 2008). For FDR's silver policy, see Chapter 8, "Financial Interference." Silver-producing states included Arizona, California, Colorado, Idaho, Nevada, Montana, New Mexico, and Utah.

26. Groves, *Now It Can Be Told*, 107.

27. Groves, *Now It Can Be Told*, 109; Rhodes, *The Making of the Atomic Bomb*, 490.

28. Rhodes, *The Making of the Atomic Bomb*, 497.

29. *New York Times*, August 7, 1945, p. 1; Rhodes, *The Making of the Atomic Bomb*, 451.

30. Rhodes, *The Making of the Atomic Bomb*, 451–52.

31. Rhodes, *The Making of the Atomic Bomb*, 451–52.

32. Groves, *Now It Can Be Told*, 65, 151.

33. Rhodes, *The Making of the Atomic Bomb*, 460. Italics in the original.

34. Rhodes, *The Making of the Atomic Bomb*, 458, 464.

35. *New York Times*, January 15, 1943, p. 11.

36. *New York Times*, February 2, 1943, p. 1.

37. R. Elberton Smith, *The Army and Economic Mobilization* (Washington, D.C.: Government Printing Office, 1959), 158.

38. Elberton, *The Army and Economic Mobilization*, 583–84; 597. Two basic data sets gave the WPB more accurate information—and most important, enough lead time—to plan where resources would go: first, "bills of materials" by industry estimated what resources they needed and how many months ahead of time, in order to fulfill military orders; and second, master production schedules gave time lines for producing those items.

39. Keith E. Eiler, *Mobilizing America* (Ithaca, N.Y.: Cornell University Press, 1997), 370.

40. *New York Times*, February 11, 1943, p. 18.

41. Eiler, *Mobilizing America*, 385; *Mayfield Messenger*, March 3, 1943, p. 4.

42. *Mayfield Messenger*, March 24, 1943, p. 1. The quotation is accurate as given.

43. *Mayfield Messenger*, February 15, 1943, p. 1.

44. *Mayfield Messenger*, February 9, 1943, p. 1.

45. *New York Times*, January 7, 1943, p. 1.

46. Brinkley, *Washington Goes to War*, 108.

47. *New York Times*, September 26, 1942, p. 1.

48. Brinkley, *Washington Goes to War*, 186.

49. Nancy Caldwell Sorel, *The Women Who Wrote the War* (New York: Arcade, 1999), 184–92.

50. Eiler, *Mobilizing America*, 374–75.

51. *Mayfield Messenger*, June 10, 1943, p. 1.

52. Donald Nelson, *Arsenal of Democracy* (New York: Harcourt Brace, 1946), 38–41; Eiler, *Mobilizing America*, 272–81.

53. John C. Culver and John Hyde, *American Dreamer: A Life of Henry Wallace* (New York: W. W. Norton, 2000), 284–86; Fleming, *The New Dealers' War*, 217–18.

54. Jesse Jones, *Fifty Billion Dollars* (New York: Macmillan, 1951), 396–402; Culver and Hyde, *American Dreamer*, 286.

55. Jones, *Fifty Billion Dollars*, 402–4; Culver and Hyde, *American Dreamer*, 284–86.

56. Jones, *Fifty Billion Dollars*, 405; Fleming, *The New Dealers' War*, 217–25. The president also let Harold Ickes lead a national drive to collect scrap rubber, which might be used until Jones's synthetic rubber or Wallace's Latin American rubber proved successful.

57. Jones, *Fifty Billion Dollars*, 402, 414–16.

58. Jones, *Fifty Billion Dollars*, 418–27; Fleming, *The New Dealers' War*, 217–30.

59. *New York Times*, July 16, 1943, p. 1; Fleming, *The New Dealers' War*, 230.

60. Claude Pepper, *Pepper* (New York: Harcourt Brace Jovanovich, 1987), 59, 112–13.
61. *New York Times*, September 5, 1943, p. E3.
62. *New York Times*, February 11, 1943, p. 1.
63. *New York Times*, May 4, 1943, p. 6.
64. George H. Roeder, Jr., *The Censored War* (New Haven, Conn.: Yale University Press, 1993), 9.
65. *New York Times*, April 16, 1943, p. 1.
66. Frederick S. Voss, *Reporting the War: The Journalistic Coverage of World War II* (Washington, D.C.: Smithsonian Institution Press, 1994), 26.
67. Brinkley, *Washington Goes to War*, 191; Roeder, *The Censored War*, 10.
68. *New York Times*, August 1, 1943, p. E3; Fleming, *The New Dealers' War*, 245.
69. Fleming, *The New Dealers' War*, 381.
70. *New York Times*, July 27, 1943, p. 1.
71. Marshall Clinard, *The Black Market* (Montclair, N.J.: Patterson Smith, 1952), 115–30, 187–294.
72. Clinard, *The Black Market*, 10, 26, 29–30, 43, 64, 79, 87–88, 126–28.
73. Clinard, *The Black Market*, 68, 161, 185; *New York Times*, December 19, 1943, p. 1.
74. *New York Times*, November 3, 1943, p. 19.
75. *New York Times*, December 29, 1943, p. 1; Samuel I. Rosenman, ed., *The Public Papers and Addresses of Franklin D. Roosevelt* (New York: Random House, 1950), XII, 570–71.

Chapter 8: Entrepreneurs vs. the Arsenal of Bureaucracy

1. Henry L. Stimson and McGeorge Bundy, *On Active Service in War and Peace* (New York: Harper and Bros., 1948), 353.
2. A great book on this topic (and more) is Robert Higgs, *Depression, War, and Cold War* (New York: Oxford University Press, 2006). We have learned much from talking with Professor Higgs.
3. Hadley Cantril, *Public Opinion, 1935–1946* (Princeton, N.J.: Princeton University Press, 1951), 347.
4. Richard Polenberg, *War and Society* (Philadelphia: J. B. Lippincott Co., 1972), 78.
5. For a good discussion of these issues, see Donald Nelson, *Arsenal of Democracy* (New York: Harcourt Brace, 1946); Higgs, *Depression, War, and Cold War*.
6. Polenberg, *War and Society*, 76.
7. Ted Morgan, *FDR: A Biography* (New York: Simon and Schuster, 1985), 665.

8. Morgan, *FDR*, 665; and Kenneth Davis, *FDR: The War President, 1940–1943* (New York: Random House, 2000), 453.

9. The key source for the next five paragraphs is Nelson, *Arsenal of Democracy*, 232–40 (quotations on pp. 232–33, 234, 235, 239, 240).

10. Allan Nevins, *Ford: Decline and Rebirth, 1933–1962* (New York: Charles Scribner's Sons, 1963), 195.

11. Polenberg, *War and Society*, 19.

12. Eliot Janeway, *The Struggle for Survival* (New Haven, Conn.: Yale University Press, 1951), 345.

13. Nelson, *Arsenal of Democracy*, 241.

14. Janeway, *Struggle for Survival*, 346; Dwight D. Eisenhower, *Crusade in Europe* (Garden City, N.Y.: Doubleday, 1948), 269.

15. Richard Overy, *Why the Allies Won* (New York: W. W. Norton, 1995), 201, 204.

16. Nelson, *Arsenal of Democracy*, 224–26.

17. For this section on penicillin, we are indebted to James Phinney Baxter III, *Scientists Against Time* (Cambridge, Mass.: MIT Press, 1946).

18. Baxter, *Scientists Against Time*, 347.

19. Baxter, *Scientists Against Time*, 343–51.

20. Mark S. Foster, *Henry J. Kaiser* (Austin: University of Texas Press, 1989), 10. For the discussion of Kaiser, we are indebted to Foster's excellent book, especially pages 68–89.

21. Foster, *Kaiser*, 68.

22. Foster, *Kaiser*, 82; Larry Schweikart, *The Entrepreneurial Adventure* (New York: Harcourt Brace, 2000), 379–80.

23. Foster, *Kaiser*, 85.

24. Foster, *Kaiser*, 85.

25. Foster, *Kaiser*, 72.

26. Paul Johnson, *Modern Times* (New York: HarperCollins, 1991), 402.

27. Jerry E. Strahan, *Andrew Jackson Higgins and the Boats that Won World War II* (Baton Rouge: Louisiana State University Press, 1994), 8. Strahan's book is very helpful. Also useful is John A. Heitmann, "The Man Who Won the War: Andrew Jackson Higgins," *Louisiana History* 34 (1993), 35–40.

28. Schweikart, *Entrepreneurial Adventure*, 381.

29. Strahan, *Higgins*, 3, 49, 51, 226–27.

30. Strahan, *Higgins*, 73, 76, 344.

31. Strahan, *Higgins*, 85.

32. Strahan, *Higgins*, 105.

33. Strahan, *Higgins*, 106.

34. *New York Times*, August 6, 1942, p. 13; Strahan, *Higgins*, 134.

35. Strahan, *Higgins*, 134. In the original text, "willful" is spelled with one "l."

36. Strahan, *Higgins*, 145; Nelson, *Arsenal of Democracy*, 254. For an example of

Higgins increasing his impact, see *Los Angeles Times*, November 4, 1942, part II, p. 4.

37. Strahan, *Higgins*, 96, 110–11, 136, 140, 194, 211–14, 304 (quotation on p. 140).
38. Strahan, *Higgins*, 3.
39. Strahan, *Higgins*, 3.
40. Strahan, *Higgins*, 3.
41. Bureau of Census, *Historical Statistics of the United States: Colonial Times to 1970* (Washington, D.C.: Government Printing Office, 1975), II, 1095.
42. George Gilder, *Recapturing the Spirit of Enterprise* (San Francisco: ICS Press, 1992), 26. Our telling of the Simplot story owes much to Gilder, especially pages 15–35.
43. Gilder, *Recapturing the Spirit of Enterprise*, 27–28.
44. Gilder, *Recapturing the Spirit of Enterprise*, 28.
45. Higgs, *Depression, War, and Cold War*, 73; Schweikart, *Entrepreneurial Adventure*, 377–78; Burton W. Folsom, Jr., *The Myth of the Robber Barons*, 6th ed. (Herndon, Va.: Young America's Foundation, 2010), 75–76.
46. Strahan, *Higgins*, 332.

Chapter 9: Taxes: "Government Can Take Everything We Have"

1. The tax song is available at www.blueoregon.com/2008/04/a-tax-day-messa/.
2. Carolyn Jones, "Mass-based Income Taxation: Creating a Taxpaying Culture, 1940–1952," in W. Elliot Brownlee, ed., *Funding the Modern American State, 1941–1995* (Cambridge, Eng.: Cambridge University Press, 1996), 121–22.
3. Jones, "Mass-based Income Taxation," 103, 123.
4. Jones, "Mass-based Income Taxation," 125–26.
5. Jones, "Mass-based Income Taxation," 110, 126.
6. John M. Blum, *From the Morgenthau Diaries*, 3 vols. (Boston: Houghton Mifflin, 1959–67), II, 310; Bureau of the Census, *Historical Statistics of the United States: Colonial Times to 1970* (Washington, D.C.: Government Printing Office, 1975), II, 1095.
7. Bureau of the Census, *Historical Statistics*, II, 1095; Charlotte A. Twight, *Dependent on D.C.* (New York: Palgrave, 2002), 117–18.
8. *Congressional Record*, 78th Cong., 1st sess., March 25, 1943, vol. 89, pp. H2496–97.
9. *Congressional Record*, 78th Cong., 1st sess., March 29, 1943, vol. 89, pp. H2614–15; March 25, 1943, p. H2504.
10. *Congressional Record*, 78th Cong., 1st sess., January 18, 1943, vol. 89, pp. 220–21; Beardsley Ruml, *Government, Business and Values* (New York: Harper and Bros., 1943); Amity Shlaes, *The Greedy Hand* (New York: Random House, 1999), 3–8.
11. David Brinkley, *Washington Goes to War* (New York: Ballantine, 1988), 220.

12. Hadley Cantril, *Public Opinion, 1935–1946* (Princeton, N.J.: Princeton University Press, 1951), 324–25; Twight, *Dependent on D.C.*, 110.
13. Blum, *From the Morgenthau Diaries*, II, 310.
14. Randolph E. Paul, *Taxation for Prosperity* (Indianapolis: Bobbs-Merrill, 1947), 131, 140.
15. *Congressional Record*, 78th Cong., 1st sess., March 27, 1943, vol. 89, p. H2583.
16. *Congressional Record*, 78th Cong., 1st sess., March 27, 1943, vol. 89, pp. H2582–84.
17. Paul, *Taxation for Prosperity*, 132.
18. *Congressional Record*, 78th Cong., 1st sess., May 12, 1943, vol. 89, p. S4274.
19. *Congressional Record*, 78th Cong., 1st sess., March 25, 1943, vol. 89, p. H2497.
20. *Congressional Record*, 78th Cong., 1st sess., May 14, 1943, vol. 89, pp. S4419–20.
21. *Congressional Record*, 78th Cong., 1st sess., March 30, 1943, vol. 89, p. H2754.
22. Paul, *Taxation for Prosperity*, 132.
23. *Congressional Record*, 78th Cong., 1st sess., March 25, 1943, vol. 89, p. H2508.
24. *Congressional Record*, 78th Cong., 1st sess., March 27, 1943, vol. 89, p. H2598.
25. *Congressional Record*, 78th Cong., 1st sess., May 12, 1943, vol. 89, p. S4274.
26. *Congressional Record*, 78th Cong., 1st sess., June 1, 1943, vol. 89, pp. H5160–61.
27. *Congressional Record*, 78th Cong., 1st sess., March 30, 1943, vol. 89, p. H2755.
28. *Congressional Record*, 78th Cong., 1st sess., May 14, 1943, vol. 89, p. S4438.
29. *Congressional Record*, 78th Cong., 1st sess., May 14, 1943, vol. 89, p. S4438.
30. *Congressional Record*, 78th Cong., 1st sess., May 14, 1943, vol. 89, p. S4431.
31. Senate Committee on Finance, *Revenue Act of 1942: Hearings on H. R. 7378*, vol. 1, 77th Cong., 2nd sess., July–August 1942, p. 137. We are indebted to Charlotte Twight for calling our attention to this source.
32. *Congressional Record*, 78th Cong., 1st sess., May 14, 1943, vol. 89, p. S4410.
33. *Congressional Record*, 78th Cong., 1st sess., May 14, 1943, vol. 89, p. S4422.
34. *Congressional Record*, 78th Cong., 1st sess., March 27, 1943, vol. 89, p. H2623.
35. *Congressional Record*, 78th Cong., 1st sess., May 4, 1943, vol. 89, p. H3926.
36. *Congressional Record*, 78th Cong., 1st sess., May 3, 1943, vol. 89, pp. H3844–46.
37. *Congressional Record*, 78th Cong., 1st sess., March 29, 1943, vol. 89, p. H2624.
38. *Congressional Record*, 78th Cong., 1st sess., May 3, 1943, vol. 89, pp. H3857–58.

39. *Congressional Record*, 78th Cong., 1st sess., May 3, 1943, vol. 89, p. H3858.

40. *Congressional Record*, 78th Cong., 1st sess., March 30, 1943, vol. 89, p. H2767.

41. *Congressional Record*, 78th Cong., 1st sess., May 13, 1943, vol. 89, p. S4344.

42. *Congressional Record*, 78th Cong., 1st sess., May 12, 1943, vol. 89, pp. S4268–71; May 13, 1943, pp. S4347–49; and May 14, 1943, p. S4446; Paul, *Taxation for Prosperity*, 138–40.

43. Burton Folsom, Jr., *New Deal or Raw Deal?* (New York: Simon & Schuster, 2008), 202–4.

44. *Congressional Record*, 78th Cong., 1st sess., May 14, 1943, vol. 89, p. S4446.

45. *Congressional Record*, 78th Cong., 1st sess., May 18, 1943, vol. 89, p. H4566; Paul, *Taxation for Prosperity*, 140.

46. *Congressional Record*, 78th Cong., 1st sess., June 2, 1943, vol. 89, p. S5208.

47. *Congressional Record*, 78th Cong., 1st sess., June 2, 1943, vol. 89, p. S5203; Paul, *Taxation for Prosperity*, 141–42.

48. *Congressional Record*, 78th Cong., 1st sess., May 14, 1943, vol. 89, p. S4394.

49. *Congressional Record*, 78th Cong., 1st sess., June 2, 1943, vol. 89, p. S5207.

50. *Congressional Record*, 78th Cong., 1st sess., May 18, 1943, vol. 89, p. H4567.

51. Paul, *Taxation for Prosperity*, 146, 149–50.

52. *Congressional Record*, 78th Cong., 1st sess., March 27, 1943, vol. 89, pp. H2576–78; Paul, *Taxation for Prosperity*, 147–48.

53. Paul, *Taxation for Prosperity*, 154–55.

54. Paul, *Taxation for Prosperity*, 160.

55. Paul, *Taxation for Prosperity*, 160–62. For a study of the tension during the war between FDR and Congress, see John Robert Moore, "The Conservative Coalition in the United States Senate, 1942–1945," *Journal of Southern History* 33 (August 1967), 368–76.

56. Claude Pepper, *Pepper* (New York: Harcourt Brace Jovanovich, 1987), 116; Blum, *From the Morgenthau Diaries*, III, 75–76.

Chapter 10: FDR and Civil Liberties

1. Arthur Krock, *Memoirs* (New York: Funk & Wagnalls, 1968), 145–46.

2. Robert Jackson, *That Man: An Insider's Portrait of Franklin D. Roosevelt* (New York: Oxford University Press, 2003), 74.

3. Jackson, *That Man*, 68.

4. Victor Lasky, *It Didn't Start with Watergate* (New York: Dial Press, 1977), 154.

5. Ted Morgan, *FDR: A Biography* (New York: Simon and Schuster, 1985), 523; Curt Gentry, *J. Edgar Hoover* (New York: W. W. Norton, 1991), 307; Richard Gid Powers, *Secrecy and Power: The Life of J. Edgar Hoover* (New York: Free Press, 1987), 264.

6. Joseph Persico, *Roosevelt's Secret War* (New York: Random House, 2002), 42–43; Gentry, *Hoover*, 228–29; Richard W. Steele, "Franklin D. Roosevelt and His Foreign Policy Critics," *Political Science Quarterly* 94 (Spring 1979), 15–32.

7. R. J. C. Butow, "The FDR Tapes," *American Heritage* (February/March 1982); Gentry, *Hoover*, 227–28, 237.

8. Richard W. Steele, *Free Speech in the Good War* (New York: St. Martin's Press, 1999), 127; Gentry, *Hoover*, 245–46.

9. Walter Trohan, *Political Animals* (Garden City, N.Y.: Doubleday, 1975), 182, 184.

10. Richard Norton Smith, *The Colonel: The Life and Legend of Robert R. McCormick* (New York: Houghton Mifflin, 1997), xx–xxi, 401, 421.

11. Smith, *The Colonel*, xx, 55, 427.

12. Carl Wiegman, *Trees to News* (Toronto: McClelland and Stewart, 1953), 234; David Reynolds, *Rich Relations* (New York: HarperCollins, 1995), 165; Smith, *The Colonel*, 437.

13. Smith, *The Colonel*, 426.

14. Ralph Martin, *Cissy: The Extraordinary Life of Eleanor Medill Patterson* (New York: Simon and Schuster, 1979), 419.

15. Steele, *Free Speech*, 167–68; Morgan, *FDR*, 523.

16. Steele, "Franklin D. Roosevelt," 29; Athan G. Theoharis and John S. Cox, *The Boss: J. Edgar Hoover and the Great American Inquisition* (Philadelphia: Temple University Press, 1988), 161.

17. Morgan, *FDR*, 561–62.

18. Morgan, *FDR*, 554.

19. Elliott Roosevelt, *A Rendezvous with Destiny: The Roosevelts of the White House* (New York: G. P. Putnam's Sons, 1975), 102; Smith, *The Colonel*, 360; Christopher Ogden, *Legacy: A Biography of Moses and Walter Annenberg* (Boston: Little Brown, 1999), 191, 212–13.

20. *Cleveland Plain Dealer*, November 4, 1942, p. 5.

21. Hamilton Fish, *Memoirs of an American Patriot* (Washington, D.C.: Regnery, 1991), 142–44.

22. *New York Times*, July 18, 1973, p. 36.

23. Lasky, *It Didn't Start with Watergate*, 145.

24. Lasky, *It Didn't Start with Watergate*, 149; Richard Polenberg, *War and Society* (Philadelphia: J. B. Lippincott, Co., 1972), 164; Conrad Black, *Franklin Delano Roosevelt* (New York: Public Affairs, 2003), 537; Gentry, *Hoover*, 237.

25. Robert A. Caro, *The Path to Power: The Years of Lyndon Johnson* (New York: Random House, 1982), 743–53.

26. Persico, *Roosevelt's Secret War*, 16, 56–59, 197–98. The Office of Strategic Services (OSS), the forerunner of the CIA, also began during World War II with approval from Congress.

27. Persico, *Roosevelt's Secret War*, 36, 38, 115–17; Steele, *Free Speech*, 162–66, 175; Gentry, *Hoover*, 313.

28. Persico, *Roosevelt's Secret War*, 43; Steele, *Free Speech*, 151, 206–8.

29. Francis Biddle, *In Brief Authority* (Garden City, N.Y.: Doubleday, 1962), 236, 238, 248–51; Geoffrey R. Stone, *Perilous Times* (New York: W. W. Norton, 2004), 260–72.

30. Jesse Jones, *Fifty Billion Dollars* (New York: Macmillan, 1951), 231–33; J. David Stern, *Memoirs of a Maverick Publisher* (New York: Simon and Schuster, 1962).

31. Trohan, *Political Animals*, 75.

32. Jones, *Fifty Billion Dollars*, 265–66. In his business dealings with Hall Roosevelt and David Stern, Jones explains his behavior and defends it as ethical.

33. Jones, *Fifty Billion Dollars*, 295–97.

34. Murray Rothbard, *America's Great Depression* (New York: Richardson & Snyder, 1972 [1963]), 262.

35. Krock, *Memoirs*, 182.

36. Richard W. Steele, *Propaganda in an Open Society: The Roosevelt Administration and the Media, 1933–1941* (Westport, Conn.: Greenwood Press, 1985), 134, 141.

37. Steele, *Propaganda*, 142–44.

38. Steele, *Propaganda*, 163–64.

39. Polenberg, *War and Society*, 62–63; David M. Kennedy, *Freedom from Fear* (New York: Oxford University Press, 1999), 751; Peter Irons, *Justice at War: The Story of the Japanese American Internment Cases* (New York: Oxford University Press, 1983), 7.

40. Kennedy, *Freedom from Fear*, 752; Polenberg, *War and Society*, 62; Irons, *Justice at War*, 64–67; John M. Blum, *V Was for Victory* (New York: Harcourt Brace Jovanovich, 1976), 159. Stimson largely exonerates himself and argues that Japan could have attacked California early in the war and the loyalty of the Japanese-Americans was uncertain. See Henry L. Stimson and McGeorge Bundy, *On Active Service in Peace and War* (New York: Harper and Bros., 1948), 405–7.

41. Biddle, *In Brief Authority*, 213; and Irons, *Justice at War*. Internment camps for Japanese-Americans were located in Arizona, Arkansas, California, Colorado, Idaho, Utah, and Wyoming.

42. Persico, *Roosevelt's Secret War*, 167–70; Powers, *Secrecy and Power*, 249–50; Irons, *Justice at War*, 28, 280–81; Black, *Roosevelt*, 721.

43. Eric L. Muller, *American Inquisition: The Hunt for Japanese American Disloyalty in World War II* (Chapel Hill: University of North Carolina Press, 2007), 15.

44. Persico, *Roosevelt's Secret War*, 168; Muller, *American Inquisition*, 86; Irons, *Justice at War*.

45. Kennedy, *Freedom from Fear*, 750.

46. Biddle, *In Brief Authority*, 213–19; Persico, *Roosevelt's Secret War*, 167–68; Irons, *Justice at War*, 57–58. Irons quotes John McCloy, assistant secretary of war, as saying that Roosevelt told him, "It [the Japanese internment] has got to be dictated by military necessity."

Chapter 11: Courting Stalin

1. John M. Blum, *From the Morgenthau Diaries*, 3 vols. (Boston: Houghton Mifflin, 1958–67), III, 81–82, 87.

2. Edward M. Bennett, *Franklin D. Roosevelt and the Search for Security* (Lanham, Md.: Rowman and Littlefield, 1985), 18–19, 23, 33. For a fresh look at those politicians deceived by communists, see Paul Kengor, *Dupes* (Wilmington, Del.: ISI Books, 2010).

3. Bennett, *Franklin Roosevelt*, 183.

4. Frances Perkins, *The Roosevelt I Knew* (New York: Macmillan, 1946), 87.

5. Robert Nisbet, *Roosevelt and Stalin: The Failed Courtship* (Washington, D.C.: Regnery, 1988), 6, 31.

6. Nisbet, *Roosevelt and Stalin*, 24; Tim Tzouliadis, *The Forsaken: An American Tragedy in Stalin's Russia* (New York: Penguin, 2008), 240.

7. Nisbet, *Roosevelt and Stalin*, 50, 73.

8. Nisbet, *Roosevelt and Stalin*, 47.

9. Nisbet, *Roosevelt and Stalin*, 25–26.

10. Nisbet, *Roosevelt and Stalin*, 15.

11. Werner Keller, *East Minus West Equal Zero* (New York: G. P. Putnam's Sons, 1961), 241–43; Eddie Rickenbacker, *Rickenbacker* (Englewood Cliffs, N.J.: Prentice Hall, 1967), 370.

12. Tzouliadis, born in Greece but raised in England, is a filmmaker whose book reflects pathbreaking research on the Americans who lost their lives in the Gulag.

13. Keller, *East Minus West Equal Zero*, 243–56.

14. Rickenbacker, *Rickenbacker*, 389.

15. Susan Butler, ed., *My Dear Mr. Stalin: The Complete Correspondence of Franklin D. Roosevelt and Joseph V. Stalin* (New Haven, Conn.: Yale University Press, 2005), 80.

16. Nisbet, *Roosevelt and Stalin*, 32, 34, 36. In the last quotation, "air forces" is one word in the original.

17. Butler, *My Dear Mr. Stalin*, 79.

18. Thomas Fleming, *The New Dealers' War* (New York: Basic Books, 2001), 318.

19. Nisbet, *Roosevelt and Stalin*, 60–63.

20. Butler, *My Dear Mr. Stalin*, 64, 66.

21. Nisbet, *Roosevelt and Stalin*, 40.

22. Nisbet, *Roosevelt and Stalin*, 45.

23. Nisbet, *Roosevelt and Stalin*, 64, 67.

24. Fleming, *New Dealers' War*, 303.

25. Tzouliadis, *The Forsaken*, 240.

26. Nisbet, *Roosevelt and Stalin*, 46.

27. Nisbet, *Roosevelt and Stalin*, 60.

28. Fleming, *New Dealers' War*, 435.

29. Nisbet, *Roosevelt and Stalin*, 59.

30. Nisbet, *Roosevelt and Stalin*, 59.

31. Nisbet, *Roosevelt and Stalin*, 59.

32. Much of our analysis of the communist influence in the U.S. government is drawn from the superb work of John Haynes and Harvey Klehr. See in particular Harvey Klehr, John Earl Haynes, and Fridrikh I. Firsov, *The Secret World of American Communism* (New Haven, Conn.: Yale University Press, 1995), and Haynes and Klehr, *Venona: Decoding Soviet Espionage in America* (New Haven, Conn.: Yale University Press, 1999).

33. Haynes and Klehr, *Venona*, 145–50.

34. Haynes and Klehr, *Venona*, 140–41. For a sympathetic biography of White, see David Rees, *Harry Dexter White: A Study in Paradox* (New York: Coward, McCann, & Geoghegan, 1973). For a more critical view of White, written after the opening of the Venona papers, see R. Bruce Craig, *Treasonable Doubt: The Harry Dexter White Spy Case* (Lawrence, Kan.: University of Kansas Press, 2004).

35. A thoughtful book on the Hiss case is Allen Weinstein, *Perjury: The Hiss-Chambers Case* (New York: Alfred A. Knopf, 1978). See also Whittaker Chambers, *Witness* (New York: Random House, 1952).

36. Haynes and Klehr, *Venona*, 203; Fleming, *The New Dealers' War*, 406.

37. Adolf Berle, *Navigating the Rapids* (New York: Harcourt Brace Jovanovich, 1973), 249–50, 582–84, 598–99; Sam Tanenhaus, *Whittaker Chambers* (New York: Random House, 1997); Chambers, *Witness*.

38. Tzouliadis, *The Forsaken*, 241.

39. For a thoughtful survey of these issues, see Amos Perlmutter, *FDR & Stalin: A Not So Grand Alliance, 1943–1945* (Columbia, Mo.: University of Missouri Press, 1993).

40. Christopher Andrew and Vasili Mitrokhin, *The Sword and the Shield: The Mitrokhin Archive and the Secret History of the KGB* (New York: Basic Books, 1999), 133.

41. Butler, *My Dear Mr. Stalin*, x.

42. Nisbet, *Roosevelt and Stalin*, 72.

43. Nisbet, *Roosevelt and Stalin*, 81, 83.

44. For a biographical sketch of Earle, see James T. Patterson, *The New Deal and the States* (Princeton, N.J.: Princeton University Press, 1969), 149–53.

45. Perlmutter, *FDR & Stalin*, 121.

46. Perlmutter, *FDR & Stalin*, 122; Fleming, *New Dealers' War*, 502–3.

47. Patterson, *The New Deal and the States*, 151.

48. Richard C. Keller, "The Little New Deal in Pennsylvania," in John A. Braeman, Robert H. Bremner, and David Brody, eds., *The New Deal: The State and Local Levels* (Columbus, Ohio: Ohio State University Press, 1975), 69–71.

49. Tzouliadis, *The Forsaken*, 240.

Chapter 12: The 1944 Election: A Fourth Term

1. Turner Catledge, *My Life and The Times* (New York: Harper & Row, 1971), 144–46.

2. Robert H. Ferrell, *The Dying President: Franklin D. Roosevelt, 1944–1945* (Columbia, Mo.: University of Missouri Press, 1998), 35–37.

3. Robert E. Ficken, "The Democratic Party and Domestic Politics during World War II" (Ph.D. dissertation, University of Washington, 1973), 201.

4. Ficken, "The Democratic Party," 184, 219. That same Gallup poll showed FDR beating Dewey 51 to 32 percent if the war was still going.

5. John C. Culver and John Hyde, *American Dreamer: A Life of Henry A. Wallace* (New York: W. W. Norton, 2000), 367.

6. Ferrell, *The Dying President*, 67, 72–74.

7. Ficken, "The Democratic Party," 83.

8. Ficken, "The Democratic Party," 108–12, 242; Glenn Altschuler and Stuart Blumin, *The G.I. Bill: The New Deal for Veterans* (New York: Oxford University Press, 2009).

9. Ficken, "The Democratic Party," 109.

10. Steven Fraser, *Labor Will Rule: Sidney Hillman and the Rise of American Labor* (New York: Macmillan, 1991), 501–4, 525.

11. Fraser, *Sidney Hillman*, 501–3; Ficken, "The Democratic Party," 209–11; Richard Norton Smith, *Thomas E. Dewey* (New York: Simon and Schuster, 1982), 409–10.

12. The best biography of Hillman is Fraser, *Sidney Hillman*.

13. Fraser, *Sidney Hillman*, 495–538; James G. Ryan, *Earl Browder* (Tuscaloosa, Ala.: University of Alabama Press, 1997), 237; Smith, *Thomas Dewey*, 409–10.

14. Ryan, *Earl Browder*, 238; Fraser, *Sidney Hillman*, 514–24, 528–29.

15. *New York Times*, July 21, 1944, p. 8.
16. Ferrell, *The Dying President*, 79.
17. Douglas MacArthur, *Reminiscences* (New York: McGraw-Hill, 1964), 199; Ferrell, *The Dying President*, 84.
18. Ferrell, *The Dying President*, 82; Ficken, "The Democratic Party," 245.
19. Ficken, "The Democratic Party," 246, 251–52.
20. Ferrell, *The Dying President*, 89.
21. *New York Times*, June 29, 1944, p. 10.
22. *New York Times*, July 21, 1944, p. 8; Ficken, "The Democratic Party," 255–56.
23. *New York Times*, September 24, 1944, p. 36.
24. Ficken, "The Democratic Party," 258.
25. Fraser, *Sidney Hillman*, 528–30.
26. M. Stanton Evans, *Blacklisted by History* (New York: Crown Forum, 2007), 78.
27. Evans, *Blacklisted by History*, 78–79.
28. Fraser, *Sidney Hillman*, 351, 522–30.
29. Fraser, *Sidney Hillman*, 183–85, 486 (quotation on p. 183).
30. *Washington Times-Herald*, November 2, 1944, p. 8; *New York Times*, July 25, 1944.
31. *New York Times*, September 24, 1944, p. 36.
32. *New York Times*, June 29, 1944, p. 10.
33. Smith, *Thomas Dewey*, 423–27. On September 4, 1944, the *New York Times* reported that eleven midwestern states were trending for Dewey: Illinois, Indiana, Iowa, Kansas, Michigan, Minnesota, Nebraska, North Dakota, Ohio, South Dakota, and Wisconsin.
34. Smith, *Thomas Dewey*, 426–27.
35. Smith, *Thomas Dewey*, 428.
36. Kirk H. Porter and Donald B. Johnson, eds., *National Party Platforms, 1840–1968* (Urbana: University of Illinois Press, 1970), 412.
37. Eric L. Muller, *American Inquisition* (Chapel Hill: University of North Carolina Press, 2007), 92.
38. Harold Ickes Diary, May 28, 1944, LC.
39. Muller, *American Inquisition*, 90, 93–94.
40. Muller, *American Inquisition*, 96.
41. For a good description of the Polish issue, see Ficken, "The Democratic Party," 272–75 (quotation on p. 273).
42. Ficken, "The Democratic Party," 273–75.
43. Ficken, "The Democratic Party," 275; Samuel Lubell, *The Future of American Politics* (New York: Harper & Row, 1965), 201–4, 210–14.

44. Ficken, "The Democratic Party," 275.

45. *New York Times*, October 29, 1944, p. 32.

46. Ficken, "The Democratic Party," 274.

47. *New York Times*, July 7, 1945, p. 6, and April 29, 1945, p. E6.

48. Catledge, *My Life and The Times*, 149.

49. Ferrell, *The Dying President*, 93.

50. Ferrell, *The Dying President*, 91–92.

51. Samuel I. Rosenman, ed., *The Public Papers and Addresses of Franklin D. Roosevelt* (New York: Harper, 1950), XIII, 369–70.

52. Rosenman, *The Public Papers*, 369–78.

53. *Washington Times-Herald*, November 5, 1944, p. A6.

54. *Washington Times-Herald*, November 3, 1944, p. 7.

55. *Washington Times-Herald*, November 1, 1944, p. 6.

56. *Washington Times-Herald*, November 3, 1944, p. 7. Dewey concluded, "We can and we will take the choking hands of government off of the throats of every small business in the country."

57. Lubell, *The Future of American Politics*, 45–46, 61, 200; Eugene Edgar Robinson, *They Voted for Roosevelt: The Presidential Vote, 1932–1944* (Palo Alto, Calif.: Stanford University Press, 1947). Dewey carried Maine, Vermont, Ohio, Indiana, Wisconsin, Iowa, North Dakota, South Dakota, Nebraska, Kansas, Colorado, and Wyoming.

58. Smith, *Thomas Dewey*, 436.

59. Smith, *Thomas Dewey*, 393.

Chapter 13: *The War Ends on the USS* Missouri

1. Arthur Krock, *Memoirs* (New York: Funk & Wagnalls, 1968), 181.

2. Krock, *Memoirs*, 219.

3. Krock, *Memoirs*, 222.

4. Stephen Ambrose, *Eisenhower: Soldier, General of the Army, President-Elect* (New York: Simon and Schuster, 1983), 332.

5. Alonzo L. Hamby, *Man of the People: A Life of Harry S. Truman* (New York: Oxford University Press, 1995), 323–25.

6. *New York Times*, January 28, 1944, p. 1; Henry L. Stimson and McGeorge Bundy, *On Active Service in Peace and War* (New York: Harper and Bros., 1948), 498.

7. Stimson and Bundy, *On Active Service in Peace and War*, 612–20; *New York Times*, January 28, 1947, p. 14.

8. Stimson and Bundy, *On Active Service in Peace and War*, 632–33.

9. William Manchester, *American Caesar* (New York: Dell, 1978), 520.

10. *New York Times*, September 2, 1945, p. 1.

11. Manchester, *American Caesar*, 515.

12. Manchester, *American Caesar*, 527.

13. *New York Times*, September 7, 1945, p. 1; Manchester, *American Caesar*, 526. The flag on the *Missouri* may have simply been one from the ship's stores; its origin is controversial.

14. Manchester, *American Caesar*, 528.

15. Douglas MacArthur, *Reminiscences* (New York: McGraw-Hill, 1964), 272–74.

16. *New York Times*, September 2, 1945, p. 1, and September 3, 1945, p. 3.

Chapter 14: Did the War End the Great Depression?

1. Bureau of the Census, *Historical Statistics of the United States: Colonial Times to 1970* (Washington, D.C.: Government Printing Office, 1975), II, 1140.

2. Charles E. Merriam, "The National Resources Planning Board: A Chapter in American Planning Experience," *American Political Science Review* 38 (December 1944), pp. 1075–88; Philip W. Warken, *A History of the National Resources Planning Board, 1933–1943* (New York: Garland, 1979).

3. John Maynard Keynes, *The General Theory of Employment, Interest and Money* (New York: Harcourt, Brace, and World, 1936).

4. Herbert Stein, *The Fiscal Revolution in America* (Chicago: University of Chicago Press, 1969), 162.

5. Paul Samuelson, *Economics: An Introductory Analysis* (New York: McGraw-Hill, 1948).

6. Merriam, "The National Resources Planning Board," pp. 1079–80. Merriam is describing rights for returning soldiers, but he applies these rights to all citizens. See also Barton J. Bernstein, "The Debate on Industrial Reconversion," *American Journal of Economics and Sociology* 26 (1967), pp. 167–72; and Alan Brinkley, *The End of Reform* (New York: Vintage, 1995), 231–51. Brinkley helpfully discusses the nuances among the different Keynesians on the subject of reconversion after the war.

7. Samuel I. Rosenman, *The Public Papers and Addresses of Franklin D. Roosevelt* (New York: Harper and Bros., 1950), XIII, 374.

8. Rosenman, *Public Papers*, XIII, 40–42.

9. Rosenman, *Public Papers*, XIII, 371–74, 376.

10. Rosenman, *Public Papers*, XIII, 374.

11. Henry A. Wallace, *Sixty Million Jobs* (New York: Reynal and Hitchcock, 1945), 8–9.

12. Wallace, *Sixty Million Jobs*, 14–15.

13. "Jobs for All," *New Republic*, January 29, 1945, p. 138.

14. "The Budget Message," *Nation*, January 20, 1945, p. 61.

15. Seymour Harris and Alvin Hansen, "The Price of Prosperity," *New Republic*, January 15, 1945, pp. 73–76; Leo Barnes, "The Anatomy of Full Employment," *Nation*, May 26, 1945, p. 593.

16. Arthur Krock, *Memoirs* (New York: Funk & Wagnalls, 1968), 145, 148.

17. "The Fight for S 380," *Nation*, June 16, 1945, pp. 664–65.

18. I. F. Stone, "Washington Faces Peace," *Nation*, August 28, 1945, pp. 151–52. Compare Stone in August 1945, with one year earlier in I. F. Stone, "On Reconversion," *Nation*, August 12, 1944, p. 76.

19. "Mr. Truman's Challenge," *New Republic*, September 17, 1945, p. 335.

20. Stone, "Washington Faces Peace," pp. 151–52.

21. Mary Hinchey, "The Frustration of the New Deal Revival, 1944–1946" (Ph.D. dissertation, University of Missouri, 1965), 215.

22. Hinchey, "New Deal Revival," 125–34; Darrel Cady, "The Truman Administration's Reconversion Policies, 1945–1947" (Ph.D. dissertation, University of Kansas, 1974), 94.

23. *New York Times*, September 7, 1945, pp. 1, 15.

24. *New York Times*, September 7, 1945, pp. 15–18.

25. *New York Times*, September 7, 1945, pp. 15–18.

26. William E. Leuchtenburg, *In the Shadow of FDR* (Ithaca, N.Y.: Cornell University Press, 1985), 9.

27. *Wall Street Journal*, September 7, 1945, p. 5.

28. Herman E. Krooss, *Executive Opinion: What Business Leaders Said and Thought, 1920's–1960's* (Garden City, N.Y.: Doubleday, 1970), 214–15.

29. Cady, "Truman Administration's Reconversion Policies," 24, 41–42, 56–57, 85.

30. *Wall Street Journal*, September, 7, 1945, p. 5.

31. Randolph E. Paul, *Taxation for Prosperity* (Indianapolis: Bobbs-Merrill, 1947), 192. See also Burton Folsom, Jr., and Anita Folsom, "Did FDR End the Depression?" *Wall Street Journal*, April 12, 2010, p. A17.

32. *Congressional Record*, 79th Cong., October 24, 1945, p. S9948.

33. Carl S. Shoup, "The Revenue Act of 1945," *Political Science Quarterly* 60 (December 1945), p. 490.

34. Shoup, "The Revenue Act of 1945," pp. 481–91; George E. Lent, "Excess-Profits Taxation in the United States," *Journal of Political Economy* 59 (December 1951), pp. 481–97.

35. *Congressional Record*, 79th Cong., October 24, 1945, p. S9986.

36. *Congressional Record*, 79th Cong., October 24, 1945, p. S9948.

37. *Congressional Record*, 79th Cong., October 24, 1945, p. S9948; Bureau of the Census, *Historical Statistics*, I, 126; Burton W. Folsom, Jr., *The Myth of the Robber Barons*, 6th ed. (Herndon, Va.: Young America's Foundation, 2010).

38. Andrew Mellon, *Taxation: The People's Business* (New York: Macmillan, 1924), 16.

39. *Congressional Record*, 79th Cong., October 24, 1945, p. S9958.

40. Folsom, *The Myth of the Robber Barons*.

41. *Congressional Record*, 79th Cong., October 24, 1945, pp. S9991–92, S9998–S10000; Paul, *Taxation for Prosperity*, 195.
42. Krooss, *Executive Opinion*, 221.
43. Hinchey, "New Deal Revival," 156–62, 192–93, 208, 211–12.
44. Alonzo Hamby, *A Man of the People: A Life of Harry S. Truman* (New York: Oxford University Press, 1995), 370–85.
45. Hinchey, "New Deal Revival," 220–25; Cady, "Truman Administration's Reconversion Policies," 153–73.
46. Cady, "Truman Administration's Reconversion Policies," 128–32.
47. Cabell Phillips, *The Truman Presidency* (New York: Macmillan, 1966), 105.
48. Susan M. Hartmann, *Truman and the 80th Congress* (Columbia, Mo.: University of Missouri Press, 1971), 115.
49. Cady, "Truman Administration's Reconversion Policies," 108–12.
50. Robert Higgs, *Depression, War, and Cold War* (New York: Oxford University Press, 2006), 108. See also Stein, *Fiscal Revolution*, 209.
51. *Congressional Record*, 79th Cong., October 24, 1945, pp. S9948, S9986. See also Stein, *Fiscal Revolution*, 209.
52. Higgs, *Depression, War, and Cold War*, 113; Krooss, *Executive Opinion*, 219.
53. Leo Barnes, "How Sound Were Private Postwar Forecasts?" *Journal of Political Economy* 56 (April 1948), pp. 161–65.
54. Higgs, *Depression, War, and Cold War*, 114.
55. Allen J. Matusow, *Farm Policies and Politics in the Truman Years* (Cambridge, Mass.: Harvard University Press, 1967), 6, 13–14, 27–28, 149–51.
56. *New York Times*, November 13, 1945, pp. 1, 13; Matusow, *Farm Policies*, 14, 27–28.
57. Higgs, *Depression, War, and Cold War*, 101.

Conclusion

1. *New York Times*, November 9, 1941, p. XX5.
2. Robert Dallek, *Franklin D. Roosevelt and American Foreign Policy, 1932–1945* (New York: Oxford University Press, 1979), 289. On the whole, however, Dallek supports Roosevelt and his strategy of deception.
3. *New York Times*, July 21, 1940, p. E8.
4. James O. Richardson, *On the Treadmill to Pearl Harbor* (Washington, D.C.: Department of the Navy, 1973), 434.
5. Forrest Pogue, *George C. Marshall: Ordeal and Hope, 1939–1942* (New York: Viking Press, 1966), 31–32.
6. *New York Times*, September 5, 1943, p. E3.
7. R. Elberton Smith, *The Army and Economic Mobilization* (Washington, D.C.: Government Printing Office, 1959), 215.

8. Smith, *The Army and Economic Mobilization*, 29.

9. Robert Higgs, *Depression, War, and Cold War* (New York: Oxford University Press, 2006), 71. The 30 percent increase in "disabling injuries" occurred in manufacturing from 1940 to 1943.

10. Richard Polenberg, *War and Society* (Philadelphia: J. B. Lippincott, Co., 1972), 173.

11. "The Avery Problem," *Time*, June 19, 1944.

12. *New York Times*, May 1, 1944, p. 14.

13. Robert Messenger, "The German Way of War," *Weekly Standard*, February 18, 2008, p. 37.

14. Paul Fussell, "Thank God for the Atomic Bomb," *Washington Post*, August 23, 1981, p. C4. We thank Ronald H. Spector for his excellent book on the war in the Pacific, *Eagle Against the Sun*, which calls attention to Paul Fussell's article.

15. *New York Times*, August 7, 1945, p. 1. Richard Frank's *Downfall: The End of the Imperial Japanese Empire* (New York: Penguin Books, 1999) gives an excellent account of the final days of the war. For a behind-the-scenes view of Truman, the news media, and the atomic bomb, see Eben Ayers Diary, August 6, 7, 8, 9, 10, 1945, Harry S. Truman Presidential Library.

ACKNOWLEDGMENTS

We are husband-and-wife historians, who come to this project from different angles. For Burt, this is the second volume in his history of the FDR presidency. His special interest is the huge economic and political impact of Roosevelt's presidency on American life. For Anita, she has had a lifelong interest in World War II, which was deepened in 1977 in graduate school when she spent a summer in Europe and saw the continued impact of the war, especially in East Germany. She has also explored Singapore, Beijing, Corregidor, Manila, and many other World War II sites. Our joint interests dovetailed, and this book is the result. This modest three-hundred-plus-page history is in no way a comprehensive survey of FDR or World War II, but we do describe the economic, political, military, and social history of the United States during World War II, and at different points we discuss every region of the country and every state.

We have been blessed with help from many sources. We are privileged to teach and work at Hillsdale College, which is a great environment for studying history and the role of government. Larry Arnn is a first-rate president, and he has supported our work from the start. Special thanks also go to John Cervini, Ellen Donohoe, and Doug Jeffrey for their encouragement with this book. The staff at the Hillsdale College Library, especially Dan Knoch and Judy Leising, have helped locate key sources for us. For creating a productive work environment, we also thank the staffs at the Library of Congress in Washington, D.C., and the Franklin D. Roosevelt Presidential Library and Museum in Hyde Park, New York, the Harry S. Truman Presidential Library & Museum in Independence, Missouri, and the Graves County Public Library in Mayfield, Kentucky. The Earhart Foundation and the Koch Foundation gave support for travel and student assistance.

In the world of academia, we have benefited from wise counsel from Robert Higgs, Allen Matusow, Larry Schweikart, John Willson, Will Morrissey, Joseph Rishel, Margaret Britt, and the late Gary Dean Best. The ten-member history department at Hillsdale College has been collegial and supportive. During a series of lectures for the Young America's Foundation, we toured the Normandy beaches on the sixty-sixth anniversary of the Allied landings and visited the American cemetery there, a very moving experience. We thank our agent, Alex Hoyt, and also Anthony Ziccardi, Kathy Sagan, Jean Anne Rose, Natasha Simons, and Melissa Gramstad, who are part of the excellent team at Simon & Schuster. Sean Devlin did an excellent job copyediting this book. Rusty Humphries, a great voice in talk radio, has interviewed us several times about this book, and we value his friendship. William F. Buckley, Jr., supported this FDR project financially more than ten years ago, and we regret that he didn't live to see the final result. Our Hillsdale students—especially Jim Nesbitt, Thomas Waters, Julia Spiotta, Marianna Ernst, Victoria Bergen, Virginia Phillips, and Alexi Treu—survived Burt's seminars and wrote papers helpful to our study of FDR and World War II. Also, we have had timely encouragement from Mitchell Rutledge, David Kent, Ron Coen, and Larry Dye. We thank our family members for their continued encouragement. Burt's sister, Sally Eveland, alerted us to some of the history of World War II in Nebraska.

Finally, we thank our son, Adam, for setting up our blog, BurtFolsom.com, and for inspiring us to keep working. For months, Adam asked, "How many words did you write today?" In many ways, we wrote this book for him. His generation is the one coming into leadership, and it must deal with the persistent impact of FDR and World War II on our world today.

BURTON AND ANITA FOLSOM
February 26, 2011

INDEX